THE MAKING OF THE MODERN BRITISH HOME

The Making of the Modern British Home

The Suburban Semi and Family Life between the Wars

PETER SCOTT

OXFORD
UNIVERSITY PRESS

Great Clarendon Street, Oxford, OX2 6DP,
United Kingdom

Oxford University Press is a department of the University of Oxford.
It furthers the University's objective of excellence in research, scholarship,
and education by publishing worldwide. Oxford is a registered trade mark of
Oxford University Press in the UK and in certain other countries

© Peter Scott 2013

The moral rights of the authors have been asserted

First Edition published in 2013

All rights reserved. No part of this publication may be reproduced, stored in
a retrieval system, or transmitted, in any form or by any means, without the
prior permission in writing of Oxford University Press, or as expressly permitted
by law, by licence or under terms agreed with the appropriate reprographics
rights organization. Enquiries concerning reproduction outside the scope of the
above should be sent to the Rights Department, Oxford University Press, at the
address above

You must not circulate this work in any other form
and you must impose this same condition on any acquirer

Published in the United States of America by Oxford University Press
198 Madison Avenue, New York, NY 10016, United States of America

British Library Cataloguing in Publication Data

Data available

Library of Congress Control Number: 2013936238

ISBN 978–0–19–967720–7

Links to third party websites are provided by Oxford in good faith and
for information only. Oxford disclaims any responsibility for the materials
contained in any third party website referenced in this work.

In memory of Francesca Carnevali (1964–2013), one of the most talented economic and business historians of my generation and a person of enormous integrity, compassion, and wit. She was the best of friends and an inspiration to myself and many others. Francesca faced her long battle with cancer with characteristic courage, fortitude, and humour. Almost to the end she continued to work, particularly on an innovative research project that has the potential to transform our understanding of Britain's household goods industries prior to 1914. She will be missed as a scholar, teacher, and, above all, as a friend.

Preface

It is now some twelve years since I first became interested in the impact of suburbanization, and the genesis of the modern semi, on British family life between the wars. It was then widely believed that the considerable expansion in home ownership during the 1930s was essentially confined to the middle classes, as purchasing a modern semi-detached house was beyond the financial reach of working-class households. In 1998 I had been fortunate to act as external examiner for Alan Crisp, whose Oxford MLitt thesis had thrown serious doubt on this view and had convinced me that this was an area where the received wisdom was in error. Two years later a doctoral thesis by another Oxford scholar, George Speight, comprehensively demolished the received wisdom, proving beyond doubt that working-class people could (and did) purchase modern suburban housing during the 1930s.

I was intrigued that what must have been a major break with traditional working-class housing practices had hitherto gone largely unrecognized by economic and social historians, and wanted to discover what impacts owner occupation had on other areas of working-class life. It soon became apparent that the large volume of personal testimonies from people who had pioneered migration to the suburbs, ranging from contemporary interviews to autobiographies and contributions to oral history projects, offered a promising route for exploring these issues. Assembling a database, with relevant information from a large sample of such testimonies, soon became an objective in its own right. However, from an early stage in the project I realized that migrants to owner-occupied suburbia had strong commonalities with people who moved out to early suburban council estates—in terms of the extra costs they faced, the nature of the houses and communities they moved to, and long-term lifestyle impacts, for both themselves and their children. I therefore widened the project to also include early suburban council tenants. I also rapidly became aware that some of the estates to which my working-class families moved also contained large numbers of lower-middle-class households, often on incomes that were not greatly above those of the highest paid working-class families. The project was thus further broadened, to include white-collar workers.

Life history testimonies revealed that moves to suburbia had far-reaching impacts on family life, constituting one of the major cleavages between the 'traditional' working class and the post-war 'new working class'. Nor were these findings particularly original—they had already been identified in social studies of new municipal estates conducted in the 1920s and 1930s. Moreover, a number of historical studies of interwar suburban localities, including excellent theses by Audrey Kay, Margaret Judith Giles, Madeline McKenna, and Lesley Whitworth, had produced similar findings.

A major breakthrough in exploring these issues nationally occurred when I discovered several hundred original returns from Britain's first detailed national household expenditure survey, conducted by the Ministry of Labour over the year beginning October 1937. These were believed to have been destroyed, but had in fact been given to a researcher and eventually deposited in the University of Bangor Library. Together with 99 returns from the same survey, preserved at the National Archives, this gave me a usable sample of over 600 households, providing data on family size, housing, and weekly household spending, for working-class families renting their accommodation, buying it on mortgage, or owning it outright.

My subsequent research on the new interwar suburbs and their pioneer migrants has taken me into such diverse areas as the history of family planning, household leisure, gardening, marketing, and the spread of new consumer durables. Some of these topics have been explored in collaboration with my colleagues at the Henley Business School's Centre for International Business History, particularly James Walker, Lucy Newton, Anna Spadavecchia, and Peter Miskell. This work mainly involved articles in academic journals, yet I was aware that looking at these issues in isolation failed to do justice to the interconnected and mutually reinforcing nature of the processes under consideration. I have therefore devoted increasing time over the past few years to drawing my work together in this book. I hope that its contents will do justice both to the topics under discussion and to the people involved—who made difficult choices and, sometimes, considerable sacrifices to achieve what they perceived to be a better life for themselves and their children.

Acknowledgements

Parts of the research connected with this project were funded by ESRC Grant RES-000-22-0152 and Nuffield Foundation Social Sciences Small Grants Scheme Award H502620; thanks are due to Fatima Cardias Williams, Nat Ishino, and Natalie Anderson for research assistant work in relation to these awards. I have also consistently received generous financial support from the University of Reading for travel and other research expenditure. I am indebted to a great many people for help with this book, including the staff of the archives and libraries mentioned in the Bibliography, anonymous referees who commented on various draft papers, and to numerous writers who have influenced my ideas or provided information for this study. I also owe a debt of gratitude to two groups of, often anonymous, people—those early pioneer migrants to new suburban estates who set down personal testimonies of their experiences in autobiographical writings or through participation in oral history projects, and those who sought to record others' testimonies of life on the early estates—capturing experiences that are now beginning to pass from living memory and, without which, our understanding of this important phase of British social history would be greatly impoverished.

I would like to give special thanks to the following people. James Walker, Lucy Newton, Anna Spadavecchia, Peter Miskell, Ian Gazeley, and Andrew Newell made valuable contributions to this project via jointly authored articles on related topics, in addition to more general support and advice. A number of people generously made their unpublished research or archival materials available to me, including Matthew Boot, Sue Bruley, Alan Crisp, Judy Giles, Michael Heller, Steve Humphries, Audrey Kay, Len Holden, Duncan Nimmo, Chris Pond, Luke Samy, Pam Schweitzer, George Speight, and Fred Wellings. Thanks are also due to various organizations which allowed me to reproduce photographs and contemporary publicity artwork; these are individually acknowledged alongside the relevant images—though I would like to give particular thanks to John Laing plc, Leeds Library and Information Service, Lloyds Banking Group plc Archives, London Metropolitan Archives, London Transport Museum, Nottingham City Council and <http://www.picturethepast.org.uk>, and Oxfordshire County Council Photographic Archive. Reproducing images from my own ephemera collection was greatly assisted by the expert help of Laura Bennetto.

My work has hugely benefited from the comments and advice of other scholars. I fear that my imperfect memory will lead to the omission of many people who should be acknowledged, though (in addition to those mentioned above) I would like to pay particular thanks to Francesca Carnevali, Leslie Hannah, Peter Hart, Jane Humphries, Stuart Mitchell, Sean O'Connell, Avner Offer, Chris Reid, Stefan Schwarzkopf, Pat Thane, Frank Trentmann, Laura Ugolini, Fred Wellings, Fatima Cardias Williams, and Lesley Whitworth. Valuable feedback was also gained from presentations at the annual conferences of the Association of Business Historians, Economic History Society, and Social History Society, together with seminar presentations at the Institute of Historical Research, London School of Economics, and the Universities of Oxford, Portsmouth, and Reading. Finally, thanks are due to my wife, Fong, for her love, support, and for putting up with me.

Contents

List of Illustrations	xiii
List of Tables	xv
List of Abbreviations	xvii
A Note on Currency	xviii

1. The New Suburban World   1
    Introduction   1
    Suburban migration and social change   7
    Marketing suburbia to the masses   12
    Reconstructing interwar suburbia   13
    The structure of this book   14

2. The Road to 'Homes Fit for Heroes'   18
    Introduction   18
    The Victorian housing legacy   18
    Scotland: a different country   25
    Crisis and reform in Edwardian Britain   29
    War accelerates change   34
    The life and death of 'homes fit for heroes'   36
    Conclusion   42

3. Municipal Suburbia   43
    Introduction   43
    Post-Addison council house development in the 1920s   43
    From general needs housing to slum clearance   46
    The characteristics of municipal housing   48
    Communities without amenities   52
    The joy of suburbia   57
    Rents, affordability, and making ends meet   61
    Conclusion   67

4. Developing Owner-Occupied Suburbia   69
    Introduction   69
    The speculative suburban house   69
    The interwar speculative house-builder   76
    Scotland—still a different country   83
    Development finance   88
    The development process   90
    'Building down' to a working-class market   94
    Conclusion   97

Contents

5.	**Marketing Owner Occupation to the Masses**	98
	Introduction	98
	A transformation in housing tenure	99
	Making houses affordable—the introduction of 'easy terms'	102
	The marketing process	108
	Marketing house-hunting as a leisure activity	116
	Lifestyle marketing	120
	Conclusion	127
6.	**Life in Owner-Occupied Suburbia**	128
	Introduction	128
	The suburban house purchaser	128
	'Keeping ourselves to ourselves' and 'keeping up with the Joneses'	135
	Making ends meet in owner-occupied suburbia	140
	Smaller, 'better' families	142
	Conclusion	151
7.	**Equipping the Suburban Home**	152
	Introduction	152
	Marketing furniture to new suburban families	153
	Hire purchase	156
	Furniture acquisition strategies and costs	160
	Labour-saving appliances in labour-saving homes	166
	Conclusion	173
8.	**The Suburban Garden**	175
	Introduction	175
	Gardens in municipal suburbia	179
	Gardening in owner-occupied suburbia	181
	Sources of information, advice, and equipment	184
	Garden styles, designs, and functions	188
	Conclusion	192
9.	**Visible and Invisible Walls: Social Differentiation and Conflict in Interwar Suburbia**	194
	Introduction	194
	The affluent worker thesis	195
	Communities and social norms	196
	Suburbia as social segregation	205
	Conclusion	212
10.	**A Crisis Averted by War? Mis-selling, Consumer Protest, and the Borders Case**	213
	Introduction	213
	Building society growth and the mortgage pool system	213
	Attempts to control competition	217

	Caveat emptor	218
	Arrears and defaults	222
	The Borders case	224
	Was there a looming housing market crisis in 1939?	228
	Conclusion	232
11.	**The Legacy of the Interwar Semi**	233
	The interwar housing achievement	233
	From ideal home to tower block	238
	The end of affordable and desirable suburban housing?	243

Appendix: A Note on Sources — 247
Bibliography — 251
Index — 265

List of Illustrations

1.1. A contemporary depiction of the suburban middle-class housewife running the servantless home — 4
1.2. A non-parlour Tudor Walters type 1930s council house — 6
1.3. Annual number of houses built in England and Wales by local government and private enterprise, 1920–39 (years ending 31st March) — 9
2.1. Court housing in Liverpool — 20
2.2. An early flyer for the National Freehold Land & Building Society, c.1900 — 33
2.3. Brochure illustration for Newton Chambers & Co. pre-fabricated houses — 40
3.1. London County Council cottage estates developed before the late 1930s — 49
3.2. Layout scheme for a housing estate at Throckley, drawn up for Newburn-on-Tyne Urban District Council, c.1919–23 — 50
3.3. An example of short terraced municipal housing — 52
3.4. Photograph of the Wyther Estate, Armley, Leeds, in 1932—reflecting the bleak initial appearance of much new municipal housing — 54
4.1. A Wates' illustration of some housing designs employed during the 1930s — 70
4.2. A 'universal-plan' speculative house developed on Edgware's Old Rectory Estate — 73
4.3. An example of 'suntrap' houses advertised by Davis Estates — 75
4.4. Layout of New Ideal Homesteads' Falconwood Park Estate, Welling, London — 77
4.5. The leading lights of New Ideal Homesteads in the 1930s—Leo Meyer and Philip Shephard — 78
4.6. A 1938 advertisement for Wates' 'all in' housing terms — 81
4.7. Annual public and private sector house-building rates in England and Wales and in Scotland, as a percentage of their 1931 populations — 87
4.8. The average cost of a three-bedroom local authority house (£ per dwelling), 1925–38 — 93
4.9. Two large suburban shopping parades developed by John Laing & Sons Ltd in north-west London — 94
5.1. Examples of 1930s building society advertising promoting home ownership: (a) Halifax Building Society bookmark; (b) Leeds Permanent Building Society postcard — 111
5.2. The key to home ownership as advertising metaphor: Coventry Permanent Economic Building Society brochure c.1930s — 113
5.3. An example of a 'modern homes' feature and accompanying advertising, from a May 1936 issue of the *Bristol Evening News* — 115
5.4. Chauffeur transport offered to prospective Wates' buyers — 119

List of Illustrations

5.5. A 1924 London Underground poster advertising the attractions of Edgware (to which the Hampstead Line, now known as the Northern Line, had just been extended) by contrasting them with inner London	125
5.6. A New Ideal Homesteads' 'Super Home' brochure (early 1930s)	126
6.1. Map of John Laing's Golders Green estate under construction, showing transport links and the sites for a proposed school and park	136
6.2. The promise of 'a Brighter Outlook' as visualized by the Leeds Provincial Building Society	146
7.1. The Ideal Home as department store furniture advertising slogan	155
7.2. A Drages' hire purchase 'drawing room' furniture package	158
7.3. A combined living/dining room arrangement demonstrated in a T. F. Nash show house	162
7.4. A three-piece suite advertised by Catesbys of Tottenham Court Road for 15 guineas	164
7.5. Laing's 'De Luxe' kitchen, as illustrated in a 1935 estate brochure	165
7.6. The all-electric home, as promoted by Currys	167
7.7. 'Gas Fires on Hire' promotion by the Liverpool Gas Company	172
8.1. Aerial view of the Minver Crescent section of Nottingham's Aspley municipal estate, $c.$1930	177
8.2. The rural charms of suburban living, as depicted by Charles Paine for London Underground in 1929	178
8.3. A depiction of the ideal house set in the ideal garden on the front cover of E. L. Berg's 1936 'Ideal Home' brochure	183
8.4. The seed catalogue as advice manual—Daniel Bros' *Illustrated Guide for Amateur Gardeners*, Spring 1930	187
8.5. 'Adam', 'The Gardeners' Good Samaritan', offers his help to new suburban householders via Bees Ltd	188
8.6. 'Conspicuous gardening'—as depicted in a 1935 Halifax mortgage advert	191
9.1. One of Oxford's two Cutteslowe walls	208

List of Tables

2.1. The relationship between average rental costs and income (£ per annum), for British households included in the 1890–1 U.S. Commissioner of Labor household budgets survey, together with the number and average incomes of householders in the survey — 23

2.2. Evidence from surviving returns to the 1904 Board of Trade household expenditure survey, on owner-occupation levels and annual rents in relation to incomes — 24

2.3. A comparison of rent as a share of income for households in England and Wales and in Scotland, in the 1890–1 U.S. Commissioner of Labor household budgets survey — 25

2.4. Estimates of average floorspace per household and per person for urban working-class families in Edwardian Britain — 29

3.1. Number of houses built in England and Wales, 1 January 1919 to 31 March 1939 (thousands) — 45

3.2. Cost of cottage estate developments under the Housing, etc., Act, 1923 and the Housing (Financial Provisions) Act, 1924, by six provincial councils to 31st December 1929, and by the London County Council to 31st March 1930 — 53

3.3. Positive features of suburban housing identified in 170 life history testimonies of interwar working-class migrants to suburban estates — 58

4.1. A comparison of house-building in England and Wales and in Scotland (thousands), 1919–38 — 84

4.2. House-building in England and Wales from the armistice to 31st March 1940 by standard economic region — 85

4.3. Costs and expected profit margins for 121 suburban houses developed by Wimpey in the late 1930s (as percentage of expected selling price) — 93

5.1. Changes in average male earnings for eight occupational groups in nominal and real (1935/6) values, 1913/14 to 1935/6 — 101

5.2. Private sector house-building in England and Wales classified by rateable value—average number per year (thousands) and percentage distribution by value band — 107

6.1. The proportion of British non-agricultural working-class families buying/owning their own homes, at various levels of household expenditure, October 1937–July 1938 — 130

6.2. A regional profile of non-agricultural working-class housing in 1937/38 — 132

6.3. A profile of middle-class housing expenditures in 1938/9 — 133

6.4. The distribution of weekly household expenditure and average family size for working-class families renting their accommodation, buying it on mortgage, or owning it outright, at various levels of total expenditure, April 1938 — 143

List of Tables

10.1.	The eight largest building societies in order of asset value (£M) 1922–1939	215
10.2.	Data on arrears, repossessions and sales (percentage of all mortgages), Abbey Road and Co-operative Permanent building societies	231
11.1.	Housing affordability and owner-occupation rates since 1938	245

List of Abbreviations

Bexley Local Studies	Bexley Local Studies and Archives Centre, London
BSA	Building Societies Association
CPBS	Co-operative Permanent Building Society
CRO	Coventry Record Office
HP	Hire Purchase
LCC	London County Council
LMA	London Metropolitan Archives
NA	The National Archives, Kew
NRO	Northamptonshire Record Office
NCSRS	Nuffield College Social Reconstruction Survey Archive, Nuffield College, Oxford
PEP	Political and Economic Planning
RCAHMS	Royal Commission of Ancient and Historical Monuments, Scotland

A Note on Currency

In this text pre-decimal currency is used: £1 = 20 shillings (s) = 240 old pence (d). In contemporary writings shillings were sometimes denoted by the symbol /-. This is not used in the general text, but is retained when it appears in direct quotes.

1
The New Suburban World

INTRODUCTION

This book examines the impact of the rise of the modern suburban semi-detached house on British family life during the 1920s and 1930s, together with its longer-term influence on lifestyles, consumption patterns, aspirations, and other elements of household behaviour. Prior to the First World War most non-rural working and lower-middle-class families had lived in different versions of the terraced house, in distinctively urban environments of high-density housing. For the working classes, these often represented long-established communities—sharing strong links of kinship, background, and, often, places of work. Such neighbourhoods were characterized by common, or at least prevailing, social values, which were fundamentally conservative in that 'acceptable' behaviour was kept within the limits of what was considered 'reasonable' to the local community—thus constraining, among other things, conspicuous consumption. Meanwhile social status was based on long acquaintance and reflected a complex web of factors, in which material affluence played only a limited role.

By contrast, the interwar years witnessed extensive migration to new suburban communities of mainly semi-detached private or municipal housing. These offered a quantum leap in conditions compared to the accommodation families typically moved from, with amenities that subsequent generations were to take for granted, but which were luxuries beyond the dreams of many of their parents—such as electricity, bathrooms, hot running water, and their own front and rear gardens. Demand for such housing partly reflected a growing preference among families of all classes for more hygienic, healthier, and spacious homes, which had been evident since at least the late nineteenth century. However, it was only during the First World War that a number of rapid and inter-related political, social, economic, and technological changes made such housing a viable proposition for large numbers of manual workers and people at the bottom end of the white-collar earnings spectrum.

The conflict drew huge numbers of civilians into war-related industries and necessitated unprecedented levels of government control over the provision of basic resources such as food, coal, and transport. Government feared widespread social unrest, in an inflationary environment where living standards were initially squeezed by rising rents and other costs. It was thus compelled to pursue policies which produced substantial redistributions of income, both from the upper and middle classes to the working class and from skilled to less-skilled manual workers.

Wage rises during the war years had a significant long-term impact on living standards, raising the average growth of real wages from 0.9 per cent per annum over 1920–38 to 1.21 per cent over 1913–38.[1]

Towards the end of the war the government focused on 'homes for heroes' as a key post-war social policy to diffuse anticipated social unrest, or even revolution, when demobbed troops returned in vast numbers to a job market which might prove incapable of absorbing them. War requirements also accelerated technological development, mechanization, and other cost-reducing innovations in a number of sectors that were to play significant direct or indirect roles in the expansion of interwar suburbia, such as road transport, building, electricity supply, electrical goods, and furniture. Lower prices facilitated a substantial increase in working-class participation in the products of these industries, which were traditionally expensive but had a large potential working-class market. A third key impact of the war was a substantial expansion in urban workers' discretionary time. Despite being overlooked in many historical accounts, the introduction of the 48-hour week for industrial workers in around 1919, reducing the length of the average working day by about 1 hour, is arguably the most important humanitarian reform of the interwar years. This was part of an international campaign; in the immediate aftermath of the armistice, European workers rallied round the 48-hour week as a key 'peace dividend' for their wartime sacrifices, while employers and governments feared widespread industrial and political unrest if these demands were not met. Shorter hours paved the way for families to live further from their places of work, a trend also boosted by new transport technologies such as the motor bus, motor bike, and cheaper and more efficient bicycles.[2]

Wartime changes impacted on middle-class housing choices principally through making their traditional housing much less convenient. De-skilling of manufacturing operations during the war, to bring new types of labour without traditional craft skills into industry, together with the longer-term growth of labour-intensive assembly industries, opened up major employment opportunities for young women. Despite union efforts to reverse the wartime 'dilution' of skilled manufacturing work, many of these labour market changes proved permanent, producing a major expansion in female employment in the rapidly growing assembly industries. Under these conditions domestic service, traditionally one of the few respectable avenues of paid employment for urban women, looked much less attractive, given its low wages, long hours, and major constraints on workers' freedom. *The Daily Express* saw the writing on the wall as early as May 1919, promoting its first 'Model Homes Exhibition' with the claim that:

> Women are now at the parting of the ways in housekeeping methods. All the signs point to a new type of small house which can be worked, if necessary, without resident

---

[1] George R. Boyer, 'Living Standards 1860–1939', in Roderick Floud and Paul Johnson (eds), *The Cambridge Economic History of Modern Britain*, Vol. II: *Economic Maturity, 1860–1939* (Cambridge: Cambridge University Press, 2004), 284.

[2] Peter Scott and Anna Spadavecchia, 'Did the 48-Hour Week Damage Britain's Industrial Competitiveness?', *Economic History Review*, 64 (2011), 1266–88.

servants, and where every detail of construction has been evolved in the interests of economy in domestic labour and the comfort of the family as a whole.³

Similarly in 1920 GEC's Ideal Home Exhibition leaflet claimed that the 'All-Electric...Ideal Home' would put an end to:

> Open fires—heat-wasting, producing residues of dust and cinders that must be regularly removed; gas-burners emitting fumes that taint the atmosphere and tarnish furniture and wall-paper; these things necessitate scrubbing-brush and pail, mop and broom and dust-pan; *hard work* and *daily repeated* work. And if we add to these the labours of cooking, ironing, dish-washing and clothes-washing, we are forced to the conclusion that the average home...is anything but 'ideal'. Yet nothing is more certain than that in the course of a very few years we shall wonder at the expensive, antiquated, wasteful methods of the present day, simply because that ever-ready servant, ELECTRICITY, without dust, or smoke, or noise, 'without haste, without rest' will take charge of our domestic routine, eliminate practically all unnecessary work, and make such work as remains into a pleasure.⁴

While GEC's prediction of all-electric living was not to become a reality for most families until long after the Second World War, the *Daily Express*'s vision of a rapid switch to labour-saving homes proved far more accurate. By the mid-1920s, even those members of the lower middle class who could still afford to employ servants tended to have only a char woman or 'daily', rather than someone on a live-in basis. This new incarnation of the 'servant problem' irrevocably changed the relationship between the middle-class housewife and her home.⁵ From now on most housewives in this group had to see themselves as participants in housework to some extent, rather than purely as supervisors, directing the work of others.

Yet the most important policy or physical innovation associated with the war period from the perspective of interwar suburbia was the new 'Tudor Walters' housing standard. Prior to 1914 new working-class neighbourhoods on the edges of towns were typically developed in long terraces, at densities of thirty or more per acre, and were of similar design to inner-urban housing.⁶ The same was true of many 'superior terraces' occupied by the lower middle classes, while in many towns even the middle and upper ranks of the middle class lived in grander versions of the terraced house. During the latter years of the war leading planners and architects, some of whom were already designing housing estates for munitions workers, successfully advocated a low-density suburban solution to the post-war housing problem, embodied in the 1918 Tudor Walters Report on the standards of post-war local authority housing.

---

[3] Adrian Bingham, *Gender, Modernity, and the Popular Press in Interwar Britain* (Oxford: Clarendon, 2004), 95.
[4] Bodleian Library, Ms Marconi 3780, GEC leaflet 'The All-Electric House: How Electricity Helps in the Quest for the Ideal Home', issued for the 1920 Ideal Home Exhibition.
[5] Deborah Ryan, 'The Daily Mail Ideal Home Exhibition and Suburban Modernity, 1908–1951', PhD thesis (University of East London, 1995), 91.
[6] Alison Ravetz, *Council Housing and Culture: The History of a Social Experiment* (Abingdon: Routledge, 2001), 62.

Fig. 1.1. A contemporary depiction of the suburban middle-class housewife running the servantless home
Source: *The Housewife's Book* (London: Daily Express, 1937), Peter Scott collection.

This set out a blueprint for the new suburban home, drawing on contemporary planning ideas (pioneered in garden city and model workers' village projects), that sought to improve economic and social conditions by creating healthier and better-designed houses and communities.[7] Proposed specifications were well in

---

[7] UK, Parliament, *Report of the Committee Appointed by the Local Government Board and the Secretary of State for Scotland to Consider Questions of Building Construction in Connection with the Provision of Dwellings for the Working Classes in England and Wales, and Scotland, and Report upon Methods of Securing Economy and Despatch in the Provision of Such Dwellings* (Cd. 9191 of 1918).

advance of previous working-class building standards, including a minimum of three ground floor rooms (living-room, parlour, and scullery with larder), three bedrooms (at least two of which could take two beds), plus a bathroom. Houses were to be built at a density of no more than twelve per acre, semi-detached or in short terraces, with wide frontages to increase natural daylight and a cottage appearance enhanced by front and rear gardens.[8]

It has been claimed that the interwar speculative semi emerged 'quite independently of council housing'.[9] In fact, Tudor Walters standards embodied the basic features of both the municipal and owner-occupied interwar working-class house. Speculative developers followed them mainly on account of their popularity with purchasers, but introduced many more, largely cosmetic, variations in design between individual houses. These distinguished each house from its neighbours and the estate in general from municipal housing, which was widely viewed as being grimly uniform in appearance. In doing so, speculative developers drew heavily on the English vernacular tradition, producing the 'Tudorbethan' semi that remains, for many people, the ideal home. Conversely, councils rapidly developed a preference for a 'neo-Georgian' style of plainer houses in near-identical rows, both as a means of economizing on costs and emphasizing their municipal identity. As Dorothy Barton, who moved with her parents to the London County Council's (LCC's) St Helier Estate in 1934 recalled, 'When we arrived at 10 Rewley Road, we found it was one of a short road of square red brick boxes, all exactly alike'.[10]

Both council and owner-occupied houses came in various sizes and costs. The ambitious standards outlined in the Local Government Board's 1919 *Housing Manual*, which exceeded those of the Tudor Walters committee in some respects, produced a council house beyond the means of most working-class families.[11] Subsequent cost-saving reductions in municipal housing standards widened access to lower income groups. The proportion of houses with parlours fell, the bathroom was sometimes sacrificed for a bath in the kitchen (with a removable top so that it could serve as a table when not in use) and the dimensions of rooms became less generous. Developers for owner occupation also sought to build down to lower income groups, particularly during the mid- and late-1930s. For example, New Ideal Homesteads—Britain's most prolific speculative house-builder—offered a range of house designs on each estate, sometimes including a low-cost model based on a three bedroom non-parlour terrace with a bath in the kitchen. This was very similar to the cheaper type of non-parlour council house and, with a price of £395 (that translated into minimum weekly mortgage payments of 9 shillings 6 pence), compared well with many such houses in terms of cost.[12]

---

[8] John Burnett, *A Social History of Housing 1815–1985*, 2nd edn (London: Methuen, 1986), 222–6.
[9] Ravetz, *Council Housing and Culture*, 90.
[10] Age Exchange, Reminiscence Theatre Archive, London, autobiographical excerpt provided for Age Concern, 'Just Like the Country' project, by D. Barton, c.1987.
[11] Burnett, *Social History of Housing*, 225.
[12] Bexley Local Studies and Archive Centre, New Ideal Homesteads brochure, 'Super 1933 Homes: Barnehurst Estate, Barnehurst, Kent' (1933).

Fig. 1.2. A non-parlour Tudor Walters type 1930s council house
Source: 'Small houses', scrapbook of house plans, (*c*.1939), Peter Scott collection.

Despite these variations, the Tudor Walters standard constituted the basic suburban housing template—three bedrooms plus bathroom; modern amenities and kitchen; a smallish front garden and larger back garden—that encompassed most of the four million or so suburban houses built in interwar Britain. Indeed this new standard became so popular that it rendered even better-quality older houses obsolete. In 1939 the government's Committee on Valuation for Rates reported that the interwar semi's improved design and superior amenities had made pre-war housing technically 'obsolescent and less attractive to tenants'.[13] Similarly, in 1945 Marion Bowley noted that middle-class houses of 'the great Victorian age...are now considered unsatisfactory and inconvenient.'[14]

SUBURBAN MIGRATION AND SOCIAL CHANGE

One of the main themes of this book is the social consequences of the first phase of mass British suburban migration. This process encompassed two major changes in housing tenure. The 1920s witnessed the advent of local government as a major provider of new rented housing. Municipal housing expanded from less than 1 per cent of the 1914 housing stock for England and Wales to around 10 per cent in 1938, with over 90 per cent of the 1.1 million new interwar council houses located on suburban estates.

The second key change was a dramatic expansion in owner occupation. Britain traditionally had a tenure pattern more similar to that of continental Europe than to 'new world' countries—with relatively few people owning their own homes. The interwar years, and particularly the 1930s, witnessed the start both of a trend towards Britain becoming a nation of owner-occupiers and of a popular perception that ownership constituted a socially superior tenure to renting. Owner-occupied dwellings, conventionally put at around 10 per cent of the 1914 housing stock, rose to around 32 per cent by 1938, mainly due to new developments (an estimated 1.8 million new houses were built for owner-occupiers, compared to 1.1 million existing houses transferred from the privately rented to the owner-occupied sector).[15] The 1914 owner-occupation rate is subject to a substantial margin of error as it is based on an assumption regarding the volume of pre-1914 housing transferred from the privately rented to owner-occupied stock by 1938, for which there are no direct estimates.[16] Yet a low 1914 owner-occupation rate is strongly corroborated by contemporary household surveys, as discussed in the next chapter. As with council houses, the vast majority of new owner-occupied housing was located on suburban estates. Around 900,000 houses were also developed for private renting, again mainly in the suburbs.[17]

These developments both radically changed the appearance and physical scale of many towns and cities and altered the overall balance between urban and rural Britain. Over the interwar period the urban area of England and Wales increased by around 26 per cent, well in advance of the 15 per cent increase in the urban

---

[13] Ministry of Health, *Report to the Minister of Health by the Departmental Committee on Valuation for Rates, 1939* (London: HMSO, 1944), paragraph 11.
[14] Marion Bowley, *Housing and the State 1919–1944* (London: George Allen & Unwin, 1945), 36–7.
[15] Stephen Merrett, *Owner Occupation in Britain* (London: Routledge & Kegan Paul, 1982), 1.
[16] Michael Ball, *Housing Policy and Economic Power: The Political Economy of Owner Occupation* (London: Methuen, 1983), 25; A. D. McCulloch, 'Owner-Occupation and Class Struggle: The Mortgage Strikes of 1938–40', PhD thesis (University of Essex, 1983), 109.
[17] Merrett, *Owner Occupation*, 1, 16; Andrzej Olechnowicz, *Working Class Housing in England between the Wars: The Becontree Estate* (Oxford: Oxford University Press, 1997), 1.

population. Some 862,500 new houses were built in rural districts, together with more expensive developments of greenfield areas on the fringes of towns.[18] Between 1927–8 and 1933–4 housing development took an average of 38,000 acres of land each year, while over 1934–5 to 1938–9 this rose to 50,000 acres.[19]

Middle-class households constituted the majority of new suburban residents. However, working-class families were also important participants in this process. The interwar years are often depicted as a period of depression and stagnation for the working class, characterized by mass unemployment, especially during the early 1920s and early 1930s. There is a great deal of truth in this depiction, though it masks considerable regional and local variations, together with important variations between industries. In 1932, when national unemployment peaked, some 36.5 per cent of insured workers in Wales were unemployed, together with more than a quarter of workers in Scotland and northern England. Yet unemployment in London, and in the rest of the South East, stood at only 13.5 and 14.3 per cent, respectively. By 1937 unemployment in these regions had fallen to 6.4 and 6.7 per cent, respectively, yet remained at 23.3 per cent in Wales and 16.0 per cent in Scotland.[20]

These disparities largely reflected those of the dominant industries in each region. Export-orientated staple industries such as coal mining, textiles, iron and steel, and shipbuilding faced severe contractions in production and employment. Conversely, expanding industries such as motor vehicles; electrical engineering; branded food, drink, toiletries, and other fast-moving household products; and other sectors mainly serving domestic markets were mainly based around the South and Midlands. Those fortunate enough to remain in regular employment experienced a substantial long-term increase in real earnings—mainly owing to falling retail prices for most of the period—and were often able to consider taking on the extra costs associated with renting a new suburban council house, or even buying a house on mortgage.

As Figure 1.3 shows, private development dominated new housing in England and Wales even in the 1920s—though council housing was then the main source of new suburban housing for working-class families. While council estates were initially dominated by the upper strata of the working class (and, in many cases, the lower middle class), reductions in rents, slum clearance programmes, and the migration of middle-class council tenants to owner-occupied estates transformed municipal housing into an overwhelmingly working-class tenure, encompassing a broad range of incomes.

It was during the 1930s that private speculative house-building really took off, peaking at almost 300,000 completions per year in England and Wales. The years from around 1933 to the outbreak of the Second World War witnessed Britain's

---

[18] John Lowerson, 'Battles for the Countryside', in Frank Gloversmith (ed.), *Class, Culture and Social Change: A New View of the 1930s* (Brighton: Harvester, 1980), 258; John Sheail, *Rural Conservation in Inter-war Britain* (Oxford: Oxford University Press, 1981), 24–7.
[19] David Matless, *Landscape and Englishness* (London: Reaktion, 1998), 34.
[20] W. R. Garside, *British Unemployment 1919–1939: A Study in Public Policy* (Cambridge: Cambridge University Press, 1990), 10.

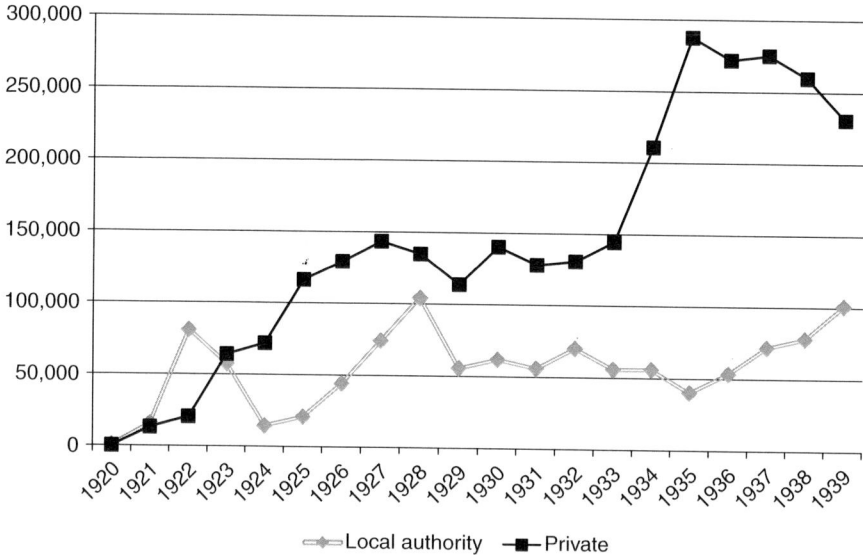

Fig. 1.3. Annual number of houses built in England and Wales by local government and private enterprise, 1920–39 (years ending 31st March)
Sources and notes: See Table 3.1.

highest ever rates of private house-building, dwarfing that for council housing. Falling interest rates, liberalized mortgage terms, reductions in building costs, and rising real incomes produced the first boom in working-class suburban home ownership. The proportion of non-agricultural workers buying or owning their own homes at least doubled over the decade, to around 18 per cent.[21] While this may not seem a huge aggregate increase, when account is taken of the fact that house purchasers were typically buying their first house, and doing so on or shortly after marriage, it represented a substantial proportion of newly formed working-class households.

Working-class suburban owner-occupation rates were highest for skilled workers, but were nevertheless significant over a broad range of working-class incomes, as discussed in Chapter 6. This trend was, however, largely restricted to England and Wales; Scotland and Northern Ireland had 1938 working-class owner-occupation rates of below 6 per cent, together with low relative proportions of owner-occupiers buying their houses on mortgage (i.e. relatively recent purchases, rather than inherited property). Interwar house-building north of the border was equivalent to only 28 per cent of Scotland's 1911 housing stock, compared to 52 per cent for England and Wales.[22] Depressed industrial areas in northern England and Wales also had markedly lower levels of house-building and suburbanization than more prosperous areas in the South and Midlands.

---

[21] National Archives [NA], LAB17/7, 'Weekly Expenditure of Working-Class Households in the United Kingdom in 1937–38', Ministry of Labour and National Service, July 1949.
[22] Bowley, *Housing and the State*, 266.

This was evident even for council housing—councils in depressed areas lacked the rateable income for major building projects, while standard council rentals were beyond the reach of many families.

Based on the available data, the proportion of non-agricultural British working-class households who moved to suburban estates during the interwar years can be very roughly estimated at around 25 per cent, with around 13 per cent taking the municipal housing route to suburbia, around 9 per cent taking the mortgage route, and perhaps 3 per cent renting privately developed suburban housing.[23] For some towns and cities in the South and Midlands, the figure would have been significantly larger. The 1937 Bristol Social Survey found that 14.2 per cent of working-class families in the survey area were living in council houses and 16.7 per cent in property built privately between the wars.[24] In Greater London (despite significant in-migration to both inner and outer areas from other parts of the country) out-migration changed the balance of population between the centre and periphery. Over 1921–37 the County of London experienced an estimated net population loss through out-migration of 708,000 (reducing its total population to 4,094,500), while outer London gained some 1,208,000 net migrants, increasing its population to 4,560,500.[25]

While this study examines the impact of suburbanization on both middle- and working-class families, its primary focus is on the working class—as suburbanization had the most dramatic economic and social impacts for this group. While middle-class migrants moved from housing that already had bathrooms, hot running water, and, often, electricity and gardens, these were typically absent from the houses which even skilled manual workers migrated from. Similarly, differences in room sizes, building standards, housing densities, and local social norms between the old and new residence were generally much greater for working-class migrants.

---

[23] Given a 1938 non-agricultural working-class owner-occupation rate of 17.8 per cent and making the conservative assumption that 50 per cent of owner-occupiers were located in the suburbs indicates that 8.9 per cent of non-agricultural working-class households took the owner-occupation route to suburbia. This estimate appears reasonable given that, of 38 accounts in the Life Histories Database involving moves to owner occupation during the 1930s (for which sufficient information was available), no fewer than 34 were new developments and almost all of these were located in the suburbs. Meanwhile, given that at least 90 per cent of interwar council houses were on suburban estates, and assuming that 90 per cent were occupied by working-class families by 1938, produces a figure of 891,000 working-class households taking the municipal housing route. As the number of working-class households in Britain can be very roughly estimated at 7.5 million, and agricultural workers comprised around 9 per cent of these, this would translate into about 13.1 per cent of non-agricultural working-class families (McCulloch, 'Owner-Occupation', 119; C. H. Lee, *British Regional Employment Statistics, 1841–1971* (Cambridge: Cambridge University Press, 1979)—using 1931 Census data). The addition of privately renting suburban residents is even more problematic, though analysis of oral history and other autobiographical accounts indicates a significant rate of tenancy by working-class families on new privately rented suburban estates. Assuming that three-quarters of the 900,000 houses developed for this sector were in the suburbs, and that 30 per cent of these were rented by working-class families, gives a figure of 202,500 households, or 3 per cent of the non-agricultural working class.

[24] Rosamond Jevons and John Madge, *Housing Estates: A Study of Bristol Corporation Policy and Practice between the Wars* (Bristol: Arrowsmith, 1946), 13.

[25] UK, Parliament, Royal Commission on the Distribution of the Industrial Population, *Report* (Cmd 6153 of 1940), 163.

Moves to new council or owner-occupied suburbs are shown to be accompanied by a transformation in working-class domestic lifestyles. As noted earlier, in inner-urban areas status was based around long acquaintance, together with a broad range of factors such as shared workplaces, and kinship, social, and other relationships, while conspicuous consumption was constrained within the limits of what was considered acceptable to the local community. In the suburbs, by contrast, a new form of working-class respectability emerged, based around maintaining minimum accepted standards of dress and other visible markers of consumption, restrained speech and behaviour, high standards of personal and domestic hygiene, 'privatized' family- and home-centred lifestyles, and an increased commitment of resources to the welfare and material advancement of the next generation.

As Jan De Vries has noted, the emergence of such new working-class lifestyles was an international phenomenon. Together with improved diets, these preferences formed a 'complex of consumption goals' which required clear household strategies to deliver them. Their importance as a 'cluster' of preferences was not due to each element being 'equally essential to achieve the ultimate goal of a longer, healthier, more comfortable life but because they were perceived to facilitate these goals and to signal to others the commitment to achieve them.'[26]

However, while most working-class suburban migrants moved by choice, this was not universally the case. During the 1930s in particular, many new council tenants moved owing to their existing housing being demolished under slum clearance programmes. Similarly, many people on council waiting lists during the 1920s sought council houses not because they were dissatisfied with inner-urban housing per se, but because they saw it as their only source of acceptable accommodation at a time of severe housing shortage. Even those who actively sought a suburban house were making a constrained choice, given that there were typically only a very limited range of housing types available. Where prospective migrants were lucky enough to have a choice between a suburban council house or a speculatively developed house, they were still likely to be faced with some variant of the three-bedroomed semi (or, sometimes, for council housing, short terrace block), with broad similarities in basic design, utilities, and gardens.

Several million migrants thus experienced moves from inner-urban housing to a distinct type of house, with broadly similar characteristics regarding suburban location, plot density, external design, internal layout, hygiene, utilities, enhanced natural daylight, generous gardens, and a neighbourhood of new migrants, drawn from different areas. These factors in turn shaped the 'habitus' (taken for granted, 'common sense' assumptions, norms, and patterns of behaviour) of these households in broadly similar ways—a process discussed throughout the book, but particularly in Chapters 3 and 6–9.[27] The suburban semi is shown to have played a key role in promoting a new, more domesticated and privatized model of working-class family life, which

---

[26] Jan De Vries, *The Industrious Revolution: Consumer Behaviour and the Household Economy, 1650 to the Present* (Cambridge: Cambridge University Press, 2008), 189.

[27] See Pierre Bourdieu, *The Logic of Practice* (Cambridge: Stanford University Press, 1990), 54–6.

was to become more generally evident after the Second World War (again, particularly in new suburban communities).

MARKETING SUBURBIA TO THE MASSES

This new cluster of social preferences and habits was also strongly influenced by new ideas regarding family life, maternity, childhood, and 'respectability', promoted by health professionals and other social commentators. There was also a strong element of more overt marketing of these values, by firms and institutions connected with the house-building industry, furniture, consumer durables, and power utilities. From around the last third of the nineteenth century the growing influence of the sanitary and hygiene movements, together with an improved understanding of the role of germs in spreading diseases, and of nutritional science, fostered an increase in the importance attached to housework and child-rearing among social policy-formers in most Western countries.[28] This led to growing social pressures for married women to focus exclusively on housework, rather than engaging in paid labour—accelerating a trend towards women withdrawing from the labour market that was already underway in Britain and several other countries.[29] These values also contributed to increased importance being placed on housing standards, by both working-class families and social reformers.

Interwar Britain witnessed an intensification of propaganda in favour of greater priority being given to childcare, family life, hygiene, and associated goods and services, via the expanding women's press, newspapers, radio, domestic education classes for girls, and a range of other channels. Commercial media were keen on promoting this agenda, partly because it tied into the messages of several of their major advertisers—including the building society movement, house-builders, retailers of furniture, consumer durables, and clothing, and gas and electricity supply concerns.

This study examines how these commercial interests marketed suburban living and owner occupation to a mass public which had hitherto typically rented their accommodation and (for the lower-income strata of this group) invested relatively little in expensive durables such as new furniture, furnishings, and appliances. The building society movement and building industry are shown to have developed a

---

[28] Joel Mokyr, 'Why "More Work For Mother?" Knowledge and Household Behavior, 1870–1945', *Journal of Economic History*, 60 (2000), 3; Carol Dyhouse, 'Working-Class Mothers and Infant Mortality in England, 1895–1914', *Journal of Social History*, 12 (1978), 248–67.

[29] This trend is often explained primarily in terms of rising working-class incomes during the second half of the nineteenth century, which led to a shift in consumption preferences from goods purchased in the market to those which could only be achieved via heavy inputs of household labour—such as improved nutrition, health, and housing (De Vries, *Industrious Revolution*, 189). Yet institutional factors, such as employers' formal and informal 'marriage-bars' (requiring female workers to leave the firm on marriage), and trade union opposition to women's employment, also played a significant role in this process (Sara Horrell and Jane Humphries, 'The Origin and Expansion of the Male Breadwinner Family: The Case of Nineteenth Century Britain', *International Review of Social History*, 42 (1997), Supplement, 48–50).

sophisticated campaign of common marketing messages, aimed at convincing the public that owner occupation was better than renting in terms of social status, cost, and as an investment. Their campaign also included a considerable element of 'lifestyle marketing', asserting that a modern suburban semi constituted a passport to a better life, for both purchasers and their children.

Suppliers of furniture, white goods, and utilities adopted similar marketing strategies, emphasizing the modern, aspirational, lifestyles which their products could facilitate—together with the 'easy' hire purchase (HP) terms on which they could be purchased. Moreover, the marketing of these goods became increasingly closely linked to that of suburban housing. Firms often engaged in cross-promotion strategies with housing developers—endorsing and advertising each other's products in their marketing material. Meanwhile show houses for new estates provided retail outlets for their goods—with a salesman in residence to close the deal. This study thus seeks to assess the role of commercial marketing in influencing and accelerating social changes associated with suburbanization, both directly and through modifying working-class expenditure priorities and related behaviour.

RECONSTRUCTING INTERWAR SUBURBIA

This study has benefited considerably from the work of previous researchers. Interwar municipal estates were subject to a number of contemporary social surveys, which yielded a great deal of valuable information.[30] Some individual council estates have also been subject to detailed historical investigation, while broader studies of interwar suburban migration from particular urban centres have also proved extremely valuable.[31] Speculative estates were not generally subject to contemporary social surveys—partly because they were seen as 'private' and thus not a legitimate area for such investigation. However, there have been some excellent subsequent studies of various aspects of life in owner-occupied suburbia, among which Alan A. Jackson's *Semi-Detached London* is a particularly fine example.[32]

---

[30] See, for example, Terence Young, *Becontree and Dagenham* (London: Becontree Social Survey Committee, 1934); Ruth Durant, *Watling: A Survey of Social Life on a New Housing Estate* (London: King, 1939); Manchester and Salford Better Housing Council, *The Report of an Investigation on Wythenshawe* (Manchester: privately published 1935); M. S. Soutar, E. H. Wilkins, and P. Sargant Florence, *Nutrition and Size of Family. Report on a New Housing Estate—1939* (London: George Allen & Unwin, 1942).

[31] For example, Olechnowicz, *Working Class Housing*; Audrey Kay, 'Wythenshawe circa 1932–1955: The Making of a Community?', PhD thesis (University of Manchester, 1993); Madeline McKenna, 'The Development of Suburban Council Housing Estates in Liverpool between the Wars', PhD thesis (University of Liverpool, 1986); Margaret Judith Giles, 'Something That Bit Better: Working-Class Women, Domesticity, and "Respectability", 1919–1939', PhD thesis (University of York, 1989); Lesley Whitworth, 'Men, Women, Shops and "Little, Shiny Homes": The Consuming of Coventry, 1930–1939', PhD thesis (University of Warwick, 1997).

[32] Alan A. Jackson, *Semi-Detached London: Suburban Development, Life, and Transport, 1900–39*, 2nd edn (Didcot: Wild Swan, 1991).

Extensive use is also made of primary sources. Chief amongst these are life history accounts of people who moved to the suburbs during the 1920s and 1930s, either as children moving with their parents or as adults setting up their own households. These include published autobiographies and contemporary interviews, though the vast majority were compiled for oral history projects. Some 170 biographical accounts of working-class people who moved from inner-urban areas to council estates or into owner occupation were examined and key information entered into a textual database (hereafter referred to as the Life Histories Database). I am deeply indebted to the (sometimes anonymous) researchers who compiled these and made them available either to myself or, more commonly, to researchers in general—by depositing them in archives or libraries.

Personal testimonies often vividly illuminate various aspects of life in interwar suburbia which are not easily accessible using other sources. Unfortunately, in common with their neglect in contemporary social studies, middle-class migrants are often poorly represented in oral history archives, with the exception of studies concerning working lives. Similarly, middle-class autobiographies for this period tend to concentrate on working, political, or social activities rather than household management. Thus, despite an exhaustive search, it only proved possible to identify some nineteen relevant and useful testimonies for middle-class suburban migrants. The Appendix provides a discussion of the Life Histories Database and how oral history material was used in this research, the procedures followed to avoid potential problems with such sources, and the locations of some of the major collections. Oral history repositories constitute a very valuable and somewhat under-utilized resource for research on the history of the household and I hope that this information may encourage their wider use.

Other, more conventional archival resources used in this study are also discussed in the Appendix. Briefly, these included the corporate archives of building firms, ephemera from house-builders (particularly estate brochures), the records of central and local government, together with the archives of various organizations and individuals involved with housing policy and social issues.

THE STRUCTURE OF THIS BOOK

In order to understand the economic and social impact of interwar suburbanization, some discussion of earlier housing provision is essential. Chapter 2 reviews housing development in Britain before 1914: the characteristic types of working- and lower-middle-class housing found in different areas of Victorian Britain, and their implications for domestic and social life. The exceptional nature of Scotland, where—in common with much of Europe—the tenement apartment dominated urban housing, is also examined.

Experiments with new housing formats towards the end of this period are shown to have foreshadowed more radical changes in housing policy during and immediately after the First World War. The impact of the government's 'homes for heroes' campaign and the short history of the first national municipal housing programme are then discussed, together with the emergence, and impact, of the new Tudor Walters suburban housing standard. While shortages and other problems limited the success of the first (Addison) housing programme, in terms of the number of homes built, it is shown to have nevertheless been of crucial importance in establishing a new model of mass suburban housing development.

Chapter 3 discusses the development of municipal housing following the end of the Addison programme. Key themes include estate and housing development policy, the advantages and costs of municipal suburban living, and the impacts of migration to municipal suburbia on household behaviour and family life. The evolution of housing policy is charted, including a progressive reduction in building standards to make houses more affordable to working families and a switch in the emphasis of provision during the 1930s from general needs to slum clearance. Council housing is shown to have been a relatively expensive option for working-class families throughout the period, compared to the inner-urban properties they typically migrated from. This was reflected not only in higher rental payments but in other additional costs that many households had not reckoned on, such as transport, furniture, and higher food prices. Costs were accentuated by perceptions that families' existing furniture and clothing did not meet the 'standards' of the new estate and that conspicuous expenditure was required to 'keep up with the Joneses'. Meanwhile suburban living had a number of other major impacts on working-class household behaviour, fostering a more privatized and domesticated pattern of family life than was found in inner-urban working-class communities.

Chapters 4–6 focus on owner-occupied suburbia. Speculative housing development is examined in Chapter 4, including the factors influencing the layout and design of owner-occupied estates and houses, the structure of the speculative building industry, the housing estate development system, and efforts by builders to produce a lower-priced product in order to broaden their market. The chapter also shows how the speculative building system acted to minimize the capital tied up in houses at each stage of development. This both facilitated entry into the sector by small firms and reduced overall capital constraints, in an industry where even the largest firms were still medium-sized entrepreneurial concerns.

Marketing owner occupation to a public who hitherto generally took renting for granted is the theme of Chapter 5. The building industry and building society movement launched an intensive campaign to sell the virtues of owner occupation, based around a number of key marketing messages, such as the ease and low cost of house purchase on mortgage, the superiority of owner occupation to renting, the investment value of a house, and, above all, the health and other lifestyle advantages of modern suburban housing. The chapter examines how the building societies and housing developers collaborated to extend the market by providing mortgages on 'easy terms'—with 5 per cent deposits and 25-year repayment terms. It also outlines how houses were marketed and how their promoters used 'lifestyle marketing' techniques to associate owner occupation with modern, aspirational, suburban lifestyles.

Chapter 6 explores family life in owner-occupied suburbia. As with municipal housing, moving to a new owner-occupied estate typically incurred increased costs not only for accommodation, but for furniture and travel. Meanwhile there were even stronger pressures to 'keep up with the Joneses' by displaying standards of dress, other visible markers of consumption, and behaviour deemed appropriate to the estate. Families often felt obliged to cut back on areas of expenditure which were less easily observed by neighbours, including 'essentials' such as food and heating, to meet these costs. One commonly used long-term strategy was family limitation. Smaller families enabled suburban migrants to both economize on their non-housing costs and improve their children's prospects, by opting for fewer, but better-resourced, offspring. Owner occupation thus promoted the adoption of longer-term planning horizons and strategies. By doing so it acted as a catalyst for one of the most fundamental breaks between the 'traditional' working-class household—for whom chronic economic uncertainty had imposed very short-term planning horizons—and the typical post-1945 household, characterized by long-term and intergenerational strategies for material and social advancement.

Equipping the suburban house is examined in Chapter 7. Retailers and producers of furniture and labour-saving durables realized the market potential of the new, larger suburban houses and intensively promoted the idea that a modern suburban house required smart, modern furnishings and appliances. Furniture retailers developed collaborative agreements with speculative developers and, sometimes, local councils. Show houses were furnished 'for free' by the retailer, in return for having their salesman on hand to meet prospective purchasers. As with home ownership, furniture was offered on 'easy payments', via HP agreements which often spread costs over four years. Similar strategies to cash in on new estate development were also widely used by suppliers of household appliances, during an era of vigorous competition between the electricity and gas supply industries. The chapter also examines the strategies families adopted to furnish their homes and the ways in which furniture and appliances were used by families to meet both functional and status objectives.

Chapter 8 then examines suburban gardening. While the interwar years saw the development of some four million suburban houses, it probably created at least as many new gardeners. Gardening became a mass leisure activity for the first time and, at a time when people had relatively little money for leisure expenditure, suburban gardens served a number of valuable functions. This chapter examines the range of attitudes among suburban families towards gardens which could be seen as a resource and/or a chore. Garden provision by local authorities and speculative housing developers is reviewed. Typical uses of the front and back garden are then discussed, together with sources of gardening materials and advice; garden styles, designs, and functions; and the role of gardens in encouraging both neighbourly cooperation, rivalry, and, in some cases, resentment.

Chapter 9 explores the timing and nature of the initial transition from a 'traditional' to a 'new' working class in twentieth-century Britain, arguing that these changes were initiated in the interwar years, on new suburban estates. Drawing on the work of Pierre Bourdieu, it also shows how moves to new residential communities undermined the habitus governing working-class consumption patterns in inner-urban areas, allowing new, more materially and domestically orientated values to emerge.

New estates also played a major role in filtering people into communities of broadly similar incomes, in contrast to inner-urban areas where streets housing the poor could sometimes be only short distances from the homes of the relatively affluent. Yet suburbanization was accompanied by growing anxieties regarding 'invasion' by new lower-status housing and neighbours, fostering intolerance towards those who did not meet the 'standards' of the estate. The few physical barriers separating different classes of housing, such as Oxford's infamous Cutteslowe walls, are shown to have formed merely the tip of a much stronger iceberg of anxiety regarding proximity to people perceived as being different. Interwar suburbia thus witnessed the start of a progressive trend towards stronger residential segregation, both between the working and middle classes and between different groups within the working class.

The dark side of the speculative housing system is explored in Chapter 10, which examines the problem of 'jerry-built' interwar speculative housing, the ways in which close relationships between building societies and builders accentuated the mis-selling of such houses; and the eventual crisis which threatened to bring this relationship to an end and, potentially, cause a significant housing market crash. Close relationships between building societies and speculative developers, who sometimes effectively acted as their retail agents, are shown to have created significant conflicts of interest, which acted to the customer's disadvantage. Concern regarding abuses culminated in the celebrated Borders case, where Mrs Elsy Borders, the wife of a London taxi driver, conducted a legal battle against the Bradford Third Equitable Building Society regarding the mis-selling of a house on a mortgage which (like most mortgages offered on speculative estates) turned out to be of questionable legality. The case threatened to make the majority of British residential mortgages null and void and, by doing so, bring down the speculative housing system. Moves towards reform of the sector at the end of the 1930s are also discussed, together with the likelihood of a housing market crash at the close of the decade had war not intervened.

The concluding chapter draws together this study's findings regarding the role of the interwar suburban semi as a catalyst for social change, the importance of commercial marketing in this process, and the relationship between the social consequences of this first phase of British mass suburbanization and longer-term changes in household behaviour, lifestyles, and priorities. Interwar suburban housing development is also compared with post-1945 patterns of housing provision to show why, despite its flaws, this era constituted the high watermark of British housing construction, from both a quantitative and qualitative perspective. A long, disastrous experiment in mass high-rise housing during the 1950s and 1960s was followed by an era of subdued housing development, sharply rising prices, and housing densities that remained significantly greater than the eight to twelve per acre of the 1920s and 1930s. It is thus hardly surprising that, despite almost three-quarters of a century of further progress in building technology, the interwar semi remains many people's vision of the 'ideal home'.

2
The Road to 'Homes Fit for Heroes'

INTRODUCTION

This chapter outlines the development of housing provision and policy in Britain from the nineteenth century to the early 1920s. Rising living standards are shown to have produced a steady improvement in the size and quality of housing in England and Wales from the mid-nineteenth century to 1914, while the role of government in the housing sector was also gradually extended. Improvements in housing quality were also evident in Scotland, though its urban centres retained a pattern of housing provision which was both distinct from that south of the border and entailed communal living practices which were declining elsewhere in Britain.

In contrast to this pattern of gradual change, the First World War proved a watershed, as in many areas of British economic and social life. Capitalizing on ideas that had been restricted to small-scale experiments prior to 1914, government—seeking to appease what was seen as a potentially revolutionary post-armistice working class—introduced a 'homes fit for heroes' policy. This led to the first large-scale development of suburban housing estates, which set the pattern for both the inter-war municipal and owner-occupied suburban house.

THE VICTORIAN HOUSING LEGACY

Pre-1914 working-class housing varied widely in form, including houses which had started life as rural cottages before being swallowed up by expanding towns, premises that had initially encompassed industrial activities such as hand-loom weaving in addition to accommodation, and houses originally built for the wealthy but later sub-divided between many families after the area became unfashionable. However, as a 1908 Board of Trade investigation showed, some broad regional patterns of working-class housing forms can be identified.[1]

Through terraces were the most common type of working- and lower-middle-class housing. Typical working-class terraces originally had two rooms on each floor, but became more generous in scope later in the nineteenth century, often having two reception rooms plus a scullery on the ground floor and two or three

---

[1] Board of Trade, Enquiry into Working Class Rents, Housing, and Retail Prices, *Report* (London: HMSO, 1908), xvii–xviii.

bedrooms above. For towns in southern and (to a lesser extent) eastern England and Wales, through terraces with back projections were typical. Bay and forecourt through terrace designs were common in the South even among relatively cheap houses. In the Midlands these features were restricted to better-class housing—ordinary workmen's terraces generally having flat fronts and doors which opened directly onto the street. Many cheaper terraces also lacked external access to backyards, thus requiring coal deliveries and refuse to pass through the front door.

In Yorkshire the four- or five-room terrace was generally restricted to well-paid artisans and the most common house form was the three- or four-room 'back-to-back'. These also accounted for a substantial proportion of older housing in cities such as Liverpool, Manchester, and Birmingham.[2] Despite a decline in new construction by the late Victorian period, in 1914 back-to-backs still represented 71 per cent of the housing stock in Leeds. While the most modern versions were not very different from Edwardian terraces in terms of their number of rooms or building densities (around 40 per acre), back-to-backs built in the 1870s and 1880s were at 50–60 houses per acre, while the bulk of Leeds' 1914 housing stock was built before 1866 and consisted of densely packed long rows or enclosed courts at densities of up to 70 or 80 per acre.[3] Six areas of such housing in Sheffield, demolished in the 1920s, had an average density of 73 houses per acre—one street having the equivalent of 126 per acre.[4]

Meanwhile Tyneside was dominated by the 'Tyneside flat'—a peculiar form of housing similar to a terraced 'maisonette'—which comprised around 60 per cent of the 1911 housing stock for South Tyneside. Each two-storey property had pairs of front doors, one leading to a flat on the ground floor and the other to a flat on the first floor. Flats originally consisted of two rooms each, but new developments from the 1880s were of 3–4 rooms. Shared backyards often contained toilets and wash houses for use by both families.[5]

From the late Victorian period there was a clear trend towards the terrace with parlour becoming the typical desirable working-class urban dwelling in most parts of the country. The parlour was generally at the front of the house and had a more public and symbolic function than the rear living room and adjacent kitchen.[6] It was used for special occasions, entertaining guests and, of course, funerals (its dimensions generally being suitable for the public display of a coffin) and was the respectable, visible, face of the house. Its importance stimulated working-class

---

[2] Board of Trade, Enquiry into Working Class Rents, xvii–xviii; John Burnett, *A Social History of Housing 1815–1885*, 2nd edn (London: Methuen, 1986), 166.

[3] Robert Finnigan, 'Council Housing in Leeds, 1919–39: Social Policy and Urban Change', in Martin J. Daunton (ed.), *Councillors and Tenants: Local Authority Housing in English Cities, 1919–1939* (Leicester: Leicester University Press, 1984), 103.

[4] A. D. K. Owen, *A Report on the Housing Problem in Sheffield* (Sheffield: Sheffield Social Survey Committee, 1931), 26.

[5] Robert Ryder, 'Council House Building in County Durham, 1900–39: The Local Implementation of National Policy', in Martin J. Daunton (ed.), *Councillors and Tenants: Local Authority Housing in English Cities, 1919–1939* (Leicester: Leicester University Press, 1984), 43.

[6] Martin J. Daunton, 'Introduction', in Martin J. Daunton (ed.), *Councillors and Tenants: Local Authority Housing in English Cities, 1919–1939* (Leicester: Leicester University Press, 1984), 27.

Fig. 2.1. Court housing in Liverpool
Source: Henry R. Aldridge, *The National Housing Manual: A Guide to National Housing Policy and Administration* (London: National Housing and Town Planning Council, 1923), 274.

purchases of status-related consumer durables. Working-class luxuries such as pianos, overmantles, and better quality furniture were said to be less evident in the back-to-backs of Yorkshire and Lancashire than in districts with parlour terraced housing.[7] There was also a strong trend for newer vintages of working-class houses to be larger than their predecessors; by the time of the 1901 census some 60.1 per cent of the population in England and Wales occupied homes of five or more rooms, while a further 21.9 per cent were in four rooms. However, substantial numbers of people remained in older, smaller houses—with 9.8 per cent occupying three rooms, 6.6 per cent two rooms, and 1.6 per cent still living in single-room dwellings.[8]

Victorian house-building was a small-scale, localized activity, most of what were then regarded as relatively large builders constructing only several dozen houses a year and even the very largest only reaching an output of 300–400 per year towards the end of the century.[9] The sector was also subject to very little building or planning regulation. Pre-1914 housing legislation focused on 'sanitary reform'—a view of the slums as being problematic mainly on account of their association with

---

[7] Burnett, *Social History of Housing*, 173–4.
[8] Board of Trade, Enquiry into Working Class Rents, 592.
[9] For a review of the available evidence, see Fred Wellings, *British Housebuilders: History and Analysis* (Oxford: Blackwell, 2006), 35.

disease and vice. By the 1860s local by-laws had begun to restrict the development of particularly dense or small houses, under powers conferred in the Local Government Act of 1858.[10] These led to improvements in building standards, densities, and numbers of rooms, without generally marking any radical break with traditional working-class housing forms.

The Artizans and Labourers' Dwellings Act of 1868 gave local authorities general powers to demolish properties unfit for human habitation, while the 1875 Artizans and Labourers' Dwellings Improvement Act empowered them to draw up urban improvement schemes—providing that at least as many working-class people were re-housed as were displaced. Yet these Acts had limited effectiveness, as many 'slum' tenants found it difficult to pay the higher rents of the replacement dwellings. The 1890 Housing of the Working Classes Act eased this problem by allowing councils to develop houses for purposes other than slum clearance and thus opened the way for low-density suburban developments. The rationale was that by re-housing higher-income working-class families, their existing accommodation would be freed-up for lower-income households. The higher costs of low-density 'garden' estates made their extension to working-class families impractical. Those councils, such as the London County Council (LCC), who experimented with suburban municipal housing, generally employed much higher densities, of around twenty-two to twenty-five or more houses per acre, which entailed traditional house designs rather than the wider frontages advocated by Raymond Unwin and his colleagues.[11]

Organized labour pressed councils for municipal housing; in 1898 the Workmen's Housing Council (later the Workmen's National Housing Council) was established to coordinate the various local campaigns.[12] Further Acts of 1900, 1903, and 1909 facilitated municipal development, though local authorities were still not obliged to engage in housing provision.[13] Private philanthropy was also very limited in its impact. Tenants of model tenement blocks run by philanthropic housing trusts ('5 per cent philanthropists') had to pay their rent in advance and were immediately evicted if they fell into arrears, thus effectively limiting occupancy to families with relatively high and secure incomes.[14] Moreover, rental levels alone excluded most households who would have been viewed as 'poor' in the eyes of contemporaries.

Renting from a private landlord remained the standard housing tenure for all classes. Yet the social status of the relatively few owner-occupiers at the turn of the century was broad, ranging from the aristocracy to people who might be considered working class by some definitions. Michael Ball has argued that there was relatively

---

[10] Burnett, *Social History of Housing*, 158.
[11] Mark Swenarton, *Homes Fit for Heroes: The Politics and Architecture of Early State Housing in Britain* (Gateshead: Heinemann, 1981), 34–5.
[12] Swenarton, *Homes Fit for Heroes*, 29.
[13] Bernard Harris, *The Origins of the British Welfare State: Social Welfare in England and Wales 1800–1945* (Basingstoke: Palgrave Macmillan, 2004), 132–3.
[14] Paul Johnson, 'Conspicuous Consumption and Working-Class Culture in Late-Victorian and Edwardian Britain', *Transactions of the Royal Historical Society*, 38:5 (1988), 34.

little social kudos associated with owner occupation prior to the First World War, or social stigma attached to renting. He also identifies quite wide regional variation in the extent of owner occupation, with significant working-class home ownership concentrated in a relatively few manufacturing and mining districts.[15]

Two household expenditure surveys provide snapshots of working-class housing costs and owner-occupation rates prior to the First World War. The first was undertaken by the U.S. Commissioner of Labor in 1890–1, as part of a wider exercise to examine international variations in labour costs for export industries. This covered 1,024 British households headed by males in eight staple industries: pig iron, bar iron, steel, bituminous coal, coke, glass, cotton textiles, and woollen textiles. Almost all (98.1 per cent) were married and 88.9 per cent had children living at home.[16]

The second survey was conducted by the Board of Trade in 1904. This covered one week during July–September and, like the 1890–1 survey, encompassed the whole of Britain, including Ireland.[17] This first large-scale official British household expenditure survey received returns from almost 2,000 working-class families. The published data for the 1904 survey covered only food consumption, family size, and household incomes, information collected on rents not being formally tabulated. However, Gazeley and Newell have digitized some 1,033 surviving returns from the survey (including some rejected from the official sample, owing to incomplete information), of which 991 contained sufficient information to examine working-class accommodation costs in relation to incomes.[18]

Table 2.1 shows the data from the 1890–1 survey and Table 2.2 shows that extracted from the 1904 survey returns (converted from weekly into annual sums, to make them comparable with the 1890–1 survey). As the surviving 1904 budgets substantially oversample households in Scotland and Ireland relative to their populations, these are tabulated separately from those for England and Wales. Like the 1890–1 data, these returns have a bias towards families with incomes higher than the average for urban workers at this time, the head of household's income peaking in the range of 30–35 shillings per week, compared to 20–25s according to a 1906 Board of Trade enquiry into the wages of adult male industrial workers.[19]

---

[15] Michael Ball, *Housing Policy and Economic Power: The Political Economy of Owner Occupation* (London: Methuen, 1983), 25.

[16] United States, *Sixth Annual Report of the United States Commissioner of Labor* (Washington, DC: USGPO, 1890, 1891); *Seventh Annual Report of the United States Commissioner of Labor* (Washington, DC: USGPO, 1891, 1892); T. J. Hatton, G. R. Boyer, and R. E. Bailey, 'The Union Wage Effect in Late Nineteenth Century Britain', *Economica*, 61 (1994), 439–41.

[17] Board of Trade, Enquiry into Working Class Rents, *Report*.

[18] In common with Ian Gazeley and Andrew Newell, 'Poverty in Edwardian Britain', *Economic History Review*, 64 (2011), 52–71, using the data set for this analysis required the removal of some returns with missing or non-standard information. I rejected budgets lacking data on household location, rental payments, or household income; cases where the head of household's income was recorded as zero for reasons which appeared to be temporary in nature; and instances where households were living at a free or reduced rent in property provided by their employers (as such accommodation involved payment in kind). This left a sample of 991 budgets, only marginally different in size from the sample of 990 found to be usable for Gazeley and Newell's purposes.

[19] Gazeley and Newell, 'Poverty in Edwardian Britain', 65–7.

Table 2.1. The relationship between average rental costs and income (£ per annum), for British households included in the 1890–1 U.S. Commissioner of Labor household budgets survey, together with the number and average incomes of householders in the survey

Annual income	Great Britain (includes Ireland)			England and Wales		
	No.	Income	Rent/income	No.	Income	Rent/income
A. Renters						
Under £60	80	52.3	15.6	71	52.2	16.0
£60–75	171	67.5	13.3	155	67.4	13.6
£75–85	127	79.7	11.9	109	79.8	12.2
£85–100	158	90.8	10.9	144	90.9	10.9
£100–25	180	109.8	9.5	146	109.9	9.7
£125–50	105	136.3	7.9	85	136.6	8.0
£150–200	127	168.6	7.1	96	168.3	7.1
Over £200	55	234.6	5.6	33	236.1	5.4
Total	1003	108.3	9.4	839	104.4	9.8
B. Home-owners	21	168.3	n.a.	18	175.8	n.a.

Source: Data set compiled by Ian Gazeley—from Sixth Annual Report of the United States Commissioner of Labor (Washington, DC: USGPO, 1890, 1891); Seventh Annual Report of the United States Commissioner of Labor (Washington, DC: USGPO, 1891, 1892).

Both surveys show extremely low working-class owner-occupation levels. The 1890–1 survey gives a figure of 2.05 per cent, while the 1904 survey returns provide figures of 4.5 per cent for England and Wales, 2.4 per cent for Scotland, and 4.4 per cent for Ireland. It is possible that some of those listed as renting may have been making mortgage payments, though the figures for people owning their houses outright are sufficiently low as to indicate that working-class owner occupation was exceptional. Both surveys indicate that mean earnings for owner-occupiers were significantly higher than those for renters.

Comparison of the surveys reveals a substantial increase in rent-to-income ratios between 1890–1 and 1904. This is partly due to the higher average incomes of workers in the 1890–1 survey—given that the share of household expenditure taken by accommodation tends to fall as income rises. However, this change is also evident when similar income ranges are compared (the data are broadly comparable, as retail prices rose by only 2 per cent over this period). While general prices may have been fairly stable, aggregate dwelling rentals in England and Wales rose by 36.7 per cent between the two surveys, greatly outstripping the 15 per cent rise in average earnings.[20] It thus appears that accommodation costs were taking up a rapidly growing share of working-class incomes, with particularly strong adverse impacts on families at the bottom end of the income scale.

[20] Sources: retail prices and earnings, Lawrence H. Officer, 'Five Ways to Compute the Relative Value of a UK Pound Amount, 1830 to Present', *MeasuringWorth*, 2011, available at <http://www.measuringworth.com/ukcompare/>; rentals, Avner Offer, 'Ricardo's Paradox and the Movement of Rents in England, c.1870–1910', *Economic History Review*, 33 (1980), 251, dwellings series.

Table 2.2. Evidence from surviving returns to the 1904 Board of Trade household expenditure survey, on owner-occupation levels and annual rents in relation to incomes

Annual income (£)	England and Wales			Scotland			Ireland		
	No.	Income	Rent/income	No.	Income	Rent/income	No.	Income	Rent/income
A. Renters									
Under £65	79	53.0	22.1	53	54.9	12.5	20	50.9	14.6
£65–86.67	89	74.8	18.7	188	75.6	12.2	28	76.2	13.1
£86.67–108.33	85	96.9	16.2	138	95.1	11.5	43	95.9	15.2
Over £108.33	89	146.1	12.6	107	145.8	9.0	38	147.6	12.7
Total	342	93.8	16.0	486	94.3	10.9	129	99.8	13.7
B. Home-owners	16	117.1	n.a.	12	153.0	n.a.	6	112.6	n.a.

Notes: Conversion from weekly data assumes a working year of 52 weeks.

Source: Data set compiled by Ian Gazeley and Andrew Newell from surviving returns submitted to the 1904 survey. See Ian Gazeley and Andrew Newell, 'Poverty in Edwardian Britain', *Economic History Review*, 64 (2011), 52–71.

Table 2.3. A comparison of rent as a share of income for households in England and Wales and in Scotland, in the 1890–1 U.S. Commissioner of Labor household budgets survey

	England and Wales			Scotland		
	No.	Income	Rent/income	No.	Income	Rent/income
Under £100	479	75.0	12.5	31	79.1	9.9
£100–50	231	119.7	9.0	45	117.7	7.7
Over £150	129	185.6	6.6	49	196.0	6.5
Total	839	104.4	9.8	125	138.8	7.3

Sources and Notes: As for Table 2.1.

Another finding which emerges from the two surveys is the very different pattern of accommodation expenditure in England and Wales compared to that in Scotland. In 1904 Scottish households for which usable returns survive devoted just 10.9 per cent of income to accommodation, compared to 16.0 per cent in England and Wales, or 13.2 per cent in Ireland. This difference was particularly notable for workers on low incomes: for example, households in England and Wales on £65–£86.67 spent 18.7 per cent of their income on accommodation, compared to 12.2 per cent in Scotland and 13.1 per cent in Ireland. To see whether this trend was already evident in 1890, Table 2.3 provides a comparison of Scotland and England and Wales data from the 1890–1 survey (disaggregated into only three income groups, owing to the limited number of returns for Scotland). A clear pattern of lower rent-to-income ratios north of the border is evident, though the differentials are less marked than in the later survey (possibly due to the fact that, given the focus on staple industries, northern industrial towns are over-represented in the England and Wales sample).

Remarkably, this difference was not the result of lower rental costs north of the border—where rentals per room were actually higher. Average Scottish urban working-class rents per room in 1904 were 24.0 pence, compared to 12.7 pence in the Midlands, 13.6 pence in northern England, and 13.7 pence in the rest of provincial England and Wales. Rents per room in Glasgow averaged 29.8 pence, even higher than the figure for Greater London (28.8 pence). Meanwhile 85 per cent of Scottish households had three or fewer rooms, compared to only 19 per cent of households in the rest of Britain and Ireland.[21]

SCOTLAND: A DIFFERENT COUNTRY

Marked differences between the proportions of household income devoted to accommodation in Scotland and those in the rest of Britain reflect the more cramped conditions of urban Scottish workers. Scottish households had much

---

[21] Ian Gazeley, Andrew Newell, and Peter Scott, 'Why was Urban Overcrowding Much More Severe in Scotland than in the Rest of the British Isles? Evidence from the First (1904) Official Household Expenditure Survey', *European Review of Economic History*, 15 (2011), 134–5.

higher incidences of overcrowding—according to the official standard used in England and Wales (more than two persons per room)—which, among other things, reflected contemporary standards of 'decency' regarding the need for parents and their male and female children to sleep in separate rooms. Cramped conditions were evident even for white-collar workers; in 1901 a mere 6.81 per cent of the population within Glasgow's old city boundaries lived in houses of five or more apartments, implying that a large proportion of its middle-class population inhabited four or fewer rooms.[22]

Scotland's principal urban centres had witnessed heavy in-migration of unskilled rural workers in the wake of the second round of Highland clearances and the Scottish and Irish potato famines. Meanwhile the Scottish land system acted to release land for their accommodation at prices so high that tenements constituted the only economic form of construction. Land was sold outright (rather than on lease), though the vendor retained the right to an annual payment (the feu) in perpetuity. Subsequent vendors of the land, such as the land developer and the builder, could also add their own feu duties. Consequently land was released only slowly for building, at high prices (in order to maximize the feu, the long-term value of which would inevitably be eroded by inflation), and tenements constituted the only form of working-class housing with sufficiently high ratios of tenants to ground area to cover both the high land prices and feu liabilities.[23]

Densely packed tenements were, in turn, divided into very small apartments. Yet there does not appear to have been much unsatisfied demand for larger accommodation; rents for dwellings of more than two rooms were not significantly higher in Scotland than in the rest of Britain.[24] Richard Rodger proposes a demand-side explanation of Scottish overcrowding, based on the interaction between the characteristics of its rental system and the type of accommodation sought.[25] A labour market characterized by a high proportion of low-skilled, casual jobs produced high rates of unemployment and underemployment, including severe problems of seasonal and cyclical unemployment.[26] Scotland also had a tenancy system based on the 'long-let'—a yearly rental from Whitsunday, which had to be contracted up to four months before the lease commenced. This system, which covered around 80 per cent of all working-class houses, involved monthly, quarterly, or half-yearly rental payments, requiring tenants to produce large sums of money at infrequent

---

[22] Board of Trade, Enquiry into Working Class Rents, 534–5.
[23] Richard Rodger, 'The Victorian Building Industry and the Scottish Working Class', in Martin Doughty (ed.), *Building the Industrial City* (Leicester: Leicester University Press, 1986), 172–4.
[24] Gazeley, Newell, and Scott, 'Why was Urban Overcrowding Much More Severe', 137–8.
[25] Richard Rodger, 'Employment, Wages and Poverty in the Scottish Cities 1841–1914', in G. Gordon (ed.), *Perspectives on the Scottish City* (Aberdeen: Aberdeen University Press, 1985), 25–63.
[26] Clive H. Lee, 'Scotland 1850–1939: Growth and Poverty', in Roderick Floud and Paul Johnson (eds), *The Cambridge Economic History of Britain*, vol. 2: *Economic Maturity, 1860–1939* (Cambridge: Cambridge University Press, 2004), 436; Richard Rodger, 'Employment, Wages, and Poverty in the Scottish Cities 1840–1914', in R. J. Morris and Richard Rodger (eds) *The Victorian City: A Reader in British Urban History* (Harlow: Longman, 1993), 102.

intervals.[27] Given these conditions, workers might prudently select cheaper accommodation to reduce their risk of eviction.

Furthermore, Scottish local rates (equivalent to about 5s in the pound of rental) were typically levied directly on occupiers, and therefore not included in rent. These taxes were legally due on the 11th of November each year and constituted a major annual financial burden on working-class households that was unique to Scotland. Scottish landlords had a legal right to sell the possessions of defaulting tenants, providing a further deterrent to taking on tenancies that might prove beyond their means if work was interrupted. Even should incomes remain buoyant, families in poverty often found it extremely difficult to engage in long-term savings (to meet annual lump-sum payments) in the face of pressing short-term needs.

Gazeley, Newell, and Scott found that Scottish households in the 1904 survey returns had almost identical average incomes to those in the rest of Britain. Furthermore, there was a much lower variance in incomes, suggesting that, at least for those workers surveyed, incomes were relatively stable by British standards. Yet they nevertheless spent a smaller share of their income on rent.[28] This suggests that accommodation was accorded lower priority in Scotland than in England. Further evidence is provided by a 1911 national household budget survey of 611 married railway clerks—a group with particularly high occupational stability, but average incomes well within the range covered by the 1904 budget survey. Expenditure on 'housing' (here comprising rents and rates, plus travelling costs to and from work, fuel and lighting, household equipment and furniture, and cleaning materials) accounted for 31.4 per cent of household budgets for clerks in England and Wales, but only 25.9 per cent for Scottish clerks, corroborating the findings of the 1904 survey that households south of the border devoted roughly 5 per cent more of total expenditure to housing than was the case in Scotland.[29]

Joseph Melling identified a cultural preference among Scottish households for prioritizing other areas of consumption over accommodation.[30] The explanation probably lies in the earlier co-evolution of housing types and associated social norms. The rapid population growth of major Scottish cities in the early and middle decades of the nineteenth century overwhelmed the capacity of the existing housing stock and led to a pattern of more intensive development both of new properties and of existing buildings (through subdivision). The wage gap between Scotland and England, which was markedly higher in the mid-nineteenth century than in the Edwardian period, also contributed to the preponderance of one- or two-bedroom apartments.[31] In 1871 over three-quarters of Scotland's population

---

[27] Richard Rodger, 'Crisis and Confrontation in Scottish Housing 1880–1914', in Richard Rodger (ed.), *Scottish Housing in the Twentieth Century* (Leicester: Leicester University Press, 1989), 39–40.
[28] Gazeley, Newell, and Scott, 'Why was Urban Overcrowding Much More Severe', 138–9.
[29] For further details of this analysis, see Gazeley, Newell, and Scott, 'Why was Urban Overcrowding Much More Severe', 143–4.
[30] Joseph Melling, 'Clydeside Rent Struggles and the Making of Labour Politics in Scotland, 1900–39', in Rodger (ed.), *Scottish Housing in the Twentieth Century*, 60.
[31] Lee, 'Scotland 1850–1939', 435.

lived in houses of three or fewer rooms, and some 82.6 per cent were in houses of four or fewer rooms.[32] Thus the vast majority of adults at the time of the 1904 budget survey would have grown up in small tenements and would have taken the social norms and mores of tenement life for granted.

These involved the sharing of a wide variety of utilities, including toilets, water supplies, cooking, washing, and laundry facilities, while the high costs of supplying gas to high-rise dwellings delayed the development of gas lighting and hot water. This added to the daily workload of the housewife, which was further compounded both by the necessity for most housewives to make frequent trips up and down the staircases of multi-storey tenements and by the need to change the layout of rooms on a daily basis so that one or two rooms could function for all the family's day- and night-time needs.[33]

Women adapted to these conditions with strategies such as sharing childcare in the inner courts and alleys. The smooth running of such arrangements involved distinctive social routines, to ensure that the rights and obligations of each family were understood and observed.[34] For example, use of the communal wash house, in the back court or basement, was organized on a rota basis and adhering strictly to the rota was key to peaceful coexistence.[35]

Living arrangements within each flat also necessitated distinct routines and norms. Flats of one or two rooms made it difficult to have segregated sleeping arrangements for parents and children and for male and female children. Indeed, Frank Worsdall argues that even many families occupying two apartment 'room and kitchen' tenements effectively lived and slept in the kitchen, with the 'room' being reserved for special occasions, in a similar manner to the parlour of the English terrace.[36] Living in one or two rooms thus necessitated distinctive patterns of housework, child rearing, play, sleeping, and sex.[37] This differentiated the habitus of Scottish households from that of their southern counterparts, in terms of expected and acceptable social practices and related consumption norms. In particular, having sufficient bedrooms for the parents and for children of each gender to sleep in separate rooms did not assume the same importance for ensuring 'decency' and 'respectability' as was the case in England. As Table 2.4 shows, Gazeley, Newell, and Scott estimate that average floorspace per person was lower even than in Ireland and only around two-thirds that for southern England, the Midlands, and Wales.

Scotland's severe overcrowding was associated with high mortality, especially infant mortality, plus higher incidences of child malnutrition, rickets, heart disease,

---

[32] Rodger, 'Crisis and Confrontation', 48.   [33] Rodger, 'Crisis and Confrontation', 29.
[34] Richard Rodger, 'Building Development: Urbanisation and the Housing of the Scottish People, 1800–1914', in Miles Glendenning and Diane Watters (eds), *Home Builders: Mactaggart and Mickel and the Scottish Housebuilding Industry* (Edinburgh: RCAHMS, 1999), 201–2.
[35] Frank Worsdall, *The Tenement: A Way of Life: A Social, Historical, and Architectural Study of Housing in Glasgow* (Edinburgh: Chambers, 1979), 34.
[36] Worsdall, *Tenement*, 46.
[37] Richard Rodger, 'The Victorian Building Industry and the Housing of the Scottish Working Class', in Martin Doughty (ed.), *Building the Industrial City* (Leicester: Leicester University Press, 1986), 199.

Table 2.4. Estimates of average floorspace per household and per person for urban working-class families in Edwardian Britain

	Average floor-space per household (sq. ft)	Average square feet per person
Scotland	392	97
North of England	591	133
Midlands	639	146
Rest of England and Wales	612	155
Ireland	511	103

Source: Ian Gazeley, Andrew Newell, and Peter Scott, 'Why was Urban Overcrowding Much More Severe in Scotland than in the Rest of the British Isles? Evidence from the First (1904) Official Household Expenditure Survey', *European Review of Economic History*, 15 (2011), 150–1.

bronchial conditions, and a range of other illnesses, together with incidences of stunted height and physical deformities.[38] Overcrowding in one-room apartments showed a particularly strong association with infant mortality, probably mainly due to the lack of physical separation between eating, sleeping, and sanitation. Meanwhile the poor ventilation, inadequate lighting, bad sanitation, and dampness characteristic of many tenements were major contributors to a range of diseases.[39] These problems strongly outweighed any positive health impact from the fact that Scottish households used the income saved by low rental expenditures on higher food budgets. Another consequence of the extremely limited floorspace and undifferentiated room functions of many Scottish tenements was that families typically had very modest levels of furniture and furnishings. It was said that moonlight flits from a Glasgow tenement could be accompanied using only a coal cart.[40]

CRISIS AND REFORM IN EDWARDIAN BRITAIN

Between 1851 and 1911 the urban population of England and Wales increased roughly threefold, from 9,688,000 to 28,468,000, or from 54 to 79 per cent of the total.[41] Meanwhile rising living standards led to demands for larger and better houses. The perceived failure of the private rental market to meet these demands, without a continuing increase in the proportion of household incomes required as rent, eventually led to an economic and political crisis for private landlords and Britain's housing system.

Avner Offer has identified a serious crisis in the supply of houses in large urban centres over the Edwardian period, with property values in London falling by some 40 per cent. This was accompanied by a slump in housing-building. Conversely, house rents remained relatively stable, following a significant rise over the 1890s.

---

[38] Rodger, 'Building Development', 203.
[40] Rodger, 'Building Development', 202.
[39] Rodger, 'Crisis and Confrontation', 31.
[41] Burnett, *Social History of Housing*, 140–1.

Offer explains this apparent contradiction between rental and capital movements as a result of the collapse in the attractions of property as an investment medium, particularly after 1905. Rising interest rates and construction costs substantially raised the minimum expected yields (ratios of rental income to house prices) required by housing investors, while rising local rates reduced the share of working-class income available to pay rent.[42]

Landlords consequently became subject to increasingly severe political attacks, which served to further undermine their economic role. Martin Daunton identifies a process of progressive political isolation of small urban landlords during the decades to 1914, as their interests came to be seen by both the Liberal and Conservative parties as inconsistent with their broader political goals. Such problems were intensified by the development of the Liberal Land Campaign and policies developed by the Conservatives in reaction to it.[43]

The Edwardian era witnessed a major downturn in the building cycle and a slowing in the pace of real income growth. Meanwhile transport improvements that increased the accessibility of the suburbs, such as the tram and motor omnibus, undermined the premium value of houses located close to places of work.[44] Despite the crisis, there was no real willingness among either central or local government for the public sector to play a major role in housing provision. In 1910 the Local Government Board had sanctioned loans for a mere 789 houses, to be built by only two local authorities. By 1914 the number of houses sanctioned had increased to 2,465 and the number of participating councils had risen to 79.[45] Yet local authority housing development comprised less than 5 per cent of new house-building in England and Wales over 1890–1914 and accounted for only around 0.3 per cent of the 1914 housing stock.[46] These developments did, however, provide valuable experiments in municipal provision. Meanwhile the Edwardian period also witnessed a number of experiments in suburban estate development, low-density working-class housing, and mortgage lending to manual workers, all of which were to influence the later emergence of mass suburbanization.

By the late nineteenth century suburbs had already become popular among the middle classes, offering fresh air, more spacious homes, and a better environment for children.[47] Marketing of new suburbs intensified during the Edwardian era. Illustrated adverts for suburban houses had appeared in the *London Evening News* from 1905, while the Great Northern Railway issued the booklet *Where to Live: Illustrated Guide to Some of London's Choicest Suburbs*, from 1906—a technique widely copied by various other railway companies operating London suburban lines.[48] Suburbs to the east of the City, such as Ilford, Leyton, and Leytonstone,

---

[42] Avner Offer, *Property and Politics 1870–1914: Landownership, Law, Ideology and Urban Development in England* (Cambridge: Cambridge University Press, 1981), 254–71.
[43] Daunton, 'Introduction', 4–6.
[44] Offer, *Property and Politics*, 281.
[45] Swenarton, *Homes Fit for Heroes*, 30.
[46] Harris, *Origins of the British Welfare State*, 133.
[47] Burnett, *Social History of Housing*, 193.
[48] Alan A. Jackson, *Semi-Detached London: Suburban Development, Life, and Transport, 1900–39*, 2nd edn (Didcot: Wild Swan, 1991), 159.

proved successful in attracting white-collar workers seeking more spacious houses and a healthier environment. For example, while the typical houses developed in Ilford from 1890–1914 were still terraces, they boasted three to four bedrooms, front and back gardens, indoor toilets, and hot water systems.[49]

Economic and institutional developments opened up the possibility of working-class suburbanization. The late nineteenth century and Edwardian era witnessed rising living standards, greater stability of employment, and some reduction in working hours. Meanwhile the Cheap Trains Act of 1883 introduced 'Workmen's fares' at a quarter of the standard rail fair (though some railway companies tried to limit their impact by compelling workers who used them to travel at 5 or 6 a.m.). From the turn of the century electric trams, with reduced return fairs, opened up suburban locations that were not easily accessible by rail, further increasing the potential land available for both working-class and white-collar suburban development.[50]

In Edwardian London working-class suburbs such as Walthamstow, Tottenham, Wood Green, Edmonton, Aton, and Willesden, a common form of new housing was the 'half-house', providing accommodation for one family on the ground floor and another on the first floor. Flats were self-contained, but sometimes shared the same street door (or porch, with the doors placed side by side).[51] These were to enjoy continued popularity in the interwar period (with the addition of a fireproof external staircase to the upper level) as 'maisonettes', providing a cheaper two-bedroom alternative to the standard three bedroom suburban semi.

Model workers' villages, such as Lever Brothers' Port Sunlight (1888); Bourneville, developed by Cadbury from 1895; and Rowntree's New Earswick (1901), represented a more radical departure from traditional working-class housing. At Bourneville, for example, three-bedroom houses, either semi-detached or in small blocks of three or four, were built six to the acre, gardens comprising at least three-quarters of each plot. Like some cheaper interwar council houses, the smallest had a 'cabinet' bath in the kitchen, rather than a separate bathroom.[52]

There was a degree of philanthropy behind these developments, reflected in the close links between several of the pioneering employers and the emerging town planning and garden city movements. Yet employers were also motivated by a belief that better living conditions would be reflected in higher productivity and improved industrial relations. Similar thinking underpinned moves by some employers to introduce shorter working hours in the years up to 1914—based on a calculation that the lost time would be more than offset by higher hourly productivity, reduced absenteeism, and a lower incidence of accidents and substandard work.

Garden city and garden suburb projects provided a further opportunity for architects to experiment with low-density housing, largely based on the semi or short

---

[49] Michael Heller, 'Suburbia, Marketing, and Stakeholders: Developing Ilford, Essex 1880–1914', *Urban History* (forthcoming).

[50] Stefan Muthesius, *The English Terraced House* (New Haven, CT: Yale University Press, 1982), 39.

[51] Jackson, *Semi-Detached London*, 11–12.   [52] Burnett, *Social History of Housing*, 183.

terrace. Hampstead Garden Suburb, developed from 1906, was an important pioneering development; however, despite its founders' intention to create a socially mixed community, its housing proved beyond the reach of most Edwardian working-class families. The architect and town planner Raymond Unwin played a major role in popularizing the practicality of such low-density developments. His 1912 pamphlet *Nothing Gained by Overcrowding!* argued that road costs were lower (owing to the reduced amount of road frontage necessary for intersections), while the much larger plots the householder received more than repaid the extra overall cost.[53]

Architects and planners also sought to develop a lower-cost version of the 'garden city' house, within the reach of the typical working-class family. In 1906 both Unwin and Bourneville's architect, Alexander Harvey, published proposals for reducing costs via the simplification of design and standardization of building components—ideas that were to be further developed during the First World War. The new standards did not always meet working-class expectations. For example, at New Earswick Barry Parker and Raymond Unwin developed short terraces of cottage-type housing, with the parlour eliminated in favour of a single living room.[54] This clashed with respectable working-class values, which saw a well-maintained parlour as a key symbol of respectability and status. This debate was to continue during the 1920s and 1930s when most council houses (and some of the cheaper speculative houses) were developed without parlours.

There were also signs that some rapidly expanding building societies were beginning to turn their attention towards working-class borrowers. Building societies were mutual organizations that had developed from 'building clubs', established to enable working- and lower-middle-class people to purchase or build their own homes. Their growth accelerated from the mid-nineteenth century, following their transition from 'terminating societies' (that were disbanded after their original members had all made house purchases) to permanent societies—which financed mortgage lending by taking deposits from savers.

This transition is often seen as having been accompanied by a switch in mortgage lending to middle-class borrowers. However, as recent work by Luke Samy has revealed, the late Victorian and Edwardian period also witnessed the development of a successful model of mortgage lending to working-class families by at least one society—the Co-operative Permanent Building Society (CPBS). Founded in 1884 as an offshoot of the Co-operative movement, CPBS used its close association with the movement as a source of savings and mortgage business and, crucially, agents. Agents constituted the principal means of the society's expansion, both accepting deposits and recommending potential borrowers. By 1905 CPBS had 170 agencies in 49 counties (thus avoiding risks inherent in geographically concentrated lending, when depression hit local industries). Agents were typically managers of local Co-operative stores who used their intimate knowledge of their customers' credit and saving history (the Co-op's 'divi' to its

---

[53] Cited in Swenarton, *Homes Fit for Heroes*, 14.
[54] Swenarton, *Homes Fit for Heroes*, 20–4.

Fig. 2.2. An early flyer for the National Freehold Land & Building Society, *c.*1900
Source: Peter Scott collection.

members was often left to accumulate as savings) to screen against unreliable borrowers. Meanwhile borrowers had strong incentives to maintain payments, as in the event of default they might lose not only their house, but access to credit at their local Co-op.

The CPBS's low arrears and repossession rates, compared to other building societies, is testament to the success of these mechanisms, despite lending to lower-income customers on more generous terms. Its loans were typically small, mainly below £300 in value, for single working-class dwellings of six or seven rooms. Samy estimates that 70 per cent of borrowers were manual workers, including some in industries vulnerable to the trade cycle.[55]

Such families were able to afford houses owing to the presence of secondary incomes, which often made household income substantially higher than that of the main 'breadwinner'. Samy estimated that almost 60 per cent of borrowers used secondary incomes, from other working family members (mainly children), from subletting, and/or from accepting rent-paying boarders. The society increased the 'affordability' of mortgages by liberalizing terms, a strategy which was to prove crucial to the interwar expansion of working-class owner occupation. Over half of its mortgages were for periods of 20 years or more, with a quarter over 25 years (which often made buying a house no more expensive than renting). Loan-to-value ratios were also generous, a quarter of loans being in excess of 85 per cent of the purchase price and almost one in ten being in excess of 90 per cent.[56]

By 1914 the Co-operative Permanent had become Britain's thirteenth largest building society, only 30 years after its foundation. Despite the Edwardian property market slump, its formula of lending to owner-occupiers, with small loans on liberal terms, and tapping the Co-operative movement's local intelligence networks regarding household credit-worthiness, had proved extraordinarily successful. Other rapidly growing and, often, relatively new, London-based building societies such as Abbey Road (established in 1874), Westbourne Park (1885), and the National (1849) were also more focused on small loans than their northern counterparts, mortgages of under £500 constituting more than 60 per cent of overall lending by each society in 1913.[57]

WAR ACCELERATES CHANGE

In August 1914 Britain entered a war which was to prove unprecedented in terms of both the number of casualties and the extent of government intervention in the day-to-day running of the economy. The long-term economic effects proved far-reaching. Wartime expansions in industrial production by both belligerents and

---

[55] Luke Samy, 'Extending Home Ownership before the First World War: The Case of the Co-operative Permanent Building Society, 1884–1913', *Economic History Review*, 65:1 (2012), 178–9.
[56] Samy, 'Extending Home Ownership', 13–21.
[57] Samy, 'Extending Home Ownership', 5.

neutrals, accentuated by dislocations in trade, led to a major rise in international competition for key British export industries concentrated in northern Britain and Wales, such as coal, iron and steel, textiles, and shipbuilding. Meanwhile the war accelerated technical change and development in a range of new assembly industries such as motor vehicles and electrical goods, based in the Midlands and South. The resulting regional imbalance was to intensify during the interwar years, culminating in the mass unemployment of outer Britain, and the relative prosperity of the South East and West Midlands.[58]

The war also had major direct and indirect impacts on the state's role in the housing market. Government initially adopted a 'business as usual' policy of minimal economic intervention. Yet the inability of private enterprise to meet wartime munitions demand led to the 'Shell Scandal' of spring 1915, the collapse of Asquith's Liberal government, and the establishment of a much more interventionist approach to economic management, symbolized by the creation of the Ministry of Munitions.

War production required extensive relocations of labour, producing severe housing problems in many moderately sized towns, such as Barrow-in-Furness (home to a Vickers engineering factory) where the working population rose from 16,000 to 35,000 during the first three years of war.[59] Sharp rent rises for poor quality private housing in Glasgow and other munitions centres led to a number of rent strikes, prompting government intervention via the Increase in Rent and Mortgage Interest (War Restrictions) Act of 1915. Rents for houses of low rateable value were fixed at levels paid on 3 August 1914.[60] Mortgage interest rates were also fixed, while the calling-in of mortgages was prohibited, to prevent lenders from switching to more lucrative investments.

Although the 1915 Act was set to terminate six months after the end of hostilities, rent controls proved far more enduring. As the gap between controlled and economic rents increased over 1915–19, and the housing shortage grew, the impact of decontrol on working-class incomes was viewed as too severe to make this politically realistic. The Increase in Rent and Mortgage Interest (Restrictions) Act, 1919, extended controls to 1923, while allowing rents to be increased by 10 per cent and mortgage interest by an additional 0.5 per cent (up to a maximum of 5 per cent per annum). Meanwhile the rateable value ceiling for rent controls was extended to higher value houses. The Increase in Rent and Mortgage (Restrictions) Act of 1920 further raised the rateable value ceiling for controlled rents, while enabling rents to be raised up to 40 per cent above 1914 levels and mortgage interest rates by 1 per cent—up to a maximum of 6.5 per cent. These measures protected working-class incomes, but had a devastating effect on private landlords. Between 1910–14

---

[58] See Peter Scott, *Triumph of the South: A Regional Economic History of Britain During the Early Twentieth Century* (Aldershot: Ashgate, 2007), Chapter 4.

[59] Laurence F. Orbach, *Homes for Heroes: A Study of the Evolution of British Public Housing, 1915–1921* (London: Seeley, 1977), 11.

[60] John McKee, 'Glasgow Working-Class Housing between the Wars, 1919–1939', MLitt thesis (University of Strathclyde, 1977), 5–8.

and 1921–4 labour's share of GNP rose from 55.3 to 67.4 per cent, partly owing to a decline in the share of rent from 11.0 to 6.8 per cent.[61]

Rent control was further extended under the Rent and Mortgage Interest Restrictions Act, 1923, though controls were now imposed on 'tenancies', rather than houses—allowing decontrol once a house became vacant. Yet only 6 per cent of houses had been decontrolled by the end of 1928, and 11 per cent by the middle of 1930.[62] The Act placed many tenants in the dilemma of having to decide whether to stay in housing which was cheap but no longer suited to their needs, or move to better housing and face a much sharper rise in rents than would be expected given the differences between their present and desired accommodation.

Rent controls remained for the rest of the interwar period—the 1931 Marley Committee on the Rent Restriction Acts found that the housing shortage was still severe enough to prevent decontrol of small working-class dwellings, while as late as 1937 the Ridley Committee found that only gradual decontrol might be countenanced. The 1933 Rent Restriction Act led to the immediate decontrol of rents on over 500,000 'middle class' houses.[63] Yet it prevented decontrol on change of tenancy for the cheapest houses, thus effectively broadening the scope of permanent rent control.

Housing shortages around key Royal Ordnance factories and other munitions facilities necessitated some wartime government house-building. Despite Treasury pressure to limit such developments to low-cost temporary structures, the War Office succeeded in pushing through some schemes for permanent housing, such as projects to house workers at the Woolwich and Gretna Royal Ordnance Factories. Some 10,000 permanent houses were built in connection with munitions factories, on thirty-eight estates, generally along 'garden city' lines. These provided both influential examples of low-cost, low-density developments and initial experience in mass housing for a group of architects who were to play an influential role in interwar municipal estate design. Costs were lowered partly through simplifications in design, producing a 'neo-Georgian' or, more negatively, 'brick box' appearance which was to become characteristic of many interwar municipal estates.[64] Architects seized on the neo-Georgian style as offering a means of expressing community through built form—the collective appearance of the houses, rather than that of individual dwellings, setting the aesthetic tone of the estate.

THE LIFE AND DEATH OF 'HOMES FIT FOR HEROES'

From 1916 government had begun to plan for post-war housing needs. Rising industrial and political unrest in areas such as Clydeside during 1917 and 1918 increased the importance attached to housing policy as a means of placating the working class and reducing what many in government saw as a potentially explosive

---

[61] Daunton, 'Introduction', 8–9.   [62] Harris, *Origins of the British Welfare State*, 244.
[63] Harris, *Origins of the British Welfare State*, 245.   [64] Swenarton, *Homes Fit for Heroes*, 60.

political situation that might give rise to widespread civil unrest or even a potential Bolshevik revolution. As Laurence Orbach noted, government sought 'to induce the calming effects of football by building houses'.[65] This would, it was hoped, both meet working-class grievances and help avoid mass unemployment during demobilization.

The war had both considerably raised building costs and shifted relative costs in favour of low-density development. Over 1914–19 the cost of road and sewer development had doubled, while land costs were little changed, increasing the financial attractions of low-density schemes, which economized on road costs but required much greater land per house. In December 1919 Unwin estimated that the additional cost per plot of developing at twelve houses per acre rather than twenty-one had fallen from 19 per cent in 1914 to less than 4 per cent.[66]

The 1918 Tudor Walters committee report on the provision of dwellings for the working classes set out the blueprint for interwar local authority and, to a considerable extent, private sector suburban housing development. The report was largely the work of Unwin, echoing his pre-war experience with low-density working-class housing and drawing on the lessons of wartime munitions factory housing developments. Tenements or two-storey flatted houses (maisonettes) were rejected in favour of self-contained cottages, generally with at least three bedrooms, a bathroom, scullery kitchen, and, wherever possible, a parlour. Simple rectangular plans dispensed with out-buildings and back projections, while low densities (twelve or fewer per acre) enabled the provision of generous gardens.[67]

April 1919 saw the publication of the Local Government Board's *Manual on the Preparation of State-Aided Housing Schemes*, which was designed as a guide to local authorities preparing housing programmes under the 1919 Act. This was essentially a re-statement of the Tudor Walters report. The Ministry of Labour issued five principal plan types for council houses, classified alphabetically into 'A' (non-parlour) and 'B' (parlour) houses, and by number—according to the number of bedrooms. The most popular designs on the early estates were the A3 and then B3 houses, while most estates included a small proportion of B4s and, sometimes, a very small proportion of A2s.[68]

The Housing and Town Planning Act of 1919 (known as the Addison Act, after the Minister for Housing, Christopher Addison) required local authorities to survey local housing needs and implement plans for providing the necessary homes (subject to Ministry of Health approval). This constituted the first obligatory, rather than permissive, local authority housing legislation. Addison's was the only interwar Act to relate the volume of municipal house-building to the needs of each area. The cost to local ratepayers was set at the same percentage of rateable value for each district (the balance being financed via national taxation). Conversely,

---

[65] Orbach, *Homes for Heroes*, 94. [66] Swenarton, *Homes Fit for Heroes*, 143.
[67] Local Government Board for England and Wales, and Scotland, *Report of the Committee Appointed by the President of the Local Government Board and the Secretary of State for Scotland to Consider Questions of Building Construction in Connection with the Provision of Dwellings for the Working Classes in England and Wales, and Scotland . . .* (Cd. 9191 of 1918).
[68] Burnett, *Social History of Housing*, 227.

subsequent interwar legislation was based on flat rate subsidies, which limited the participation of depressed areas.[69]

The Act contained a government subsidy, covering all losses incurred by local authorities, in excess of those funded by levying a penny rate. Meanwhile rents were fixed independently of costs—very loosely based on the level of controlled rents of working-class houses—but reflecting the new houses' superior amenities and the incomes of their prospective tenants.[70] Rent levels had to be approved by the Ministry of Health, cases where the local authority and Ministry failed to reach agreement being referred to a tribunal. Yet the Addison Act also required local authorities to raise finance for housing development from private sources. This proved difficult during the immediate post-armistice period, forcing many authorities to postpone or curtail their housing programmes.[71]

Average rents (excluding rates) on houses built under the Act were between 9 and 10s, though there was wide local variation—from under 5s in some (mainly rural) areas to 11–12s (mainly in Greater London). Marion Bowley estimated that a considerable proportion of Addison houses were let at 7–9s.[72] Another feature of the 1919 housing programme was encouragement of 'satellite town' development, prompting several major councils to launch some of the most ambitious municipal housing developments of the twentieth century, including Manchester's Wythenshawe satellite town and the LCC's Becontree Estate.[73]

Addison's first housing Act was reinforced by a second, the Housing (Additional Powers) Act, 1919. This offered a small lump sum subsidy per house for private enterprise developments which met certain size criteria, to assist potential owner-occupiers on relatively low incomes (by the standards of contemporary house purchasers). However, most potential private developers were put off by high building costs. Municipal housing development was similarly limited by shortages of building materials, labour, and finance. For example, brick prices were driven up by a shortage of labour for the brickfields. Demobilization did not resolve the problem, as the brickyards had hitherto relied on cheap, casual labour, and, given the temporary economic boom, men who had done this work before enlisting generally sought better paid and more secure factory employment. For the same reasons, those workers who did return to the building industry staunchly opposed the 'dilution' of traditional craft demarcations and restrictions to speed up housing construction. An official committee informed the cabinet that only 14 per cent of the 53,000 bricklayers in England and Wales were engaged in house-building at the end of May 1920.[74] However, the onset of economic depression soon prompted a return of trained building workers, as the downturn in manufacturing employment was much more severe than in construction.

---

[69] Ryder, 'Council House Building in County Durham', notes that the 1930 Housing Act represented a partial exception, as subsidies were linked to the number of slum-dwellers re-housed.
[70] Marion Bowley, *Housing and the State 1919–1944* (London: George Allen & Unwin, 1945), 17. However, after March 1927 tenants were to be charged an economic rent if they could afford it, as it was believed that by then the post-war housing problem would have been solved.
[71] Daunton, 'Introduction', 10. [72] Bowley, *Housing and the State*, 25.
[73] Swenarton, *Homes Fit for Heroes*, 143. [74] Orbach, *Homes for Heroes*, 96–111.

There was considerable initial enthusiasm for unconventional building techniques, capitalizing on developments in the erection of temporary buildings for the war effort. In November 1919 the Ministry of Health launched a publicity campaign for alternative building techniques and established a demonstration centre in Acton where local authority representatives could see houses built using the new methods. Steel, cast-iron, concrete, and timber-frame technologies all received serious consideration, as they offered the possibility of housing development using unskilled labour and available materials at a time when both bricks and bricklayers were in very limited supply. Yet, despite grand claims regarding the various systems, most failed to either achieve any substantial reduction in building costs or overcome negative perceptions regarding their appearance and rapid depreciation.[75]

One popular method was the Dorman Long system, originally developed by Dorman Long & Co. for housing its own workers. Kits of steel girders were sold to councils, who had them assembled and added walls and floors made from concrete slabs. Several councils in County Durham experimented with this system (encouraged by their proximity to the firm's 'Dormanstown' housing estate at Redcar, where it had been pioneered). Yet the houses proved liable to cracking and dampness (and eventually rusting of the steel frame), usually necessitating extensive repairs within 10–15 years. Ironically, the solution to this problem was found to be the addition of a protective shell of brickwork.[76]

Yet two of the largest and most prestigious British house-building firms, John Laing and Henry Boot, made extensive use of concrete housing in their contract work for municipal estates, with a considerable degree of success. Both used cavity wall systems—Laing's 'Easiform' system and the 'Boot Pier and Panel Continuous Cavity System'. Boot's chief executive, Charles Boot, claimed to have erected over 8,000 concrete houses during 1924–30, for large municipalities such as London, Birmingham, Liverpool, Sheffield, and Glasgow. He argued that a key factor behind their success was supervision of the building process by people trained in the use of concrete and that the lack of such supervision had been responsible for the poor general reputation of concrete housing.[77]

Building materials and labour costs did not fully account for the rising cost of municipal house-building, which was further inflated by unscrupulous building contractors. Price rings were used to avoid competitive tendering and contractors also insisted on clauses in their contracts which enabled them to artificially inflate costs. For example, the Bristol Association of Building Trades Employers (BABTE) successfully negotiated a contract with the council which included an 'elastic clause' that both guaranteed a minimum profit even where the cost per house

---

[75] David Jeremiah, *Architecture and Design for the Family in Britain, 1900–70* (Manchester: Manchester University Press, 2000), 45–9.
[76] Ryder, 'Council House Building in County Durham', 63.
[77] Henry Boot plc company archives, Charles Boot, 'Housing Built by Private Enterprise', Memorandum for the Ministry of Health's Sub-Committee on Private Enterprise Housing, October 1943, 14–16. For Laing's concrete houses see Roy Coad, *Laing: A Biography of Sir John W. Laing, CBE (1879–1978)* (London: Hodder & Stoughton, 1979), 74–7.

Fig. 2.3. Brochure illustration for Newton Chambers & Co. pre-fabricated houses, built from cast-iron plates covered by cement rough cast—a system developed to employ spare foundry capacity previously used for shell casings (no date, *c.*1919)
Source: Peter Scott collection.

exceeded the agreed figure and did not oblige contractors to keep detailed, audited accounts.[78]

There is also strong evidence that materials suppliers sought to charge councils inflated prices (especially during the early 1920s). For example, in 1924 Bristol's Housing Committee—following advice from the Ministry of Health—conferred with local brick manufacturers about prices and supply. Despite Bristol's brick production being at record levels, only one brick manufacturer offered to supply the corporation. Yet once the committee decided to start using concrete all the manufacturers suddenly felt able to meet its needs—at a lower price.[79]

By February 1920 the Ministry of Health perceived that builders' rings had removed competition in contracting for municipal housing.[80] The Ministry thus reversed its initial opposition to councils employing direct labour, given that this sometimes constituted the best way of weakening the power of local builders'

---

[78] Madge Dresser, 'Housing Policy in Bristol, 1919–30', in Martin J. Daunton (ed.), *Councillors and Tenants: Local Authority Housing in English Cities, 1919–1939* (Leicester: Leicester University Press, 1984), 155–216, esp. 177–8.

[79] Dresser, 'Housing Policy in Bristol', 186. [80] Swenarton, *Homes Fit for Heroes*, 126.

federations. Despite claims by local business groups and newspapers that direct labour developments were characterized by lax supervision and low productivity, evidence indicates that (at least during the 1920s) its use produced significant savings compared to paying private contractors.[81] For example, Liverpool built 500 houses by direct labour (under a Ministry of Health scheme to ascertain the most economical method of house-building), which proved to be significantly cheaper than Liverpool's contractor-built houses.[82] Nevertheless, most municipal housing during the 1920s was undertaken by private contractors.[83]

The 1919 Act was designed to produce some 500,000 new municipal houses. Yet, as a result of the above problems, by December 1919 not a single house had been built under the new legislation.[84] Fears of Bolshevik revolution rapidly receded during 1919 and, with post-war boom giving way to severe slump from the summer of 1920, the power of organized labour waned. Government felt sufficiently confident to introduce deflationary economic policy in an effort to restore pre-war 'normalcy' by returning the pound to the gold standard at its 1914 parity (which it had fallen considerably below, owing to wartime and post-war inflation). The ambitious Addison Act, with its generous Treasury subsidy, rapidly became a target of the expenditure cuts. July 1921 marked the end of the 'homes fit for heroes' era; the number of houses to be developed under the Act being limited to 170,000—only slightly in excess of the number for which contracts had already been signed.[85]

The average all-in cost of the 160,000 municipal houses contracted for by the end of April 1921 was around £1,000 per dwelling, while building contract prices had increased from about £740 in the summer of 1919 to around £930 at their peak in autumn 1920. Ironically, by the time construction had begun in earnest the decline in building activity was sufficient to prevent any significant upward pressure on building industry capacity and costs—though as many contracts had already been signed, the chief beneficiaries of falling costs were the contractors.[86] Britain's severe housing shortage continued.

The Addison Act had failed to seriously address a housing shortage which had been compounded by a virtual cessation of non-defence-related house-building during the war years. By 1921 some 30 per cent of all households were in dwellings of not more than three occupied rooms and 20 per cent were sharing the same dwelling with at least one other family (compared to 15.7 per cent in 1911).[87] Yet, while limited in volume, Addison Act houses did provide a blueprint for the interwar suburban home. These typically had the most generous dimensions and highest building specifications of any interwar municipal housing. Although the Ministry had recommended a 900-sq. ft average floorspace for a typical three-bedroom

---

[81] Ryder, 'Council House Building in County Durham', 65–6.
[82] Madeline McKenna, 'The Development of Suburban Council Housing Estates in Liverpool between the Wars', PhD thesis (University of Liverpool, 1986), 80–1.
[83] Ruth Issacharoff, 'The Building Boom of the Interwar Years: Whose Profits and Whose Cost?', in Michael Harloe (ed.), *Urban Change and Conflict* (London: CES, 1978), 304.
[84] Orbach, *Homes for Heroes*, 88.   [85] Bowley, *Housing and the State*, 22.
[86] Bowley, *Housing and the State*, 30–1.   [87] Burnett, *Social History of Housing*, 221.

Addison house, their actual floorspace ranged from around 950–1,400 sq. ft, making them among the most spacious council houses ever developed in Britain.[88] This was an increase of over 50 per cent compared to the average floorspace per household in England and Wales before 1914 (as shown in Table 2.4).

CONCLUSION

The Addison Act famously failed in providing 'homes fit for heroes' on a scale that came anywhere close to meeting potential demand. Yet, in the longer term, it succeeded in establishing a new housing standard, which would eventually lead to the construction of four million homes broadly along Tudor Walters lines before war once again intervened. The first wave of interwar council houses had played a vital role in demonstrating a new model of housing, based on three-bedroom semi-detached houses with large gardens in a semi-rural environment. There would be no going back to the pre-war terrace.

However, the suburban semi was to evolve along two divergent paths. Municipal housing was to become somewhat smaller and even more standardized—while keeping the basic essentials of the Tudor Walters standard. Conversely, privately developed housing was to use ornamentation, variegation, and other attributes (such as garage spaces) as a means of distinguishing itself from its municipal counterpart, though again remaining essentially Tudor Walters houses. The following chapters examine the reasons behind the emergence of these two distinct but related 'species' of interwar suburban semi, starting with the subsequent evolution of the council house.

[88] Harris, *Origins of the British Welfare State*, 248.

3
Municipal Suburbia

INTRODUCTION

Council housing comprised over 30 per cent of the 4.3 million new homes built in Britain over the interwar period, while dominating total house-building in Scotland. Moreover, it popularized the suburban semi during the early 1920s (a time of very limited private sector house-building) and brought it within the financial reach of working-class households. For the first time large numbers of ordinary working people were given access to new suburban houses with hot running water, bathrooms, gas, electricity, and substantial gardens, creating aspirations that, for many people, had become expectations by the late 1930s.

This chapter charts the post-Addison history of the interwar council house and the impacts of municipal suburban living on the new council tenants. It also examines how employing council houses for slum clearance and relieving overcrowding during the 1930s changed public perceptions of this form of housing from being aspirational to something clearly inferior to owner occupation.

POST-ADDISON COUNCIL HOUSE DEVELOPMENT IN THE 1920S

The 1920s and 1930s witnessed a rapid succession of new housing legislation. The Conservatives introduced Neville Chamberlain's 1923 Housing Act, providing a relatively modest subsidy of £6 per house annually for 20 years, for houses built by 1 October 1925. This was available both to private and local authority developers and for houses built for either letting or sale. Qualifying houses had to meet certain minimum standards and not be over a specified maximum size. Local authorities were only allowed to build houses if they could convince the Minister of Health that it would be better for them to do so than to leave house-building to private enterprise. The Act also empowered local authorities to assist owner-occupiers and private landlords—by advancing down payments for people who did not have sufficient funds for a mortgage deposit, by guaranteeing mortgage instalments, and by providing loans to landlords for repair and reconstruction of dwellings.

The election in 1924 of Britain's first minority Labour government saw further legislation—the Housing (Financial Provisions) Act, 1924, generally known as the Wheatley Act, after the current Minister of Health. This retained the Chamberlain subsidy. It also introduced a new subsidy (of £9 per house per annum in urban areas and £12 10s in rural areas) available only for houses built for letting, by local authorities or public utility societies. Qualifying houses were to be rented at an average level fixed in relation to prevailing controlled rents on pre-1914 houses. Local authorities were required to meet a maximum loss of £4 10s per year on each house built, thus (together with the Treasury subsidy) obliging them to set average rents at levels which prevented any overall deficit in excess of £13 10s per house, or £17 in rural parishes.[1] Rents for Liverpool's Wheatley houses were very much lower than those for its Addison houses, due to both falling building costs and their smaller dimensions (950 sq. ft for parlour houses and 768–814 sq. ft for non-parlour houses). Yet their rents remained beyond the reach of many working-class families.[2]

The Act repealed Chamberlain's clause requiring local authorities to show that the private sector could not adequately meet housing demand before commencing development on their own account and extended the period over which grants would be available for new houses to those completed before 1 October 1939. Wheatley also reached a 'gentleman's agreement' with the building trade unions, promising an increase in building work in return for a relaxation of rules limiting the entry of skilled men into the trade. A steady increase in house-building was envisaged, from 63–95,000 houses per year in 1926 to a peak of 150–225,000 by the mid-1930s.[3]

The Conservative administration of 1924–9 advised local authorities to concentrate development on cheaper houses, aimed at the lowest-paid workers (partly to avoid competition with the private sector). Yet they offered no incentives, or compulsion, to achieve these ends. They also reduced the Chamberlain and Wheatley subsidies from 30 September 1927 and then, in 1928, abolished the Chamberlain subsidy for houses completed after 30 September 1929 and further reduced the Wheatley subsidy from this date (though this was prevented by the election of a new minority Labour government). Some councils followed the government's advice, mindful of the difficulties their tenants were facing in meeting the rents of the Addison and Wheatley houses. By the end of the 1920s non-parlour houses of 710 and 620 sq. ft were being constructed in Liverpool, with rents of 10s 11d and 9s 6d a week, respectively. Yet tenants still found it difficult to afford rent payments and agitation for lower rents by tenants associations continued.[4]

As Table 3.1 shows, around 580,000 new municipal houses were built in England and Wales under the 1923 and 1924 Acts, though over the lifetime of these Acts annual completions only surpassed the peak annual level under the Addison Act in one year (ending 31 March 1928).

---

[1] Marion Bowley, *Housing and the State 1919–1944* (London: George Allen & Unwin, 1945), 36–42.
[2] Madeline McKenna, 'The Development of Suburban Council Housing Estates in Liverpool between the Wars', PhD thesis (University of Liverpool, 1986), 106.
[3] Bowley, *Housing and the State*, 41.
[4] McKenna 'Development of Suburban Council Housing Estates', 107.

Table 3.1. Number of houses built in England and Wales, 1 January 1919 to 31 March 1939 (thousands)

Year ending 31st March	By local authorities[a]					By private enterprise[b]						All housing
	1919 Act	1923 Act	1924 Act	1930–8 Acts	Total	1919 Acts	1923 Act	1924 Act	1930–8 Acts	Un-subsidized[c]	Total	
1920[d]	0.6				0.6	0.1					0.1	0.7
1921	15.6				15.6	13.0					13.0	28.6
1922	80.8				80.8	20.3					20.3	101.1
1923	57.5				57.5	10.3				53.8[c]	64.1	121.6
1924	10.5	3.8			14.3		4.3			67.5	71.8	86.1
1925	2.9	15.3	2.5		20.7		47.0			69.2	116.2	136.9
1926	1.1	16.2	26.9		44.2		62.4	0.4		66.4	129.2	173.4
1927	0.9	14.1	59.1		74.1		78.4	1.2		63.9	143.5	217.6
1928	0.2	13.8	90.1		104.1		73.1	1.5		60.3	134.9	239.0
1929		5.1	50.6		55.7		48.4	0.7		64.7	113.8	169.5
1930		5.6	54.6	1.6	61.8		49.1	1.1		90.1	140.3	202.1
1931			52.5	3.4	55.9			2.6		125.4	128.0	183.9
1932			65.2	4.9	70.1			2.3		128.4	130.7	200.8
1933		1.4	47.1	7.4	55.9			2.4	0.1	142.0	144.5	200.4
1934			44.8	11.2	56.0			2.8		207.9	210.7	266.7
1935			11.1	29.1	40.2			0.8	0.3	286.4	287.5	327.7
1936				53.5	53.5				0.2	271.7	271.9	325.4
1937				71.8	71.8				0.8	274.4	275.2	347.0
1938				78.0	78.0				2.6	257.1	259.7	337.7
1939				100.9	100.9				4.2	226.4	230.6	331.5
Total	170.1	75.3	504.5	361.8	1111.7	43.7	362.7	15.8	8.2	2455.6	2886.0	3997.7

Source: Marion Bowley, *Housing and the State 1919–1944* (London: George Allen & Unwin, 1945), 271.

[a] Excluding 15,365 houses built for persons displaced by reconstruction and improvement schemes under the 1890 and 1925 Acts.
[b] Excluding houses with rateable values exceeding £78 (£105 in the Metropolitan Police Area).
[c] Total for all years includes 21,500 houses built by private enterprise with Local Authority guarantees under the Housing (Financial Provisions) Act, 1933, not shown separately.
[d] Including the three months January to March 1919.
[e] Includes 30,000 houses built from the armistice to October 1922. As 23,800 were built in the five months to March 1923, an annualized figure based on these months would exceed 53,800.

FROM GENERAL NEEDS HOUSING TO SLUM CLEARANCE

Between 1921 and 1931 overcrowding in England and Wales (according to the official definition, a density of more than two persons per room) had declined from 497,133 to 396,850 families. However, if a more stringent 1.5 persons per room was taken as the standard, 1,174,607 families (or 7 million people), some 19 per cent of the population, would be considered overcrowded.[5] Overcrowding rates were substantially higher in many areas of rapid population growth. The 1931 census showed that 40.1 per cent of all dwellings in the County of London, though structurally undivided, nevertheless accommodated more than one family. Some 63.2 per cent of families lived in dwellings of at least two families and 32.0 per cent in dwellings accommodating three or more families.[6]

Until 1930 only around 11,000 slum dwellings had been demolished and replaced under interwar housing programmes. Yet the issue assumed increasing political importance from the late 1920s, featuring in Labour's 1929 election programme. Labour's new Minister of Health, Arthur Greenwood, focused on slum clearance. The 1930 Housing Act provides a variable Treasury subsidy to local authorities, based on the number of people displaced and re-housed. This had the twin functions of ensuring that displaced families were re-housed (a notable flaw in pre-1914 slum clearance programmes) and facilitated the re-housing of large families, as it was paid per person, rather than per family. Local authorities made a fixed annual contribution per dwelling of £3 15s for 40 years and rental policy was left to their discretion, subject to what slum clearance tenants could be reasonably expected to pay.[7] Addressing the problem of the slums was considerably facilitated by declining building costs. A Tudor Walters-type house cost more than £1,000 to build in 1920; by 1932 the same house could be built for about £350, thus bringing it within reach of lower-income families.[8]

The Greenwood Act was originally introduced to run alongside the Wheatley subsidy, thus providing both a general and a slum clearance element to local authority housing provision. Yet under the new national government, the Housing (Financial Provisions) Act, 1933, repealed the Wheatley subsidy on all houses for which plans were approved after the end of December 1932 and restricted central government housing subsidies to slum clearance projects. A five-year slum clearance and re-housing programme was outlined, funded by the Greenwood subsidy, local authorities being obliged to draw up plans to abolish their slums over this period.

In 1935 this policy was supplemented by a programme to abolish overcrowding. The Housing Act of that year imposed a specific duty on local authorities to survey

---

[5] J. H. Marshall, 'The Pattern of Housebuilding in the Inter-war Period in England and Wales', *Scottish Journal of Political Economy*, 15 (1968), 196.

[6] London School of Economics, *The New Survey of London Life and Labour*, Vol. VI: *Survey of Social Conditions (2) The Western Area* (London: P. S. King, 1934), 158.

[7] Bowley, *Housing and the State*, 135–45.

[8] Norman Williams, 'Problems of Population and Education in the New Housing Estates, with Special Reference to Norris Green', MA dissertation (Liverpool University, 1938), 11.

overcrowding in their areas and prepare plans to relieve what overcrowding was identified—over the five years following the five-year slum clearance programme. By the end of the programme it was to be made illegal to have overcrowded dwellings, both landlords and tenants facing penalties. Subsidies were only provided where it was necessary to build flats on expensive central urban sites, where the burden imposed on local rates was deemed unreasonable, and where, in certain cases, houses were provided for overcrowded agricultural workers. Yet the legislation used such a restrictive overcrowding standard that only 3.8 per cent of working-class families were so classified.

In 1936 government tried to rationalize the use of municipal housing developed under the various interwar Housing Acts. Local authorities were instructed to pool subsidies received under all these Acts and use this pool to adjust rents on individual houses as they deemed suitable. This would enable them to, for example, set a standard rent for all housing and then adjust this according to tenants' capacity to pay by using the subsidy pool to make up the difference. It also enabled local authorities to place slum clearance tenants in Addison, Greenwood, and Wheatley houses which would otherwise command rents beyond their means.[9]

As Table 3.1 shows, annual housing completions in England and Wales under the 1930–8 Acts did not exceed those under the 1924 Act until the year ending March 1935, and the volume of building only returned to that during the most active years of the 1924 programme from around 1937, then accelerating to a peak of just over 100,000 houses in the year to 31 March 1939. The slums were not entirely abolished—by March 1939 the number of people re-housed fell 239,000 short of that originally proposed. Nevertheless, more slum dwellers had been re-housed in the five years up to this date than under all earlier slum clearance programmes. Meanwhile a further 439,000 houses had been renovated to make them fit for human habitation.[10]

Local authority housing and government financial support made a particularly strong relative contribution to new housing in Scotland. Of the 311,510 houses built in Scotland over 1920–38 some 251,404 involved public subsidy, of which 208,337 were municipal houses.[11] There was also significant regional and local variation in municipal house-building within England and Wales—according to both the attitude of the local authority and its financial resources. For example, councils in depressed areas such as County Durham had both greater difficulties in borrowing money to develop municipal housing and a weaker rates base to subsidize housing provision.[12]

---

[9] Bowley, *Housing and the State*, 144.
[10] Bowley, *Housing and the State*, 152.
[11] See Table 4.1.
[12] Robert Ryder, 'Council House Building in County Durham, 1900–39: The Local Implementation of National Policy', in Martin J. Daunton (ed.), *Councillors and Tenants: Local Authority Housing in English Cities, 1919–1939* (Leicester: Leicester University Press, 1984), 55–7.

THE CHARACTERISTICS OF MUNICIPAL HOUSING

Flats represented only 5 per cent of interwar subsidized housing, though the proportions were much higher in London (40 per cent) and Liverpool (20 per cent). They became more popular in the 1930s, receiving increasing support from the architectural elite—inspired by the modern movement and the Viennese workmen's flats. Yet they were not attractive from a financial viewpoint, five-storey flats being between a third and two-thirds dearer than non-parlour council houses (and almost double per square foot).[13] As subsequent experience was to prove, they were also problematic with regard to maintenance, accommodating families with small children, and in creating harmonious communities.

Conversely, over 90 per cent of interwar council housing was located on suburban estates. These were sometimes much larger than typical privately developed estates. The London County Council (LCC) developed eight 'cottage estates' of semi-detached housing from the 1920s, as well as completing three smaller pre-1914 estates. Lacking sufficient land within the County of London, the LCC placed almost two-thirds of its interwar housing on so-called 'out-county' estates, beyond the county's borders. As Figure 3.1 shows, these constituted major residential areas. The largest, Becontree in Dagenham, comprised 25,769 dwellings (out of a total of around 61,000 developed by the LCC over the interwar period), and had a population of around 116,000 by 1939.[14] Manchester's Wythenshawe 'satellite town' was almost as large, being planned to incorporate about 25,000 houses and around 100,000 persons.[15]

Yet the few massive estates developed nationally were exceptional. A review of developments by the Nottingham, Birmingham, Birkenhead, Leicester, Liverpool, and Manchester councils to the end of 1929 found few housing schemes covering more than 1,000–1,500 units on a single site. Numbers were more commonly in the hundreds, which kept costs for roads and sewers to a lower figure than that for the LCC's out-county estates.[16] Liverpool developed thirty-one municipal estates over the interwar period, ranging from 14 to 7,689 dwellings. Nine had less than 100 dwellings each, twelve had between 100 and 1,000, while the remaining ten each had more than 1,000.[17] Leeds developed twenty-four council estates, ranging from 33 to 3,478 dwellings—with some 70 per cent of houses located in eight large estates of over 1,000 dwellings each.[18] Conversely Sheffield focused more on smaller estates; of the thirteen commenced over 1913–31, only two (Manor and

---

[13] John Burnett, *A Social History of Housing 1815–1885*, 2nd edn (London: Methuen, 1986), 247–8.
[14] Alan A. Jackson, *Semi-Detached London: Suburban Development, Life, and Transport, 1900–39*, 2nd edn (Didcot: Wild Swan, 1991), 133–4 & 235.
[15] Manchester and Salford Better Housing Council, *The Report of an Investigation on Wythenshawe* (Manchester: privately published, 1935), 4.
[16] London Metropolitan Archives, HSG/GEN/1/23, London County Council, Joint Housing and Finance Committee Report, 15 March 1932.
[17] McKenna, 'Development of Suburban Council Housing Estates', 266–7.
[18] Robert Finnigan, 'Council Housing in Leeds, 1919–39: Social Policy and Urban Change', in Martin J. Daunton (ed.), *Councillors and Tenants: Local Authority Housing in English Cities, 1919–1939* (Leicester: Leicester University Press, 1984), 134.

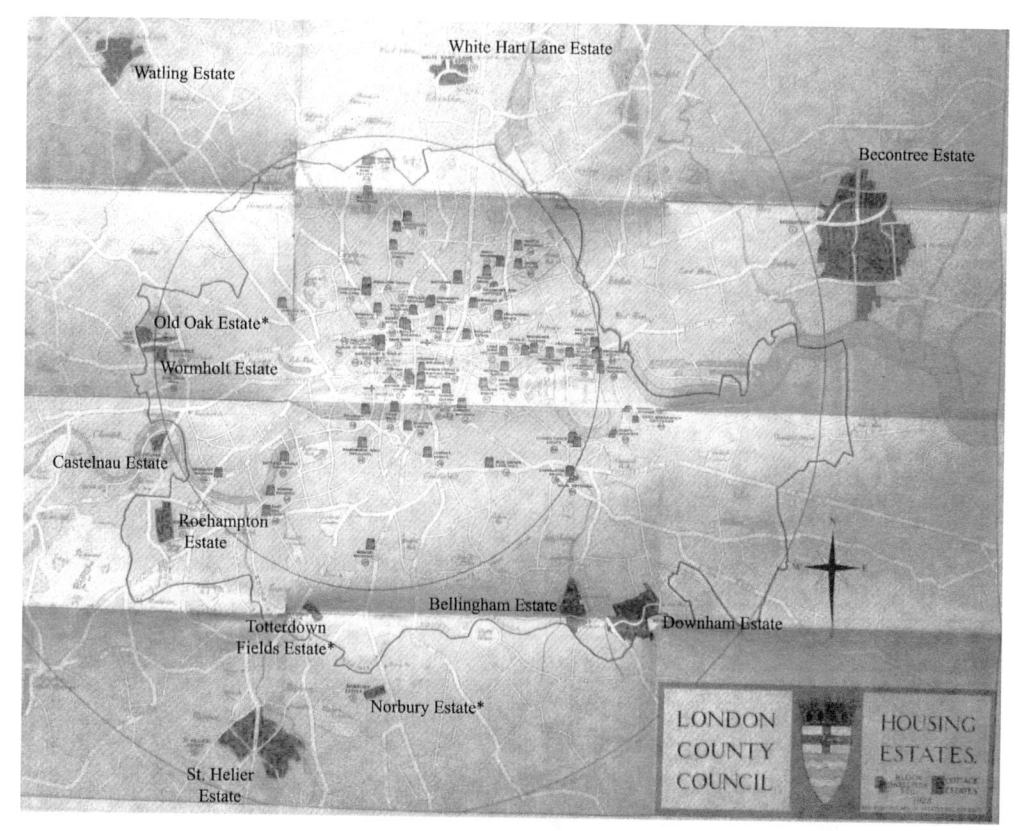

Fig. 3.1. London County Council cottage estates developed before the late 1930s

Source: London Metropolitan Archives, HSG/GEN/03/007, London County Council map showing housing estates, 1928.

Notes: Reproduced by kind permission of London Metropolitan Archives. * indicates cottage estates commenced before 1914. Smaller symbols show the council's urban 'block dwelling' developments.

Longley) had populations of over 1,000 in April 1931—though these accounted for over half of all tenants.[19] The larger estates in particular provided local authority architects with opportunities to develop sophisticated estate plans, sometimes involving geometric designs that incorporated parks, public buildings, and significant landscaping, as shown by the example of an early Newburn-on-Tyne estate plan in Figure 3.2.

Estates were much more homogenous in terms of their houses. As Judy Giles noted, 'The most striking characteristic of inter-war council housing was its uniformity across the country: Becontree, Birmingham, York, Leicester—the houses are fairly indistinguishable.'[20] A study of Bristol's interwar municipal estates found

---

[19] A. D. K. Owen, *A Report on the Housing Problem in Sheffield* (Sheffield: Sheffield Social Survey Committee, 1931), 64.

[20] Margaret Judith Giles, 'Something That Bit Better: Working-Class Women, Domesticity, and "Respectability", 1919–1939', DPhil thesis (University of York, 1989), 203.

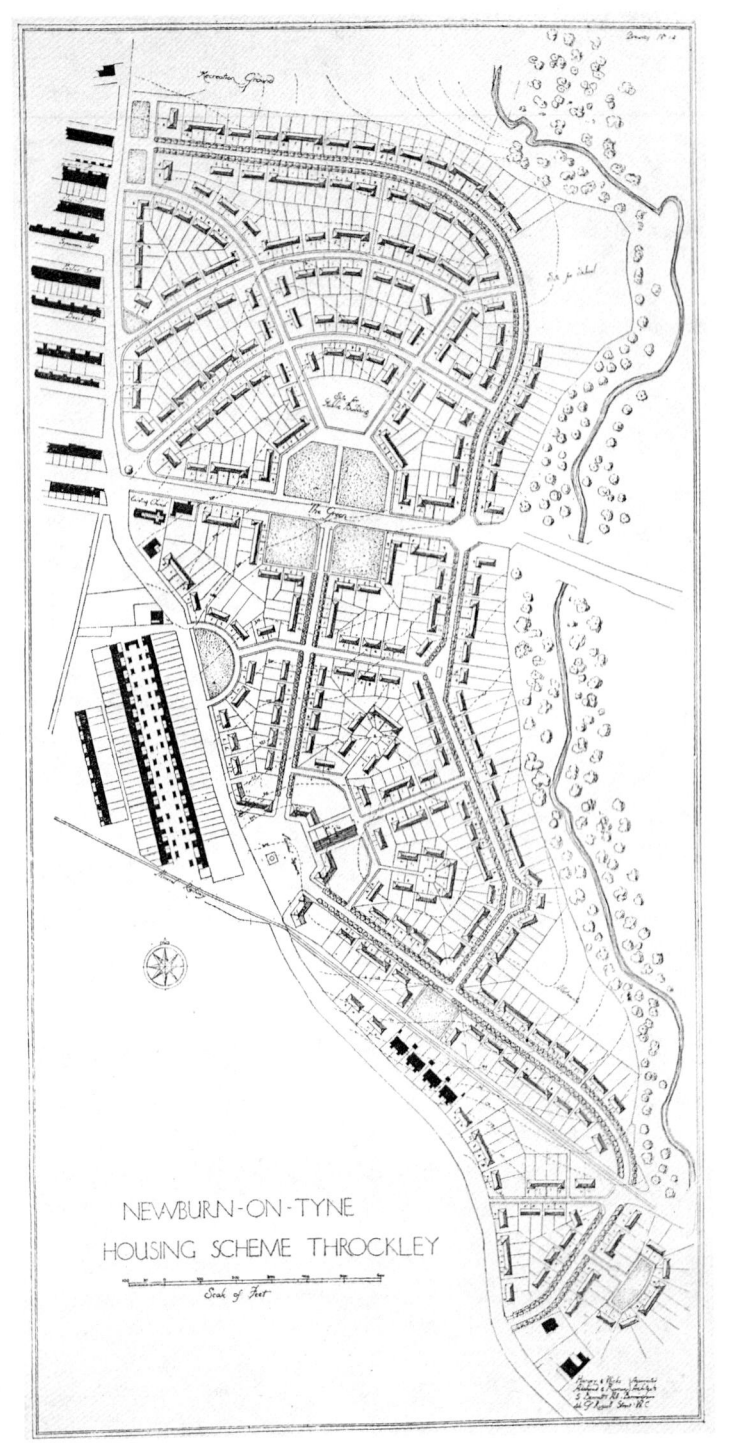

Fig. 3.2. Layout scheme for a housing estate at Throckley, drawn up for Newburn-on-Tyne Urban District Council, *c.*1919–23

Source: Henry R. Aldridge, *The National Housing Manual: A Guide to National Housing Policy and Administration* (London: National Housing and Town Planning Council, 1923), 167.

that 'The typical Bristol Council houses are of plain neo-Georgian type. The majority are faced with red brick... Parts of the estates are undoubtedly monotonous in appearance; as some tenants say, the houses are "barrack-like". The uniformity of materials and elevations is not relieved by any variety in colour.'[21]

Some councils, such as Leeds, placed the small proportion of better-designed and parlour houses in prominent locations such as the entrance to the estate or areas adjacent to main roads, to create a better visual appeal than would be provided by their standard houses.[22] Some councils also introduced a limited degree of variegation in their houses. Nottingham's Aspley estate had as many as thirteen different house designs, largely based on a common ground plan and distinguished by decorative elements such as differences in roofings, windows, and facade details.[23]

While many council estates were visually unappealing, there is no doubt that, in terms of building specifications, internal layouts, and dimensions, they were an enormous step forward compared to pre-war working-class housing. House designs aimed to move away from the narrow frontages and long party walls of the standard pre-war terrace with back projection, using lighter, better-ventilated designs with the front and rear walls being the longest and semi-detached or short terraced construction further increasing natural daylight. This was assisted by low housing densities, typically around twelve per acre.[24]

The most common house designs were the 'A3' and 'B3' (B denoting the presence of a parlour, which was absent from the A houses, and the number referring to the number of bedrooms). Parlours tended to be an early casualty of cutbacks in housing costs; in Leeds the proportion of parlour houses fell from 52 per cent for Addison houses to 11.6 per cent for council houses built between 1924 and 1933.[25] The one reception room format of the non-parlour council house offered a larger, unified living area, but frequently sacrificed privacy—as in many designs the living room also served as a circulation route to other parts of the house.[26]

Table 3.2 shows a comparison of the average cost per house of cottage estates developed under the 1923 and 1924 Acts, by the LCC to the end of March 1930, and by six large provincial councils up to the end of 1929. Councils are arranged according to their ratios of parlour houses to all houses developed, to show the influence of eliminating parlours on housing costs. Leicester, with parlour houses comprising 57 per cent of its new housing developments, paid an average of £564 per house, while Nottingham, which had only 19 per cent, paid

---

[21] Rosamond Jevons and John Madge, *Housing Estates: A Study of Bristol Corporation Policy and Practice between the Wars* (Bristol: Arrowsmith, 1946), 21–2.
[22] Finnigan, 'Council Housing in Leeds', 27.
[23] Georgina E. Couch, 'The Cultural Geography of the Suburban Garden: Landscape and Life History in Nottingham, c.1920–1970', PhD thesis, (University of Nottingham, 2004), 88.
[24] B. S. Rowntree, *Poverty and Progress: A Second Social Survey of York* (London: Longmans, 1941), 226 & 234; Manchester and Salford Better Housing Council, *Report of an Investigation on Wythenshawe*, 4.
[25] Finnigan, 'Council Housing in Leeds', 127.
[26] Ian Bentley, 'The Owner Makes his Mark: Choice and Adaption', in Paul Oliver, Ian Davis, and Ian Bentley, *Dunroamin: The Suburban Semi and its Enemies* (London: Pimlico, 1981), 151.

Fig. 3.3. An example of short terraced municipal housing
Source: Henry R. Aldridge, *The National Housing Manual. A Guide to National Housing Policy and Administration* (London: National Housing and Town Planning Council, 1923), 177.

£414. Standardization and simplicity in design also reduced costs, the most economical councils having eliminated costly architectural features, expensive materials, and embellishments. Their estate layouts were also generally simpler, with less expenditure on items such as greens, paths, and fencing.[27]

Houses with two, or four, bedrooms generally formed a small minority of units on council estates, if they were provided at all. Sheffield was exceptional in that some 27.3 per cent of its 8,377 council houses built between the armistice and 1 April 1930 had only two bedrooms. Such houses failed to meet the 'decency standard' of enabling parents, and children of each gender, to sleep in separate rooms, but were financially attractive to workers facing low wages and/or insecure employment—typically being rented for 7s (or 10s 9d when council and water rates were added), compared to 8s 6d (12s 11d) for three-bedroom non-parlour houses, or 10s (15s 11d) for three-bedroom houses with small parlours.[28]

COMMUNITIES WITHOUT AMENITIES

Madeline McKenna has characterized early Liverpool municipal estates as 'bleak utilitarian dormitories, lacking the facilities that were required to foster a new community.'[29] A similar picture emerges for many other councils. In order to economize on land costs, municipal estates were typically built further from urban boundaries or transport links than most owner-occupied housing. Families thus faced significant transport costs. In Manchester a single tram fare into the city from even the nearest big municipal estates, Anson and Wilbraham (located

---

[27] London Metropolitan Archives, HSG/GEN/1/23, London County Council, Joint Housing and Finance Committee Report, 15 March 1932.
[28] Owen, *Report on the Housing Problem in Sheffield*, 19.
[29] McKenna, 'Development of Suburban Council Housing Estates', 298.

Table 3.2. Cost of cottage estate developments under the Housing, etc., Act, 1923 and the Housing (Financial Provisions) Act, 1924, by six provincial councils to 31 December 1929, and by the London County Council to 31 March 1930

Local authority	Houses erected or under contract	% Parlour houses	Average cost per house (£): Houses	Roads & sewers	Establishment charges	Total
Leicester	4,696	57	465.95	86.99	10.75	563.69
Liverpool	12,829	46	467.79	59.00	7.00	533.79
London County Council	26,731	42.5	447.68	60.53	11.02	519.24
Manchester	11,156	20	435.68	62.91	7.26	505.84
Birkenhead	2,040	27.5	432.70	45.77	2.94	481.41
Birmingham	30,724	15	397.66	65.55	[a]	463.21
Nottingham	4,748	19	369.42	43.53	1.19[b]	414.14

Source: London Metropolitan Archives, HSG/GEN/1/23, London County Council, Joint Housing and Finance Committee Report, 15 March 1932.

[a] Included under the previous two columns.
[b] Part only, the balance being included under the previous two columns.

Fig. 3.4. Photograph of the Wyther Estate, Armley, Leeds, in 1932—reflecting the bleak initial appearance of much new municipal housing
Source: courtesy of Leeds Library and Information Service.

2.25 miles from the centre) was 2.5d, while the journey from Wythenshawe (7 miles from the centre) involved an 8d return bus fare (equivalent to a 2010 value of around £1.60 in terms of retail prices, or around £5 relative to average earnings). Some cities had lower fares; tram fares from Leeds to any municipal estate were a maximum of 2d, and bus fares were 3.5d or less (fares in Liverpool also being around this level). An ordinary return fare from Brighton's Moulsecoomb estates was 5d, or 4d for a workmen's ticket. However, even the workmen's fares imposed a 2s a week commuting cost, while many people started work at times when these were not available.[30]

While buses were expensive, they did provide an avenue for social interaction among estate tenants. A Mass Observation report on a Bolton housing estate emphasized the lively atmosphere on the buses, especially the late buses leaving town for the estate on Saturday nights:

> The impression created by these late buses, brilliantly lit, noisily happy...flying over Thicketford Bridge like a bird to its nest, is a peculiar one, if one happens to be a fellow passenger. The bus appears to be the connecting link between two worlds as typified by the town & the estate, & is the scene of more exchanged intimacies than any other place. In this respect, it partially takes the place of the absent pub. It is the 'meeting

---

[30] Frances Thompson, 'A Study of the Development of Facilities for Recreation and Leisure Occupation on New Housing Estates, with Special Reference to Manchester', Diploma in Social Studies dissertation (University of Manchester, 1937), 4–6.

place of the estate' & the 'bus stop' at the shopping centre becomes to a limited degree, the centre around which the estate revolves.[31]

Transport difficulties were compounded by the fact that people typically worked several miles from their new homes, while there was little work available close to most estates, especially for adult males. In 1931 (prior to the opening of the Ford complex) over two-thirds of working males at Becontree had to travel at least 5 miles to work and a third had to travel at least 10 miles. Meanwhile 55.8 per cent of working women had to travel at least 5 miles and 28.2 per cent at least 10 miles. Even in 1939 some 42 per cent of tenants at Becontree lived over 5 miles from their work.[32] Residents of the LCC's Watling estate at Hendon found that there were ample jobs for women on the new local industrial estates of assembly and other light industries. However, adult males, particularly skilled workers, found little work locally. As Ruth Durant noted, 'unskilled labour is almost exclusively employed by these newly installed factories. Family fathers, therefore, have scarcely profited from the openings they provided: only their wives, their sons and their daughters are wanted.'[33] This situation was not limited to Greater London. A 1935 social survey of Wythenshawe noted that the local labour supply

> consists almost entirely of men, most of whom at present are skilled or semi-skilled workers...the new [local] factories, by contrast, are of the 'light industry' type, employing principally female labour; the actual proportions in employment are...35 per cent men and 65 per cent women...if development continues in this way, there will be a situation in which on the one hand thousands of Wythenshawe residents spend an hour or more daily in travelling to and from Manchester, while...local factories are being staffed largely with workers who travel from Manchester and other surrounding districts to Wythenshawe.[34]

The slow development of schools constituted a major grievance. Families with young children were usually given priority in council house allocation, which led to most estates having relatively large proportions of children. In 1937 some 30.4 per cent of all Bristol children aged under 15 lived in Corporation houses, compared with only 6.5 per cent of those aged 55 or over.[35] Meanwhile almost half the population of Becontree was under school leaving age and almost half the residents of the LCC's Watling estate were under 18.[36]

At Liverpool the development of schools lagged well behind municipal housing, especially on the early estates. There was also a long delay in developing

---

[31] Mass Observation Archive, Worktown Project, Box 44A, 'The Housing Estate', observer account, n.d., c.1938.
[32] Terence Young, *Becontree and Dagenham* (London: Becontree Social Survey Committee, 1934), 121; Andrzej Olechnowicz, *Working Class Housing in England between the Wars: The Becontree Estate* (Oxford: Oxford University Press, 1997), 96.
[33] Ruth Durant, *Watling: A Survey of Social Life on a New Housing Estate* (London: King, 1939), 12.
[34] Manchester and Salford Better Housing Council, *Report of an Investigation on Wythenshawe*, 18.
[35] Jevons and Madge, *Housing Estates*, 27.
[36] Young, *Becontree and Dagenham*, 114; Durant, *Watling*, 14.

denominational, especially Catholic, schools, though as McKenna noted, 'it probably had a long term beneficial effect since it forced children of different religions to mix together thereby reducing prejudice and bigotry.'[37] As one of her interviewees recalled:

> down Scotland Road way, Catholics and Protestants only came together to fight. The Catholics lived in certain streets and Protestants in others and no one mixed. Out here though the Corporation forced us all to mix because all the children at first had to go to Council Schools. Well, when people started to mix a lot of the old hatreds start to go and out here the Orangemen and Catholics never fought like back down town.[38]

There is evidence of a similar trend away from denominational schools and activities on owner-occupied estates. For example, the Coney Hall estate in West Wickham, Kent, experienced a political struggle over whether schools should be run by the Church of England or the local authority. A plebiscite organized by the Residents' Association produced a 91 per cent vote against a Church school and a state infants' school was opened despite determined opposition from the local rector.[39] The influence of religious organizations in pressing for denominational schools and organizing denominationally based youth and other social activities was also weakened by delays in developing churches on new estates, the dispersion of potential local congregations among scattered existing churches, and the less community-orientated outlook of many residents.[40]

One of the amenities most central to the social life of inner-city communities, and most objectionable to social reformers, the public house, was often deliberately barred from estate developments. The Ministry of Health had recommended that, to achieve good town planning, licensed premises must form part of the amenities of new estates. Yet some councils objected to pub provision, which might encourage 'reckless' expenditure and behaviour by their tenants. For example, Liverpool did not allow any public houses, despite the large size and physical remoteness of many of their estates.[41]

Access to shops was also very limited, a situation which many tenants capitalized on by setting up shops in their houses—despite councils prohibiting such activity. Liverpool Corporation introduced a ban on fish and chip shops on its estates, resulting in a boom in 'back-kitchen' fish and chip shops.[42] Formal shop provision was usually restricted, by councils mindful of the income they could gain from developing shopping parades. As a result local shops were generally more expensive than in inner-urban areas, where bargains could be picked up at markets or the local Woolworths and Marks & Spencer. Mobile shops thus found estates to be

---

[37] McKenna, 'Development of Suburban Council Housing Estates', 278–82.
[38] McKenna, 'Development of Suburban Council Housing Estates', Appendix 13, interview 53.
[39] A. D. McCulloch, 'Owner-Occupation and Class Struggle: The Mortgage Strikes of 1938–40', PhD thesis (University of Essex, 1983), 258–9.
[40] Olechnowicz, *Working Class Housing*, 81–2 & 193–4.
[41] McKenna, 'Development of Suburban Council Housing Estates', 292.
[42] Williams, 'Problems of Population', 17.

particularly attractive prospects and made vigorous efforts to secure the custom of new arrivals. As a migrant to Wythenshawe recalled:

> When we first came up here on all the doorsteps there was loafs of bread with cards and bottles of milk...and inside there was more paraphernalia, advertising material for stuff and that...I should think there was 3 or 4 bottles of milk and all with the different milk people.[43]

THE JOY OF SUBURBIA

The slow development of council housing, relative to the post-armistice housing shortage, enabled councils to select new tenants from a long waiting list of applicants. Government initially encouraged councils to give the families of ex-servicemen top priority—to fulfil its 'homes for heroes' pledge.[44] However, other criteria, such as family size and medical need, assumed greater priority as the decade progressed. Ability to pay the higher rentals of the new estates also assumed increasing priority, as councils found growing numbers of tenants struggling to make ends meet.[45] Formal criteria were not the only factors influencing people's position on the housing list; it was far from unknown for members of municipal Housing Committees to receive council houses, which inevitably raised suspicion of malpractice. There were also often allegations and suspicions of more widespread corruption, bribery, and favouritism.[46]

The working and (initially) lower middle classes enthusiastically embraced this new form of housing. Contemporary and life history accounts suggest that most early migrants welcomed their move from inner city to suburban living, frequent mention being made of the strong emotional commitment that housewives, in particular, felt towards their new homes. For example, the wife of a railway labourer, who moved to a small (non-parlour) house on Liverpool's Fazakerley estate in 1930, stated, 'I loved it. Everything was new. We had a bath to ourselves, hot water and lots of space. I can remember the range in the kitchen. All the neighbours used to polish it to see who could get the steel edges the cleanest. We were very proud of our new houses.'[47]

Decisions to move to suburban estates (both municipal and owner-occupied) appear to have been largely motivated by dissatisfaction with the previous residential environment. Joanna Bourke's analysis of applications for Bolton council housing showed that dislike of the applicant's existing neighbourhood was the most common reason given for wanting to move.[48] Suburban estates offered a number

---

[43] Tameside Local Studies Library, transcripts of interviews conducted by Mike Harrison, c.1975–6, interview with Mr Pennington.
[44] Ryder, 'Council House Building in County Durham', 74.
[45] Madge Dresser, 'Housing Policy in Bristol, 1919–30', in Martin J. Daunton (ed.), *Councillors and Tenants: Local Authority Housing in English Cities, 1919–1939* (Leicester: Leicester University Press, 1984), 205; McKenna 'Development of Suburban Council Housing Estates', 89.
[46] Ryder, 'Council House Building in County Durham', 73–4.
[47] McKenna, 'Development of Suburban Council Housing Estates', Appendix 13, interview 30.
[48] Joanna Bourke, *Working-Class Cultures in Britain 1890–1960: Gender, Class and Ethnicity* (London: Routledge, 1994), 158.

of major environmental advantages, which collectively constituted a strong positive attraction to migrants. These included labour-saving designs, more spacious rooms, better natural lighting, modern plumbing and utilities, front and rear gardens, and a semi-rural environment.

Analysis of the Life Histories Database accounts for working-class families included an attempt to classify the positive environmental features people associated with their new houses and neighbourhoods. This proved problematic for a number of reasons. It was sometimes difficult to distinguish positive mentions of particular features from mere description; descriptions lacking clear positive statements were thus disregarded. Furthermore, as the life histories were assembled from a wide range of sources, the detail with which the house was discussed varied considerably, some accounts making little or no reference to its characteristics. Finally, factors associated with certain pursuits, such as gardens, were more likely to receive positive mention than others, for example mains electricity.

Nevertheless, the data, shown in Table 3.3, do provide a broad indication of the major environmental attractions of suburban housing. Among council tenants the presence of a bathroom or fitted bath ranked particularly high, mentioned by almost 60 per cent of accounts that noted any positive features. Running, or hot, water was also mentioned in a substantial proportion of accounts, as was mains electricity and an indoor toilet. Most urban working-class accommodation lacked bathrooms and indoor (or, often, individual) toilets, while many flats and older houses lacked hot, or even running, water.

Table 3.3. Positive features of suburban housing identified in 170 life history testimonies of interwar working-class migrants to suburban estates

Percentage of house move descriptions mentioning any positive feature, which included positive mention of:	Municipal tenants	Owner-occupiers
Bathroom/fitted bath in kitchen	59.4	38.9
Toilet	22.9	5.6
Running/hot water	31.3	11.1
Electricity	32.3	16.7
Gas	9.4	11.1
Kitchen	12.5	5.6
Space	19.8	5.6
Lightness	7.3	11.1
Garden	60.4	55.6
Rural surroundings	35.4	38.9
Number identifying any positive features	96	18
Total number of relevant house moves	116	58

Source: UK Data Archive, AHDS History, SN 5085, Peter Scott, 'Analysis of 170 Biographical Accounts of Working-Class People Who Moved into Owner-Occupation or Suburban Council Housing during the Inter-war Period' (2005).

Notes: The 170 accounts include 174 relevant house moves.

Mass Observation's *People's Homes* survey found that the lack of a bathroom (or the bath being in the scullery) stood out as the largest single specific grievance about housing, despite the fact that less than a third of houses in the sample (which mainly excluded poor-quality inner-urban accommodation) had no separate bathroom. This was followed by grievances concerning the water system (mentioned by just over half as many people as those who mentioned bathrooms), stoves, kitchens, and toilets.[49] Problems of inadequate water utilities in older houses persisted into the post-war era; the 1951 census indicated that over 40 per cent of British homes still lacked a fixed bath, while almost two million people lived in accommodation without a private water closet.[50]

Regular bathing and cleanliness (and, by extension, access to indoor plumbing and a bathroom) had become important markers of respectability by the interwar period, their role in ensuring cleanliness and hygiene being symbolically reinforced by the clean, white, tiled and spartan design aesthetic of suburban bathrooms.[51] Indoor plumbing also had a major impact in reducing housework (or freeing up additional time for other housework), as it removed two of the housewife's most time-consuming tasks—heating water for washing and bathing purposes and carrying it through the house. Many accounts also stress the importance of getting away from negative environmental factors associated with previous housing, such as dampness, vermin infestations, and cramped conditions—space receiving much more frequent mention as a negative feature of previous accommodation than as a positive feature of new housing.

For working-class families moving to owner-occupied suburbia, positive mentions of specific environmental factors feature less frequently in testimonies. Some involved moves from municipal, or other better-quality, accommodation, which already had at least some of these attributes, while a larger proportion of accounts, relative to the municipal sample, did not discuss the house in any detail. Nevertheless, the presence of a bathroom still constituted a major attraction, being highlighted by almost 39 per cent of accounts that noted any positive factor.

The estate's external environment receives more frequent mention than the house's interior, for both tenures. Gardens receive positive mention in a larger proportion of accounts than any other environmental factor, while the area's rural environment is also often highlighted—some people placing considerable emphasis on this. Again, external environmental factors sometimes featured as the absence of a previous negative. Several people mention their old neighbourhood's unhealthy environment, especially with regard to the needs of children—dangers including pollution, and traffic on busy urban streets. Indeed a significant number of migrants to council housing moved following medical advice regarding a child's chronic health problems.

---

[49] Mass Observation, *An Enquiry into People's Homes* (London: John Murray, 1943), 67–8.

[50] Vanessa Taylor and Frank Trentmann, 'Liquid Politics: Water and the Politics of Everyday Life in the Modern City', *Past and Present*, 211 (2011), 238.

[51] Elizabeth Shove, *Comfort, Cleanliness and Convenience. The Social Organization of Normality* (Oxford: Berg, 2003), 100–6.

In common with contemporary social surveys, the life history accounts give lie to the myth that early council tenants did not value their amenities and might, for example, store coals in the bath. As a report for Mass Observation's study of Bolton noted, 'With very isolated exceptions, a pride in living & appearance is adopted, that in the previous house, flat, or rooms, had no room for expression.'[52]

These environmental priorities are broadly indicative of what has been termed the 'suburban aspiration', defined by Mark Clapson as comprising a wish to escape from inner-city living, a desire for a suburban-style house and garden, and 'social tone'—the appeal of a high-quality residential environment, in terms of both its material qualities and type of people.[53] Another important aspect of 'social tone' was a strong preference for greater privacy and private space—many moves having been at least partially motivated by a wish to get away from intrusive neighbours. Audrey Kay's study of Wythenshawe concluded that people typically moved 'not to found a community but for three bedrooms, a bath, and a smoke-free environment. Neighbours were less important than private space.'[54]

Neighbourliness became regarded as an activity which occurred outside the home—in gardens, whilst cleaning front paths and sills, at local shops, and when taking the children to school.[55] Durant emphasized the rarity of mutual house visiting: 'A Watling woman who had lived four years in the same cottage and is on very good terms with her neighbour has, nevertheless, not been in her house. Their boys play together, but each in his own garden, the fence separating them.'[56] This trend was evident even in towns with particularly strong traditions of neighbourliness, such as Bolton. A Mass Observation account noted that in inner-urban districts 'gossiping...is seldom done in the street itself, but in the house; a woman will make some excuse to call on a neighbour & then spend the afternoon exchanging small talk.' On the municipal estate, by contrast, 'where gossip is indulged in, it usually takes place at some neighbours' garden gate.'[57]

Neighbourliness was, however, still seen as an important duty in times of crisis. As a man who had migrated to the LCC's Castleneau Estate as a child recalled, 'it wasn't a kind of East End spirit with you living in each other's place. [But] if you wanted any help you knew that you could always get it. When my brother died I went down to a friend's down the road and she gave me meals and looked after me...while they were going to hospital.'[58] Similarly, Becontree resident Grace

---

[52] Mass Observation, Worktown Project, Box 44A, 'The Housing Estate', observer account, n.d., c.1938.
[53] Mark Clapson, *Suburban Century. Social Change and Urban Growth in England and the United States* (New York: Berg, 2003), 51–2 & 69.
[54] Audrey Kay, 'Wythenshawe circa 1932–1955: The Making of a Community?', PhD thesis (University of Manchester, 1993), 461.
[55] Giles, 'Something That Bit Better', 319.
[56] Durant, *Watling*, 88.
[57] Mass Observation Archive, Worktown Project, Box 44, observer account, 'Transition from Street Dwelling to Housing Estate', April 1938.
[58] Age Exchange, Reminiscence Theatre Archive, interview conducted for 'Just Like the Country' project, c.1987, with members of the Breeze family.

Foakes recalled the help received from neighbours when her husband was on strike for six weeks:

> They, like us, found it hard to manage from one week to another, yet help they did. One day my near neighbour, after doing her weekly shopping, decided she must share it with us. She halved everything she had brought and insisted we take it. Then in the evenings she would dig up some potatoes and fry a large pan of chips. That too was halved and passed over the garden fence to us... Another neighbour, having had her weekly supply of coal in, filled a dustbin with some, saying she must share it with us. Yet another asked us in for a game of cards, then provided supper before we went home.'[59]

Yet contemporary sources indicate that many tenants who became unemployed did suffer much greater hardship than their inner-urban counterparts, as they faced both greater isolation from traditional support networks and higher fixed commitments for both rents and, often, hire purchase debts. The Pilgrim Trust found that such problems could be even more severe for white-collar workers, who sometimes felt obliged to hide their poverty from neighbours. They cited the example of an unemployed Liverpool clerk, who received 36 shillings a week from the Unemployment Assistance Board for himself and his wife and son, of which just over half went on rent. Another child had died, partly due to being malnourished: 'At the clinic they told his wife that the child was in need or extra nourishment, but—as he alleged—when the officer came round and saw a home of middle-class character, he said that no extra nourishment could be allowed.'[60] Yet appearances had to be maintained and, despite being forced to sell off many of their best items of furniture, 'He conceals the fact of being out of work from all his friends, if possible, and from his neighbours, and even the boy is not allowed to know the real position. He is dreaming of the day when he goes to College!'[61]

A collective preference for privacy in day-to-day life was, in part, motivated by fears of one-sided borrowing, intrusive neighbours who might spread gossip, and the possibility that frequent contact might lead to conflict. A taboo against mutual visiting may also have reflected fears that the entry of neighbours into the home would reveal the family's true standard of living. This preference for privacy reinforced the constraints placed on tenants by their physical remoteness from urban centres and lack of local public houses, in fostering a trend towards home-centred, rather than community-centred, leisure.[62]

RENTS, AFFORDABILITY, AND MAKING ENDS MEET

Council housing allocation policies that prioritized families with children produced estates characterized by households composed of a working husband, a housewife who (like most interwar married women) did not undertake paid work,

---

[59] Grace Foakes, *My Life with Reubin* (London: Shepheard-Walwyn, 1975), 44.
[60] Pilgrim Trust, *Men without Work* (Cambridge: Cambridge University Press, 1938), 93.
[61] Pilgrim Trust, *Men without Work*, 93.
[62] Olechnowicz, *Working Class Housing*, 214.

and a relatively large number of children. The *New Survey of London Life and Labour* found that the average size of families occupying LCC suburban estates was 4.7, compared with 3.67 for wage-earning working-class families in its (inner-urban) survey area. Meanwhile the ratio of wage-earners to all family members was only 32 per cent in the LCC cottage estates, compared to 47 per cent for families in the survey area.[63]

Given larger family sizes and heavy reliance on single incomes, council tenants were typically in somewhat precarious financial circumstances (despite being more weighted towards skilled workers than the overall working-class population, particularly during the 1920s). As such, councils carefully policed tenancy applications, so as to minimize risks of rent arrears and removals. Prospective tenants for Wythenshawe were asked to show their rent books as proof of regular payments, their incomes also being typically checked via correspondence with the breadwinner's employer.[64]

Nevertheless, the costs of moving to suburbia and meeting the economic and social requirements of the new estates often proved onerous. Council houses were generally substantially more expensive than the 'rooms' or small houses from which their occupants had migrated. Some thirty-six Life Histories Database accounts for working-class migrants to municipal estates, that include both their new and previous rent, indicate that moving to a council house involved an average rise in rental costs of 21.2 per cent.

McKenna's analysis of several thousand Liverpool council tenants' house cards, showing the rent paid in the new and previous accommodation, indicated that tenants moving to houses built under the 1919 Housing Act experienced average rental rises of 26.2 per cent. The average number of rooms in their previous dwellings was 3.15, compared with 4.65 in the new Addison houses. They thus obtained a 47 per cent increase in accommodation for a 26 per cent increase in rent. The average rise in rents on moving to Liverpool council estates fell to 19.7 per cent for houses built under the 1923 and 1924 Acts and only 7.5 per cent for the small number built under the 1925 Act. Yet it increased to 44.1 per cent for houses built under the 1930 and 1935 Acts—which were primarily aimed at slum clearance tenants.[65] Evidence from other municipalities also indicates a substantial increase in rents following moves to council housing. For example, in 1931 Bristol's Housing Committee reported that tenants then paying 11s 6d per week for Corporation houses had been paying an average of 8s 3d per week for their previous accommodation.[66]

Strategies to make ends meet included a heavy reliance on credit, reducing food expenditure, and taking in lodgers (despite the fact that this typically violated their conditions of tenancy).[67] As discussed in Chapter 7, furniture and, often, furnish-

---

[63] London School of Economics, *New Survey of London Life and Labour*. Vol. VI, 209–10.
[64] Kay, 'Wythenshawe', 194.
[65] McKenna, 'Development of Suburban Council Housing Estates', 85 & 196–220.
[66] Jevons and Madge, *Housing Estates*, 44.
[67] Olechnowicz, *Working Class Housing*, 7.

ings and appliances were typically purchased on HP. Tenants felt that acquiring suitable furniture was necessary to meet both physical needs and the expectations of their neighbours. As the Watling survey noted, 'The new house needs new linoleum, new curtains and even new furniture, and all is bought on hire purchase. In the old "mean street," people were not tempted by the example of their neighbours to acquire fresh impedimentia. At Watling...the wireless next door becomes an obligation to bring home a wireless.'[68] Similarly, a 1939 survey of a Birmingham municipal estate found high levels of HP debts. Migrants' old furniture was said to look:

> very shabby and dirty when it is set out in a new light room. One of the first outlays of the rehoused family is often on curtains with which to hide their dilapidated possessions from the inquiring eyes of the neighbours. A greater number of rooms may call for more furniture, and many people feel that new beds are a necessity. The fear of being accused of bringing vermin into new houses seems to be sufficiently strong to make some housewives undertake instalments on new beds for the whole family.[69]

Young's Becontree survey estimated that families spent between 3s and 5s on furniture, usually on HP,[70] while Jevons and Madge's Bristol municipal estates' survey put the figure at 2s 6d.[71] Similar pressures were evident regarding clothing. As Durant noted, 'clothes lend social status, assurance and even personality to the wearers, whose standards of judgement upon frocks and suits are determined by films and magazines depicting the rich and leisured. Many Watling residents...are deterred from mixing with others because of the embarrassing consciousness that their outfits are shabby.'[72] Again, these were often purchased on credit, through 'clothing clubs', mail order catalogues, or provident checks (credit vouchers accepted by various shops).

As noted earlier, the isolation of many suburban estates, together with the absence of suitable local jobs, often imposed substantial travel expenses. A 1939 survey of Birmingham's Kingstanding estate found that tenants generally paid 2s 6d–3s per week on commuting to work; Andrzej Olechnowicz found that the median figure for LCC cottage estates was in the region of 3–6s in 1937; while McKenna estimated that Liverpool council tenants during the 1920s had to pay about 2s per week extra on transport to work and a total of about 6s for all additional transport and food costs.[73] Transport costs for families on Brighton's three Moulsecoomb estates commonly amounted to 2–3s per week (though for families with several earners this could rise as high as 8s). Despite the fatiguing nature of their work, 55 per cent of manual workers on the North Moulsecoomb estate,

---

[68] Durant, *Watling*, 7–8.
[69] M. S. Soutar, E. H. Wilkins, and P. Sargant Florence, *Nutrition and Size of Family: Report on a New Housing Estate—1939* (London: George Allen & Unwin, 1942), 42.
[70] Young, *Becontree and Dagenham*, 216.
[71] Jevons and Madge, *Housing Estates*, 45.
[72] Durant, *Watling*, 89.
[73] Soutar, Wilkins, and Florence, *Nutrition and Size of Family*, 51; McKenna, 'Development of Suburban Council Housing Estates', 244.

surveyed in 1939, used bicycles (some purchasing these via HP payments of 2s 6d per week). Meanwhile unemployed men on the East Moulsecoomb estate faced a 3-mile walk to the Employment Exchange, which reduced their chances of finding work, as they could have called in daily had they lived more centrally.[74]

Similar shifts in expenditure patterns following moves to new suburban estates are recorded in the Life Histories Database. A significant number of accounts mention squeezing food budgets to make ends meet, or other behaviour aimed at reducing daily costs, such as going to bed early to cut down on fuel and lighting expenses. A woman who had moved to a Hull council estate recalled that many ex-slum dwellers found themselves 'having to pay excessive rents, for which they had not budgeted…The new Preston Road Housing Estate was duly christened "Corned Beef Island", that being in many cases, the menu throughout the week, the said commodity costing only 2.5d per quarter pound.'[75] A contemporary survey of Liverpool's Norris Green estate noted that: 'The extra 2/- for transport and the extra 4/- for rent have got to be found somehow and the only way…is to pay less on food; which is usually what happens.'[76]

Taking in lodgers was one common means of dealing with financial difficulties.[77] Unauthorized subletting was reported to be widespread on Bristol Corporation estates during the 1920s, partly due to high rents.[78] At Becontree about 4 per cent of households were found to contain boarders (though this figure, based on the 1931 census, may be subject to under-reporting in the case of unauthorized sublettings).[79] Some tenants organized to protest against excessive rents—a prime motivation behind the formation of tenants, associations.[80] These provided both a collective voice for tenants in addressing common grievances with their council landlords and a base for social and community activities. Yet membership was often relatively low; the Wythenshawe survey noted that while there were two residents' associations on the estate, 'their existence does not appear to be very widely known.'[81]

Many families fell into rent arrears. In 1925 some 20 per cent of tenants on Liverpool suburban council estates were in arrears; by 1928 this figure had risen to nearly 30 per cent and, by the beginning of 1932, 40 per cent.[82] For some, financial problems culminated in eventual voluntary or compulsory removal from the estate. Families who suffered interrupted earnings through unemployment or illness were particularly vulnerable. The *New Survey of London Life and Labour* noted, 'a constant replacement by removals of unemployed persons by employed persons.'[83]

---

[74] Marion Fitzgerald, *Rents in Moulsecoomb: A Report on Rents and other Costs of Living in Three Brighton Housing Estates* (Brighton: Southern Publishing, 1939), 17–38.
[75] Kay Pearson, *Life in Hull from Then till Now* (Hull: Bradley, 1979), 117.
[76] Williams, 'Problems of Population', 39.
[77] Durant, *Watling*, 17–18.
[78] Dresser, 'Housing Policy in Bristol', 201.
[79] Young, *Becontree and Dagenham*, 112.
[80] McKenna, 'Development of Suburban Council Housing Estates', 87.
[81] Manchester and Salford Better Housing Council, *Report of an Investigation on Wythenshawe*, 15.
[82] McKenna, 'Development of Suburban Council Housing Estates', 108 & 134.
[83] Young, *Becontree and Dagenham*. 142.

During most years between 1922/3 and 1931/2 annual removals from Becontree (which had the highest removal rates of any LCC cottage estate) involved around 10–12 per cent of households, though they fell as low as 7 per cent in 1924/5 and peaked at 17 per cent in 1928/9.[84]

From 1930 national policy turned away from 'general needs' council housing towards slum clearance and eliminating overcrowding. At local level, however, the preference given to slum clearance tenants was sometimes qualified by requirements that tenants should be 'desirable', i.e. that they had a good record of keeping up with rental payments and a clean and tidy disposition.[85] For example, Brighton's Medical Officer of Health noted in his 1932 report that of the 221 families re-located from the Carlton Hill area and paying an average rent of 7s 9d per week before removal, 70 per cent were re-housed centrally, while only 23 per cent were moved to the council's suburban Whitehawk estate. Yet even those selected for Whitehawk faced great financial difficulties, with an average rent increase of around 50 per cent, together with commuting costs. His predictions proved prescient—a year later he reported that 21 per cent of these tenants had vacated Whitehawk for financial reasons.[86]

Councils also often adopted policies of allocating lower status families to less desirable estates (usually more recent estates, or those composed of non-parlour houses). This marked the start of what was to become a common post-1945 local authority policy of grading tenants and allocating their best houses on their most pleasant estates to those considered most desirable.[87] The focus on slum tenants from the 1930s played a significant role in giving council housing a negative public image and in producing a second wave of migration, on the part of more affluent early council tenants, to owner-occupied estates. This process, and its implications for social segregation, are discussed more fully in Chapter 9.

The Housing Act, 1930, empowered local authorities to introduce differential rent schemes, relating rents to tenants' incomes. By 1938 some 112 local authorities in England and Wales operated some programme for adjusting rents according to the family's capacity to pay, most being limited to tenants re-housed under the slum clearance and overcrowding schemes. Some 84 Scottish local authorities also operated rent rebate schemes by 1938, with around 20 per cent of their 51,951 council houses being subject to rebates.[88] Only a handful applied this to their entire municipal housing stock—Leeds was particularly exceptional in not requiring any rent from families whose incomes fell below an official subsistence level. Yet this was widely interpreted as imposing a 'means test' on rents and was regarded as a key factor in Labour's loss of control of the city council in November 1935.[89]

---

[84] Young, *Becontree and Dagenham*. 210.
[85] Ryder, 'Council House Building in County Durham', 75.
[86] *Annual Report of the Medical Officer of Health for 1932 and 1933* (Brighton, 1933 and 1934), cited in Ben Jones, 'Slum Clearance, Privatisation and Residualisation: The Practices and Politics of Council Housing in Mid-Twentieth-Century England', *Twentieth Century British History*, 21 (2010), 520–1.
[87] McKenna, 'Development of Suburban Council Housing Estates', 258.
[88] Department of Health for Scotland, *Tenth Annual Report*, 1938 (Cmd. 5969 of 1939), 183.
[89] Finnigan, 'Council Housing in Leeds', 116–18.

A similar attempt to impose differential renting on both slum clearance and general purpose municipal housing in Birmingham led to a 13-week rent strike in 1939, involving 6–8,000 council tenants.[90]

Slum clearance tenants faced the greatest difficulties in adapting to life on the new estates. Characterized by low and/or irregular incomes and, often, large numbers of dependents, they were particularly ill-placed to meet the high rental and other costs of council housing. Municipal estates also represented a particularly sharp break with their established patterns of living. Inhabitants of high-density courts of back-to-back housing had a mode of life that bore strong similarities to that of the Scottish tenements. As sociologist A. D. K. Owen noted, the slum areas of Sheffield he investigated in 1929 were characterized by poor housing and sanitation, congestion, overcrowding, and associated health problems. However, this did not exhaust their essential features:

> The same congestion of families and houses within a small area... produces an extraordinary sense of neighbourliness and social intimacy. Crises of birth and death as well as the details of everyday life are shared in a way which would appear strange to most middle class people, and the dwellers in a slum court sometimes unconsciously form a social group, on the basis of contiguity, to which they are surprisingly loyal both in times of adversity and in the cross currents of doorstep and beer shop chatter. Life in congested areas is intensely social. It is extremely difficult, if not impossible, to live entirely to oneself, and those who attempt to do so are usually made the subject of incredibly malicious gossip. On the other hand, despite its crudeness, the common life of slum courts and streets regularly produces extraordinary examples of distress communism and genuine charity as between family and family.[91]

Families relocated from slums to municipal estates faced the loss of traditional community networks and the weakening of kin relationships, undermining their ability to access support in times of crisis.[92] Higher living costs and fixed weekly commitments accentuated their vulnerability. An extreme example concerned 152 families re-housed from a slum area in Stockton-on-Tees to a new municipal estate in 1927. An investigation by the local Medical Officer of Health, G. C. M. M'Gonigle, found that the standardized death rate over the 5 years prior to the move (22.91 deaths per thousand population) had risen considerably during the following 5 years to 33.55. Meanwhile death rates in the town as a whole, and in an area adjoining the demolished houses, had actually fallen.

Rising death rates were attributed to an almost doubling in accommodation costs, from 4s 8d in the old slum area to 9s 0d on the Mount Pleasant Estate. Over 90 per cent of families on the estate were unemployed, many for prolonged periods. These were facing ratios of accommodation costs to total income of 31.3 per cent, compared to only 20.8 per cent for unemployed families in the area

---

[90] Martin J. Daunton, 'Introduction', in Martin J. Daunton (ed.), *Councillors and Tenants: Local Authority Housing in English Cities, 1919–1939* (Leicester: Leicester University Press, 1984), 23.
[91] Owen, *Report on the Housing Problem in Sheffield*, 37.
[92] Ross McKibbin, *Classes and Cultures: England 1918–1951* (Oxford: Oxford University Press, 1998), 190–1.

neighbouring the demolished houses. M'Gonigle concluded that their high mortality rates stemmed from malnutrition, as there was not enough money left after rent and other essentials to provide anything like an adequate diet.[93]

Mount Pleasant was atypical in terms of the chronically high levels of unemployment faced by its tenants. However, such problems do not appear to have been confined to Britain's depressed regions. In Brighton, where, as noted earlier, the Medical Officer of Health made repeated criticisms of the council's policy of re-housing slum tenants on high rental estates (even by the standards of suburban council housing), a 1939 journalistic investigation reported severe poverty: 'I heard of housewives with empty larders, of sick and ailing people in homes without the bare necessities of life, of children who sat in lightless, fireless kitchens, because there is no money for the gas-meter, no coal for the grate.'[94]

A few councils addressed this problem by developing houses more suitable to the needs of low income families. Sheffield Corporation's 60-acre Wybourn Estate, commenced in 1925 to re-house slum clearance families, was located only a mile from the centre of Sheffield, providing reasonable proximity both to the town and to major local employers, such as the Nunnery Colliery. While houses were built at low densities (less than ten per acre), the majority were two-bedroom non-parlour houses, thus keeping down rentals. Installing gas, rather than electric, lighting further lowered costs. Yet many families nevertheless had difficulties in adapting to the new conditions. By September 1931, 109 families re-located to the 564 houses then built had returned to central Sheffield. Only 18 were evicted owing to their unsatisfactory behaviour, while a few others found it impossible to adapt to social conditions on the estate (while many who remained also regretted the loss of their old way of life). However, most left owing to economic problems; by the end of 1930 almost 20 per cent of household heads were out of work, while some others experienced short-time working or low wages (rarely exceeding 45s a week).[95]

CONCLUSION

Council housing offered an immense improvement in the dimensions, quality, and amenities of working-class housing—at the costs of markedly higher rents, some increase in other living expenses, and longer journeys to work and to access retail, social, and other amenities. While some families struggled to cope, for others the suburban council house opened up a new world of bathrooms, electricity, gardens, and modern living. Suburban council housing accelerated the transition from the communal and street-orientated life of the Victorian working class to the family- and home-centred lifestyles characteristic of post-1945 households. Yet, as noted

---

[93] G. C. M. M'Gonigle, *Poverty and Public Health* (London: Gollancz, 1936), 108–29.
[94] *Brighton Gazette*, 1 April 1939, cited in Jones, 'Slum Clearance', 522.
[95] Owen, *Report on the Housing Problem in Sheffield*, 38–41.

earlier, for some families the suburban council house marked only one step on a journey towards a new, more affluent lifestyle, embodied in the owner-occupied semi. Meanwhile many other working-class people who married in the 1930s moved directly from the traditional inner-urban housing of their parents to a new owner-occupied estate. This alternative route to suburbia is explored in the following chapters.

4
Developing Owner-Occupied Suburbia

INTRODUCTION

Almost all the three million privately developed interwar British houses were speculative developments. Many were the work of relatively small firms, while even most of the largest house-builders operated at a regional, rather than national, level. Yet they succeeded in producing what was, fundamentally, a relatively standardized product, which was then marketed using standardized techniques and sales pitches.

This chapter examines the characteristics of the speculative suburban house, briefly outlines the histories of some of the most important speculative builders, and discusses the similarities and differences between speculative development north and south of the Scottish border. Sources of development finance, and the housing development process, are then explored. Finally, the chapter briefly reviews attempts by speculative builders to extend the market to lower income groups, and to renters, during the 1930s. The following chapter examines the marketing campaign used by the industry to 'sell' the idea of owner occupation to a hesitant public, while Chapter 6 explores life on the new owner-occupied estates.

THE SPECULATIVE SUBURBAN HOUSE

The Tudor Walters report proved very influential for speculative, as well as municipal, developers. It provided a blueprint for a characteristically modern house, with detailed practical advice on both low-density house design and economical site layout, based on the work of leading architects and planners. Yet, in addition to the influence of mass housing pioneers such as Unwin and Parker, the owner-occupied semi was also strongly influenced by the English vernacular building style of much Edwardian suburban middle-class housing, pioneered by Philip Webb, C. F. A. Voysey, and Ned Lutyens.

Developers used features such as bays, half-timbering, leaded windows, and similar ornamentation to create the characteristic mock-Tudor semi that became emblematic of the superior social status of speculatively built suburbia—in contrast to the grimly uniform neo-Georgian facades of local authority estates. Timber was almost always entirely decorative rather than structural, but had important status connotations. It placed the house both in the lineage of earlier garden suburb developments and in a certain cost bracket—as extensive and convincing simulated

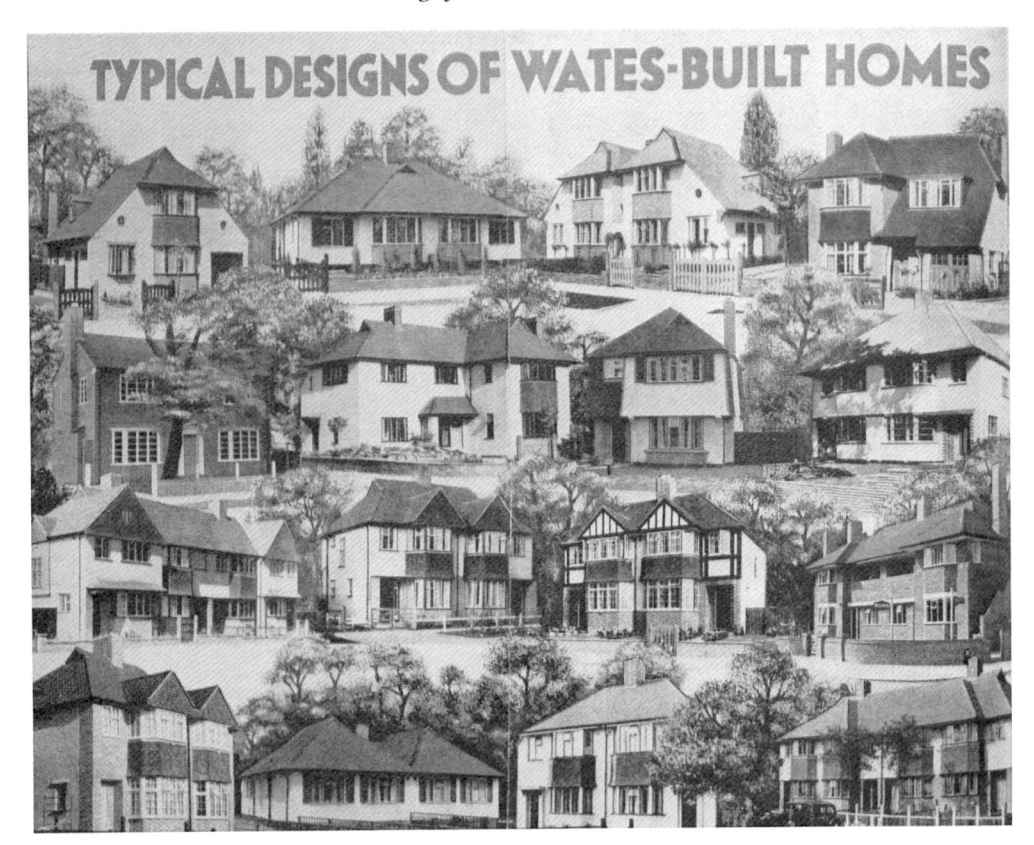

Fig. 4.1. A Wates' illustration of some housing designs employed during the 1930s
Source: Wates Ltd, 'Guaranteed Houses: Morden Common Estate', brochure (1939), Peter Scott collection.

timber framing was relatively expensive.[1] Private developers also created a more aspirational environment by mixing different styles of house to produce a more natural streetscape, in contrast to the planned collectivity of municipal suburbia.[2] The horizontal flow of the street created by conventional end-gable housing was broken via swept gables and hipped roofs projecting at the front. Hipped roofs also served to define the individuality of each dwelling in a pair of semis.[3]

One of the most visible differences between speculative and council houses was the ubiquitous front (and often rear) bay window. Most local authorities looked on bays as an unnecessary extravagance, which also increased maintenance costs.

---

[1] Paul Oliver, 'The Galleon on the Front Door', in Paul Oliver, Ian Davis, and Ian Bentley, *Dunroamin: The Suburban Semi and its Enemies* (London: Pimlico, 1981), 155–72, esp. 162.

[2] Deborah Ryan, 'The Daily Mail Ideal Home Exhibition and Suburban Modernity, 1908–1951', PhD thesis (University of East London, 1995), 138; Bexley Local Studies and Archives Centre (Bexley Local Studies), *Bexley between the Wars*, interview with Mr & Mrs Mehew.

[3] Ian Davis, 'A Celebration of Ambiguity: The Synthesis of Contrasting Values', in Oliver, Davis, and Bentley, *Dunroamin: The Suburban Semi and its Enemies*, 86.

However, Godfrey Way Mitchell of Wimpey, responding to criticism of their use, argued that:

> if we could get an equally pleasing effect inside and out without the use of a bay, we'd make a much more efficient house. On the other hand, the bay—if taken up to the bedroom as well as down—only costs per super foot about as much as the rest of the house (in other words it isn't expensive to make if it is wide and shallow though it is a sort of structural weakness in the front wall of the house). And it does, for some reason, make a house easier to look a bit high class both outside and in. It responds outside to various kinds of treatment; and inside it gives a woman a better chance with her curtains. Another reason why the bay was always a selling point was that inasmuch as Council houses had no bay, the mere possession of a bay moved you the right way, from the Council house atmosphere.[4]

Speculative houses were built at slightly lower densities than municipal estates (typically eight to ten per acre, compared to twelve per acre for council houses). However, like municipal housing, they were fairly uniform in plan, once cosmetic variation is ignored. In 1936 architect Gordon Allen discussed the 'universal plan' of most speculative suburban housing. This was attractive to developers as it minimized the floor area necessary to embody buyers' expectations, using a basic rectangular pattern to keep down building costs. Universal plan semi-detached houses were typically developed with two reception rooms of roughly equal size, placed back-to-back. One or both usually had bay windows and the rear room was often fitted with French doors to provide access to the garden. This contrasted with the design of most post-Addison council houses, which had only one reception room, without bay windows. A small staircase hall led from the front door of the typical speculative semi (at the side of the house furthest from the party wall) and to the rear of this was a small working kitchen, often at the side of the rear reception room. This also had a window facing the back garden (partly so that the housewife could supervise children playing in the garden), while the bathroom was commonly placed above it, to minimize plumbing costs.

According to Allen this house served a broad range of demand, being priced from £400 to £900 in the London region (varying according to dimensions, quality of finish, and features such as bay windows, porches, and gables).[5] Two reasonably sized bedrooms were provided, together with a smaller third bedroom, while the ground and first floors were equal in area. Four-bedroom houses were almost as scarce on cheaper speculative estates as on municipal estates. As Mitchell explained:

> We have never been able to find a market on...[lower-priced] estates for the four-bedroomed house even when we sold it for only about £80 more than the three-bedroomed house because although it only costs 2/- a week more in repayments, it also costs something more in rates; and even if people can afford that, they don't like

---

[4] Circa Trust, George Wimpey archives, G. W. Mitchell, letter file. Comments by G. W. Mitchell on E. V. Collins, 'Interim Report Concerning Speculative House Construction', 1 May 1944.
[5] Gordon Allen, 'Building to Sell', in Ernest Betham (ed.), *House Building 1934–1936* (London: Federated Employers' Press, 1934), 145.

the fourth bedroom which throws on them the obligation to put up all and sundry—or even to have the mother-in-law permanently.[6]

Semis dominated the speculative market. Detached houses on speculative estates were essentially detached versions of the semi, with a similar internal layout, but with the advantage of physical separation from any other dwelling (though the distance to the next house was often little greater than that typically separating one pair of semis from its neighbours). These often appeared on estates largely composed of semis, taking the more prominent and slightly more spacious corner plots. More upmarket estates occasionally had entire sections composed of detached houses and in some cases these were the only type of houses developed—both scenarios often involving slightly more generous plots and separations.[7]

Developers, especially those serving the bottom end of the market, sometimes also included a proportion of lower-cost housing solutions than the semi, such as the short terrace (again, typically with a similar internal layout to the semi-detached houses). The bungalow and its variants, the 'semi-bungalow' (with one bedroom in the roofspace) and chalet (two bedrooms in the roof space), were popular in seaside areas—particularly those attracting large numbers of retired people. As a cheaper building form it was well-suited to cheaper plots in outer suburban and coastal areas, where it was generally developed in detached units. Chalets were generally built to a standard plan, with two large bedrooms in the roof space and a further, very small one on the ground floor. They were typically semi-detached, with main entrances at their sides. During the 1930s another low-cost solution, the maisonette, also gained popularity. While superficially similar to the semi in external appearance, these marked the re-emergence of the half-house of the Edwardian era, in that they comprised two flats, one on top of the other. Each had two bedrooms, making them attractive to single people or childless couples who did not need the third bedroom of the typical semi.[8]

Speculative semis were always near-symmetrical in appearance and near-identical in their facades, though they were commonly differentiated from the neighbouring pairs of semis. As Allen noted, while the tastes of the speculative purchaser regarding external appearance varied, 'It is safe to say he desires his home to look different from his neighbour's, and, above all, unlike the municipal house, owing to his sense of social dignity.'[9] Some architects considered that speculative developers took cosmetic differentiation too far. A 1944 report commissioned by Wimpey criticized their 1930s estates'

> strained attempt to obtain variation. Seldom are two similar elevations trusted alongside each other. A round bay follows a square bay, with possibly a played one next in

---

[6] Mitchell, comments on Collins, 'Interim Report Concerning Speculative House Construction'.
[7] Alan A. Jackson, *The Middle Classes 1900–1950* (Nairn: David St John Thomas, 1991), 53.
[8] Alan A. Jackson, *Semi-Detached London: Suburban Development, Life, and Transport, 1900–39*, 2nd edn (Didcot: Wild Swan, 1991), 100–2.
[9] Allen, 'Building to Sell', 149.

Fig. 4.2. A 'universal-plan' speculative house developed on Edgware's Old Rectory Estate
Source: 'Small houses', scrapbook of house plans (*c*.1939), Peter Scott collection.

rotation[,] rendering jumps from lower to upper sill level, often changing colour and texture while doing so and just to make doubly sure, at fairly regular intervals, along comes a gable fronted house.[10]

---

[10] Circa Trust, George Wimpey archives, G. W. Mitchell, letter file, E. V. Collins, 'Interim Report Concerning Speculative House Construction', 13 April 1944.

Mitchell agreed that a better architect might handle the variations 'more quietly', but countered that at the later stages of the estate's development:

> when people have planted their gardens—all this merges in and isn't too startling. During the early vital stages of the estate, when the buyers are coming round and it is being built, any 'sameness' does get most awfully drab. Another difficulty is that a woman sees the one house that she likes, says she will have it if it is like that, and that is why, three houses up, the same design can be found repeated.[11]

'International style' houses, with flat roofs and austere, streamlined facades, attracted some interest from speculative builders during the early 1930s, who hoped that their simplicity of form might translate into low building costs. Six different firms exhibited international style show houses at the 1934 Ideal Home Exhibition, including the 'Sunspan House' designed by the celebrated modernist architect and designer Wells Coates. Yet, despite combining the houses into a 'Village of Tomorrow', promoting them with extensive marketing, and setting relatively low prices, these radical departures from the popular idea of what the semi should look like externally were almost universally rejected by the public.[12] E. & L. Berg included Sunspan houses in their range of designs offered to purchasers, but lack of interest rapidly led to the experiment being dropped.[13] The closest that the speculative semi typically came to what later generations were to call 'art deco' was the 'suntrap' house, with long, curved windows to maximize internal sunlight, as shown in Figures 4.2 and 4.3.

One of the leading high-end speculative developers, Laings (who marketed at least 40 different designs of house each year), had up to nine or ten furnished show houses on some of their estates to illustrate their model range. Building several basic models of house (which were each then customized via variations in design details) also enabled developers to offer a broad range of house prices and thus widen their potential market. For example, a New Ideal Homesteads estate at Barnehurst, Kent, offered a three-bedroom terraced house, with a bath in the kitchen (similar in design to the cheaper type of non-parlour council house), for £395; a three-bedroom non-parlour semi, with downstairs bathroom, for £495; and several more expensive designs based on the semi with upstairs bathroom, to a maximum of £695.[14] Yet the bath and garden were virtually universal features, as was a low-density, aspirational, and often semi-rural environment.

One key attraction of the speculative semi was its superior embodied services— the bathroom with indoor water closet, modern kitchen, hot water, and electricity and/or gas. The pre-1914 house generally came with little equipment for heating, lighting, power, washing, or cooking, beyond such basic facilities as

---

[11] Mitchell, comments on Collins, 'Interim Report Concerning Speculative House Construction'.
[12] Ian Bentley, 'Arcadia Becomes Dunroamin: Suburban Growth and the Roots of Opposition', in Paul Oliver, Ian Davis, and Ian Bentley, *Dunroamin: The Suburban Semi and its Enemies* (London: Pimlico, 1981), 74–5.
[13] Jackson, *Middle Classes*, 55.
[14] Bexley Local Studies, New Ideal Homesteads, *Super 1933 Homes: Barnehurst Estate Barnehurst, Kent* (1933).

Developing Owner-Occupied Suburbia 75

Fig. 4.3. An example of 'suntrap' houses advertised by Davis Estates
Source: Davis Estates Ltd, 'The Davis Estate, Ensbury Park, Bournemouth', brochure (1935). Peter Scott collection.

fireplaces and windows, or, possibly the coal range, which integrated space heating for the main room, water heating, and cooking. Yet a strong upward trend in the contribution of utilities to overall building costs was evident from around 1900 (following a more gradual increase over the previous century). The inter-war period witnessed a further acceleration and by the 1930s heating, lighting, plumbing, and other utilities accounted for around one-third of a new house's total cost.[15] Kitchens were typically 9 to 10 ft 6 in. long and 5 to 8 ft wide; a size which could accommodate an inbuilt kitchen cabinet, a larder, a sink (often with cupboards underneath), and space for the cooker, washing boiler, and wringer.[16]

THE INTERWAR SPECULATIVE HOUSE-BUILDER

Rowntree found that in York speculative semi-detached houses priced from £450 to £600 were typically built on small estates, ranging from as few as twenty houses to between one and two hundred. These were built eight or ten to the acre, the builder developing his piece of land gradually, as he was able to sell the houses. Rather than employing an architect, he would typically work from existing plans, either from housing or architectural journals, or drawn up for one of his previous developments.[17]

Although the 1930s witnessed an all-time peak in private sector housing construction, developers remained primarily local in scope, with even most of the largest firms mainly confining their operations to a single region. Fred Wellings has developed a 'league table' of private sector house-builders in the 1930s. As he acknowledges, given the substantial data limitations for this period, the estimates can only be taken as indicating broad orders of magnitude. Yet they are based on a very comprehensive range of sources (including some privately held business archives) and can be expected to be as accurate as the surviving evidence will allow for. Only around ten developers appear to have achieved an annual output of 1,000 or more units at any point during the decade and even at the height of the boom the top ten were estimated to be developing only 16–18,000 private houses a year, or around 6–7 per cent of the national total. Even the largest remained essentially family firms, managed by entrepreneurial chief executives who (with a few exceptions, such as Frank Taylor and William Leach) generally had their origins in property-related professions, such as contracting, general building, surveying, carpentry, or architecture.[18]

While developers were typically smaller than their modern counterparts, the freer availability of large tracts of building land led the major house-builders to concentrate on relatively large projects compared to the typical, cramped, modern housing development. Speculative estates often comprised hundreds (and, in a few cases, thousands) of houses per site.[19] Yet estate layouts were often somewhat basic compared to the geometric designs and substantial landscaping elements favoured by some council architects—as shown by comparing Figure 4.4 with the council estate layouts shown in Figures 3.2 and 8.1.

[15] John Burnett, *A Social History of Housing 1815–1885*, 2nd edn (London: Methuen, 1986), 261.
[16] Suzette A. Worden, 'Furniture for the Living Room: An Investigation of the Interaction between Society, Industry, and Design in Britain from 1919 to 1939', PhD thesis (Brighton Polytechnic, 1980), 74.
[17] B. S. Rowntree, *Poverty and Progress: A Second Social Survey of York* (London: Longmans, 1941), 226.
[18] Fred Wellings, *British Housebuilders: History and Analysis* (Oxford: Blackwell, 2006), 42 & 123–4.
[19] Wellings, *British Housebuilders*, 41 & 106.

Developing Owner-Occupied Suburbia 77

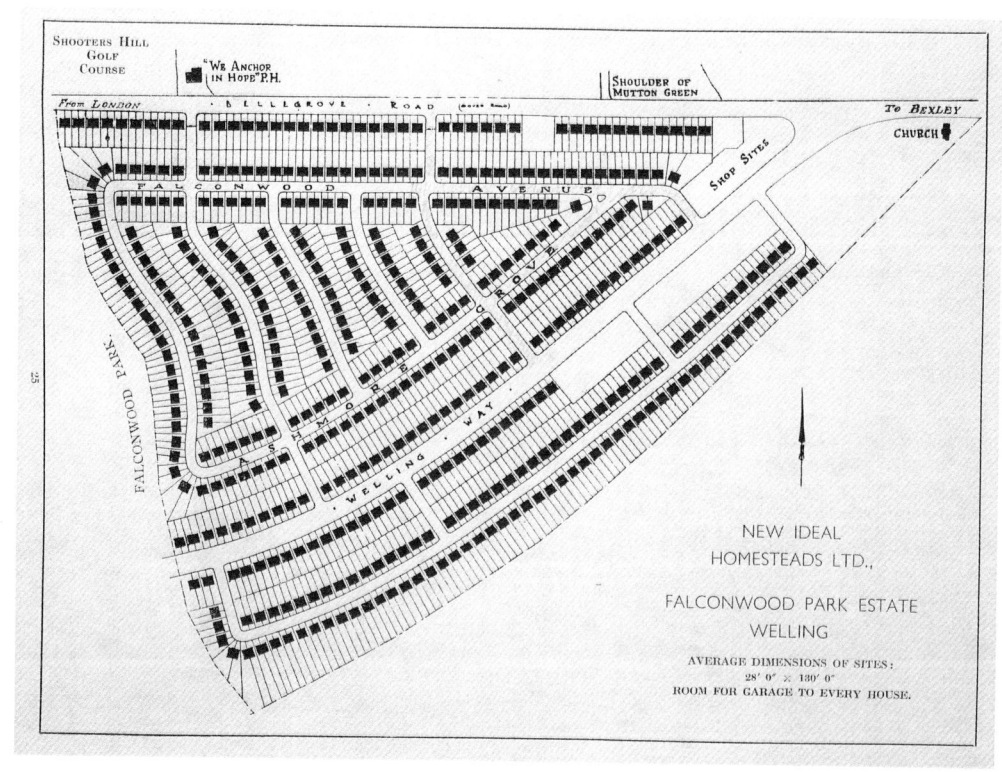

Fig. 4.4. Layout of New Ideal Homesteads' Falconwood Park Estate, Welling, London
Source: New Ideal Homesteads' 'Super Home' brochure for the Falconwood Park Estate, Welling (*c.*early 1930s). Peter Scott collection.

Fred Wellings' *Dictionary of British Housebuilders* explores the histories of Britain's housing developers and provides much of the information for the following summary biographies of the leading interwar speculative builders.[20] New Ideal Homesteads Ltd, Britain's most prolific interwar speculative housing developer, built around 36,000 houses by 1939. Founded in October 1929 by Leo Meyer (an Assistant Surveyor for Erith Council who had launched an earlier, unsuccessful building company) and Philip Edward Shephard (an insurance inspector and former railway clerk), it began developing estates in Metropolitan Kent from an office in Bexleyheath.[21] Their first estate, in Shepherds Lane, Dartford, was followed by estates in Welling, Orpington, Sidcup, and Erith. Within four years the firm had produced some 7,000 houses for sale, priced between £300 and £1,000. Many were below £500; New Ideal Homesteads generally serving the low end of

---

[20] Fred Wellings, *Dictionary of British Housebuilders: A Twentieth Century History* (Trowbridge: Cromwell Press, 2006).
[21] Wellings, *Dictionary*, 152.

the market.[22] According to one of their competitors, Godfrey Mitchell, 'New Ideals built their whole business on what they called their "semi-bungalow" i.e. with their bathroom downstairs and two big rooms in the roof upstairs, approached by a stairway running between the front and back bedroom.'[23]

Fig. 4.5. The leading lights of New Ideal Homesteads in the 1930s—Leo Meyer and Philip Shephard

Source: New Ideal Homesteads' 'Super Home' brochure for the Falconwood Park Estate, Welling (*c*.early 1930s). Peter Scott collection.

[22] Michael Furnell, *The Diamond Jubilee of Ideal Homes* (privately published, 1989), 8.
[23] Mitchell, comments on Collins, 'Interim Report Concerning Speculative House Construction'.

In 1934 alone they sold 5,700 houses, almost one-twelfth of Greater London's private sector output.[24] By this time around sixteen estates were under development in and around the London suburbs. The year 1934 also witnessed their launch as a public company, Ideal Building & Land Development Co., with the aid of the financier and share promoter Jimmy Dunn. Dunn used techniques such as 'paid puffing' (arranging for favourable articles to be carried by the press) and stock 'pyramiding' (transactions whereby a speculator increases his holdings by using their rising market value as margin for further purchases) for his new issues, and it is interesting to speculate whether these techniques contributed to a disappointing longer-term share performance.[25] Ideal's share price fell sharply during the mid- to late 1930s, as profits failed to meet expectations.[26] Perhaps partly to combat market saturation, Ideal began developments in the Midlands, Crewe, and Southampton, while also diversifying into public works contracting and houses for rental.[27]

Henry Boot & Sons was Britain's second largest speculative housing developer and was the first to be floated as a public company—in 1919. Established in around 1886 by Henry Boot, a farmer's son from Sheffield who had served a joinery apprenticeship, the firm expanded from jobbing builder to independent contractor, soon taking on public works and housing projects. Henry was later joined by his son, Charles Boot—who was responsible for the firm's interwar growth. The firm was a major local authority housing contractor, municipal housing accounting for most of the 20,000 or so houses they built from 1919 to 1930.[28] However, by 1924 speculative development had also commenced, with an estate at Elstree. In 1933 it set up two development subsidiaries—Henry Boot (Garden Estates) Ltd, which developed housing for sale, and First National Housing Trust, formed to develop estates for letting, at low rentals, under the Housing (Financial Provisions) Act, 1933.[29] Henry Boot (Garden Estates) built around 4,400 houses on nine developments, mainly around London but including an estate of 1,408 houses in Garrowhill on the outskirts of Glasgow and a small estate in Litherland on Merseyside. Meanwhile First National Housing Trust (whose record is discussed in more detail later in this chapter) built 7,582 houses over 1933–9.[30]

Another of Britain's largest speculative house-builders, Davis Estates, was founded by the builder Arthur Felix Davis. He entered the speculative housing sector by launching two estates in Kingsbury, in north-west London, in 1929. By the time of their public flotation in 1935 Davis Estates were advertising twenty different estates in the London area (while also being active in Luton, Kent, Sussex,

---

[24] Jackson, *Semi-Detached London*, 66–9.
[25] Fred Wellings, *The History of Marley* (Cambridge: Woodhead, 1994), 34.
[26] Wellings, *Dictionary*, 153.
[27] Furnell, *Diamond Jubilee of Ideal Homes*, 14–15.
[28] Wellings, *Dictionary*, 52–6.
[29] Henry Boot plc company archives, Charles Boot, 'Housing Built by Private Enterprise', memorandum for the Ministry of Health's Sub-Committee on Private Enterprise Housing, October 1943, 2.
[30] Henry Boot plc company archives, Henry Boot plc collation of numbers of houses built by Henry Boot and associated companies, 1920–39.

and Hampshire).[31] Further geographical expansion during the late 1930s took them as far as Birmingham and Plymouth.

Wates was established in 1901 by four brothers who began building in a small way in and around Croydon. During the 1920s management of the company began to pass to the second generation, particularly Norman Wates (1905–69), who was the architect of its interwar expansion. From the mid-1920s major housing estates were developed in the areas around Sidcup, Catford, Lewisham, New Malden, Streatham, and Croydon, with later extensions to Oxford and Coventry.[32] Wates was selling on some twenty south London estates in 1939 and had developed around 30,000 houses. At least half of those developed in the 1930s were sold to working-class customers, while production had declined from around 2,000 houses in 1934 to around 1,700 in 1937, owing to the market downturn.[33]

Costain was a Liverpool-based firm of building contractors, which moved into speculative house-building after the First World War to counterbalance fluctuations in local authority contracting work. In 1922 they extended their speculative developments to the South East and a year later they launched their first large London estate at Kingswood, Croydon. Richard Costain & Sons Ltd was established to undertake their speculative activities and during the 1920s it developed at least four further estates around Croydon, together with an estate at Brent Water, which—unlike Costain's earlier developments—consisted of smaller, cheaper houses, designed to attract high-wage manual workers.[34] During the early 1930s they extended their operations to Sudbury and Dagenham, including an estate of at least 700 acres between Dagenham and Hornchurch stations comprising 7,500 planned dwellings, a railway station, eight schools, five shopping centres, two churches, a public house, a cinema, and a recreation ground.[35] Shortly before launching this project, in April 1933, Costain obtained a stock exchange listing.[36]

John Laing & Sons, one of the most reputable interwar speculative developers, principally targeted the lower-middle-class market. This long-established Carlisle-based firm of builders and contractors rose to national prominence under John W. Laing (1879–1978). The firm expanded via wartime government contracts and, in the 1920s, extensive local authority contracting work. Operations were extended to London in 1921, which became the main focus of their interwar expansion. Speculative development in the capital commenced in 1927 when Laing purchased the Colin Park estate, near its new Mill Hill headquarters. In 1929 Laing launched

---

[31] Wellings, *Dictionary*, 110; Jackson, *Semi-Detached London*, 107.
[32] Wellings, *Dictionary*, 286–7.
[33] Nuffield College, Oxford, Nuffield College Social Reconstruction Survey Archive, NCSRS/C1/179, survey of the building industry in south London, interview with C. G. Allsopp of Wates Ltd, 13 August 1941; Jackson, *Semi-Detached London*, 72.
[34] Wellings, *Dictionary*, 87; Jackson, *Semi-Detached London*, 65.
[35] J. D. Bundock, 'Speculative Housebuilding and Some Aspects of the Activities of the Suburban Housebuilder within the Greater London Outer Suburban Areas 1919–1939', MPhil thesis (University of Kent, 1974), 477–8. Development of this estate was still in progress at the outbreak of the Second World War.
[36] Wellings, *Dictionary*, 88. The new company included the firm's London assets and the Walton Health Land Co. (acquired by William Costain in 1922), but not the Liverpool business.

Fig. 4.6. A 1938 advertisement for Wates' 'all in' housing terms
Source: Daily Mail Ideal Home Exhibition brochure (1938), back cover. Peter Scott collection.

their first major group of housing developments, focusing on north-west London, with two estates at Colindale, two at Sudbury, and one at Golders Green (plus another estate at Woodford in north-east London).[37] A second group of estates

---

[37] Roy Coad, *Laing: A Biography of Sir John W. Laing, CBE (1879–1978)* (London: Hodder & Stoughton, 1979), 103.

were launched in the mid-1930s—including six in London's north-west suburbs (two at Canons Park, two at Mill Hill, and estates at Queensbury and Colindale), together with Cranford in west London, Southgate in north London, Shooters Hill in the south-east, and Purley in south London.[38] A final group of estates was launched in the late 1930s—at Elstree, Edgware, Stanmore, and Hatch End. Laing's speculative estates had an average completion rate of 930 houses per year over 1930–8, declining from a peak of 1,450 in 1934 to 706 in 1938.[39]

Laing's houses were in a slightly higher price bracket than those of typical large speculative developers, ranging from around £595 to £1,300 (though on some of their more upmarket estates prices could go as high as £1,700).[40] However, their most ambitious project, a 470-acre 'garden city' at Elstree, developed from 1937, offered cheaper houses, including short terraces from £545 and semis from £565.[41] Laing was known for their high building standards, using 11-in. cavity walls, rather than the 9-in. solid brick wall then common in the South East, which was prone to dampness (a factor which encouraged the rendering of external walls).[42] Meanwhile their brochures were more restrained than most of their competitors', focusing on building standards and amenities rather than emotive advertising copy.

Taylor Woodrow was established by Frank Taylor, a greengrocer's son, born in Hatfield in 1905. At the age of 14 his family moved to Blackpool and two years later he commenced housing development by building his own home. The firm switched its attention to the booming London market in 1930, concentrating on large housing estates.[43] Their first London project—the Grange Park Estate, Hayes—aimed to develop 1,248 houses, priced at £445 and £550, plus a parade of twenty-three shops and an 808-seat cinema.[44] During the second half of the decade Taylor Woodrow expanded into the provinces, including developments at Bristol, Plymouth, West Bromwich, and Scunthorpe. The firm was launched as a public company in 1935 (again with the help of share promoter Jimmy Dunn), its completions rising from around 400 houses a year in the early 1930s to around 1,200–1,500 towards the end of the decade.[45]

Wimpey came to prominence under the management of Godfrey Mitchell, who purchased this paving and roadworks firm after returning from France as a young army captain in 1919. Contracting work on speculative estates led Mitchell to believe that he could develop houses more efficiently than the competition and that development was potentially more lucrative than contracting. After experimenting with a private venture he launched the Greenford Park Estate in 1928. Houses were priced at £550, utilizing the government's £50 per house subsidy.[46] The firm focused on a small number of large estates in west and north-west London. Wimpey was launched on the Stock Exchange in 1934, at which time it had a

---

[38] Coad, *Laing*, 109–10.   [39] Wellings, *Dictionary*, 165.
[40] Coad, *Laing*, 110; notes on Laing's interwar developments by J. A. Parfitt, November 1979.
[41] John Laing & Sons Ltd, 'Laings 10 Estates', brochure (n.d., *c*.1937).
[42] Coad, *Laing*, 105.
[43] Wellings, *Dictionary*, 265–6.
[44] Jackson, *Semi-Detached London*, 69.
[45] Wellings, *Dictionary*, 265–6; Wellings, *History of Marley*, 34.
[46] Valerie White, *Wimpey: The First Hundred Years* (London: Wimpey News, 1980), 11–12.

turnover of around £2 million, on which it earned pre-tax profits of £81,000. By 1938 profits had more than doubled to £188,000 (assisted by the firm's large contracting business).[47] Wimpey claimed to have built an average of 1,200 houses a year in the South East during the ten years to 1939 (though Alan Jackson puts the firm's output to this date at the slightly lower figure of around 10,000), with houses being advertised on about a dozen estates over 1935–7.[48]

Most provincial speculative developers operated on a smaller scale than the major London-based firms. Wellings estimates that Newcastle-based William Leech, a former window cleaner who commenced speculative development in 1932 (reportedly because he noticed—when going into pubs—that the only people who could afford to buy whisky were builders), became one of the region's largest house-builders within a few years. By 1937 a building rate of 500 units a year probably placed him among the top three or four provincial speculative housing developers.[49] Only Scotland boasted a developer whose activities rivalled those of the major London firms.

SCOTLAND—STILL A DIFFERENT COUNTRY

Scotland suffered from severe economic depression during the interwar period, with mass unemployment and chronic job insecurity. Meanwhile house prices were markedly higher than in the rest of Britain, reflecting higher development costs. This is generally attributed to Scotland's system of local rates, which shared the rates burden between the occupier and owner, owner-occupiers having to take on both burdens (though the owner's burden would presumably have been passed on to tenants indirectly, in the form of higher rents). Moreover, the owner's rate had to be paid even if the house was unoccupied, thus speculative house-builders were liable until their houses were sold (in addition to their liability for feu duty, a further burden of the Scottish system).[50]

Charles Boot, the chief executive of Henry Boot Ltd (the only major housebuilder to undertake significant speculative housing development in both Scotland and England), recalled the factors which led him to abandon plans for developing cheap houses for renting in Scotland, under the Housing (Financial Provisions) Act, 1933. His investigations showed the owner's rate to be the key factor behind prohibitive building costs. However, more stringent building standards north of the border (presumably reflecting regulations designed with tenements in mind) were also problematic—increasing construction costs by around £20 per house.[51]

Tables 4.1 and 4.2, and Figure 4.7, compare public and private sector housebuilding in England and Wales, and in Scotland, over 1919–38. Some 311,500

---

[47] Wellings, *Dictionary*, 304–5.
[48] White, *Wimpey*, 12; Jackson, *Semi-Detached London*, 72.
[49] Wellings, *Dictionary*, 174.
[50] Annette O'Carroll, 'Social Homes, Private Homes: The Reshaping of Scottish Housing, 1914–39', in Miles Glendinning and Diane Watters (eds), *House Builders: Mactaggart & Mickel and the Scottish Housebuilding Industry* (Edinburgh: RCAHMS, 1999), 217–18.
[51] Boot, 'Housing Built by Private Enterprise', 1 & 16.

Table 4.1. A comparison of house-building in England and Wales and in Scotland (thousands), 1919–38

Year	England and Wales[a] Local authority	Private	Total	Scotland Local authority	Private[b]	Total[b]	Great Britain Local authority	Private[b]	Total[b]
1919	0.6	0.1	0.7	0.0	0.0	0.0	0.6	0.1	0.7
1920	15.6	13.0	28.6	0.8	0.9	1.8	16.4	13.9	30.4
1921	80.8	20.3	101.1	4.3	2.0	6.4	85.1	22.3	107.5
1922	57.5	64.1	121.6	9.5	2.2	11.7	67.0	66.3	133.3
1923	14.3	71.8	86.1	6.5	1.4	7.8	20.8	73.2	93.9
1924	20.7	116.2	136.9	3.0	2.5	5.4	23.7	118.7	142.3
1925	44.2	129.2	173.4	4.8	4.6	9.4	49.0	133.8	182.8
1926	74.1	143.5	217.6	8.4	6.6	14.9	82.5	150.1	232.5
1927	104.1	134.9	239.0	15.8	6.1	21.9	119.9	141.0	260.9
1928	55.7	113.8	169.5	14.7	5.1	19.8	70.4	118.9	189.3
1929	61.8	140.3	202.1	14.3	4.8	19.2	76.1	145.1	221.3
1930	55.9	128.0	183.9	7.9	4.2	12.1	63.8	132.2	196.0
1931	70.1	130.7	200.8	8.3	3.8	12.1	78.4	134.5	212.9
1932	55.9	144.5	200.4	11.6	5.6	17.3	67.5	150.1	217.7
1933	56.0	210.7	266.7	15.8	7.8	23.6	71.8	218.5	290.3
1934	40.2	287.5	327.7	15.2	9.2	24.4	55.4	296.7	352.1
1935	53.5	271.9	325.4	18.8	6.6	25.4	72.3	278.5	350.8
1936	71.8	275.2	347.0	16.0	7.3	23.4	87.8	282.5	370.4
1937	78.0	259.7	337.7	13.3	7.6	21.0	91.3	267.3	358.7
1938	100.9	230.6	331.5	19.2	6.9	26.1	120.1	237.5	357.6
Total (thousands):	1,111.7	2,886.0	3,997.7	208.3	103.2	311.5	1,320.0	2,989.2	4,309.2
% of 1931 population	2.79	7.24	10.03	4.30	2.13	6.43	2.95	6.69	9.64

Sources: England and Wales, see Table 3.1. Scotland, Department of Health for Scotland, *Tenth Annual Report, 1938* (Cmd. 5969 of 1939), 178.

[a] Data for England and Wales are for years ending 31 March of the following year.

[b] Scottish data for individual years cover houses of five apartments or less. Total includes 7,934 privately developed houses of more than five apartments developed over this period. Data for Scottish private house-building from 1920 to 1924 are partly based on estimates.

Table 4.2. House-building in England and Wales from the armistice to 31 March 1940 by standard economic region

Region	Numbers			Percentage of 1931 population		
	Local Authority	Private	Total	Local Authority	Private	Total
South East	291,626	1,333,574	1,625,200	2.18	9.96	12.14
South West	71,765	185,978	257,743	2.51	6.51	9.03
East Anglia	43,828	68,073	111,901	3.71	5.77	9.48
East Midlands	94,328	223,272	317,600	3.13	7.40	10.53
West Midlands	166,254	282,276	448,530	4.44	7.54	11.99
Yorkshire and Humberside	155,226	241,088	396,314	3.96	6.15	10.11
North West	183,796	418,771	602,567	3.00	6.83	9.83
Northern Region	102,251	152,016	254,267	3.36	5.00	8.36
Total: England	1,109,244	2,904,958	4,014,202	2.98	7.79	10.77
Wales	50,061	96,410	146,471	1.93	3.72	5.65
Total: England and Wales	1,159,305	3,001,368	4,160,673	2.91	7.53	10.44

Source: Derived from J. H. Marshall, 'The Pattern of Housebuilding in the Inter-war Period in England and Wales', *Scottish Journal of Political Economy*, 15 (1968), 199–200.

houses were built in Scotland, equivalent to only 28 per cent of total dwellings in 1911, or 6.4 per cent of Scotland's 1931 population. In England and Wales, by contrast, new interwar houses were equivalent to 52 per cent of 1911 dwellings, or 10.0 per cent of 1931 population.

Table 4.2 shows the variation in house-building in the various regions of England and Wales from the armistice to 31 March 1940, derived from county-level data compiled by J. L. Marshall. All regions of England are shown to have significantly higher levels of house-building than Scotland (relative to their 1931 populations), though Wales—which was suffering severe depression and heavy out-migration—had a significantly lower rate. Yet in terms of private sector housing development, even Wales significantly exceeded Scotland's record. Table 4.2 also shows that the South East was the only region of England with a rate of private sector development, relative to its population, above the average for England (though it had the lowest municipal house-building rate of any English region). The West Midlands had both high private and municipal house-building, bringing its total interwar housing development close to that of the South East. Meanwhile, the depressed northern region and the largely rural regions of the South West and East Anglia had relatively low overall housing completions.

Scotland is thus shown to be an outlier from all regions of England and Wales in terms of private house-building, while having the highest public sector housing development per head of population of any UK region except the West Midlands (though as Table 4.2 covers a longer period than Table 4.1 the figures for these two regions are probably roughly similar). Interwar private sector house-building was equivalent to only 2.1 per cent of Scotland's 1931 population, compared to 7.2 per cent for England and Wales. Migration to the suburbs was also much less common than south of the border, even for middle-class households, as demonstrated by the small proportion of houses with a number of rooms equivalent to the typical English semi.[52] Only 27.3 per cent of interwar private enterprise houses in Scotland were of more than four apartments, while the majority of Scotland's local authority housing had only three apartments.[53]

Yet Scotland did have one spectacularly successful house-builder, Mactaggart & Mickel, which completed almost 1,000 units per year in the 1930s, for sale and letting. Mactaggart & Mickel began developing speculative housing from the mid-1920s, following extensive work as a housing contractor for Glasgow Corporation.[54] During the late 1920s it faced no real competition in the Glasgow market, but found it necessary to aggressively promote owner occupation to a hesitant public. In selling the virtues of home-ownership to Glaswegian

---

[52] Marion Bowley, *Housing and the State 1919–1944* (London: George Allen & Unwin, 1945), 266.

[53] Department of Health for Scotland, *Tenth Annual Report, 1938* (Cmd. 5969 of 1939), 179. Private sector totals also include public utility societies and housing associations.

[54] Wellings, *Dictionary*, 202.

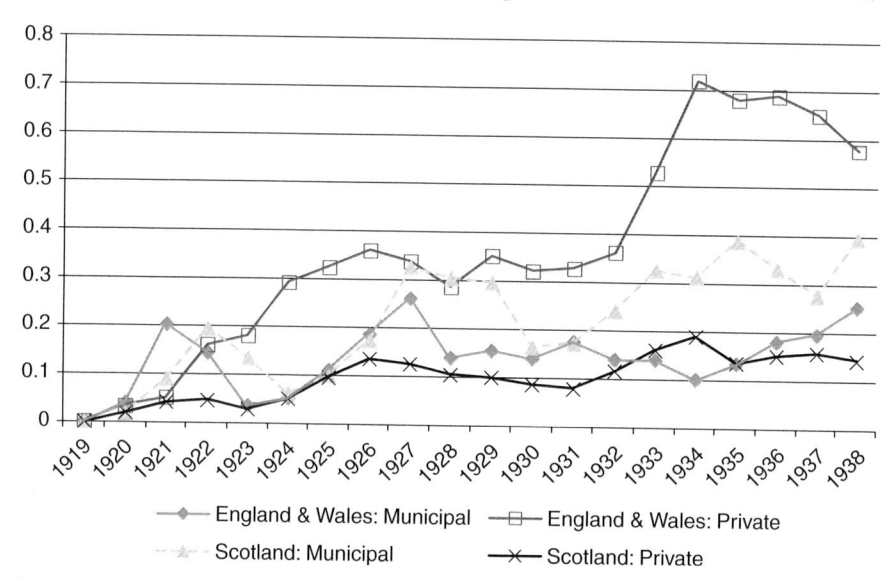

Fig. 4.7. Annual public and private sector house-building rates in England and Wales and in Scotland, as a percentage of their 1931 populations

Sources and notes: As for Table 4.2.

tenants, it adopted a marketing pitch that strongly echoed its London counterparts. By the late 1920s it was already using show houses, with modern bathrooms and 'kitchenettes' as key selling points, backed up by substantial print advertising to market its £750 houses.[55]

During the early 1930s Mactaggart & Mickel broadened its market, developing some significantly cheaper homes—such as three-apartment semi-detached bungalows, priced at £500 and available for a £25 deposit. Annual outgoings for these in 1931 amounted to £4 5s feu duty, £35 10s interest and repayments for a 25-year £493 mortgage,[56] £12 13s 2d in rates and taxes, and 7s 6d insurance.[57] Bungalows proved particularly popular, possibly reflecting Scotland's inheritance of single-floor living in tenement flats. Mactaggart & Mickel claimed to have introduced the all-in-one house purchase scheme to Scotland, with an inclusive price that covered legal fees, road charges, and removal expenses. This allowed them to claim that house purchase was even easier than renting. Yet they also built large numbers of houses for letting, both on their own account and for their associated company, Western Heritable Investment Co.

---

[55] Diane Watters, 'Mactaggart & Mickel: A Company History', in Miles Glendinning and Diane Watters (eds), *House Builders: Mactaggart & Mickel and the Scottish Housebuilding Industry* (Edinburgh: RCAHMS, 1999), 37.

[56] The fact that the loan was higher than the purchase costs minus deposit may indicate that it also covered some additional legal fees.

[57] Watters, 'Mactaggart & Mickel', 56.

Mactaggart & Mickel's only significant rival was Edinburgh-based Miller Homes, established by James Miller and his brother John. In 1927, aged 23, James Miller commenced his first speculative development of 16 houses, which sold almost immediately following an advert in the *Scotsman*. With financial support from Edinburgh Council, the firm built some 1,922 houses on subsidy schemes over 1927–34, more than ten times as many as its nearest Edinburgh rival. Its peak interwar sales were achieved in 1933, with 705 completions.[58]

Despite the limited development of new suburban owner-occupied housing in Scotland, working-class families do appear to have participated significantly in the market for those houses that were available. Analysis by Annette O'Carroll indicates that around 40 per cent of 'average cost' houses (with a selling price of around £600) on estates developed in Edinburgh during the 1930s were owned by manual workers—mostly in skilled occupations.[59]

DEVELOPMENT FINANCE

One of the speculative developer's main tasks was to secure finance, as much working capital was inevitably locked up in land and buildings. In 1935 the chairman of Taylor Woodrow Estates Ltd stated that land holdings for future development accounted for a third of their overall assets and houses in the course of construction represented a considerable proportion of the balance.[60] Unlike many other industries, housing developers generally received a warm reception from financial institutions. Building societies actively sought out speculative builders and estate agents—who were vital intermediaries with regard to securing mortgage business—by placing advertisements in their trade publications, circularizing them, and by personal calls.[61]

In addition to providing mortgages for their customers, building societies were often prepared to offer development finance. A study of the Bradford Equitable and the Bingley building societies found that both were involved in building finance. For example, in 1928 Bradford Equitable approved a scheme to provide a London building firm with 80 per cent of the development (excluding land) costs of an estate at 6 per cent interest—in five instalments during construction.[62] Southern societies were also active in this market; for example, in January 1935 Abbey Road's directors agreed in principle to consider applications for building finance, generally at an interest rate of 6 per cent.[63]

[58] O'Carroll, 'Social Homes, Private Homes', 219; Wellings, *Dictionary*, 214.
[59] O'Carroll, 'Social Homes, Private Homes', 221.
[60] Minutes of statutory meeting of Taylor Woodrow Estates Ltd, 26 April 1935.
[61] Sydney J. Walter, 'British Building Society Methods of Publicity and Advertising', *Building Societies Gazette* (September 1931), 668.
[62] Colin Pooley and Michael Harmer, *Property Ownership in Britain c.1850–1950: The Role of the Bradford Equitable Building Society and the Bingley Building Society in the Development of Home Ownership* (Cambridge: Granta, 1999), 227–8.
[63] London Metropolitan Archives, Abbey Road Building Society papers, 10/32, Finance Committee minutes, copy of Board minute, 17 January 1935.

Ruth Issacharoff has argued that building society development finance was particularly important for smaller builders who could not raise bank loans in the 1920s, and for firms in the early stages of development before becoming public companies in the 1930s.[64] The system enabled builders to minimize the capital locked up in estates. Until development was completed, building societies usually required only payment of interest on the instalments advanced. Once the final instalment had been provided, the whole loan became repayable and the completed properties usually remained mortgaged to the society until their sale. Developers also avoided excessive up-front costs by obtaining supplies from builders' merchants on credit.

Land market practices also minimized the developer's immediate financial burden. During the 1920s it became possible to take possession of developed land on payment of a deposit, paying the balance of the purchase money on a plot-by-plot basis, only after selling the house in question. George Cross, who developed the Canons Park estate in Harrow from around 1926, not only agreed to wait for payment until the buildings were sold, but actually raised the majority of the building costs for some of his speculative builders.[65] This enabled land developers to both accelerate sales and free capital otherwise tied up in land. Having sold the land (or, rather, received the deposit on it) to a speculative builder, the land developer was in the position to obtain a bank loan on the security of the 'sold' plots and thus plough his capital back into new sites. There is evidence that some land developers charged builders interest on the outstanding balance, while their capital was protected by 'default' clauses, along the following lines:

> If any purchaser shall make a default in payment of the balance of his purchase money or any instalment thereof...his deposit and all instalments (if any) paid up by him shall be absolutely forfeited and the vendors shall be at liberty...to realise the lot or lots sold to him either by public auction or private contract and the deficiency (if any) arising on such a resale and all expenses attending the same or any attempted resale shall be made good and paid by the Purchaser...as liquidated damages and any increase in price on such sale shall belong to the vendor.[66]

Thus, in effect, default entitled the land developer not only to take back the land, but the full value of any payments already made, plus ownership of any fully or partially developed buildings. J. D. Bundock noted that some developers exploited the potential for opportunism in such contracts by making it easy for small, undercapitalized developers to start house-building work, but difficult for them to finish, thus gaining the value of their accumulated investment and work once a payment was missed.[67]

---

[64] Ruth Issacharoff, 'The Building Boom of the Interwar Years: Whose Profits and Whose Cost?', in Michael Harloe (ed.), *Urban Change and Conflict* (London: CES, 1978), 308.
[65] George Cross, *Suffolk Punch: A Business Man's Autobiography* (London: Faber & Faber, 1939), 389.
[66] Lewisham Public Library, Local History Collection, A61/4/10, conditions of sale of West Chislehurst Park Estate, 1926, cited in Bundock, 'Speculative Housebuilding', 621.
[67] Bundock, 'Speculative Housebuilding', 622–3.

Large building firms often purchased virgin land and generally did so outright, rather than via staggered or deferred payments. Instead they obtained a loan on the security of the land—real estate being favoured collateral for banks and other financial institutions. Clearing banks were the main sources for such loans, though building societies also became involved. For example, both Bradford Third Equitable and the Halifax provided substantial mortgage funding to New Ideal Homesteads on the security of its development sites.[68] However, securing a loan on land already purchased was infinitely easier than taking out a loan to buy land, without the security of its ownership. Firms thus needed sufficient capital to pay deposits, which gave larger firms with stronger financial resources an advantage over smaller rivals.

THE DEVELOPMENT PROCESS

Land development companies typically laid out the necessary roads, sewers, and other public utilities required for residential development, before dividing the land into sections for sale—generally to speculative builders. The physical nature of the process differed little compared to the pre-1914 era, though there were important legal differences. Land development companies generally bought land freehold, whereas leasehold sales had been common before the First World War. Similarly, they sold the land to the builder freehold, rather than on a building lease. Thus full legal ownership passed from landowner to land developer at the point of sale, and then from land developer to builder.

The decline of the building lease system (with the property reverting to the lessor at the end of, say, 99 years) was partly due to the removal of legal constraints that inhibited landowners from selling land outright. Meanwhile agricultural depression, high taxation (by pre-1914 standards), and relatively attractive alternative investment opportunities made it more attractive to maximize immediate gains from land sales than secure a very distant bonanza for their descendants. Sites developed during the interwar period were also typically much larger than before the First World War. Transport improvements and reduced working hours greatly increased the distances over which workers could commute daily, bringing large areas of agricultural land within the radius of new development. Meanwhile severe agricultural depression from the early 1920s increased landowners' willingness to dispose of large tracts of land.

Various organizations and individuals were drawn to land development. Bundock found that estate agents often played an active role; for example, one Golders Green agent, P. H. Edwards Ltd, developed estates at Mill Hill, Sudbury, Northolt, Kenton, and Queensbury over the decade to the mid-1930s. It is often unclear whether agents were acting as principals (which ran counter to their professional code if it involved taking a leading financial role) or were working on behalf of

---

[68] Bundock, 'Speculative Housebuilding', 635–8.

clients. Acting for clients was probably far more common; one Essex agent recalled that his practice would organize, design, and supervise land development projects, including the sale of the plots, for a fee amounting to around 5 per cent of the cost of the project.[69] However, agents were often involved in the land development, or housing development, companies they assisted—thus blurring the line between principal and agent.

In contrast to the post-war era there were no 'green belt' or other substantial planning restrictions on moving land from agricultural to residential use. Bundock found that from the late 1920s land development companies were being increasingly displaced by large speculative house-builders who undertook the whole process from acquiring virgin land to developing and marketing finished housing estates—though land companies remained significant players in the market, especially for smaller house-builders. Their site development activities enabled entrepreneurs with little detailed knowledge of the technical and organizational aspects of house-building to enter the sector. Such knowledge could effectively be bought-in, by subcontracting site preparation and house construction to building firms and employing estate agents to oversee operations. Builders might be employed on either a labour-only basis or a contract where they undertook responsibility for providing both labour and materials. Some developers preferred to employ a number of separate builders, each being responsible for perhaps fifteen to twenty houses.[70] Even if the developer operated using direct labour, organizational and technical expertise could be bought-in by employing a builder or architect as project manager.

Part of the interwar decline in building costs was achieved through increased use of unskilled labour by speculative developers who employed techniques such as pebble-dashing or rough rendering of external walls partly to disguise poor brickwork. Innovations first introduced before 1914, such as the substitution of iron for lead piping (which greatly simplified plumbing work, enabling it to be done by electricians rather than skilled plumbers) and the introduction of ferro-concrete on-site processes, assisted de-skilling. Shortages of skilled building labour in the immediate aftermath of the First World War fostered further de-skilling innovations, such as the introduction of plasterboard.[71] De-skilling in turn allowed developers to employ non-union labour and thus free themselves from union restrictive practices.[72] Census data indicate an increase in the proportion of building employees who were unskilled labourers, from 31.5 per cent in 1911 to 44 per cent in 1931, together with a decrease in the proportion of craftsmen from 48.6 to 39.8 per cent; accompanied by a decline in apprenticeships.[73]

---

[69] Bundock, 'Speculative housebuilding', 442–7. Bundock also notes that agents also commonly put a clause into all sales agreements with builders for the improved land—giving them the agency rights on the sale of the completed dwellings.
[70] Bundock, 'Speculative Housebuilding', 470–88.
[71] Issacharoff, 'Building Boom', 284–92.
[72] Alan Crisp, 'The Working Class Owner-Occupied House of the 1930s', MLitt thesis (University of Oxford, 1998), 145–61.
[73] Issacharoff, 'Building Boom', 316.

Post-war shortages of building materials also stimulated innovations in building products. For example, shortages of the standard roofing materials—Welsh slate and clay tiles—led to the rapid diffusion of concrete roof tiles, which comprised around 25 per cent of the pitched roof market by 1935. The largest supplier, Marley (which accounted for between 42 and 50 per cent of production over the mid-late 1930s), had grown via an innovative 'supply and fix' marketing strategy, whereby they not only sold direct to builders, but supplied the labour force to fix the tiles. This solved the key difficulty with concrete tiles—which were prone to snap if sat on by the tiler and thus needed to be layed using a different technique—while also removing the need for the builder to find his own tilers.[74]

According to a 1934 estimate by Political and Economic Planning, labour constituted only around 32 per cent of total (labour and materials) house-building costs.[75] Movements in total building costs can be proxied using data on the average cost of a three-bedroom non-parlour council house, shown in Figure 4.8. However, this almost certainly underestimates the downward trend in costs for speculative builders—as these had greater scope for savings via cheaper materials, substituting unskilled labour on piecework for apprenticed building workers, and engaging in extensive subcontracting of activities such as painting to small gangs of workmen.[76] The council house cost index, nevertheless, shows a considerable fall in building costs, at a time of fairly stable retail prices. House costs, which had peaked at around £1,000 in the immediate post-armistice period, had fallen to £510 during 1925 and 1926. During the following years (a period of only very modest falls in general retail prices), costs fell to a low of £361 in 1934, after which they again rose significantly, returning to the levels of the late 1920s by 1937.[77]

House prices included both costs and profit margins. Alan A. Jackson estimated builders' profits (net of an allowance of around 6 per cent for interest on capital) to be in the region of about 10 per cent of turnover in the London region.[78] Similarly, John Burnett estimated that net profits for speculative builders averaged around 10 per cent, with a range of between 7 and 14 per cent.[79] A document prepared by Wimpey in 1943 provides rare archival evidence of the structure of costs and profits. This is based on houses unsold at the outbreak of war, which were then let and later requisitioned. The data must be treated with some caution, as the analysis is based on expected, rather than actual, selling prices. However, it suggests that land costs comprised just over 20 per cent of the retail price of houses and building costs just under 60 per cent. Legal and sales costs accounted for a further 5 per cent, leaving a profit of just over 15 per cent. It is not clear whether this

---

[74] Wellings, *History of Marley*, 12–134, 50–3, 62–6.
[75] Political and Economic Planning, *Housing England* (London: PEP, 1934), 59.
[76] Crisp, 'Working Class Owner-Occupied House', 145; British Library of Economic and Political Science Archive, ABS 352, private evidence to Oxford Economists' Research Group by Sir Malcolm M'cAlpine and Mr Bennett, 28 May 1937.
[77] Bowley, *Housing and the State*, 30 & 278.
[78] Jackson, *Semi-Detached London*, 150.   [79] Burnett, *Social History of Housing*, 263.

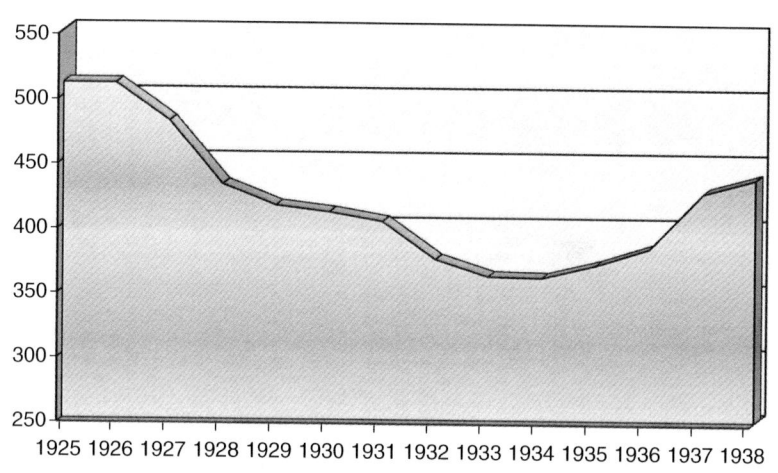

Fig. 4.8. The average cost of a three-bedroom local authority house (£ per dwelling), 1925–38

Source: Marion Bowley, *Housing and the State 1919–1944* (London: George Allen & Unwin, 1945), 278.

Notes: Data represent the annual average of quarterly contract prices for 3-bedroom non-parlour houses (excluding flats), plus £70 for land and drainage etc. (as assumed by the Ministry of Health).

'profit' also includes interest on capital. If so, the figure matches very closely with those given by Jackson and Burnett.

In contrast to the pre-war tradition of the corner shop, private estates, like their municipal counterparts, had their shops concentrated on 'parades' rather than interspersed among the houses. A 200-house estate was considered sufficient to support a small parade with the six 'essential trades' of the butcher, baker, grocer, greengrocer, dairyman, and newsagent/tobacconist/confectioner. A larger suburban parade on a main road might attract one of the multiples as an anchor

Table 4.3. Costs and expected profit margins for 121 suburban houses developed by Wimpey in the late 1930s (as percentage of expected selling price)

	Semis	All
Number of houses	100	121
Percentage distribution of expected revenue		
Plot costs	21.3	21.3
Building costs	58.2	58.3
Legal & sales costs	5.0	4.9
Profit	15.6	15.5
Total	100.0	100.0

Source: Circa trust, CWACL H, unsigned memorandum, 'Wimpey houses and land', 31 August 1943.

Notes: Based on unsold houses subsequently let by Wimpey, which had then been requisitioned by civil or military authorities, on its Barn Hill, Bullsmoor, Eastcote, Lake Farm, Roxeth, Stanmore, and Mote Farm (Mill Hill) estates. 'Semis' represent houses which could definitely be identified as being semi-detached from their coding; some of the other houses may have also been semi-detached.

Fig. 4.9. Two large suburban shopping parades developed by John Laing & Sons Ltd in north-west London

Source: Northamptonshire Record Office, John Laing & Son Ltd, 'The New Shopping Parade at Queensbury' (brochure, 1935), 7. Reproduced by kind permission of the Laing Charitable Trust.

tenant—such as Sainsbury's, Woolworths, or W. H. Smith, who would be granted a preferential deal on account of the trade they would draw (and the consequent rise in rental values for surrounding shops). With the exception of shop development—which proved particularly lucrative owing to the initial absence of local competitors—developers rarely undertook provision of other social amenities such as pubs, churches, libraries, and schools (though sites were commonly set aside for these).[80] In practice it was often many years before another party (usually the local authority) stepped in to meet the gap in local services.

'BUILDING DOWN' TO A WORKING-CLASS MARKET

Burnett estimated that the speculative housing market generally catered for families on incomes of £200–600 per year, which translated into purchase prices in the region of £500–1,500 (more affluent households commissioned architecturally

[80] Jackson, *Semi-Detached London*, 89–91.

designed houses).[81] Much activity was towards the bottom end of this range. As one informed contemporary noted, 'In travelling through England in 1936 and 1937 this was brought home very clearly by the innumerable signs advertising houses for sale at £400, 425, 475, 500, 525, but rarely at higher prices.'[82] As speculative housing aimed at the middle classes and the upper strata of the working class approached market saturation, developers began to look at ways of providing owner-occupied housing to lower income groups.

New Ideal Homesteads marketed a three-bedroom terraced house, with a bathroom in the kitchen (similar in design to many non-parlour council houses) for £395 (or £295 leasehold on some estates) from around 1932.[83] Several other developers soon began offering houses priced from around £395 in London, or £350 in the provinces. Many working-class families could afford houses substantially in excess of this minimum price and quality threshold; the mean house price given in the Life Histories Database for working-class purchases during the 1930s was £600, with a standard deviation of £173, while the median price was £575.[84] Minimum prices continued to fall; by 1938 New Ideal Homesteads were advertising two-bedroom maisonettes in eighteen different suburban locations around London, from £355.[85] There is evidence that by the end of the decade developers were turning their attention to even lower income groups. In 1939 *The Builder* reported that:

> A plan... [for] making house purchase practicable for unskilled workers and others earning only £2 or £3 a week has been launched by Davis Estates Ltd...estates of well-built houses purchasable at an all-in cost, which, in the main, will be less than the unskilled worker now pays in rent for similar accommodation. The estates are to be established throughout the country...each will have at least 200 houses of a new standardised design, and will have not less than three rooms, kitchen, bathroom, and garden. The purchase price will be in the neighbourhood of £330, and the houses will be purchasable for a small deposit and all-in payments as low as 12s 11d a week. Work...has already begun on seven new estates at Birmingham, Leicester, Rugby, Chatham, Plymouth, and Yeovil, where show-houses of the new type are nearing completion. The initial objective of the company is the disposal of some 10,000 houses on 40 to 50 estates.[86]

Another means of widening the market was a return to the pre-war practice of developing speculative housing for rental. Government attempted to revive the private rental market via the Housing (Financial Provisions) Act, 1933, which enabled building societies to lend up to 90 per cent of the value of properties constructed by private developers for letting at low rents to working-class tenants.

---

[81] Burnett, *Social History of Housing*, 252.
[82] W. F. Stopler, 'British Monetary Policy and the Housing Boom', *Quarterly Journal of Economics*, 56:1 (1941), 20.
[83] Bexley Local Studies, New Ideal Homesteads brochure, 'Super 1933 Homes: Barnehurst Estate, Barnehurst, Kent' (1933); Jackson, *Semi-Detached London*, 66–9 & 152.
[84] This information is available for thirty-three accounts.
[85] Jackson, *Semi-Detached London*, 102.
[86] 'Housing the unskilled worker', *The Builder*, 31 March 1939, 627.

Advances were partially guaranteed by the relevant local authority and Ministry of Health, while the building societies received an interest rate of 4.5 per cent (around 0.5 to 1 per cent below their normal lending rates). Between June 1933 and March 1939, only 21,482 houses were built under the Act, its failure generally being ascribed to limited interest on the part of the building societies (once the 4.5 per cent interest rate was inserted into the legislation) and antipathy by local authorities who saw themselves as the main providers of working-class housing.[87]

A substantial proportion of these were developed by Henry Boot's subsidiary First National Housing Trust, which was set up specifically to build houses under the Act and appears to have operated on a non-profit basis. First National built some 7,582 houses, on nine estates varying from 52 to 2,204 houses, at an all-in cost of £300–£440 per house. Most were in the South and Midlands, though they included an estate of 1,540 houses in Frecheville, Sheffield. An innovative element was the inclusion of a community centre in the larger estates, run by a company-employed secretary/administrator and funded by an additional 2d per house on weekly rentals.[88]

Their chief executive, Charles Boot, recalled that while some local authorities had supported their plans, others had been indifferent or hostile. However, he regarded the attitude of the building societies as a more formidable barrier, most, including the large societies, not being prepared to provide finance under the Act. He claimed that the building societies' initial support for the legislation had reflected their fears of weakening demand in the housing market and that when conditions improved they were unwilling to lend at preferential interest rates to social housing providers, especially where this involved very large loans to a single borrower.[89]

First National's experience also indicates the practical limitations of providing low rental housing without government subsidy. It was originally intended to let houses at rentals (inclusive of rates) of 10s per week. However, higher costs and interest rates resulted in inclusive rentals that ranged from 11s 2d to 13s 9d at their Frecheville estate in Sheffield and 15s 10d to 17s 8d at their Addington estate in Croydon (reflecting higher land and building costs in London). Figures for these two estates, plus Perry Beeches in Birmingham, indicate that 55 per cent of rental income went on covering interest and sinking fund costs; 26 per cent on general and water rates; and 19 per cent on repairs, management, insurance, bad debts, and so forth. Assuming that these figures are broadly representative of the costs faced by commercial landlords, where tenants paid their rates directly the administrative costs of managing rental property would thus be equivalent to just over a quarter of break-even costs.[90]

More homes were developed for rental outside the provisions of the 1933 Act. Mactaggart & Mickel (and its associated company, Western Heritable Investment

---

[87] Crisp, 'Working-Class Owner-Occupied House', Chapter 2.
[88] Boot, 'Housing Built by Private Enterprise', 2–6.
[89] Boot, 'Housing Built by Private Enterprise', 3.
[90] Boot, 'Housing Built by Private Enterprise', 4.

Co.) developed a large number of houses for renting in Scotland, while New Ideal Homesteads moved into developing for rental in the late 1930s.[91] A significant rental market was also evident in York; Rowntree found that 118 of the 670 occupiers of speculative houses he surveyed had bought them in full, 388 were buying them on the instalment system, and 164 were renting them.[92] Yet letting experienced only a very limited national revival, due to continuing fears regarding rent control. In 1939 Norman Wates told the Departmental Committee on Valuation for Rates that 'modern weekly rented properties are not saleable which show a return of less than about 8.5 per cent', whereas the pre-1914 rate of return was later given as only 5 per cent. Thus it was generally cheaper to buy than to rent such properties.[93]

CONCLUSION

During the 1930s speculative house developers devised a system whereby semi-detached housing could be offered for sale at prices within the reach of not only the middle classes but (given liberalized mortgage terms) many skilled and semi-skilled workers. In an era when planning restrictions were virtually absent, transport innovations were rapidly widening the radius of viable locations for daily commuting, and the de-skilling of building trades substantially reduced costs (partially at the expense of declining quality), developers found themselves able to provide houses at successively lower prices. However, any major expansion in home ownership required a willingness on the part of potential purchasers to undertake a costly long-term investment in a new and unfamiliar tenure, whilst also moving to new communities that were very different to those where they had grown up. How developers and mortgage providers succeeded in persuading large numbers of families to embrace this transition is explored next.

---

[91] Wellings, *British Housebuilders*, 40–1. [92] Rowntree, *Poverty and Progress*, 229.
[93] The National Archives, HLG56/157, Departmental Committee on Valuation for Rates, oral evidence from John Laing; Norman Wates, and Gilbert F. Armitage (Secretary of the National House Builders Registration Council), 16 March 1939.

5

Marketing Owner Occupation to the Masses

INTRODUCTION

'New world' societies have long-established traditions of widespread owner occupation; by 1911 46 per cent of households in the United States and 50 per cent in Australia owned their own homes, while in 1921 owner-occupation rates had reached around 58 per cent in Canada and almost 60 per cent in New Zealand. In these nations an 'ideology of home ownership' is said to have been strongly associated with the spread of middle-class lifestyles, the diffusion of class tensions, and the emergence of common socio-political values.[1] As US President Herbert Hoover stated in 1931, 'to possess one's home is the hope and ambition of almost every individual in our country'.[2] Conversely, in many Western European nations home ownership per se has relatively little social significance, as reflected in its slower development and lower current levels.[3] Indeed, in countries such as West Germany, Sweden, and Switzerland, owner-occupation rates actually declined during much of the post-1945 'long boom' period, despite rapidly rising living standards.[4]

Britain represents an unusual case—in 1914 it strongly conformed to the European pattern, most working- and middle-class families living in privately rented accommodation and social status being dependent on the type of house occupied rather than its tenure. However, the interwar period, and particularly the 1930s, witnessed a major break with this trend, a high proportion of new households being established in new suburban owner-occupied housing. The emergence of a marked British 'ideology of home ownership' also first became evident during this period, marking the start of a long-term transition in housing tenure that has

---

[1] Ann Dupuis and David C. Thorns, 'Home, Home Ownership and the Search for Ontological Security', *Sociological Review*, 46 (1998), 24–5; Richard Harris and Chris Hamnett, 'The Myth of the Promised Land: The Social Diffusion of Home Ownership in Britain and North America', *Annals of the Association of Amercian Geographers*, 77 (1987), 177; Ian Winter and Lois Bryson, 'Economic Restructuring *and* State Intervention in Holdenist Suburbia: Understanding Urban Poverty in Australia', *International Journal of Urban and Regional Research*, 22 (1998), 64.

[2] Herbert Hoover, opening address, President's conference on home-building and home ownership, Washington, 2 December 1931, cited in Niles Carpenter, 'Attitude Patterns in the Home-Buying Family', *Social Forces*, 11 (1932), 76.

[3] Harris and Hamnett, 'Myth of the Promised Land', 175.

[4] Jim Kemeny, *The Myth of Home Ownership: Private versus Public Choices in Housing Tenure* (London: Routledge & Kegan Paul, 1981), 6.

culminated in a current owner-occupation rate around the new world, rather than the European, norm.[5]

This chapter examines the spectacular success of building societies' and speculative housing developers' promotional initiatives in creating a market for new owner-occupied houses. Despite the huge financial burden involved (compared to any other commitments most purchasers had hitherto taken on), aggressive promotion of 'easy terms', together with a marketing strategy that portrayed the suburban semi as an essential component of a new, aspirational, form of working-class respectability, produced the first major boom in working-class owner occupation. Purchasers typically came from cramped, rented, inner-urban accommodation, and, only a few years previously, would not have considered the possibility of buying a suburban house.

A TRANSFORMATION IN HOUSING TENURE

The 1914 British owner-occupation rate is often cited as being in the order of around 10 per cent.[6] While this is no more than a 'guesstimate', the evidence in Chapter 2 concerning late Victorian and Edwardian working-class owner-occupation levels is consistent with an aggregate figure of around this magnitude. For England and Wales, housing tenure patterns were transformed during the interwar period and, in particular, the 1930s. On the eve of the Second World War some 32 per cent of houses were estimated to be owner-occupied, 10 per cent owned by local authorities, and 58 per cent privately rented.[7] Much of this change represented new houses; around one-third of the 1938 housing stock of England and Wales is estimated to have been built after 1914 (with 67 per cent of new private sector houses, and 47 per cent of all new houses, developed for owner occupation).[8] Speculative developers tapped into popular enthusiasm for modern suburban homes. As a 1934 estate developer's brochure noted:

> On all sides there is the demand for a break-away from the old style of terrace house with its useless gable, wasted roof space and a layout just like every other house. All that belongs to thirty years ago. We are alive to-day to the need for sunshine; we bask in it whenever we can, let into our houses the life-giving rays. But to do that, a house must be built with windows flush and unobscured by brickwork, frame, or sash. Howard Houses are designed to trap the sunlight as a welcome thing.[9]

---

[5] Data collected by Maria Concetta Chiuri and Tullio Jappelli ('Financial Market Imperfections and Home Ownership: a Comparative Study', Universita Delgi Studi Di Salerno, Centre for Studies in Economics and Finance Discussion Paper 44 (2000), 27) gives owner-occupation rates of 68.56 per cent for the UK, an average of 66.67 per cent for the USA, Canada, and Australia, and an average of 58.78 per cent for 10 European nations.

[6] Stephen Merrett, *Owner Occupation in Britain* (London: Routledge & Kegan Paul, 1982), 1.

[7] Merrett, *Owner Occupation*, 16.

[8] Department of the Environment, *Housing Policy: Technical Volume Part I* (London: HMSO, 1977), Table I.23.

[9] Bodleian Library, John Johnson Collection, Building Estates, Box 1, brochure for Howard Houses Upper Farm Estate, Hampton Court, 1934.

The First World War and subsequent two decades witnessed changes in the growth and distribution of earnings that considerably increased the number of families for whom such housing was affordable. The major changes in male earnings are outlined in Table 5.1 (male earnings being shown because, in most sectors, women typically did not remain in employment after marriage). The highlighted columns show real earnings, i.e. adjusted for inflation to show earnings at 1935–6 retail prices. Between 1913–14 and 1922–4 average real earnings rose by 13 per cent. However, unskilled manual workers did substantially better than skilled and semi-skilled workers, or clerks, thus reducing earnings differentials between these groups. By 1935/6 average earnings had risen considerably, being 43 per cent greater in real terms relative to 1913/14. Unskilled workers still retained a slight improvement in their relative position compared to other manual workers and clerks in 1914, while these other groups failed to achieve the average rise in earnings for all classes of employee.

Yet earnings data underestimate the economic position of clerical workers. In addition to higher typical incomes than manual workers, this group had much greater stability of employment, at a time when unemployment or the threat of unemployment limited the capacity of many working-class families to fully translate higher real earnings into rising living standards. The clerical workforce was undergoing rapid expansion, the number of male clerks rising by 4 per cent from 1911 to 1921 and a further 11 per cent from 1921 to 1931, by which time they numbered around 817,000. There was no census in 1941, though it appears likely that a significant proportion of the 21 per cent increase in clerical employment from 1931 to 1951 occurred in the 1930s.[10] As the army of clerks grew faster than the entry of clerks' children into the workforce, much of the deficit was drawn from the ranks of the working class, principally the skilled workforce. Growing numbers of clerks formed part of a broader trend for the expansion of the middle classes to occur mainly towards the lower end of its income spectrum—the group who would look to speculative, rather than architecturally designed, housing.[11]

The building of several hundred thousand municipal suburban houses during the 1920s had contributed to the rapid technical obsolescence of pre-war terraced housing lacking bathrooms, other modern utilities, and gardens. Demonstrating that working-class families could access housing with this level of amenities played an important role in popularizing the modern suburban semi among manual workers. Lower-middle-class families were also attracted to new, modern housing, but for different reasons. Many felt themselves to be under increasing financial pressure. The standard rate of income tax had risen from 5.83 per cent on the eve of the First World War to 20–5 per cent over the interwar years, while there had also been rapid rises in the costs of services such as private education, local rates, and, especially, employing live-in servants.

---

[10] Guy Routh, *Occupation and Pay in Great Britain 1906–60* (Cambridge: Cambridge University Press, 1965), 25.
[11] John Burnett, *A Social History of Housing 1815–1885*, 2nd edn (London: Methuen, 1986), 251.

Table 5.1. Changes in average male earnings for eight occupational groups in nominal and real (1935/6) values, 1913/14 to 1935/6

Period	1913/14 Nominal £	1913/14 Real £	1922/4 Nominal £	1922/4 Real £	1922/4 % of 1913/14	1935/6 £	1935/6 % of 1913/14
Professional:							
(A) Higher	328	463	582	475	102	634	137
(B) Lower	155	219	320	261	119	308	141
Managers etc.	200	283	480	392	139	440	156
Clerks	99	140	182	149	106	192	137
Foremen	113	160	268	219	137	273	171
Manual workers:							
Skilled	99	140	180	147	105	195	139
Semi-skilled	69	97	126	103	105	134	137
Unskilled	63	89	128	104	117	129	145
Average (all sectors)	92	130	180	147	113	186	143

Source: Earnings, Guy Routh, *Occupation and Pay in Great Britain 1906–60* (Cambridge: Cambridge University Press, 1965), 104; retail prices, Charles Feinstein, *National Income, Expenditure, and Output in the United Kingdom, 1855–1965* (Cambridge: Cambridge University Press, 1972), T140.

Notes: Average is weighted by the number of people in each class.

By the 1930s many working- and lower-middle-class families both were attracted to new suburban housing and had the potential to afford it, on the right terms. The prospects for creating a 'mass market' in owner occupation were thus considerably greater than in the Edwardian Britain—if a means could be found to spread the cost of house purchase over a sufficiently long period and make buying on mortgage acceptable to socio-economic groups who had generally hitherto seen renting as the norm.

MAKING HOUSES AFFORDABLE—THE INTRODUCTION OF 'EASY TERMS'

As Chapter 2 noted, some major London-based building societies were beginning to develop a working-class mortgage base before 1914. However, it was during the interwar years, and particularly the 1930s, that a general shift of building society lending towards this group became evident. This period witnessed a boom in building society savings, partly owing to a historical compromise between the movement and the Inland Revenue, whereby interest on building society shares and deposits was paid net of tax (levied at a favourable rate for substantial investors, who accounted for a growing proportion of building society savings).[12]

While there were around 1,000 building societies during the interwar period, the movement became increasingly dominated by its giants. The largest societies were the Halifax, with total assets of £128,242,000 by 1939 (£32 million higher than ICI's consolidated assets and equivalent to 25.2 per cent of the total assets of Britain's largest clearing bank) and Abbey Road, with assets of £51,948,000. The Leeds Permanent, Woolwich Equitable, National, and Co-operative societies each had 1939 assets in excess of £30 million, while the Leicester Permanent, Burnley, Bradford Third Equitable, Huddersfield, Westbourne Park, and Leeds Provincial all had assets in excess of £10 million. These twelve societies collectively controlled £411.3 million of the movement's total assets of £758.9 million and dominated lending on speculative estates.[13]

Rapid growth in building society lending on new houses during the 1920s catered for a mainly middle-class customer base. However, there was a substantial increase in lending to working-class home-buyers for existing rented houses, offered to sitting tenants by landlords faced with the continuation of wartime rent controls. As these were mainly older-style terraced properties, lacking bathrooms and modern utilities, often in a poor state of repair and, crucially, subject to rent control, prices were generally low—making them affordable to people with insufficient incomes to purchase new houses.[14] Despite limited government financial support for private housing development under the 1923 Housing Act, house

---

[12] Jane Humphries, 'Inter-war House Building, Cheap Money, and Building Societies: The Housing Boom Revisited', *Business History*, 29 (1987), 330–4.
[13] 'Building Societies since 1925', *Economist* (1 July 1939), 10.
[14] Herbert Ashworth, *The Building Society Story* (London: Franey, 1980), 70–2.

prices remained too high for any significant development of the working-class market by the time subsidies were phased out in the late 1920s. The overall growth of working-class home ownership remained modest; while no national figures are available, a review of fragmentary local evidence by George Speight indicated that a 1931 working-class owner-occupation rate of 8 or 9 per cent is an upper-bound estimate.[15]

Middle-class households were already finding owner occupation financially attractive by the mid-1920s, as evidenced by the substantial increase in private-sector house-building from around 1923 (see Table 4.1). From 1926 building society borrowers could use their mortgage interest costs to reduce their income tax liability, providing a powerful incentive for house purchase. However, given that a married couple with two children only became liable to tax on incomes from employment if they earned £375 or more a year, and only paid tax at the standard rate on incomes in excess of £500 per year, the benefits were only relevant to a small proportion of the population—most of whom would probably have followed the trend towards owner occupation even in their absence.[16]

Of greater importance was the long-term fall in house prices over the 1920s and early 1930s, discussed in the previous chapter. Yet while this greatly facilitated house purchase for lower-middle-class families, it was insufficient, of itself, to open up the market to most working-class households. It has been estimated that in 1930 buying a new house would still have required a weekly income in excess of £4, limiting access to white-collar employees and some highly paid manual workers.[17] The key remaining obstacles for workers earning £2 10s–£4 per week were the substantial deposit and heavy instalments. The reduction in interest rates during the early 1930s—following Britain's departure from the gold standard and the government's adoption of a cheap money policy—reduced minimum instalments, but was again insufficient to substantially widen accessibility.

Building societies played a crucial role in expanding access, as a response to intense competition in the mortgage market. Following the onset of the National Government's cheap money policy, they were viewed as relatively high-interest, low-risk savings vehicles and thus faced heavy inflows of funds. Many were so overwhelmed that they were forced to place temporary restrictions on deposits.[18] Lowering interest rates in line with general reductions was viewed as high risk, given that building societies borrowed short and lent long—at fixed interest rates—and would thus face difficulties if cheap money proved transitory.[19] Instead they

---

[15] George Speight, 'Who Bought the Inter-war Semi? The Socio-economic Characteristics of New-House Buyers in the 1930s', University of Oxford, Discussion Paper in Economic and Social History 38 (December 2000), 14.

[16] Bernard Harris, *The Origins of the British Welfare State: Social Welfare in England and Wales 1800–1945* (Basingstoke: Palgrave Macmillan, 2004), 256.

[17] London School of Economics, *New Survey of London Life and Labour*. Vol. VI, 164; Speight, 'Who Bought the Inter-war Semi?', 10.

[18] Ashworth, *Building Society Story*, 87.

[19] Alan A. Jackson, *Semi-Detached London: Suburban Development, Life and Transport 1900–39*, 2nd edn (Didcot: Wild Swan, 1991), 155–6.

extended the market for mortgages by liberalizing terms and promoting the advantages of home ownership.[20] This process was intensified by competitive pressures to undercut each other on 'easy terms' in order to expand their market share; a process discussed in detail in Chapter 10. Mortgage periods were extended from around 20 years to 25, or even 30, substantially reducing weekly payments. Meanwhile a number of devices were employed to reduce the minimum deposit.

House-buyers could pay a reduced deposit by taking out an insurance policy, paying a single premium in return for a guarantee to compensate the building society for any loss on the sum loaned in excess of the society's normal maximum ratio of mortgage to house price (generally 75 or 80 per cent).[21] Local authorities provided similar guarantees. Yet these still required a minimum deposit of at least 10 per cent.[22] Of much greater importance were guarantees provided by estate developers, commonly known as builder's pool arrangements (as guarantees were typically pooled over many properties), which reduced deposits to around, or sometimes below, 5 per cent of the purchase cost.

Under the pool scheme developers made cash deposits with building societies, originally equal to the difference between the society's normal maximum ratio of mortgage to house price and the new 95 per cent ratio. However, as competition between societies intensified, builders successfully renegotiated terms, lowering deposits to one-third or even one-quarter of this excess.[23] Government sources indicate that by 1938 40–60 per cent of current building society mortgage business was being conducted via pool schemes, and a higher proportion for relatively cheap properties.[24] This is corroborated by the Life Histories Database; purchasers of new houses during the 1930s typically report deposits of around 4.0–6.7 per cent of the purchase price, which were only available on pool schemes.

Pool arrangements played a key role in opening up owner occupation to manual workers. As one building society luminary noted, 'Innumerably more people can find a 5 per cent deposit than ... 10 per cent ... it is much easier to scrape together £25 than £50 and experience has shown us that ingenious methods of finding a small deposit have certainly obtained.'[25] Making an initial payment of £25–£30 to secure a property was also more in keeping with working-class expectations, as it had a parallel in the house rental market: 'key money', the money landlords sometimes demanded for handing over the keys to accommodation.[26] In some cases deposit requirements were reduced to below £25, through devices such as

---

[20] Humphries, 'Inter-War House Building', 325–45.
[21] Cited in Merrett, *Owner Occupation*, 15.
[22] T. H. Chandler, 'How Building Societies Assist the Builders', in Ernest Betham (ed.), *House Building 1934–1936* (London: Federated Employers' Press, 1934), 81–5.
[23] Jackson, *Semi-Detached London*, 156.
[24] The National Archives [NA], CAB 27/645, Committee on Building Societies, report of Cabinet Committee, 9 December 1938.
[25] Frank L. Lee, 'The Changes in Building Society Practice to Meet Changed Business Conditions', *Building Societies Gazette* (October 1936), 937.
[26] Howard Marshall, *Slum* (London: Heinmann, 1933), 52; Nuffield College, Oxford, Nuffield College Social Reconstruction Survey Archive (NCSRS), C5/12, M. P. Fogarty, 'Birmingham Housing', report, c.1939.

using a life assurance policy as additional collateral, or the developer loaning the purchaser part of the deposit.[27] Costain advertised houses available for possession on payment of only £10. A permit was issued to move in on receipt of this sum, while the balance of the full deposit was paid in 13 or 15 weekly instalments after the move. The building society mortgage became active only after completion of this arrangement, thus avoiding the need to make mortgage payments while deposit instalments were still due.[28]

Customers with particularly secure incomes were offered even more generous terms. For example, New Ideal Homesteads advertised 'Special "No Deposit" terms for civil servants and people of "pensionable position"'. One hundred per cent loans were offered, together with complete life cover throughout the term of mortgage—so that in the event of the breadwinner's death, 'the property passes to his dependents without further payment.'[29]

The liberality of British mortgage terms is illustrated by comparison with the USA, where, despite federal government support for mortgage liberalization in the aftermath of the depression, average loan-to-value ratios were still less than 70 per cent in the late 1930s. Meanwhile even insurance companies (that introduced the most liberal loan terms) increased average contract lengths to only around 18 years.[30] In comparison, Britain's 25-year, 95 per cent mortgages were truly revolutionary. The ability of building societies to introduce such radical liberalization partly reflected the relative stability of Britain's domestic financial institutions and housing market during the early 1930s. Yet Britain's more generous terms were also necessitated by its higher land values and lower wages. In contrast, 1939 US mortgage terms (which were broadly similar to those in Britain during the 1920s) would have left new houses beyond the reach of most working-class families.

Some building societies also sought to reduce the risks associated with taking on long-term mortgage liabilities. Woolwich offered protection from mortgage default for the purchaser's dependents in the event of death, via a life insurance policy. The 'Combined scheme' involved the society paying a single lump sum insurance premium, which the borrower re-paid to the society via a small addition to each instalment.[31] This was later re-packaged as 'The Endowment Plan of Home

---

[27] NA, HLG29/253, memorandum by joint committee of Building Societies Association (hereafter BSA), National Federation of Building Societies (NFBS), and important unaffiliated societies, 12 March 1938; BSA, bound volumes of circulated letters, Circular no. 4, 5 August 1936, by R. H. Marsh; Gunnersbury Park Museum, Oral History Archive, GPM/OH70, interview with Edgar Wynn.

[28] Richard Costain & Sons Ltd, 'The "Beechwood" Home, Greenford, Middx.', promotional leaflet, n.d., 1930s; *Harrow Gazette and Observer*, 9 September 1932, 15. J. D. Bundock, 'Speculative Housebuilding and Some Aspects of the Activities of the Suburban Housebuilder within the Greater London Outer Suburban Areas 1919–1939', MPhil thesis (University of Kent, 1974), 711. Budock also notes that C. T. Crouch Ltd offered a similar arrangement, which they called the 'Crouch Deposit Savings Club'.

[29] New Ideal Homesteads, 'A New Ideal Home Costs Much Less Than You Think', leaflet, n.d., 1930s (held at the British Library).

[30] Leo Grebler, David M. Blank, and Louis Winnick, *Capital Formation in Residential Real Estate* (Princeton: Princeton University Press, 1956), 234–57.

[31] Barclays Bank Archive, 1023/868, 'Woolwich Equitable Building Society: The Key to a Home of Your Own', brochure.

Ownership'.[32] Meanwhile Abbey Road offered 'complete security of tenure' to its mortgagees; repudiating the right building societies normally reserved to call in the mortgage (provided that repayments were maintained and the usual covenants observed).[33] At least one major builder, Henry Boot, also moved in this direction, introducing a free insurance policy for house-purchasers aged 50 or under from 1936 to cover repayments in the event of death for the first 5 years of the mortgage.[34]

Building society mortgage debt had risen from £120 million in 1924 to £316 million in 1930, involving some 720,000 borrowers. By 1937 it was to expand to £636 million and 1,392,000 borrowers.[35] Meanwhile private-sector house-building reached an all-time peak of almost 300,000 houses per year during the mid-1930s. The role of mortgage liberalization in this expansion is well known. However, for a long time there was a consensus that this did not involve any significant broadening of the market beyond the middle class.[36] Conversely, recent studies have highlighted the large numbers of working-class families who entered this market for the first time during the 1930s and their importance to the expansion of house-building, which increasingly involved 'building down' to lower income groups.[37]

As Table 5.2 shows, only 1.3 per cent of new private sector houses built in England and Wales from January 1919 to March 1931 were in the lowest rateable value band, equivalent to a sale value of below around £400 (or £600 in London), while almost a third of houses were in the highest band (involving a sale price of over £750, or £1,000 in London). Yet over the subsequent 8 years building in the highest value band stagnated, the lowest band expanded to 38.2 per cent of new construction, while building for the middle band underwent considerable absolute growth.

Working-class households accounted for virtually all houses in the lower value band, while also comprising a substantial proportion of the middle band. Of twenty-two people in the Life Histories Database who purchased properties in Greater London (for which the purchase price is known), ten paid more than £600, while of nineteen purchasers in the rest of Britain, fifteen paid more than £400. More broadly based data are available from the Abbey Road Building

---

[32] Barclays Bank Archives, 1023/1272, Woolwich Equitable, 'The Endowment Plan of Home Ownership', brochure (1 October 1938).
[33] Peter Scott collection, Abbey Road Building Society, *Home Ownership: A Simple Guide to the Abbey Road Mortgage Service*, brochure (n.d., c.mid-late 1930s), 7.
[34] Henry Boot plc company archives, 'Henry Boot Garden Estates Ltd, Hayes Place Estate—Hayes—Kent', brochure (n.d., c.1936). It was stated that this might be subject to medical examination.
[35] Marian Bowley, *Housing and the State 1919–1944* (London: George Allen & Unwin, 1945), 279.
[36] Mark Swenarton and Sandra Taylor, 'The Scale and Nature of the Growth of Owner-Occupation in Britain between the Wars', *Economic History Review*, 38 (1985).
[37] George Speight, 'Building Society Behaviour and the Mortgage Lending Market in the Interwar Period: Risk-Taking by Mutual Institutions and the Interwar House-Building Boom', DPhil thesis (University of Oxford, 2000); Alan Crisp, 'The Working Class Owner-Occupied House of the 1930s', MLitt thesis (University of Oxford, 1998).

Table 5.2. Private sector house-building in England and Wales classified by rateable value—average number per year (thousands) and percentage distribution by value band

Rateable Value[a]	Up to £13		£14–26		£27–78		Total
Estimated sale price	Under £400		£400–750		Over £750		
	No.	%	No.	%	No.	%	No.
Jan. 1919–March 1931	1.2	1.3	58.1	65.8	29.1	32.9	88.4
April 1931–Sept. 1934	74.6	41.1	80.8	44.4	26.3	14.5	181.8
Oct. 1934–March 1939	98.0	36.7	136.1	50.9	33.3	12.4	267.4

Sources: Housing data—Marian Bowley, *Housing and the State 1919–1944* (London: George Allen & Unwin, 1945), 272. Estimated sale price equivalents—George Speight, 'Who Bought the Inter-war Semi? The Socio-Economic Characteristics of New-House Buyers in the 1930s', University of Oxford, Discussion Paper in Economic and Social History 38 (December 2000), 15 (using a formula published by Harold Bellman, general manager of the Abbey Road Building Society, in 1935).

[a] Houses in Greater London were classified under different rateable value bands—up to £20, £21–35, and £36–105, respectively.

Society (Britain's second largest building society during the 1930s and the only one to provide any information on the socio-economic composition of borrowers). In 1933 fewer than 23 per cent of its new mortgages involved houses costing below £500, yet 42 per cent of borrowers were 'wage-earners and labourers'. Moreover, the proportion of Abbey Road's mortgage portfolio accounted for by working-class borrowers rose from 35.6 per cent in 1930 to 49 per cent in 1939.[38] Building industry estimates reveal a similar trend; for example, one of Britain's largest house developers, Wates, stated that around 50–75 per cent of their 1930s houses were intended for the 'steady working class'.[39] Most purchases involved new houses; of thirty-eight accounts in the database regarding houses known to have been bought during the 1930s, no fewer than thirty-four were new developments.[40]

New private housing was both more plentiful and cheaper during the 1930s than any time before or since, it being estimated that during the mid-1930s the cost of a new house would be equivalent to around 2.5 years' income for a man earning the average industrial wage.[41] Indeed it became generally cheaper (from the perspective of weekly payments) to buy a new house on mortgage than to rent it.[42] A major Ministry of Labour household expenditure survey found that by 1937/8 around 17.8 per cent of non-agricultural working-class households either

---

[38] Speight, 'Who Bought the Inter-war Semi?', 13 & 27.
[39] NCSRS, C1/179, interview with C. G. Allsopp of Wates Ltd, 13 August 1941.
[40] Excluding a few accounts where it was unclear whether the property was newly developed.
[41] J. C. Weston, 'International Comparisons of the Cost of Housebuilding', *Journal of Industrial Economics*, 12:1 (1963), cited in Burnett, *Social History of Housing*, 252.
[42] NA, HLG56/157, Departmental Committee on Valuation for Rates, oral evidence from John Laing, Norman Wates, and Gilbert F. Armitage, 16 March 1939; NCSRS, C5/12, M. P. Fogarty, 'Birmingham Housing', report, c.1939; BSA, verbatim reports of National Association of Building Societies' discussions, 1934–6, paper delivered at AGM, 2–5 June 1936, by R. Bruce Wycherley.

owned or were purchasing their own homes.[43] Thus the proportion of working-class owner-occupiers appears to have at least doubled since 1931. Such growth is dramatic, given that purchases were strongly associated with the household formation stage of the family life cycle. The average interval between marriage and house purchase, available for thirty-six families in the Life Histories Database, was only 2.7 years, while some of these had initially lived with their parents after marriage.[44]

The housing boom is widely recognized as having had a considerable impact in boosting economic growth and employment in the wake of the 1929–32 depression. Increased house-building accounted for around 17 per cent of GNP growth from 1932 to 1934, while if the expansion of construction materials is added, it is estimated to have accounted for 30 per cent of the increase in employment during the first three years of the recovery.[45] This is sometimes pointed to as evidence of the success of the national government's recovery policy—though there is little evidence that Treasury officials appreciated the impact cheap money was likely to have (in conjunction with building society mortgage liberalization) in boosting house-building and thereby stimulating economic growth. Meanwhile, in common with downplaying the role of working-class purchasers in this boom, the importance of producers' marketing campaigns in overcoming the perceived economic and cultural barriers to owner occupation, and thereby enabling the market to be extended to this new class of purchaser, has been similarly neglected in many accounts.

THE MARKETING PROCESS

Longer mortgage terms and smaller deposits made home ownership accessible to a substantial section of the working class. Yet merely because a product is affordable to a new mass market does not imply that large numbers of consumers will necessarily be prepared to purchase it. In the early 1930s owner occupation was still alien to most working-class families and ran counter to entrenched cultural orthodoxies. It involved dealings with middle-class professionals and institutions and entering into complex legal contracts—activities viewed with fear and suspicion by many working people.[46] The chief objection, however, was to taking on a massive and very long-term debt. Traditional 'respectable' working-class values emphasized

---

[43] NA, LAB17/7, 'Weekly Expenditure of Working-Class Households in the United Kingdom in 1937–38', Ministry of Labour and National Service, July 1949.

[44] The dates of marriage and house moves are generally only known to the nearest year. One owner-occupier who purchased a house (originally jointly with his brother) before marriage is treated as having moved there on marriage.

[45] Barry Eichengreen, 'The British Economy between the Wars', in Roderick Floud and Paul Johnson (eds), *The Cambridge Economic History of Modern Britain*, Vol. II: *Economic Maturity, 1860–1939* (Cambridge: Cambridge University Press, 2004), 334–5.

[46] For a discussion of British working class attitudes to debt see Peter Scott, 'The Twilight World of Interwar Hire Purchase', *Past & Present*, 177 (2002); Margot C. Finn, *The Character of Credit: Personal Debt in English Culture, 1740–1914* (Cambridge: Cambridge University Press, 2003).

keeping out of debt, which could greatly increase the risks of falling into destitution during periods of hardship.[47] Several database accounts reflect these concerns, young couples being warned by friends or relatives that a mortgage was 'a millstone round your neck'.[48]

A mortgage was also much less flexible than a tenancy. There were heavy 'sunk costs' of the deposit, various transactions fees, and accumulated capital payments, plus a continuing legal liability to repay the loan (even if the house was surrendered to the building society). These made it difficult and expensive to switch to cheaper accommodation during periods of reduced income, or when a change of job required a new location. Urban working-class families typically made frequent house moves; it has been estimated that before 1914 around 30–40 per cent of London's population changed residence annually.[49]

Many lower-middle-class people considering house purchase for the first time also had real anxieties, especially those whose occupations might involve periodic house moves. A 1930 article for members of the Association of HM Inspectors of Taxes noted that while in minor provincial towns there were still people prepared to invest in housing and accept a moderate rent in return for a 'desirable' tenant, in larger towns this class of investor was almost extinct and a house available at a reasonable rent was likely to be unsaleable: 'Too frequently the only choice lies between paying a high rent for a house which seems to consist entirely of stairs, and purchasing a modern house of the type which might, not inaptly, be called "labour saving" '.[50] However, the writer added, 'the purchase of a house takes three months to settle down and fifteen years to settle up.' Nor were the immediate financial benefits at all clear-cut (at least for employees such as tax inspectors, who might be required to move between districts). The annual costs of a freehold house priced at £1,250 (excluding capital repayments) would be equivalent to an annual rental of £106, owing to:

	£
Interest, £1,250 at 5.5%	69
Repairs and decorations	14
Reserve for depreciation (1.5%)	18
Legal costs of purchase and sale (excess over amount allowed on removal claim, £25 spread over 5 years)	5
Total	106[51]

[47] Simon Szreter, *Fertility, Class and Gender in Britain, 1860–1940* (Cambridge: Cambridge University Press, 1996), 528.
[48] Coventry Record Office [hereafter CRO], 1647/1/36, female born 1913; Museum of London Archive, material collected for Gavin Weightman and Steve Humphries, *The Making of Modern London 1914–1939* (London: Sidgwick & Jackson, 1984), letter from, and transcript of interview with, G. R. Matthews.
[49] Andrzej Olechnowicz, *Working Class Housing in England between the Wars: The Becontree Estate* (Oxford: Oxford University Press, 1997), 49–52.
[50] 'On Purchasing Houses', *Quarterly Journal of HM Inspectors of Taxes*, 26 (1930), 228–9.
[51] 'On Purchasing Houses', 229–30.

Yet renting generally involved living in an 'obsolete' house, which incurred additional costs for labour, heating, cleaning, and decorating. Large gardens and rooms too big for the family's current furniture presented additional costs. Taking these factors into account, the article concluded, a suitable house offered for sale at £1,250 was generally a better bet than an obsolete house offered at an annual rental of £70 or more.

To overcome cultural and practical aversions to owner occupation, the building industry and building society movement engaged in an aggressive marketing crusade to sell both the idea of home ownership and the appeal of new suburban estates to the working public. The basic techniques were pioneered in the marketing of middle-class housing during the 1920s, though during the 1930s the targeting of working-class customers involved a much greater emphasis on 'easy terms' and the lifestyle benefits of modern suburban housing. There was also a general move towards more sophisticated marketing techniques, embodied, for example, in more extensive and lavishly illustrated brochures, with greater emphasis on emotive messages regarding the lifestyle advantages of owner occupation and suburban living.

Scott and Newton estimated that building society advertising expenditure (including both mortgage and other advertising) rose from around 1.0 per cent of their mortgage interest income over 1909–13 to around 2.1 per cent over 1919–28 and 2.8 per cent over 1929–38.[52] In 1935 building societies were estimated to account for 0.58 per cent of all press display advertising, equalling the combined expenditures of the banking, insurance, and trustee company sectors. Yet the building industry proved the key player in selling owner occupation to a mass public; building estate companies' direct advertising accounted for 1.08 per cent of press display advertising, while an unknown volume of additional advertising was conducted via estate agents.[53] Both building societies' and builders' advertising tended to emphasize common themes, with relatively little brand differentiation. As such, their advertising tended to reinforce a number of key messages, such as the advantages of modern suburban housing, the superiority of owning over renting, the ease with which houses could be bought on mortgage, and the investment value of a home.

Traditionally there had been no strong social kudos from owner occupation or social stigma attached to renting, as demonstrated by the broad social composition of tenants prior to 1914.[54] It was during the interwar years that owner occupation came to be perceived as a markedly superior tenure—due, at least in part, to a concerted effort by the building industry to imbue it with a new symbolic meaning.

---

[52] Peter Scott and Lucy Newton, 'Advertising, Promotion, and the Rise of a National Building Society Movement in Interwar Britain', *Business History*, 54 (2012).

[53] Nicholas Kaldor and Rodney Silverman, *A Statistical Analysis of Advertising Expenditure and the Revenue of the Press* (Cambridge: Cambridge University Press, 1948), Table 69. This included advertising aimed at depositors as well as borrowers.

[54] Michael Ball, *Housing Policy and Economic Power: The Political Economy of Owner Occupation* (London: Methuen, 1983), 25.

Despite the limited size of even the largest house-building firms, the industry collectively developed a sophisticated portfolio of marketing messages. This was fostered through strong inter-firm marketing knowledge 'spillovers', via housing exhibitions, movement of sales staff, the activities of advertising agencies and estate agents as market intermediaries, and direct observation of competitors' estates and publicity material. Thus, despite its fragmented nature, best practice rapidly spread between firms, which employed similar and mutually reinforcing broad marketing pitches.

Fig. 5.1. Examples of 1930s building society advertising promoting home ownership: (a) Halifax Building Society bookmark; (b) Leeds Permanent Building Society postcard

Source: Peter Scott collection.

A barrage of advertising, including an increasing proportion of large, illustrated adverts, was brought into working-class homes via national, regional, and local newspapers, sometimes in the form of extensive property supplements.[55] Newspaper advertising covered a wide range of themes, though the 'easy terms' on which attractive, modern houses could be purchased tended to feature most prominently.

Adverts for new housing estates became larger, more sophisticated, and more elaborately illustrated, including photographs, more eye-catching slogans, and greater use of symbolism and emotional appeal, compared to the simple line drawings or text announcements of the 1920s.[56] Moreover, they embraced new, emotive arguments regarding the benefits and superiority of owner occupation and suburban life. For example, a 1938 Mactaggart & Mickel advert showed a white-collar worker together with the slogan:

> WHOSE KEY DO YOU CARRY IN YOUR POCKET. YOUR OWN OR YOUR LANDLORDS? Are you whiling away the years in a home owned by another man? A home which, even if you stay in it for 20–25 years, will be no more your own than it is now? Are you handing a considerable portion of your hard-earned income to a landlord for a house that will always be on loan?[57]

Roadside hoardings constituted another important advertising medium. As one house-buyer recalled, travelling through south-east London one encountered 'huge hoardings...First Wates—£5 down secures your house. From £300 leasehold, £350 freehold. Show House Open. Then...Ideal Homesteads, same kind of wording still £5 down. These adverts were very colourful and eye catching'.[58] Hoardings were particularly effective in alerting people to the presence of a new estate in their vicinity and in stressing the easy terms on which houses were available. They proved successful in enticing people who were not actively seeking a house; for example, Jane Walsh (the wife of an Oldham cotton piecer) recalled how seeing a hoarding during a Saturday evening walk led to her house purchase:

> a big signpost...said: 'Own Your Own House. Price £449. Deposit £20. Repayments, rates, taxes, 18s. weekly. Exhibition House now open.' We went and had a look at the exhibition house...How we admired and exclaimed! We discussed ways and means of raising the £20 deposit—which seemed an impossible sum. And if we could raise it, what about the 18s rent? It would mean that I should have to go on working for

---

[55] J. R. Gold and M. M. Gold, '"A Place of Delightful Prospects": Promotional Imagery and the Selling of Suburbia', in L. Zonn (ed.), *Place Images in Media: Portrayal, Experience, and Meaning* (Savage, MD: Rowman & Littlefield, 1990).

[56] Ian Davis, 'A Celebration of Ambiguity: The Synthesis of Contrasting Values', in Paul Oliver, Ian Davis, and Ian Bentley, *Dunroamin: The Suburban Semi and its Enemies* (London: Pimlico, 1981), 93–8.

[57] Royal Commission of Ancient and Historical Monuments, Scotland (RCAHMS), Mactaggart & Mickel, MMX/1, copy of advertisement in *Edinburgh News*, 21 January 1938.

[58] Museum of London Archive, material collected for Weightman and Humphries, *Making of Modern London*, letter from and transcript of interview with G. R. Matthews.

Fig. 5.2. The key to home ownership as advertising metaphor: Coventry Permanent Economic Building Society brochure (*c.*1930s)
Source: Peter Scott collection.

years.... In comparison with our present rent of 6s 9.5d a week it was tremendous. But then so was the difference between the exhibition house and our present slum.[59]

Having attracted the customer's initial interest, sales messages were delivered in a more elaborate form via the estate brochure. Brochures often ran to many pages and adopted a glossy format with large photographs or other good quality illustrations. They were used to convey a number of messages, yet easy terms again typically featured prominently. For example, the front cover of a 1933 New Ideal Homesteads brochure had the slogan '9'6 Weekly £395 freehold'—together with a large house (not the one available for £395).[60] Brochures and advertisements further asserted affordability by portraying house purchase as an investment—in effect suggesting that a mortgage made long-term savings less necessary. For example, Davis Estates claimed that:

> The money wasted in paying rent over a period of years will surprise you... To invest part of your savings in the best of all securities—a home—is a sound policy, as your building society repayments are usually less than the rent demanded for similar accommodation. You are, therefore, **acquiring your own home at no additional cost** and in many cases at an actual saving, and **making your rent pay for your house**.[61]

The investment value of a house was also sometimes presented as a means of avoiding rental payments in old age. As a Henry Boot (Garden Estates) brochure noted: 'When you purchase a house *built by Boots* you buy security for the days when your earning capacity shall have diminished; you invest your money in a tangible asset instead of wasting it in rent, and you buy peace of mind for yourself and your wife when you become your own landlord.'[62]

One particularly powerful means of demonstrating affordability was by recruiting existing purchasers as agents. Several developers began to offer purchasers commission for introducing new customers, typically £5 (approximately 1 per cent of the purchaser price). Ivy Willis recalled that her husband, a postal sorter, introduced about eight or nine buyers to their developer, earning around £40–£45.[63] This practice appears to have been an important source of customers for at least some estates; for example, W. H. Wedlock claimed that '80 per cent of our Sales are through the direct recommendation of our satisfied purchasers.'[64] New Ideal Homesteads also noted that a high proportion of new purchasers were recommended by existing clients.[65] Similarly, Gleesons claimed that 'out of five hundred

---

[59] Jane Walsh, *Not Like This* (London: Lawrence & Wishart, 1953), 55–6.
[60] Bexley Local Studies, New Ideal Homesteads brochure, 'Super 1933 Homes: Barnehurst Estate, Barnehurst, Kent' (1933).
[61] Bodleian Library, Oxford, John Johnson Collection, Davis Estates brochure (1934). Emphasis in original.
[62] Henry Boot plc company archives, 'Henry Boot Garden Estates Ltd, Hayes Place Estate—Hayes—Kent', brochure (n.d., c.1936).
[63] Museum of London Archive, material collected for Weightman and Humphries, *Making of Modern London*, unpublished memoir by Ivy Willis, c.1980s, plus project interview with Ivy Willis.
[64] Bexley Local Studies, W. H. Wedlock Ltd, 'Mayplace Estate', undated brochure (c.1934).
[65] Michael Furnell, *The Diamond Jubilee of Ideal Homes* (privately published, 1989), 12.

Fig. 5.3. An example of a 'modern homes' feature and accompanying advertising, from a May 1936 issue of the *Bristol Evening News*
Source: Peter Scott collection.

odd houses... sold this year, nearly half have been sold to friends of previous purchasers of Gleesons Homes.'[66]

Another aspect of 'easy terms' was simplifying the purchase process. This had traditionally involved dealings with building societies, solicitors, and estate agents, which both mystified and intimidated many working people and incurred substantial transactions fees that increased up-front costs. Developers began to offer an 'all-in' product, that included arranging the mortgage and incorporating legal and other fees into the house price and, therefore, the mortgage. Some even offered free furniture removal over a certain distance.[67]

It was also common for developers to reduce 'moving-in' costs by installing wallpaper and fittings for free, the purchaser being allowed to choose from a range of designs. Purchasers were often also offered the choice of items such as fireplaces, kitchen and bathroom fittings, leaded glass panels, or even doors and windows.[68] The range of choices became progressively wider over the interwar years, owing to the growth of the building components industry, the 'industrialization' of supply for some components that had traditionally been made on site or locally, such as windows, and their marketing via large builders' merchants who provided developers with catalogues to display their range to house purchasers. A 1938 catalogue for James & Co. (Catford) Ltd, in south-east London, extended to 380 pages, including 80 pages of fireplaces and similar items (mantles, ranges, gas fires, and so forth).[69]

MARKETING HOUSE-HUNTING AS A LEISURE ACTIVITY

Building estates were the crucial venues for turning a purchaser's initial curiosity into a firm commitment to purchase. People were drawn in by marketing strategies which portrayed estate visits as a leisure activity. Sometimes the initial 'day out' took place at a venue other than the estate, such as the Daily Mail Ideal Home Exhibition, or various similar local and regional exhibitions. For example, the North London Exhibition boasted two miles of stands, covering 'every aspect of progress in the planning, building, equipping, furnishing, and running of the home' and drew large audiences with gimmicks such as the presence of radio stars.[70]

Some London developers had their own permanent exhibitions in the form of centrally located show houses. Davis Estates opened show houses adjacent to

---

[66] Cited in Fred Wellings, *Dictionary of British Housebuilders: A Twentieth Century History* (Trowbridge: Cromwell Press, 2006), 139.

[67] Bexley Local Studies, *Bexley between the Wars*, unpublished two-volume collection of interviews with interwar Bexley residents, c.1986–7, interview with Mr Bollon; A. D. McCulloch, 'Owner-Occupation and Class Struggle: The Mortgage Strikes of 1938–40', PhD thesis (University of Essex, 1983), 214.

[68] Ian Bentley, 'The Owner Makes his Mark: Choice and Adaption', in Paul Oliver, Ian Davis, and Ian Bentley, *Dunroamin: The Suburban Semi and its Enemies* (London: Pimlico, 1981), 143.

[69] Source: Peter Scott collection, James & Co. (Catford) Ltd, *Catalogue* (July 1938).

[70] 'The North London Exhibition', *St. Pancras Chronicle*, 11 October 1935, 10.

Charring Cross and Victoria stations to attract buyers to its various estates in London's suburbs and satellite towns.[71] New Ideal Homesteads established a small bureau at Waterloo Station to provide information regarding their developments and dispense vouchers—exchangeable for railway tickets to their estates. Clapham Junction Station—through which many trains passed on their way to the southern suburbs—hosted E. & L. Berg's 'model rooms' and G. T. Crouch's show house.[72]

In 1934 John Laing opened a detached show house on the forecourt of Kings Cross Station, with floodlighting at night. Open until 8 p.m. (and later 10 p.m.) it attracted many evening commuters and was claimed to have received over 70,000 visitors in around its first three years.[73] The house came complete with a garage—which was used to exhibit films of Laing's estates—while cars were available to take prospects to estates in which they showed interest.[74] In February 1937 this was supplemented by a more ambitious New Homes Exhibition in Oxford Street, hosting three full-size furnished show houses, each built on one level. In the Oxford Street window of the exhibition a colour film provided a conducted tour of the estates and show houses. This was claimed to attract such audiences that on many occasions the police had to move the crowds on for obstruction.[75]

Nor was this method of bringing the suburban house into the city centre limited to London. As early as June 1931 Mactaggart & Mickel opened a show house (complete with gardens) and a sales office at the busy crossroads at Elington Toll, Glasgow, to entice prospects to their suburban estates. They claimed that this proved so popular that it enabled them to set 'A World Record in House Sales' by selling over 130 houses within 24 working hours.[76] In 1934 they erected another show house, this time on the concourse of Glasgow's Central Station.

Promotional material emphasized a low-pressure sales approach. Laing's told prospective viewers that 'The attendants are "helpers" rather than salesmen, and will be pleased to show you round and give the fullest information regarding Laing Estates, Laing Houses and Laing House Purchase. If after inspection you desire to visit an Estate, a car is at your service without obligation.'[77] Similarly, a New Ideal Homesteads brochure claimed, 'You will not be pressed in any way, or worried to buy, but you will be met with a spirit of helpfulness, actuated by a desire to give

---

[71] Peter Scott collection, Davis Estates Ltd, 'The Davis Estate, Ensbury Park, Bournemouth', brochure (n.d., c.1935).

[72] Jackson, *Semi-Detached London*, 163.

[73] Bodleian Library, John Johnson Collection, Building Estates Box 1, John Laing & Co., 'The Laing Washington House', brochure (c.1937); Simon Pepper, 'John Laing's Sunnyfield Estate, Mill Hill', in Boris Ford (ed.), *Early Twentieth Century Britain: The Cambridge Cultural History* (Cambridge: Cambridge University Press, 1992), 297.

[74] Roy Coad, *Laing: A Biography of Sir John W. Laing, CBE (1879–1978)* (London: Hodder & Stoughton, 1979), 109.

[75] Notes on Laing's interwar developments by J. A. Parfitt, November 1979; Northampton Record Office, Laing advertisement scrapbook, c.1935–9; Coad, *Laing*, 110.

[76] Diane Watters, 'Mactaggart & Mickel: A Company History', in Miles Glendinning and Diane Watters (eds), *House Builders: Mactaggart & Mickel and the Scottish Housebuilding Industry* (Edinburgh: RCAHMS, 1999), 60.

[77] John Laing & Co., 'The Laing Washington House'.

you the fullest information on any subject dealing with houses and their cost.'[78] This removal of a perceived obligation to purchase was crucial to the presentation of estate visits as a leisure activity. It followed contemporary trends in retailing, evident among department stores and, most notably, 'variety stores' such as Woolworths and Marks & Spencer.[79] Opening hours that included Sundays and evenings further increased the leisure appeal of an estate visit.

A chauffeur-driven car was generally offered for at least the customer's first visit. At a time when very few working-class people owned cars, this was a considerable novelty and helped to emphasize the aspirational nature of owner occupation. It also avoided having prospects make the journey from the station on foot or by public transport, which would have given them a more realistic idea of the effort normally involved in travelling there. Estates often provided further entertainment, such as firework displays, concerts, visits from politicians, and launch events hosted by film or radio stars.[80] Several database accounts mention the fairground atmosphere of the estate visit, which was intended only as a day out but resulted in their becoming home-owners. For example, Grace Foakes recalled that before inspecting the real show house, she and her husband were invited to a novelty show house:

> which was a representation of Snow White's House... together with seven dwarfs and Snow White... shaking hands and escorting you around. This was a very good sales gimmick, for after you had seen the house you were given a wonderful tea. When this was finished you were driven around the estate and invited to choose your plot of land or your house.[81]

Developers generally built one show house for each basic 'model' available on the estate, one sometimes doubling as a sales office. In addition to illustrating the different houses on offer this enabled the developer to gauge likely demand for each design and the popularity of proposed layouts for areas such as kitchens and bathrooms. After showing prospects around and getting them to select the style of house and building plot they most liked, the salesman asked for an 'initial deposit' to secure their chosen property—typically £5, but in many cases only £1.

By asking for a sum small enough for the customer to be able to pay on the day of the viewing, but large enough to make them feel committed to the transaction, the salesman was able to close the deal at the end of the sales pitch and avoid any 'cooling off' period. The balance of the deposit, typically £20–£25, was not generally required until the customer took possession (though in some cases an intermediate deposit of £5–£10 was due after a week or so). If the customer failed to find the balance, the builder would often offer a loan—as the deposit amounted to only 5 per cent of the sale price, they could afford to take this risk. Prospects who did

---

[78] Bexley Local Studies, New Ideal Homesteads, 'Albany Park Estate', brochure (c.1935).
[79] B. S. Rowntree, *Poverty and Progress: A Second Social Survey of York* (London: Longmans, 1941), 218–19.
[80] Weightman and Humphries, *Making of Modern London*, 114.
[81] Grace Foakes, *My Life with Reubin* (London: Shepheard-Walwyn, 1975), 59.

Fig. 5.4. Chauffeur transport offered to prospective Wates' buyers
Source: Wates Ltd, 'Guaranteed Houses: Morden Common Estate', brochure (1939), Peter Scott collection.

not leave a deposit on the day of the visit were typically 'followed up' after a week or two, either via mail or a personal visit from the salesman or estate agent.[82]

LIFESTYLE MARKETING

In addition to making the purchase process simple and enjoyable, and emphasizing the affordability of the product, marketing campaigns also sought to attach specific values to owner occupation and living on modern, suburban estates. In doing so, they pioneered an aspirational sales pitch, which was to become an enduring feature of house marketing. Developers both tapped into a new, aspirational family- and home-centred model of working-class respectability and played an important role in promulgating this model, selling a 'suburban dream' that had hitherto been beyond the reach of the working classes.

As Susan Strasser has noted, effective marketing campaigns generally encouraged new needs and desires, 'not by creating them out of whole cloth, but by linking the rapid appearance of new products with the rapid changes in all areas of social and cultural life.'[83] Contrary to some traditional depictions, the interwar years, and particularly the 1930s, witnessed a marked expansion in working-class occupational, geographical, and (within certain limits) social mobility. Bains and Johnson found that occupational mobility for men was substantially higher during this period than in the nineteenth century, while research on young interwar women, by Selina Todd, found a high level of occupational and geographical mobility, together with rising social aspirations—within constraints imposed by their material circumstances and class position.[84]

As discussed further in Chapter 6, working-class migration to new owner-occupied estates was strongly associated with desires for a new, aspirational, suburban model of working-class respectability. This was based around 'privatized' family- and home-centred lifestyles, an increased commitment of monetary and psychological resources to the welfare and material advancement of children, and asserting status through the display of material goods and high standards of domestic hygiene and associated behaviour.[85] This period witnessed the diffusion of a powerful 'ideology of domesticity', which had begun to influence a substantial section of the working

---

[82] Anon, 'One Hundred Not Out: The First Century of Hilbery Chaplin 1894–1994', unpublished typescript (c.1994), 24.

[83] Susan Strasser, *Satisfaction Guaranteed: The Making of the American Mass Market* (New York: Pantheon, 1989), 95.

[84] Dudley Baines and Paul Johnson, 'In Search of the "Traditional" Working Class: Social Mobility and Occupational Continuity in Interwar London', *Economic History Review*, 52 (1999); Selina Todd, *Young Women, Work, and Family in England, 1918–1950* (Oxford: Oxford University Press, 2005), 113–44.

[85] A. Hughes and K. Hunt, 'A Culture Transformed? Women's Lives in Wythenshawe in the 1930s', in A. Davies and S. Fielding (eds), *Worker's Worlds: Cultures and Communities in Manchester and Salford, 1880–1939* (Manchester: Manchester University Press, 1992), 92; Szreter, *Fertility*, 528; Diana Gittins, *Fair Sex: Family Size and Structure, 1900–39* (London: Hutchinson, 1982), 175–6, notes the importance of these new family-centred lifestyles as a factor encouraging family limitation.

class by the 1930s, promoted through the new mass-circulation women's magazines, women's sections in national newspapers, other media, health professionals, the Ideal Home Exhibition (and its local and regional counterparts), and advertisements for new consumer durables.[86] These idealized the married woman's role as 'professional housewife', providing a happy, clean, home environment for her family via labour-saving devices and efficient household management practices.[87] Such values are strongly reflected among the database accounts, when discussing motives behind moves to owner-occupied suburbia. A modern suburban house was seen as offering the ideal environment for these new values, on account of its hygienic conditions, modern, labour-saving layout, more spacious rooms, front and rear gardens, and semi-rural setting.

A range of monthly magazines promoted suburban lifestyles to middle-class women, including *Homes and Gardens* (1919), *The Ideal Home* (1920), *Good Housekeeping* (1922), *Woman & Home* (1926), *Woman's Journal* (1927), *Wife & Home* (1929), and *Harper's Bazaar* (1929). These were ostensibly aimed at more affluent sections of the middle class, but were also popular with the purchasers of higher-price speculative suburban semis, who aspired to the lifestyles they portrayed.[88] The 1930s witnessed the launch of new popular weekly magazines, such as *Woman's Own* (1932) and *Woman* (1937), which targeted a broad readership, while being more acceptable to middle-class housewives than existing popular titles such as *Woman's Weekly*. With content more directly relevant to women running a home without live-in servants, these new weeklies facilitated a further convergence in the attitudes of working- and lower-middle-class housewives.

Aspirational values were also a key motif of much building society mortgage advertising, which linked owner occupation with citizenship, domesticity, and a healthy, secure, and prosperous future for one's family.[89] For example, in around 1937 the National Association of Building Societies published *Members of Parliament in Praise of Building Societies*, a collection of endorsements from forty-seven MPs including Prime Minister Stanley Baldwin and several cabinet ministers. A typical contribution was that of Col. R. V. K. Applin: 'The man who owns his home has rooted himself in the very soil of his country: he is a productive citizen, with all his interests centred in the land. He has staked out his claim, settled his future, and is an asset in the national life, a worthy "citizen of no mean empire".'[90]

---

[86] Deborah, Ryan, 'The Daily Mail Ideal Home Exhibition and Suburban Modernity, 1908–1951', PhD thesis (University of East London, 1995), 92.

[87] Gittins, *Fair Sex*, 182–3; Margaret Judith Giles, 'Something That Bit Better: Working-Class Women, Domesticity, and "Respectability", 1919–1939', DPhil thesis (University of York, 1989), 108–9.

[88] Alan A. Jackson, *The Middle Classes 1900–1950* (Nairn: David St John Thomas, 1991), 117.

[89] J. R. Gold and M.M. Gold, ' "Home at Last!": Building Societies, Home Ownership and the Imagery of English Suburban Promotion in the Interwar Years', in John R. Gold and Steven V. Ward (eds), *Place Promotion: The Use of Publicity and Marketing to Sell Towns and Regions* (Chichester: Wiley, 1994).

[90] BSA, National Association of Building Societies, 'Members of Parliament in Praise of Building Societies', pamphlet, c.1937.

Halifax produced its own quarterly *Home Owner* magazine, based on the popular *Ideal Home* type of magazine. This was circulated to its members and distributed via the society's branches, agencies, and exhibition stands. *Home Owner* included features on advice to house buyers; house designs; housekeeping; heating the house; hobbies; plus regular columns on topics such as 'health in the home', 'the young housewife', 'the art of furnishing', and gardening. There were also items on saving, insurance, etc., but these formed only a small part of the content. Abbey similarly produced the half-yearly *Abbey Road Journal*, issued free to members and depositors.[91] Some builders pursued a similar marketing strategy. In 1934 E. & L. Berg produced a catalogue for the Ideal Home Exhibition in the form of a 'New Estates Magazine', with a cover price of 6d, to advertise their developments in Surrey (involving houses mainly priced at £895 and above). This included a short story, 'Mr & Mrs', and articles on film stars, dress design, setting up the perfect nursery, gardening, and beauty.[92]

Many aspirational features of the modern house—enhanced hygiene via the provision of a bathroom, inside toilet, and hot running water; electricity and other modern utilities; light, generously fenestrated rooms; front and rear gardens; and a suburban location—were shared by both owner-occupied and council houses. Yet speculative estate developers successfully distinguished their product via various (often largely cosmetic) design features, aspirational street and estate names, and using advertising copy to assert a superior status. As a social survey of Oxford noted: 'speculative builders pander to the weaknesses of human beings to be exclusive and are erecting a type of house which, by its appearance, will distinguish its inhabitants from those of the council houses.'[93]

Building society advertising emphasized the status pretensions of owner occupation, posters generally showing large detached villas, despite the fact that smaller suburban semis formed the backbone of the market.[94] Building estate advertising followed a similar strategy, often showing the largest type of house available on the estate, though such houses would typically account for only a small proportion of sales. Depicting a higher social setting than that of the target customer was characteristic of contemporary advertising, based on the premise that people preferred to identify with portrayals of themselves as they aspired to be rather than as they currently were.[95]

Perceptions of the social superiority of owner occupation emerge strongly from the Life Histories Database. As Ivy Willis recalled, part of the motivation behind her house purchase was 'bettering ourselves, a sort of one-upmanship from living

---

[91] Harold Bellman, *The Thrifty Three Millions: A Study of the Building Society Movement and the Story of the Abbey Road Society* (London: Abbey Road Building Society, 1935), 239.

[92] Museum of Domestic Design and Architecture, BADDA 457, E. & L. Berg, *New Estates Magazine* (1934).

[93] Barnett House, *A Survey of the Social Services in the Oxford District*, II: *Local Administration in a Changing Area* (London: Oxford University Press, 1940), 354.

[94] Gold and Gold, 'Place of Delightful Prospects', 173–5.

[95] Roland Marchand, *Advertising the American Dream: Making Way for Modernity, 1920–1940* (Berkeley: University of California Press, 1985), 166.

in rented accommodation...council houses were rather looked down on'.[96] Similarly, Ken Milne recalled that 'we felt we'd come up in the world as we'd got our own little house and I think there was a tendency for people to keep the places smarter, the gardens were more obvious and they were usually well-kept and the houses were painted up, keeping up with the Jones's'.[97]

Developers' advertising copy played on such aspirations, an extreme example being a 1935 brochure in which a two-bedroom semi, priced at £535, was described as having a 'Tradesmen's Side Door'.[98] Even New Ideal Homesteads, whose estates provided perhaps the cheapest houses offered by any of the major London speculative builders, noted in one brochure that 'Every house...will be semi-detached, so that a feeling of spaciousness will pervade the whole Estate. This will keep the property select and values will tend to increase as the years roll by, so that every purchaser may be sure of a good investment for his money.'[99] Developers also asserted status through emphasizing their estates' rural settings and scenic beauty. This both illustrated suburbia's advantages of clean air, space, and healthy living and tapped into the upsurge in popular enthusiasm for the countryside. In 1933, for example, New Ideal Homesteads advertised houses from £395 on an estate in Barnehurst, offering:

> beautiful unspoiled country in the very heart of Kent...Barnehurst enjoys all that the countryside has to offer, commanding entrancing views, while away to the North-east stretches the Thames, a silvery ribbon, winding seawards bringing fresh breezes which sweep across the countryside at every change of the tide.[100]

Scotland's leading speculative builder, Mactaggart & Mickel, used strikingly similar copy:

> For natural beauty this Estate cannot be equalled by any other in Scotland, or for that matter, in Britain. Here, in the quiet calm that Nature demands of her own, we find magnificent old oaks, stately young pines, firs, and trees of every description. In the summer months, flowering shrubs and bushes give a veritable blaze of colour, and in the dark days of winter a large variety of evergreen bushes softly shade the tone of an already magnificent landscape. To further increase its charm, picturesque streams, which have their source somewhere in the moorlands of Renfrewshire, wind gaily through the Estate, suddenly widening out into a delightful miniature lake, to mirror this picture of perfect painting.[101]

---

[96] Museum of London Archive, material collected for Weightman and Humphries, *Making of Modern London*, unpublished memoir by Ivy Willis, c.1980s, plus interview with Ivy Willis.
[97] Museum of London Archive, material collected for Weightman and Humphries, *Making of Modern London*, interview with Ken Milne.
[98] Jackson, *Semi-Detached London*, 138.
[99] Bexley Local Studies, New Ideal Homesteads, 'New Claremont. Kent's New Garden Suburb in the Making Near Sidcup', brochure (n.d., 1930s).
[100] Bexley Local Studies, New Ideal Homesteads, 'Super 1933 Homes'.
[101] RCAHMS, MS/1034/1. Mactaggart & Mickel Ltd, 'The Book of Broom Estate, Whitecraigs', brochure (n.d., c.1930s).

'Garden-city' estate planning ideas were also frequently emphasized. Morrell's—developers of the Coney Hall Estate (which became notorious for its poor building standards)—described their estates as 'veritable gardens...so cunningly planned that every one of their delightful homes has the maximum fresh air and sunshine...an environment which is ideal, and far removed from that of the crowded streets of the cities, dangerous to the health of children and parents alike.'[102] Brochures also frequently contained information regarding the area's historic heritage and access to shops, transport, local schools, and other amenities, to buttress their aspirational credentials. Other organizations with an interest in promoting suburbanization, such as passenger transport concerns, employed similar emotive appeals to persuade households to opt for the clean, healthy, and safe environment of the suburbs, as illustrated in Figure 5.5.

Another major motivation for migration to the suburbs was to provide a safe and pleasant environment for children. Mactaggart & Mickel made skilful use of this in their promotional literature. For example, a 1938 advert showed a young girl playing with a West Highland terrier in the garden, while her mother watches her through spacious bay windows, with the copy:

> HER GARDEN'S HER GUARDIAN. Protected from the dangers of city streets...guarded from the smoke-laden atmosphere, she's a happy child whose brought up in such healthy surroundings. She's got clear, fresh air to build her up, a lovely garden in which to play. No wonder she's happy and contented; no wonder her mother's at ease, because she's under her watchful eye.[103]

Estate developers also emphasized their houses' attractive fittings and 'labour-saving devices'. This appeal was aimed principally at the housewife, following a general advertising trend towards identifying the housewife as the key player in household expenditure decisions.[104] For example, New Ideal Homesteads marketed several estates with brochures entitled 'The Super Home: Designed by a _Woman_ for the _Woman_'.[105] Similarly, Mactaggart & Mickel advertised 'The house that the housewife built':

> For too long now the housewife has had to adapt herself to the home instead of the home being adapted for her needs. Realising this, *we asked over 5,000 Glasgow Housewives to give us their views on* the Ideal Home, and this New 4-Apartment Self-Contained Bungalow is the result. Every feature which was in popular demand has been embodied...[106]

In 1935 the north London developer Comben & Wakeling recruited Helen Burke, the 'Home Expert' for the *Sunday Pictorial*. Her message to 'every woman' endorsed their homes as 'honest houses—well-planned, well-built—so labour-saving and so

---

[102] McCulloch, 'Owner-Occupation', 202.
[103] RCAHMS, MMX/1, Mactaggart & Mickel Ltd, *Edinburgh News* advert, 18 February 1938.
[104] Marchand, *Advertising the American Dream*, 66–7.
[105] Bexley Local Studies, estate brochure collection.
[106] *Daily Record*, 17 August 1932, Mactaggart & Mickel advertisement for Netherlee Park Estate, reproduced in Watters, 'Mactaggart & Mickel', 57–8.

Fig. 5.5. A 1924 London Underground poster advertising the attractions of Edgware (to which the Hampstead Line, now known as the Northern Line, had just been extended) by contrasting them with inner London

Source: Reproduced courtesy of London Transport Museum.

Fig. 5.6. A New Ideal Homesteads' 'Super Home' brochure (early 1930s)
Source: Peter Scott collection.

practical as to delight a housewife's heart.'[107] The kitchen's role as a centre for efficient household management often received particular emphasis; for example, a 1934 Davis Estates brochure claimed that:

> The housewife's needs have inspired the planning and arrangement of this excellent kitchen…arranged for efficient working and equipped with gas copper for household

---

[107] *Daily Telegraph*, 6 September 1935, 23, advertisement for Comben & Wakeling, cited in Davis, 'Celebration of Ambiguity', 101.

laundry, fitted kitchen cabinet, and enamelled Sentry boiler which provides constant hot water upstairs and down... The work of cleaning has been reduced to a minimum; the walls are half-tiled and taps, switches and other fittings are chromium plated.[108]

CONCLUSION

Within less than a decade the building industry and building society movement had substantially broadened the market for new owner-occupied houses, overcome working-class cultural aversions to the mortgage system, and successfully portrayed the owner-occupied semi as the key to achieving new, aspirational, and domestically orientated working-class suburban lifestyles. Despite the limited scale of both most builders and building societies, the industry nevertheless succeeded in developing a sophisticated portfolio of marketing messages and techniques, which led large numbers of (particularly newly or recently married) working-class people to make the transition to owner-occupied suburbia and thus played a major role in extending the limits of 'consumer citizenship' to this group.[109]

Comparison of the marketing messages used to sell owner occupation and the testimonies of the fifty-eight working-class house purchasers analysed for this study corroborates Gold and Gold's finding that suburban house marketing represented neither an exact reflection of reality, nor a *Zerrspiegel* (a fairground distorting mirror), but a mirror that selected and enhanced popular aspirations.[110] This process had important impacts not only for the housing market but for the types of consumer durables found mainly in middle-class homes at the start of the interwar period—such as new suites of furniture, gas or electric cookers, and new curtains, carpets, and linoleum—which rapidly diffused to the working classes over these years. Moreover, it had major economic and social impacts on those working-class families who pioneered migration to owner-occupied suburbia, encompassing standards of dress, behaviour, leisure interests, and even family size. These form the subject of the next chapter.

---

[108] John Johnson Collection, Davis Estates brochure, 1934. The house was priced at £595.
[109] Marchand, *Advertising the American Dream*, 63–6.
[110] Gold and Gold, 'Home at Last!', 89.

6
Life in Owner-Occupied Suburbia

INTRODUCTION

Moves to new owner-occupied suburbs typically had significant impacts on lifestyles, consumption patterns, and household behaviour. While these changes were significant for the middle classes, they were most striking for working-class families. Many found that notions of 'respectability' and ways of asserting social status were markedly different even on predominantly working-class suburban estates compared to their old communities. Meanwhile suburban owner occupation entailed substantial extra costs compared to inner-urban living, which made the task of making ends meet, while meeting the expectations of their new communities, extremely challenging.

This chapter first examines the types of people who moved to suburbia. Moves are shown to have been motivated, at least in part, by a wish to escape negative environmental factors associated with inner-urban living. Patterns of neighbourliness, and of status competition, on the new estates are then examined. The chapter also looks at how working-class families balanced their tight budgets in the light of increased living costs and strong social pressures for higher standards of material display. Common solutions involved squeezing those areas of expenditure not easily observable to neighbours—including 'necessities' such as food, fuel, and light. One long-term solution was family limitation—a strategy which also allowed parents to invest greater resources in the one to three children that completed the typical 1930s working-class home-owning suburban family.

THE SUBURBAN HOUSE PURCHASER

As Lesley Whitworth has noted, studies of interwar home ownership often conflate the expansion of suburbia with the middle class, rendering working-class residents invisible.[1] Yet this period witnessed the dawn of working-class owner occupation as more than a merely localized phenomenon. The upper income strata of the working classes, together with families with lower incomes but secure jobs, were

---

[1] Lesley Whitworth, 'Men, Women, Shops and "Little, Shiny Homes": The Consuming of Coventry, 1930–1939', PhD thesis (University of Warwick, 1997), 5.

significant participants in the 1930s owner-occupation boom. Liberalized mortgage terms, falling interest rates, and reductions in building costs brought new suburban houses with bathrooms, modern utilities, and front and back gardens within the financial reach of a substantial proportion of working people. Meanwhile, rising real incomes, shortages of inner-urban accommodation, and the appeal of suburban living and modern housing—reinforced by aggressive marketing by the building industry and building society movement—made owner occupation attractive to large numbers of working-class families.

The 1937/8 Ministry of Labour working-class household expenditure survey provides the best contemporary data on working-class owner occupation.[2] This aimed to provide a representative collection of expenditure budgets for UK working-class households, covering manual wage-earners (with the exception of the long-term unemployed) and non-manual workers with salaries up to £250 a year. A total of 10,762 sets of four-weekly budgets were compiled, at quarterly intervals from October 1937, of which 8,905 covered non-agricultural households. Some 17.8 per cent of non-agricultural households were found to own, or be purchasing, their own homes, while 80.0 per cent rented their accommodation, and the remaining 2.2 per cent (mainly comprising mining families) had houses provided rent-free by their employers.

Table 6.1 shows the proportion of non-agricultural working-class owner-occupiers by level of household income. Home ownership is shown to be concentrated among higher income groups, but was significant for families on all but the lowest incomes—owner-occupiers constituted almost one in eight households even for families with a weekly expenditure of only 50–60s (compared to the working-class household average of 85s).[3] The Life Histories Database sheds further light on the socio-economic composition of house purchasers. Of fifty-four accounts that give the head of household's occupation, thirty-three concern factory workers. These ranged from skilled workers to people undertaking standardized assembly work, many being employed in the expanding motor vehicle and engineering industries.[4] Despite the risk of periodic layoffs, better-paid factory workers in prosperous sectors were targeted by speculative developers. For example, a May 1936 *Bristol Evening News* property advertising feature highlighted housing estates that were convenient for workers at the aeroplane works, the Imperial Tobacco works, and Fry's chocolate factory.[5]

The second largest group, comprising eleven accounts, was transport and utilities workers. Contemporary sources suggest that 'uniformed' workers—in

---

[2] For the most comprehensive report on the survey's findings see The National Archives [NA], LAB17/7, 'Weekly Expenditure of Working-Class Households in the United Kingdom in 1937–38', Ministry of Labour and National Service, July 1949.

[3] This figure is higher than that for individual earnings, as there were an average of 1.75 wage-earners per household.

[4] Engineering workers are probably over-represented in the sample, as a number of major engineering centres had particularly good oral history records.

[5] *Bristol Evening News*, 1 May 1936, 'Modern Homes: Attractive Labour-Saving Houses by Bristol's Best Builders', 20.

Table 6.1. The proportion of British non-agricultural working-class families buying/owning their own homes, at various levels of household expenditure, October 1937–July 1938

Total household expenditure (shillings per week)	% of households in class buying/owning their home
Under 40	2.5
40–50	3.7
50–60	12.3
60–70	13.0
70–80	17.1
80–90	17.4
90–100	24.8
100–10	22.2
110–20	26.6
120–30	30.6
130–40	27.0
140 and over	37.2
All	18.9

Source: NA, LAB17/7, 'Weekly Expenditure of Working-Class Households in the United Kingdom in 1937-38', Ministry of Labour and National Service, July 1949.

Notes: The average weekly household income recorded by the survey was 85s (with an average of 1.75 wage-earners per household). The table is based on a random sub-sample of 2,225 households, rather than the full survey sample of 8,905 households.

sectors such as public transport, the postal service, power utilities, and council services—were strongly represented among working-class owner-occupiers. Despite having wages below those of many skilled manufacturing workers, they had stable jobs and were thus less concerned about interruptions to their income. A lack of job stability constituted a significant deterrent to owner occupation for many workers. As Violet Kentsbeer, who lived as a child on the LCC's Becontree Estate, recalled, council tenants were deterred from moving to a nearby owner-occupied estate, not on account of houses being too expensive, but because 'people were frightened to take a chance and get a mortgage in case the men lost their jobs and could not continue to pay.'[6] The only other substantial group, comprising six accounts, concerned building and related trades.[7]

[6] Violet Kentsbeer, *My Dagenham Childhood* (Bicester: Bound Biographies, 2003), 67.
[7] Three building workers and three workers in building-related trades (two carpenters and a self-employed plumber). The sample also included two 'white-collar' workers—a clerk and the manager of a small shop. The shop manager earned less than £3 a week at around the time of the house purchase, while the clerk earned only £3 5s from his clerical work (his income being supplemented by his wife continuing to work after marriage—unlike most families in the sample—as a dressmaker, and from money he earned at weekends in a jazz band). These workers thus earned less than many factory workers and lived on estates where such workers were also resident. Remaining workers in the sample comprised a river man and a horse driver.

Table 6.2 compares regional patterns of working-class owner occupation and renting. This is based on the original Ministry of Labour survey report, as use of the surviving survey returns would produce an unreliably low sample size for some regions. Unfortunately the original survey report does not provide separate data for families buying their houses on mortgage and those owning them outright. Most regions of England and Wales are shown to have owner-occupation rates above the UK average. The main exception is the northern region, though this also has a low proportion of households renting their accommodation—owing to an unusually large number living 'rent-free' in employers' housing (mainly comprising colliery households, rather than urban workers). Some relatively depressed regions, such as the North West and Wales, are shown to have relatively high owner-occupation rates, though given that parts of these regions had unusually high home ownership prior to the First World War, this probably boosted observed rates.[8]

Scotland and Northern Ireland are shown to have patterns of housing tenure and accommodation costs very different to those in the rest of the UK. Both had very low owner-occupation rates (less than a third of the UK average), low average accommodation expenditures, and, in the case of Scotland, a substantially lower average number of rooms rented per household—despite the number of persons per household being higher than that for any other UK region apart from Northern Ireland. Furthermore, houses owned/purchased in these regions have relatively low average accommodation payments, suggesting that a large proportion represented traditional housing, bought by sitting tenants (including houses purchased before 1914).

Comparing the data in Table 6.2 on weekly accommodation costs for people owning or buying their homes and for people renting their accommodation provides a very rough indicator of the extent to which working-class home-owners in each region were involved in purchasing modern housing on mortgage. On this basis Greater London, the South East, and the Midlands appear to be the main regions of the interwar working-class owner-occupation boom, as was found (for all classes) in Table 4.2.

Table 6.3 provides data from a counterpart survey of lower-middle-class households, based on 1,360 civil servants, local government officers, and teachers. This followed the methodology of the Ministry of Labour survey, but was initiated six months later. Comparison with Table 6.4 shows that families on the bottom rungs of the middle-class income ladder spent a substantially higher proportion of income on accommodation than the families of manual workers with similar household incomes. To take the example of households renting their homes, 13.87 per cent of total expenditure was devoted to accommodation by the lowest income group in the table, compared to only 8.7 per cent for the highest income group in Table 6.4.

Yet the ratio of accommodation costs to total household expenditure declined as income rose for the middle classes similarly (though less steeply) to that for working-class households. Philip Massey speculated that this might reflect some

---

[8] Mark Swenarton and Sandra Taylor, 'The Scale and Nature of the Growth of Owner-Occupation in Britain between the Wars', *Economic History Review*, 38 (1985), 378–9.

Table 6.2. A regional profile of non-agricultural working-class housing in 1937/8

Region[a]	Proportion of UK households			Accommodation costs (d per week)				For rented houses[c]	
	Renting	Owning/buying	Rent-free	Renting	Owning/buying	Total[b]	No. of rooms rented	Rent per room (d)
Greater London	79.7	19.3	1.0	181.2	226.7	188.1	3.6	50.3
South East	78.6	19.5	1.9	131.3	162.2	134.8	4.5	29.3
South West	72.5	25.4	2.1	127.3	124.1	123.8	4.3	29.5
Midlands	79.0	19.8	1.2	119.2	150.6	124.0	4.4	27.3
North East	81.2	17.5	1.3	119.2	142.5	121.7	4.0	29.8
North West	78.9	20.5	0.6	126.8	137.0	128.1	4.3	29.5
Northern	72.7	16.0	11.3	120.9	142.8	110.9	3.7	32.8
Wales	77.6	20.0	2.4	111.7	110.4	108.7	4.3	26.0
Scotland	91.0	5.9	3.1	100.7	105.4	97.8	2.6	38.8
Northern Ireland	93.4	5.3	1.3	74.9	47.6	72.5	3.9	19.3
Total	80.0	17.8	2.2	127.9	153.5	129.7	3.9	32.8

Source: NA, LAB17/7, 'Weekly Expenditure of Working-Class Households in the United Kingdom in 1937-38', Ministry of Labour and National Service, July 1949.

[a] Regional classifications: South East: Those parts of Essex, Hertfordshire, Kent and Surrey outside the Metropolitan Police District, plus Bedfordshire, Berkshire, Buckinghamshire, Cambridgeshire, Huntingdonshire, Norfolk, Suffolk, Sussex, and Soke of Peterborough. South West: Cornwall, Devon, Dorset, Gloucestershire, Hampshire, Oxfordshire, Somerset and Wiltshire. Midlands: Derbyshire (except the Buxton, Chapel-en-le-Frith, Glossop, Hadfield, and New Mills districts), Herefordshire, Leicestershire, Northamptonshire (excluding Soke of Peterborough), Nottinghamshire, Rutland, Shropshire, Staffordshire, Warwickshire, and Worcestershire. North East: Lincolnshire and Yorkshire (except Cleveland). North West: Lancashire & Cheshire and the Buxton, Chapel-en-le-Frith, Glossop, Hadfield, and New Mills districts of Derbyshire. Northern: Northumberland, Durham, Cumberland and Westmorland, and the Cleveland district of Yorkshire.

[b] Includes rents/purchase instalments, ground rents, rates, and water charges (after deducting any rent received from rooms sublet).

[c] Includes households living 'rent-free'. Rent per room includes kitchens, but excludes 'sculleries', bathrooms, etc.

Table 6.3. A profile of middle-class housing expenditures in 1938/9

Group	Weekly household expenditure	Proportion of UK households				Accommodation costs (% of total)[a]			No. of rooms occupied[c]
		Renting	Buying	Owning	Rent-free	Renting	Owning/buying	All[b]	
(1)	£6 15s 11.75d	36.5	47.4	16.0	0.2	13.87	14.06	13.97	5.1
(2)	£8 13s 4.75d	34.1	46.9	18.2	0.8	11.35	11.81	11.56	5.6
(3)	£11 7s 9.75d	29.7	48.7	21.6	0.0	11.60	11.17	11.30	6.0
(4)	£16 1s 8.75d	42.4	30.1	27.5	0.0	12.87	9.32	10.83	7.6
Total	£8 12s 1.75d	35.0	46.5	18.2	0.4	12.45	12.24	12.27	5.5

Source: Philip Massey, 'The Expenditure of 1,360 British Middle-Class Households in 1938–39', *Journal of the Royal Statistical Society*, 105 (1942), 181.

[a] Includes rents/purchase instalments, ground rents, rates, and water charges (after deducting any rent received from rooms sublet).
[b] Includes households living 'rent-free'.
[c] Includes kitchens, but excludes 'sculleries', bathrooms, etc.

minimum level of middle-class rent, below which white-collar workers could not find accommodation appropriate for their status.[9] In other words, while the poorest working-class families had to devote a high proportion of their income to accommodation owing to basic economic necessity, the lowest-income middle-class families had to do likewise, owing to the 'necessity' of living in the right kind of house in the right kind of area. This was an economic as well as a social necessity, as an appropriate address was a major marker of middle-class status and, therefore, of having a legitimate claim to white-collar employment.

The proportion buying or owning their homes was found to average 64.7 per cent for lower-middle-class households, compared to only 17.8 per cent for working-class households. The proportion of middle-class households currently buying their house on mortgage is broadly stable between income bands, except for the highest income group where it is markedly lower (owing to a high proportion of survey families in the top income group being headed by men from a section of the civil service where transfers between locations were commonplace).[10] Meanwhile the proportion of households owning their houses outright rose significantly with income (partly reflecting a tendency for people who occupied the higher ranks in these professions to come from wealthier families). The significant jump in the number of rooms occupied by families in the highest income category suggests that these enjoyed a mode of living different to that of middle-class families on lower incomes. This is corroborated by their substantial expenditure on domestic servants (averaging 14s 10d per week, compared to 1s 10d for the lowest middle-class group and 6s 6d for the second highest group).[11]

The 1930s owner-occupation boom was distinguished from later growth phases in home ownership by an unusually high proportion of first-time buyers. Typical house purchasers moved from rented accommodation (rented by either themselves or their parents). Moreover, even working-class people who moved into owner occupation typically did so on or shortly after marriage. The interval between marriage and house purchase (known for thirty-five of the fifty-eight Life History Database accounts) was around 2.7 years,[12] with half the couples having made the move within a year of marriage and only a quarter moving 6 years or more after marriage.

During this period workers typically lived at their parental home prior to marriage and sometimes amassed substantial savings from that proportion of their income they retained after paying board. Indeed accumulating sufficient savings before marriage to underwrite the creation of a new household has been identified as a marker of working-class respectability.[13] A number of Life History Database

---

[9] Philip Massey, 'The Expenditure of 1,360 British Middle-Class Households in 1938–39', *Journal of the Royal Statistical Society*, 105 (1942), 169.
[10] Massey, 'Expenditure', 169.
[11] Massey, 'Expenditure', 184.
[12] Based on data rounded to the nearest year.
[13] David Levine, *Reproducing Families: The Political Economy of English Population History* (Cambridge: Cambridge University Press, 1987), 186. All the accounts involve people buying houses on or after marriage, with the exception of two people who bought jointly with other male workers—one with his brother, and one with a friend. In both cases, following arguments, the person concerned was forced to take over the mortgage, on what later became their marital home.

accounts mention very high accumulated savings relative to income: for example, Jack Aston (Colchester railway worker, earning £2 17s, saved £100);[14] or F. J. Stevens (a printer, who, together with his fiancée, a secretary, saved £150).[15] Having substantial savings was important, as home ownership involved other major costs in addition to the deposit, such as extra furniture, furnishings, house maintenance, and commuting expenses.

Working-class home buyers typically had more skilled jobs and higher and more stable incomes than migrants to municipal estates, particularly during the 1930s when council housing allocation priorities shifted decisively in favour of slum clearance tenants. However, many still moved from cramped accommodation with poor utilities and thus found access to electricity, bathrooms, or even sometimes running hot water to be a novelty. Most inner-urban housing—even better quality 'bay and forecourt' terraces—lacked bathrooms, front gardens, or rear gardens of any size, and many houses even lacked indoor toilets or internal plumbing. New suburban homes thus offered a quantum leap in amenities. As Ken Milne, who moved with his parents from gas-lit rented accommodation shared with other lodgers to a new three-bedroom house in Neasden in 1930, recalled:

> for the first time in our lives we lived in a house by ourselves... It was bright and clean and...we really enjoyed the bathroom, of course, was a great feature, first time we'd really enjoyed having baths without going out or else just makeshifting in the copper. The...electric light was very very novel to us...we had lighting in every room instead of going to bed by candle-light...and the staircases and all the little corners, dark corners that were prominent in the other house were all beautifully lit and of course it was very much cleaner, there was no gas, used to...poison the atmosphere to some extent, made the ceiling very black.[16]

'KEEPING OURSELVES TO OURSELVES' AND 'KEEPING UP WITH THE JONESES'

In common with 'pioneer' migrants to new municipal estates, purchasers of new suburban houses (especially those on larger or more isolated estates) often moved to communities that were still works in progress, with sections of the estate awaiting development and facilities such as shops, schools, or even some roads being merely lines on the map. This state of affairs is captured in Figure 6.1, which shows John Laing's Golders Green estate in mid-construction. However, within a relatively short space of time a series of social conventions and accepted standards of behaviour emerged, which showed remarkably little variation from one estate to the next.

---

[14] Essex Record Office, SA/8/1585–93, interview with Jack Aston, railway worker.
[15] Imperial War Museum, ID No. 1083, 88/8/1, unpublished typescript memoirs of F. J. Stephens, 1988.
[16] Museum of London Archive, material collected for Gavin Weightman and Steve Humphries, *The Making of Modern London 1914–1939* (London: Sidgwick & Jackson, 1984), transcript of interview with Ken Milne.

Fig. 6.1. Map of John Laing's Golders Green estate under construction, showing transport links and the sites for a proposed school and park

Source: Northamptonshire Record Office, John Laing plc Archives, L9/1/295, 'The palaces of Golders Green', promotional brochure (1931). Reproduced by kind permission of the Laing Charitable Trust.

These were the product of two key features common to almost all owner-occupied estates—the broadly similar motivations that typically led people to set up home there and the fact that they were initially communities of strangers, drawn from various parts of town and lacking any strong commonalities in terms of workplace or shared background. Owner occupation was often seen as offering a greater degree of freedom than privately rented or municipal housing. As Ivy Willis recalled, 'you had more control over your destiny, and you knew financially you would be better off one day, you wouldn't be going on paying for ever. And you could do as you liked as well.'[17] Yet in practice, this 'freedom' produced a surprising degree of conformity to new, but in their own way highly restrictive, social norms.

During the Edwardian era migration to new suburban communities by the expanding middle classes was already being identified as a factor weakening traditional markers of social standing (such as occupation and background) and increasing

---

[17] Museum of London Archive, material collected for Weightman and Humphries, *Making of Modern London*, unpublished handwritten memoir by Ivy Willis, undated, *c.*1980s, plus information from project interview with Ivy Willis.

the relative importance of status competition via conspicuous consumption.[18] A similar process was evident among interwar working-class suburban migrants, though most were anxious to 'keep up' with the Joneses, rather than to overtake them. Life History Database accounts corroborate evidence from contemporary sources that moves to suburbia were strongly associated with desires for new lifestyles based on the complex of related consumption goals associated with owner occupation and suburban living. Pre-1914 notions of working-class respectability emphasized independence from state or charitable assistance—via mutual aid networks, thrift, living within one's means, and stoically tightening one's belt during hard times. As Simon Szreter notes, compared with

> competitive and aspirational bourgeois aims and motives, this bred an economically conservative and culturally static set of values, so that working-class communities were much less 'open' and were each a law unto themselves…Ambitions for social status and consumer aspirations were contained within the very modest limits which were appropriate to the circumstances of the great majority of the community.[19]

Conversely, Hughes and Hunt have identified the emergence during the interwar period of a different model of working-class respectability, based around independence from even the local community and focused on the family as 'an intense domestic unit enclosed from the wider world'.[20] This new respectability was aspirational rather than conservative and privately rather than socially orientated. Its key features included high standards of personal and domestic hygiene, 'privatized' family- and home-centred lifestyles, and an increased commitment of material and psychological resources to the welfare and material advancement of the next generation.[21]

Working-class suburban migration often represented movement from traditional urban working-class communities to what D. J. Boorstin has termed 'consumption communities'.[22] Suburban estates were often initially communities of strangers. Lacking the long acquaintance necessary for a 'life portrait' assessment of status (including one's family background, kinship networks, occupation and/or workplace, plus community and leisure activities), the new communities adopted a much narrower yardstick, a process later observed by Young and Willmott in the 1950s.[23] Life history testimonies generally outline a status system on the new estates based around a coordinated display of appropriate material goods and

---

[18] Deborah Cohen, *Household Gods: The British and Their Possessions* (New Haven, CT: Yale University Press, 2006), 131–4.
[19] Simon Szreter, *Fertility, Class and Gender in Britain, 1860–1940* (Cambridge: Cambridge University Press, 1996), 528.
[20] A. Hughes and K. Hunt, 'A Culture Transformed? Women's Lives in Wythenshawe in the 1930s', in A. Davies and S. Fielding (eds), *Worker's Worlds: Cultures and Communities in Manchester and Salford, 1880–1939* (Manchester: Manchester University Press, 1992), 92.
[21] Hughes and Hunt, 'A Culture Transformed?', 92; Szreter, *Fertility, Class and Gender*, 528. Diana Gittins, *Fair Sex: Family Size and Structure, 1900–39* (London: Hutchinson, 1982), 175–6, notes the importance of these new family-centred lifestyles as a factor encouraging family limitation.
[22] D. J. Boorstin, *The Americans: The Democratic Experience* (New York: Vintage, 1973), 145–8.
[23] Michael Young and Peter Willmott, *Family and Kinship in East London* (Harmondsworth: Penguin, 1957), 162.

'restrained' speech and behaviour, which contrasted with the broader and less materialistic factors governing status in their old communities.[24]

While owning and displaying prestige goods was a recognized feature of status competition in traditional working-class areas, it had generally focused around one, or a few, particularly prized possessions, such as a gramophone or a piano in the parlour.[25] In contrast the new suburban working-class respectability generally involved adopting, or at least projecting to the outside world, a broader, coordinated material 'lifestyle' that encompassed all aspects of observed consumption—creating consumption communities, tied together not by background, workplace, or religion, but by shared material values.[26]

As Paul Johnson has noted, status competition was primarily based on comparisons with one's immediate neighbours.[27] Aspects of material life that received greatest attention were those most visible to external observers. For example, gardens constituted an intense arena of neighbourly competition, as discussed in Chapter 8. Within the house, those areas visible from the front door step or accessible to visitors—the hall and the parlour/front room—received most attention. One couple interviewed by Whitworth felt obliged to furnish the hall before any of the rooms so that it appeared respectable when the front door was opened.[28]

A key feature of the new suburban respectability involved a restrained pattern of neighbourliness, summed up by the ubiquitous phrase, 'keeping ourselves to ourselves'—something which was identified as a post-1945 phenomenon in the affluent worker studies of the 1950s and 1960s.[29] There is some debate regarding the real extent of close neighbourliness even in traditional working-class communities.[30] For example, Stefan Muthesius has argued that a trend towards greater privacy and more restrained neighbourliness can be identified from the late nineteenth century, linked to the displacement of traditional working-class housing designs with shared open yards, in favour of more conventional through terraces with private outdoor space.[31]

Yet the great majority of Life Histories Database accounts identify a marked change in neighbourly relations on moving to suburbia. This was partly the result of suburban migrants having a preference for greater privacy and private space—their moves having often been at least partially motivated by a wish to get away from

---

[24] Young and Willmott, *Family and Kinship*, 162.

[25] Robert Roberts, *The Classic Slum: Salford Life in the First Quarter of the Century* (Manchester: Penguin, 1971), 17; Joanna Bourke, *Working Class Cultures in Britain 1890–1960: Gender, Class and Ethnicity* (London: Routledge, 1994), 160–1.

[26] Boorstin, *Americans*, 145–8.

[27] Paul Johnson, *Saving and Spending: The Working-Class Economy in Britain 1870–1939* (Oxford: Oxford University Press, 1985), 226.

[28] Whitworth, 'Men, Women, Shops', 156.

[29] Young and Willmott, *Family and Kinship*, 128; Ferdynand Zweig, *The Worker in an Affluent Society: Family Life and Industry* (London, Heinemann, 1961), 116.

[30] Bourke, *Working Class Cultures*, 156–9.

[31] Stefan Muthesius, *The English Terraced House* (New Haven, CT: Yale University Press, 1982), 138–9.

intrusive neighbours. Couples who purchased new suburban housing generally had a more family-orientated rather than community-orientated outlook, with the husband and wife forming a more central social unit than in traditional working-class communities. Most husbands did not drink heavily, engaged in relatively few regular leisure activities outside the home, and spent much of their time on home-centred pursuits such as gardening. Both husbands and wives reported taking pride in their houses and in projecting a good standard of material display and 'respectable' behaviour to neighbours, typified as being polite and friendly, but distant.

For example, Alice Pond, who moved from Hackney to an owner-occupied estate in Chingford in 1935 recalled, 'You talked to [neighbours]...over the fence, at the shops, and if you had children. But no, it wasn't like Hackney with people dropping in.'[32] Similarly, a July 1938 article in a Surrey suburban residents' association magazine noted that women who had lived in the area for over a year hardly knew their neighbours' names and contacts were minimal: 'People just nod and pass on.'[33]

Yet as on municipal estates, mutual support was still valued, and expected, during times of crisis such as illness, bereavement, or childbirth. A woman who set up home on an owner-occupied Coventry estate recalled that 'if Mrs Sweet was ill I would go and see if there was anything I could do. And when Arthur was ill she'd come and see if I wanted anything, you know. But we never...butted in on private lives.'[34] Restrained behaviour extended beyond distant neighbourliness, encompassing a broader behavioural code, which also militated against plainness in speech, strong accents, the free use of taboo words, children who appeared poorly cared-for, over-readiness with a cuff for the children, a forthright approach in personal relations, and poor standards of housework (observed, for example, via the wash line). Having a large family was also taken as a sign of roughness, as it indicated a lack of the restraint necessary to achieve the suburban dream of a well-cared-for house and well-resourced children.[35]

As noted in Chapter 3, this more restrained pattern of neighbourliness could leave households in more severe difficulties if unemployment or other misfortunes led to loss of income, as they lacked the traditional support networks of long-established working-class communities. Another, more mundane, negative impact was the loneliness and isolation felt by many housewives (who, unlike their husbands, were generally alone or with their young children for most of the day). In a 1938 *Lancet* article, Stephen Taylor coined the term 'suburban neurosis' to describe the anxiety states—often with hysterical features and reactive depression—experienced by his patients on new estates. These he attributed to boredom (arising from a lack of friends and isolation), together with anxieties linked to financial pressures

---

[32] Notes of interview with Alice Pond, June 1985. Supplied to the author by Chris Pond.
[33] Alan A. Jackson, *Semi-Detached London: Suburban Development, Life, and Transport, 1900–39*, 2nd edn (Didcot: Wild Swan, 1991), 137.
[34] Coventry Record Office [CRO], 1647/1/72, interview for project on the social history of car workers, deposited by Paul Thompson in 1986. Female, born 1908.
[35] See Peter Scott, 'Did Owner-Occupation Lead to Smaller Families for Interwar Working-Class Households?', *Economic History Review*, 61 (2008).

arising from the new house and a 'false' set of values (failure to achieve unrealistic expectations of suburban married life culminating in general disillusionment).[36]

This phenomenon was evident on both owner-occupied and municipal estates (being mentioned in social studies of both the 1930s and the early post-war era).[37] Several Life Histories Database accounts mention women suffering from a combination of depression and anxiety, usually as a transient condition after moving house (though return migration may have reduced the reported incidence of people with longer-term symptoms). As a migrant from the Old Kent Road to an owner-occupied estate in Sidcup recalled:

> when the husband went to work say seven o'clock in the morning... they probably wouldn't get back till nearly seven o'clock at night, and the women used to get lonely, fed up... there wasn't much round here then, like... churches and things like that... no clubs or anything... and they used to get bored stiff, and often they used to kind of break down, you know, my wife found it very hard at first, but... then she got used to it by getting mixed up with the church.[38]

The radio offered a welcome break from isolation and loneliness for many housewives. For the most affluent the telephone (which was still mainly confined to the upper-middle classes) offered a valuable link with old neighbours. The Telephone Development Association capitalized on this in their marketing, one of their Ideal Home Exhibition leaflets claiming that

> Life is fuller than ever of exciting possibilities when there's a 'phone in the house—of enjoyment, of happiness, of sheer fun. Parties, trips, meetings—they can all be arranged in a minute or two... And where there's a telephone loneliness can never be. No woman can feel solitary when she can pick up the 'phone and chat to a friend. A husband is never out of reach, friends are never beyond your call, that feeling of dreariness and helpless isolation can never sweep over you.[39]

MAKING ENDS MEET IN OWNER-OCCUPIED SUBURBIA

As Avner Offer has noted, 'to be credible, a good [status] signal needs to be costly'.[40] Achieving the suburban dream of aspirational respectability was indeed an expensive business. A smart, modern, house had to be matched by similar furnishings

---

[36] Stephen Taylor, 'The Suburban Neurosis', *The Lancet* (26 March 1938), 759–61.
[37] For example, Ruth Durant, *Watling: A Survey of Social Life on a New Housing Estate* (London: King, 1939), 1 & 21; Manchester and Salford Better Housing Council, *The Report of an Investigation on Wythenshawe* (Manchester: privately published, 1935), 146. For a summary of post-war studies, see 'Suburban Neurosis up to Date' (leading article), *The Lancet* (18 January 1958), 146–7.
[38] Museum of London Archive, material collected for Weightman and Humphries, *Making of Modern London*, letter from, and transcript of interview with, G. R. Matthews.
[39] BT Archives, POST 33/1875, Telephone Development Association leaflet, 'The Ideal Home is on the Phone' (1930).
[40] Avner Offer, *The Challenge of Affluence: Self-Control and Well-Being in the United States and Britain since 1950* (Oxford: Oxford University Press, 2006), 279.

(for at least those areas visible to visitors at the door), a tidy garden, good quality clothing, and neat, well-behaved, well-spoken children. Thus, in addition to mortgage instalments and rates that were typically substantially higher than the rental costs of inner-urban working-class housing, plus maintenance expenses that would otherwise have been the landlord's responsibility, purchasers also faced higher costs for furniture, clothing, and other items necessary to 'keep up with the Joneses'. Suburban living, by distancing people from places of work and shopping centres, often also incurred a significant increase in transport costs.[41] As the daughter of a building worker recalled, her family found it hard to pay their mortgage and had to economize on food—not on account of the mortgage itself, but due to the additional expenses of suburban living, which they had not anticipated.[42]

These costs were met, primarily, by squeezing budgets for items of daily expenditure—food, drink, heating, lighting, and so forth. Families soon realized the challenges they were facing, though many received a temporary bonanza from tradesman eager to secure their custom. As Ivy Willis recalled:

> For the first two weeks all the local trades people came with free gifts... The baker gave us small brown and white bread four rolls, four sausage rolls and cakes. The butcher, sausages, two chops and 1/2 lb stewing steak; greengrocer, potatoes, cabbage, small box of fruit. The milk man, pot of cream and pint of milk 1/2 lb butter and cheese. The fishmonger brought some fish. So the first week or two we lived for free which helped; my husband would not allow me to work, although we needed the money. On being given my 30/- house keeping money I would put 5/- in the gas meter, 2/- for insurance, the bakers money and the milkman. What was left divided for each day's needs. By Friday there was only about 1/- left, so I went to Peckham market, bought 3/4 fish for 6d, 2lb potatoes for 2d, 1d suet. There was usually a small tin of baked beans in the larder, a little flour and dried fruit, so we had an enormous meal with the last 1/-.[43]

Surviving returns for the April 1938 Ministry of Labour working-class household expenditure survey allow comparison of weekly budgets for working-class families currently buying houses on mortgage (mainly in the suburbs), those owning their houses outright, and those renting accommodation. The results, presented in Table 6.4, indicate that households buying their houses on mortgage devoted a substantially higher proportion of expenditure to accommodation than households on similar incomes who rented their homes. They also spent slightly more on 'other' items (furniture, household equipment, clothing, transport, and so forth), as would be expected given their larger houses, increased commuting costs, and higher conspicuous expenditures to meet the 'standards' of the estate. Meanwhile these increased expenditures were financed by substantial economies in areas of

---

[41] The Ministry of Labour database (see below) indicates that owner-occupying households had weekly costs for transport to/from work and for other purposes of 37.6d and 9.4d, respectively, compared to 15.1d and 6.1d for families who rented their accommodation.

[42] Museum of London Archive, material collected for Weightman and Humphries, *Making of Modern London*, information regarding Joyce Leader.

[43] Museum of London Archive, material collected for Weightman and Humphries, *Making of Modern London*, interview with Ivy Willis.

expenditure usually classed as 'necessities': particularly food and, to a lesser extent, fuel and lighting.[44]

Are home buyers' lower food expenditures proportionate to family size? Prais and Houtakker have estimated relative food expenditures for individuals according to age and gender, using 2,200 budget summaries from the Ministry of Labour enquiry.[45] Applying these weightings to households in the highest income group in Table 6.4 indicates that adjusted per capita food consumption for buyers and renters accounted for a similar proportion of total expenditure (8.23 and 8.40 per cent, respectively). Roughly similar figures were also produced for buyers and renters in the medium expenditure band (12.01 and 11.41 per cent, respectively). Thus (assuming accommodation and fuel and lighting costs remain constant), for buyers in the medium expenditure group to have the same family size as renters, and maintain their adult-equivalent per capita food consumption, expenditure on items other than housing, food, fuel and light would have to have been reduced from 38.2 to only 29.7 per cent of total weekly budgets.

The survey returns also indicate that a significant proportion of home buyers used a means of making ends meet that was also popular on municipal estates—letting out rooms. Seven of the seventy-nine home purchasers in the sample let part of their accommodation, reducing their gross property outgoings by an average of 54.5 per cent. These received an average weekly income of 54.4d per room let. Yet their gross property costs averaged 41.9d per room—a margin of profit (before bad debts, etc.) sufficiently low to indicate that letting rooms generally represented a means of coping with high mortgage costs, rather than of generating a lucrative additional income.

SMALLER, 'BETTER' FAMILIES

One of the most important mechanisms for controlling household budgets on the new estates was family limitation. British fertility rates had been in long-term decline since the third quarter of the nineteenth century, a process initiated by the middle classes, but already evident among most sections of the working class by the 1870s.[46] Szreter has convincingly argued that this can be explained in terms of the rising perceived relative (material and non-material) costs of childbearing. For the middle classes these costs were measured against the need to maintain a certain observed standard of living, while for the working classes they had initially been dominated by the chronic economic uncertainty which characterized the lives of the vast majority of households, during a period when the expansion of compulsory education increased the perceived costs of childbearing.[47]

---

[44] For a more detailed analysis of this data, see Scott, 'Did Owner-Occupation'.
[45] S. J. Prais and Hendrik Houthakker, *The Analysis of Family Budgets* (Cambridge: Cambridge University Press, 1955), 125–45 (based on their preferred, Table 29, specification).
[46] Robert Woods, *The Demography of Victorian England and Wales* (Cambridge: Cambridge University Press, 2000), 116–22.
[47] Szreter, *Fertility, Class and Gender*, 514–20.

Table 6.4. The distribution of weekly household expenditure and average family size for working-class families renting their accommodation, buying it on mortgage, or owning it outright, at various levels of total expenditure, April 1938

Weekly expenditure	Number of households	% distribution of expenditure					Mean values of expenditure (d)	Household size	No. of children under 18
		Housing	Food	Fuel & light	Other			
Renters								
Under 77s	265	15.8	45.9	9.1	29.2	664	3.50	1.37
77–109s	120	13.2	42.3	8.0	36.5	1,086	4.33	1.69
109s or over	92	8.7	34.1	5.9	51.4	1,785	4.49	1.10
All	477	12.6	40.8	7.7	39.0	986	3.90	1.40
Buyers[a]								
Under 77s	25	21.0	39.6	9.0	30.4	735	3.48	1.36
77–109s	28	18.1	36.0	7.7	38.2	1,100	3.43	1.14
109s or over	26	11.4	27.8	5.5	55.3	1,998	3.81	0.69
All	79	15.2	32.5	6.8	45.5	1,280	3.57	1.06
Owners								
Under 77s	9	4.8	57.7	10.0	27.6	667	4.00	1.67
77–109s	8	5.0	46.8	5.5	42.7	1,165	3.63	0.38
109s or over	8	2.7	27.7	4.1	65.5	2,108	3.38	0.63
All	25	3.8	38.8	5.6	51.8	1,287	3.68	0.92
Buyers + Owners								
Under 77s	34	17.0	44.1	9.3	29.7	717	3.62	1.44
77–109s	36	15.0	38.5	7.2	39.3	1,114	3.47	0.97
109s or over	34	9.3	27.8	5.2	57.8	2,024	3.71	0.68
All	104	12.4	34.0	6.5	47.1	1,282	3.60	1.03

Source: Peter Scott, 'Did Owner-Occupation Lead to Smaller Families for Interwar Working-Class Households?', *Economic History Review*, 61 (2008), 115.

[a] Households buying their homes on mortgage (rather than owning them outright).

The new suburban model of working-class respectability substantially raised the costs of children, as it involved buying in to higher standards of childcare, hygiene, nutrition, clothing, and education. This group therefore strongly embraced a wider contemporary trend among working-class families of viewing family planning as a means of defending socially necessary minimum consumption standards, rather than merely safeguarding against destitution.[48] Small families represented a key feature of the new suburban working-class respectability, being both instrumental in achieving, and an important marker of, desired lifestyles.

Mass Observation's *Britain and Her Birth Rate* survey found that the high standards of housework and motherhood expected of suburban housewives and the expense of maintaining these standards (compared to the expectations placed on women in traditional inner-urban working-class communities) constituted a deterrent to large families.[49] As Judy Giles noted, 'Fewer children meant less housework, fewer mouths to feed, improved health and the possibility of a non-too-distant future freed from the responsibilities of childcare.... "Respectable" families had fewer children and aspirations to "respectable" status could be achieved by smaller families'.[50]

By the interwar period a relatively small family had become a marker of respectability even in traditional working-class communities.[51] Mass Observation reported hostile peer reactions to large families; for example, a father of five children (with a sixth pending) stated, 'what misery the wife suffers by those nasty loud remarks, not to her, but at her, concerning rabbits and their habits etc.'[52] Similar comments were reported in listeners' responses to a series of BBC radio broadcasts on population decline.[53] On new owner-occupied estates the very small family of two (or fewer) children was widely viewed as the respectable norm, larger families becoming synonymous with a lack of self-control, recklessness, or outmoded values—all features of 'roughness'.

More importantly, owner occupation had a powerful direct impact on family size by squeezing household budgets. Johnson has argued that family budgeting strategies can be explained in terms of 'procedural rationality'. Living and spending according to a very short-term economic horizon is perfectly rational in an environment of chronic economic insecurity and low incomes, whereas higher and more regular incomes promoted longer-term planning and capital accumulation according to the same rational criteria.

Meanwhile changes in the institutional environment of saving and spending could have a significant impact in shifting the balance of household budgeting

---

[48] T. H Marshall et al., *The Population Problem: The Experts and the Public* (London: Allen & Unwin, 1938), 18–24 & 36. See also Wally Seccombe, *Weathering the Storm: Working-Class Families from the Industrial Revolution to the Fertility Decline* (London: Verso, 1993), 177; Royal Commission on Population: *Report* (London: HMSO, 1949), 39–40.

[49] Mass Observation, *Britain and Her Birth Rate* (London: John Murray, 1945), 153–66.

[50] Margaret Judith Giles, 'Something That Bit Better: Working-Class Women, Domesticity, and "Respectability", 1919–1939', DPhil thesis (University of York, 1989), 270.

[51] Levine, *Reproducing Families*, 212–13.

[52] Mass Observation, *Britain and Her Birth Rate*, 75.

[53] Marshall et al., *Population Problem*, 59.

from a present-orientated to a future-orientated time frame.[54] Owner occupation appears to have produced such a shift. In addition to the considerable monetary sunk costs of the deposit, accumulated capital repayments, and additional furnishings, the psychological costs of abandoning the new suburban lifestyle, the aspirational respectability which went with it, and the perceived opportunities it offered for children were also substantial. As Jane Walsh (the wife of an Oldham cotton piecer) recalled, when a series of misfortunes made it impossible to keep up the mortgage payments on their new suburban house, handing back the keys involved closing the door 'Not only on my dream house, but on my [plans for having] dream children.'[55]

These sunk costs and psychological pressures led families who moved from inner-urban areas to suburban owner occupation to shift their spending outlook towards a future-orientated perspective. Mortgage payments and the other costs of suburban living were met by squeezing budgets for items offering immediate gratification—food, heating, lighting, and so forth, in favour of expenditure linked to the long-term aim of defending their new social status.[56] This longer time horizon also encompassed family planning, as suggested by research on 'forethought', which indicates that there are strong connections between planning one's family and the wider areas of one's life.[57] For example, a man who had married in around 1935 told Mass Observation:

> We began married life with the intention of having no children... For me work was poor three or four days a week, also to get a passable house to live in we had to buy one in a housing scheme through a building society. That also made it necessary that we had no family or we would have been in poverty for the rest of our lives... We still could have a family, but neither of us want them now, if we ever did. We want to enjoy a decent standard of living without having more encumbrances to drag us down.[58]

Small families offered women the potential to break free from the chronic uncertainty and fear of destitution that had characterized many of their childhoods and had made a future-orientated perspective unrealistic for their parents. For such women, family limitation often formed part of a wider strategy to escape economic insecurity that might also include selecting a husband with a stable job and a willingness to adopt a lifestyle centred round the family rather than the pub. As Alice Pond explained, she and her siblings had families of zero, one, or two children, in contrast to her parents' six, as 'We all saw our mothers slaving away looking after loads of children. And if the father drank or was out of work they had to scrub

---

[54] Johnson, *Saving and Spending*; Szreter, *Fertility, Class and Gender*, 41.
[55] Jane Walsh, *Not Like This* (London: Lawrence & Wishart, 1953), 65.
[56] Museum of London Archives, material collected for Weightman and Humphries, *Making of Modern London*, regarding Joyce Leader; Walsh, *Not Like This*, 56–7; North Kingston Centre, Kingston, Surrey, NKC/OH62, transcript of interview with Mr Walden (a bus driver) and his wife.
[57] M. Anderson, L. Jamieson, F. Bechhofer, and D. McCrone, 'Planning and Family Planning: Forethought and Fertility-Related Attitudes and Behaviours', summary of paper presented at the Annual Conference of the British Society for Population Studies, Leicester, 15 September 2004.
[58] Mass Observation, *Britain and Her Birth Rate*, 123–4.

Fig. 6.2. The promise of 'a Brighter Outlook' as visualized by the Leeds Provincial Building Society
Source: Leeds Provincial, 'A Brighter Outlook', brochure (1937), Peter Scott collection.

floors or sell bootlaces or go on the assistance. We weren't having that, no that sort of thing was very old-fashioned, we wanted something better.'[59]

Most contemporary studies did not directly examine the impact of housing choice on family size. An exception is a report prepared for Rowntree's 1936 York survey, which found that many working-class families, living in owner-occupied suburban semi-detached housing, 'have found that re-payments for loans, rates, and costs of repairs constitute a heavy drain on their resources. There is no doubt

---

[59] Interview supplied to the author by Chris Pond. The interviewee was a dressmaker, working in a Hackney factory, who married a clerk (earning £3 5s a week at the time of marriage) in 1935.

that this is an important factor making for restriction in the size of the family. The average size of families occupying this class of house is only 3.24.'[60]

As Table 6.4 shows, surviving original returns from the 1937/8 Ministry of Labour working-class household expenditure survey indicate that buyers had significantly fewer children than renters at each income range other than the lowest (which included a substantial proportion of former sitting tenants of inner-urban properties who had purchased their existing homes from their landlords). For example, the average number of children for families in the 77–109 s per week group (for which mean household expenditure for buyers and renters is roughly similar) is around 0.55 lower for buyers, and 0.72 lower for the combined buyers and owners group, than for renters. Further quantitative analysis of this data corroborates the relationship between owner occupation and family size, as does data on completed fertility from the Life Histories Database and database testimonies regarding family planning strategies.[61]

Strategies of cutting back on food, heating, and other daily costs to meet the expenses of suburban life have also been identified on interwar municipal estates, as discussed in Chapter 3.[62] Similarly, life history testimonies indicate that many families on council estates engaged in family planning to cope with the extra costs and material expectations of their new environment. Yet, while many council estates embodied new notions of respectability and associated spending patterns, quantifying their impact on family size is much more difficult than for owner-occupied housing. Tenant selection policies generally excluded families without children and, especially during the 1930s (when new council housing was used primarily for slum clearance and alleviating overcrowding) larger families received priority. As a result, average household size was high by contemporary working-class standards, despite any impact that suburban living might have had on fertility after families had made their house moves.[63]

Another aspect of the higher perceived costs of further births for suburban owner-occupiers involved impacts on the family's existing children. New notions of working-class respectability placed considerable emphasis on providing children with the greatest possible support for their future lives and careers. This was to be achieved by creating a better domestic environment and concentrating available monetary and psychological resources on a limited number of children. The emerging

---

[60] Borthwick Institute, York, Rowntree Archive, PP13, paper on housing in York (n.d., c.1936).

[61] For more detailed analysis of this data, see Scott, 'Did Owner-Occupation'. This article also includes a number of checks on the reliability of the data and comparison with available data on completed fertility, which corroborates the link between owner occupation and family size. The analysis excludes families living 'rent-free' in accommodation provided by their employer.

[62] See, for example, Audrey Kay, 'Wythenshawe circa 1932–1955: The Making of a Community?', PhD thesis (University of Manchester, 1993); Madeline McKenna, 'The Development of Suburban Council Housing Estates in Liverpool between the Wars', PhD thesis (University of Liverpool, 1986).

[63] For example, average household size on the LCC's Becontree and Watling estates was 4.78 and 4.70, respectively, compared to 3.67 for all London families—Terence Young, *Becontree and Dagenham* (London: Becontree Social Survey Committee, 1934), 112; Durant, *Watling*, 14. Similar patterns are evident on provincial estates—see, for example, McKenna, 'Development of Suburban Council Housing Estates', 234a.

working-class ideal of the small, well-resourced, family was influenced by changes in the general climate of opinion regarding child-rearing, which filtered down to working-class families via contact with 'professionals' such as health visitors and maternity clinic staff, together with books, magazines, the women's pages of newspapers, and radio programmes.

Medical and other expert opinion promoted an increasingly elaborate 'ideology of childhood', in which the mother played a central role in creating a happy, clean home environment. Unrestricted fertility threatened this role, by forcing the mother to spread her limited resources of money and time over an ever-increasing number of children and thus undermining the family's ability to maintain a healthy, modern house in a suitable neighbourhood.[64] Almost all working-class women would have come into some contact with the new ideas regarding child welfare, though suburban owner-occupiers would have been particularly exposed to them (and particularly receptive, given the congruence between these ideas and their wider notions of respectability).

The ideology of domesticity, enlightened parenthood, and the efficient 'professional housewife' proved one of the editorial cornerstones of the new mass-circulation women's magazines. For example, the largest, *Woman's Own*—which targeted the young, aspirational (but often working-class) housewife—provided advice via 'expert' columnists, including 'Nurse Vincent' who wrote its childcare pages. Content analysis of *Woman's Own* articles, by Greenfield and Reid, indicates that 12.3 per cent concerned childcare, 10.5 per cent housekeeping, and 12.7 per cent involved 'lifestyle' topics.[65] Meanwhile greater isolation from neighbours and the local community on new suburban estates reinforced the importance women placed on family life, domesticity, and, particularly, children.[66]

Such motivations were evident, to some extent, in encouraging family limitation among all working-class groups.[67] However, the Life Histories Database indicates that these aspirations appear to have been more fully developed and integrated into long-term household strategies by suburban owner-occupiers. This involved sacrifices of both time and money. As a motor vehicle coach painter who had purchased a house on a new suburban Coventry estate recalled, having a small family allowed him to create

> a broader based home environment, completely different to anything I enjoyed, the ability to have a separate room to study in, and a piano for the pianist in our family to play on... The ability to relax, and the chance to sit entrance exams to the King Edward VIII Grammar School and get past, and... go to University. They kept us poor at one point... I'd got two lads at University, having to pay for them both.[68]

---

[64] Gittins, *Fair Sex*, 182–3.
[65] Jill Greenfield and Chris Reid, 'Women's Magazines and the Commercial Orchestration of Femininity in the 1930s: Evidence from Woman's Own', *Media History*, 4 (1998).
[66] Gittins, *Fair Sex*, 136; Kay, 'Wythenshawe', 238.
[67] Kate Fisher, 'Uncertain Aims and Tacit Negotiations: Birth Control Practices in Britain, 1925–50', *Population and Development Review*, 26 (2000), 302.
[68] CRO, 1647/1/4, interview with male, born 1908.

Extra time and financial resources were also often devoted to children's broader social development. Several accounts mention devoting time to playing games with children and helping them with their hobbies. An extreme example was given by the wife of a Coventry sheet metal worker, who recalled that they devoted so much time to their daughter's hobby of showjumping that 'we never had a Sunday lunch at home for six months of the year'.[69]

Life history accounts indicate that a substantial proportion of the suburban pioneers' offspring obtained higher-status jobs than their parents, as noted in other studies of interwar working-class suburbia.[70] Yet this did not necessarily indicate a desire that their children should move from the working to the middle class. The Life Histories Database corroborates earlier research by Judy Giles that—like their own transition to suburbia—these parents viewed their children's prospects not in terms of transcending the working-/middle-class divide, but as 'material improvement and conformity to "respectable" values—a steady marriage, a solid and regular income and a "respectable" lifestyle.'[71]

Life histories generally provide little information on the actual mechanisms by which small families were achieved (even when this information was specifically requested by interviewers), women who married during this period often being reticent to discuss contraception in any detail.[72] Yet they indicate a generally very limited level of knowledge regarding sex and birth control at the time of marriage: for example, one woman recalled that 'When we got married...George had to teach me all I knew. I didn't know a thing 'cos Mum didn't tell you anything, and you didn't get anything from school those days.'[73] Advice from birth control clinics does not appear to have played a significant role in the family planning strategies of most women. Only one respondent mentioned attending a birth control clinic before the Second World War (following advice that her husband's mental illness would be passed on to her children).[74] Meanwhile only two of the fifty-eight accounts mentioned consulting family planning manuals.

This corroborates Kate Fisher's observations that interwar working-class couples generally had an informal approach to birth control, but not her further finding that contraception was used 'without formulating an ideal family size'.[75] Despite their limited knowledge, many couples appear to have successfully planned for a certain number of children. For example, a motor vehicle worker who had purchased a £575 house on marriage, when asked whether they had planned the family, responded, 'Well, we planned to have one or two, but two was enough.' Asked

---

[69] CRO, 1647/1/36, interview with female, born 1913.
[70] See, for example, Giles, 'Something That Bit Better', 327.
[71] Giles, 'Something That Bit Better', 293.
[72] Giles, 'Something That Bit Better', 278; Kay, 'Wythenshawe', 238.
[73] Bexley Local Studies and Archives Centre, *Bexley between the Wars*, interview with Mrs Harrington.
[74] Ruskin College Library Archives, M.ss 47, Jessie Gear, 'The Trials and Joys of an Orphan', unpublished autobiography (c.1986). Interwar working-class women often felt inhibited from seeking medical advice on how to control their fertility—A. McLaren, *A History of Contraception: From Antiquity to the Present Day* (Oxford: Blackwell, 1990), 225.
[75] Fisher, 'Uncertain Aims and Tacit Negotiations', 301.

about how they had accomplished this, he replied 'I suppose we took things to chance, you know, guessed it, and everything turned out as we wanted it.'[76]

Cryptic comments about leaving things to chance or 'being careful' usually refer to non-mechanical methods, principally coitus interruptus, abstinence, or using the 'safe' period of the menstrual cycle.[77] The use of sheaths or other mechanical methods is reported in only one account. The reticence with which most people discussed these issues may have led to their use being under-reported; Fisher found significant use of condoms among her interview sample (though withdrawal was more commonly used), while contemporary evidence corroborates the significant diffusion of appliance methods by the 1930s.[78] Similarly, reticence may account for the lack of any mention of abortion, despite contemporary evidence of its significance in limiting fertility within marriage.[79]

The prevalence of 'male' methods of contraception required the husband's initiative or, at least, cooperation.[80] As Wally Seccombe has noted, male self-restraint was a key factor behind successful family limitation—involving a willingness to limit sexual pleasure in order to meet the economic and social objectives of the household.[81] Foregoing immediate gratification in pursuit of long-term goals was an underlying feature of suburban owner-occupiers' lifestyles during this period—for example, paying the mortgage and keeping up with the standards of the estate often had to be put ahead of good quality and plentiful food, while men were required to make long commutes to work and forego the pleasures of the pub, which was not now at the end of the street.

This period witnessed a change in thinking regarding 'proper' sexual relations between married people, men being expected to exercise new standards of restraint and consideration. The diffusion of such ideas remained limited, though they had begun to enter into magazines and other literature read by working-class women.[82] Studies of interwar working-class suburban communities have highlighted the importance of more companionate and equalitarian marriages than were then the norm, with husbands being prepared to make greater sacrifices in the interests of their families.[83]

While in some ways the sacrifices made by women were even greater (for example, they often bore the brunt of any reduction in food budgets during periods of financial difficulties), the lifestyle changes required of men marked a much sharper

---

[76] CRO, 1647/1/56, interview with male, born 1906.
[77] Mass Observation, *Britain and Her Birth-Rate*, 59.
[78] Kate Fisher, ' "She was Quite Satisfied with the Arrangements I Made": Gender and Birth Control in Britain 1920–1950', *Past and Present*, 169 (2000), 161–93; McLaren, *History of Contraception*, 235.
[79] See McLaren, *History of Contraception*, 227; Seccombe, *Weathering the Storm*, 158.
[80] Fisher, 'She was Quite Satisfied'.
[81] Wally Seccombe, 'Starting to Stop: Working-Class Fertility Decline in Britain', *Past and Present*, 126 (1990), 176–7.
[82] Margaret J. Giles, *The Parlour and the Suburb: Domestic Identities, Class, Femininity and Modernity* (Oxford: Berg, 2004), 61.
[83] A. D. McCulloch, 'Owner-Occupation and Class Struggle: The Mortgage Strikes of 1938–40', PhD thesis (University of Essex, 1983), 246.

and more fundamental break with traditional patterns than those required of women. The Life Histories Database indicates that women often sought 'prudential' marriages, selecting husbands largely on account of their having the qualities necessary to make successful partners in their project of suburban respectability and securing a good long-term future for their children. This suggests that the roots of their family limitation strategies often predated marriage and migration to suburbia, new owner-occupied estates providing the environment in which these aspirations could be achieved.

CONCLUSION

For many working-class families who made the transition from being urban tenants to suburban owner-occupiers during the 1930s, the move to suburbia involved buying into a cluster of related preferences including hygiene, presenting a smart appearance to neighbours and the wider world; privatized, home- and family-centred lifestyles; restrained behaviour; and small, well-resourced families. This required a more future-orientated time horizon, epitomized by the widespread use of birth control to keep family size to a level where this lifestyle could be maintained and to concentrate available resources in fewer, 'better' children. Achieving this consumption cluster involved sacrificing current gratification—including that from less restricted fertility—for long-term benefits, which would be experienced most fully by the next generation.

These were difficult lifestyle choices, which makes it all the more remarkable that a substantial proportion of new urban working-class households chose owner-occupied suburbia in preference to inner-urban communities which were less expensive in terms of monetary costs, time spent commuting, or the psychological stresses associated with the imperatives to keep up mortgage and HP payments and avoid unplanned pregnancies. Yet there is a strong measure of consensus among life history testimonies that moving to suburbia was not only worth the sacrifice, but was key to achieving the type of lifestyles they desired, for both themselves and their children.

7
Equipping the Suburban Home

INTRODUCTION

'Conspicuous consumption' by working-class families was not a new phenomenon: social investigators at the turn of the century reported its presence even among lower-income households. For casual workers this could take the form of coloured prints, photographs, and ornaments, while for more prosperous working-class households it found expression in a parlour, used only on Sundays, with patterned linoleum, their best furniture, paintings, a mirror over the fireplace, and other symbols of 'respectability'—as interpreted by their particular reference group. However, limited resources were generally concentrated on a few prized possessions, with one high status object often dominating.[1] An extreme example was recalled by a man who grew up in a mice-infested Coventry court house. When he was a child, his mother bought a 57-guinea piano, which took up almost half their only ground-floor room, on HP—paying almost half as much on the instalments as her family paid in rent.[2]

Conversely, achieving the new, aspirational lifestyle of suburban home-owning respectability went beyond merely possessing the right house, requiring appropriate furnishings, clothing, and other observable markers of consumption and household behaviour. The lifestyles offered in estate developers' brochures, showing rooms dressed in matching modern furniture with complementary wallpaper, carpets, and light fittings, contrasted with the reality of the homes many owner-occupiers had moved from, typically furnished with an eclectic mix of new, inherited, second-hand, and home-made furniture. Firms selling furnishings and consumer durables capitalized on this, collaborating with estate developers to enable house purchasers to replicate not only the show house but its contents—which, like the house, were generally available on 'easy' HP terms.

Pressures to conform to the standards of the new suburban 'consumption communities' were evident on both owner-occupied and council estates (especially the early, general needs municipal estates of the 1920s). As a 1939 survey of a Birmingham council estate noted, people felt obliged to purchase new furniture,

---

[1] Paul Johnson, 'Conspicuous Consumption and Working-Class Culture in Late-Victorian and Edwardian Britain', *Transactions of the Royal Historical Society*, 38:5 (1988), 36–7; Clive Edwards, *Turning Houses into Homes: A History of the Retailing and Consumption of Domestic Furnishings* (Aldershot: Ashgate, 2005), 218.
[2] Coventry Record Office, Acc. 1662/3/130, Coventry Oral History Project, interview with Mr Batchelor.

partly in order 'to live up to the standard set by their new surroundings'—for example, people often prioritized furnishing the parlour, even if it was seldom used.[3] However, contemporary accounts pay relatively little attention to the 'supply side' of this process—the role played by manufacturers and (more often) distributors of furniture and household appliances in convincing new tenants that they needed to make heavy investments in furnishings. Techniques used to sell the idea that a new house required brand new furniture and appliances form one theme of this chapter. Strategies employed by households to furnish their new suburban homes are also examined, together with the types of goods typically purchased and how these were used and financed.

MARKETING FURNITURE TO NEW SUBURBAN FAMILIES

Department stores had long been aware of the advantages of displaying complete room sets (or even entire houses) in a realistic domestic context.[4] As a 1919 *Cabinet Maker* article noted, 'The customer is spared the trouble of endeavouring to imagine the room as it will look when completed.'[5] The first suburban council estates provided furnishers with an opportunity to exhibit their goods in actual houses and to target a specific market, characterized by a high propensity to purchase new furniture.

Some councils turned to organizations without a direct commercial interest to show tenants how they could furnish their new homes 'tastefully'. For example, in 1921 the Design and Industries Association collaborated with Manchester City Council to decorate and furnish a cottage on its new Anson estate, which also formed the basis for its Cottage Interior and Decoration Exhibition at Manchester City Art Gallery. However, the impact of the association's 'arts and crafts'-influenced ideals, including a large proportion of handmade content, contributed to an overall furnishing price of £160—well beyond the pocket of the typical council tenant.[6] Similarly, upmarket furniture manufacture P. E. Gane Ltd of Bristol furnished a new corporation house at 32 St John's Crescent, Bedminster, Bristol, at a cost that also amounted to about £160 (including furnishings, floor covering, etc., but not linen or crockery).[7]

Department stores soon caught on to this form of marketing. In 1925 Laidler Robsons Ltd of Sunderland announced their exhibition of a model 'subsidy' or council house, the furniture for which they supplied 'at the moderate figure of

---

[3] M. S. Soutar, E. H. Wilkins, and P. Sargant Florence, *Nutrition and Size of Family: Report on a New Housing Estate—1939, Prepared for the Birmingham Social Survey Committee* (London: George Allen & Unwin, 1942), 39–40.

[4] Susanna Goodden, *At the Sign of the Four Poster: A History of Heals* (Aldershot: Ashgate, 1984), 17; Edwards, *Turning Houses into Homes*, 137–9.

[5] 'The Decoration Department: Its Importance to Furnishing Houses', *Cabinet Maker* (18 January 1919), 62.

[6] David Jeremiah, *Architecture and Design for the Family in Britain, 1900–70* (Manchester: Manchester University Press, 2000), 69–70.

[7] 'Furnishing of Small Houses: Bristol Demonstrations', *Cabinet Maker* (22 October 1921).

£127. The cost of the living-room works out at £25 16s, the parlour at £36 9s, the first, second and third bedrooms at £30 16s 6d, £23 12s 6d and £10 6s respectively, and in all the rooms the principal articles are of oak.'[8]

Furniture suppliers were, initially, less sanguine about the opportunities which *owner-occupied* housing offered, some fearing that mortgage costs would leave families with insufficient resources to purchase their furniture new. Yet by the 1930s most had realized that owner occupation acted to boost, rather than inhibit, furniture expenditure and had begun to devise marketing strategies to collaborate with speculative developers. For example, in 1930 Chapman's of Newcastle introduced its 'Siesta Scheme for Home Lovers':

> For the convenience of all moving into new houses a system of 'Siesta' notices will be seen in the windows of good modern homes, to certify that our representative has inspected the estate, and that Messrs. Chapmans are intimately aware of the type of furnishings required. From time to time announcements will appear in these columns recommending well-built, pleasantly situated homes of reasonable price that will make ideal 'Siesta' homes.[9]

A more common strategy was for furniture retailers (most commonly department stores) to use building estate show houses as showrooms. The store would furnish the show house and have a salesman present to meet the viewers and advertise the broader selection of furniture available in their shop. Meanwhile, the department store and estate developer commonly cross-promoted their products in brochures, displays, and other publicity material. In 1935 Davis Estates opened a show house adjacent to Charing Cross Station, to attract buyers to its various estates in London's suburbs and satellite towns.[10] This was furnished by Furlongs Ltd, of Woolwich, as a large proportion of visitors were residents of the Woolwich area, who commuted in to central London via Charing Cross. Complementary publicity was placed in the windows of Furlong's Woolwich store, encouraging their customers to visit the show house. This supplemented Davis Estates' own advertising. The arrangement was formalized via a contract which stipulated that Furlongs would maintain the house furnishings for one year.[11]

One major advantage for the retailer was that, unlike a shop, a show house could remain open on Sundays. In 1934 a representative of Coventry furnishers John Anslow (which had furnished ten show houses, including three during that year) told *Cabinet Maker*, 'We make a point of having them open on Sunday... Although nothing is actually sold on that day, there are so many people who only get Sunday to look round that we find that enquiries from them are as numerous as from visitors during the other days of the week put together'.[12]

---

[8] *Furniture Record*, 23 January 1925, 101.
[9] Cited in 'Current Furniture Advertising', *Cabinet Maker* (23 August 1930), 326–8.
[10] Peter Scott collection, Davis Estates, 'The Davis Estate, Ensbury Park, Bournemouth', undated brochure (c.1935).
[11] 'Charring Cross Showhouse', *Cabinet Maker* (21 September 1935), 482.
[12] 'Furnishing a Show House: Coventry Furnishers set an Example', *Cabinet Maker* (15 September 1934), 394–5.

Department stores also began to adopt some of the marketing ideas employed by the house-builders. For example, in 1936 Reading department store Heelas held its own 'Modern Homes and Gardens' exhibition, followed the next year by a 'Beautiful Homes' exhibition. The format drew on the Ideal Home Exhibition and its local and regional counterparts, including a novelty Heath Robinson flat, and a garden, complete with lawns and fountains. It also boasted 28 furnished rooms, an 'eastern carpet market', a 'bachelor's study-bedroom', and a 'modern office'.[13]

Some stores blurred the line between their activities and those of the house-builders to an even greater extent. The well-known department store Bentalls of Kingston began to combine business ventures in the furnishing and housing markets during the 1930s. Its building department won the contract for 144 council houses for Kingston Corporation in Norbiton and also began to manufacturer timber-frame bungalows—priced at £175. These were very popular as retirement homes and its staff were frequently called to erect them on the south coast. In typical fashion for a store famous for its publicity stunts, Bentalls put a show bungalow on their roof, which was used to display furniture in a domestic context. The firm also established an estate agency, which began by dealing with estates of new small

Fig. 7.1. The Ideal Home as department store furniture advertising slogan
Source: Arding & Hobbs Ltd, 'The Ideal Home Furniture', brochure (n.d., 1930s), Peter Scott collection.

[13] John Lewis Partnership Archive, file 2075/6–7.

houses in Chessington. Bentalls had up to a dozen specially furnished show houses on these estates to promote their furnishing departments.[14]

One of Bentalls' most popular deals was a furnishing package which would equip a three-bedroom house for £100. Such 'all-in' packages were offered by many department stores and furniture retailers. For example, in 1932 Lewis's of Liverpool introduced a 'Design for Living' department, which was later extended to their Manchester and Birmingham branches. This composed room furniture displays; in 1938 their Birmingham store displayed a four-room house furnished for £65 for a family on £3 per week, together with a five-room house furnished for £165 for a family with an income of £5.[15]

HIRE PURCHASE

Migrants to suburbia relied heavily on HP to furnish their new houses. Buying on HP had become common practice for working- and lower-middle-class households by the mid-1920s. However, it appears to have been particularly heavily used on suburban estates. Many families had already stretched their cash resources in making the move to suburbia, while the relatively large size of suburban houses compared to inner-urban accommodation increased the amount of furniture required (especially if they were to live up to the 'standards' of the estate).

In 1939 evidence to the Departmental Committee on Valuation for Rates, Mr Lord of the National Federation of House Builders responded to a question about how many new house purchasers also got their furniture on the HP system with the answer, 'Nine out of ten. It is terrible really. It is really distressing.'[16] Jevons and Madge's survey of Bristol municipal estates found that the cost of equipping the house translated into weekly HP payments of around 2s 6d.[17] Meanwhile, a report on Birmingham's Kingstanding municipal estate found that more than half the families visited were currently paying for furniture acquired on HP:

> For most of them it seems to be impossible to save and pay cash for clothes, let alone beds. It is hard not to dip into savings when one of the children needs a pair of shoes or where there has been short-time working and there is no money for dinners. But once furniture has been contracted for, the instalment must be paid regularly, and for this reason the family may have to go short of immediate necessities in order to meet the weekly payments....[18]

HP terms were offered by most furniture retailers. However, a number of multiple retail chains, such as Drages, Smart Brothers, and Jay's, used this as their

---

[14] Rowan Bentall, *My Store of Memories* (London: W. H. Allen, 1974), 162–3.
[15] Cited in Edwards, *Turning Houses into Homes*, 184.
[16] The National Archives, HLG56/157, Departmental Committee on Valuation for Rates. Minutes of evidence of National Federation of House Builders, 16 March 1939.
[17] Rosamond Jevons and John Madge, *Housing Estates: A Study of Bristol Corporation Policy and Practice between the Wars* (Bristol: Arrowsmith, 1946), 45.
[18] Soutar, Wilkins, and Florence, *Nutrition and Size of Family*, 39.

main sales strategy, aggressively promoting 'easy' terms via newspaper and other advertising. These generally targeted lower-middle- and working-class customers and charged heavy interest rates, ranging from 10 to 50 per cent (mainly towards the higher end of this spectrum), often chiefly via an additional price mark-up.[19] Such high rates partly reflected the high administrative costs of recording and monitoring payments, enquiries into customers' credit worthiness, taking up references, dealing with arrears, and—for lower-income customers—door-to-door collections of payments (though bad debt ratios appear to have been relatively small).[20]

Slum clearance tenants often lost some of their furniture in the course of compulsory fumigation to remove lice and other vermin, thus placing what was generally the poorest social group to make the move to suburbia in the greatest need of new furniture.[21] Some 103 of Sunderland's 179 new municipal tenants during 1934 were required to have their furniture and bedding disinfested before moving.[22] In Halifax soft goods were put through a steam disinfector, while other articles were treated with HCN gas. Much bedding and other soft furnishings disintegrated under this treatment, in which case Halifax council offered replacements, on HP.[23]

Halifax was not alone in offering HP facilities to tenants, some of whom needed credit terms even to purchase second-hand items.[24] A number of councils established furniture supply facilities, offering HP-type systems for essential items on terms more generous than those of the furniture multiples. Gateshead council provided essential new furniture in its 1930 Act houses on HP, for 3 shillings per week over 3 years.[25] Leeds, Birmingham, Bolton, Rotherham, and some of the London boroughs also adopted variants of this scheme, as did 10 per cent of Scottish local authorities (including Glasgow).

In Birmingham the Citizen Society launched a scheme for collecting unwanted furniture to assist poor people moving into new housing. Similarly in Liverpool the Personal Service Society started a second-hand furniture store in 1938. Bristol's Housing Committee also held a stock of second-hand furniture, to help those for

---

[19] University of East Anglia Archives, Pritchard papers, Board of Trade Furniture Working Party minutes, 28 November 1945; J. B. Jefferys, *The Distribution of Consumer Goods: A Factual Study of Methods and Costs in the United Kingdom in 1938* (Cambridge: Cambridge University Press, 1950), 270–1; Board of Trade Working Party Reports, *Furniture* (London: HMSO, 1946), 33.
[20] See Peter Scott, 'Mr Drage, Mr Everyman, and the Creation of a Mass Market for Domestic Furniture in Interwar Britain', *Economic History Review*, 62 (2009), 813–14.
[21] Madeline McKenna, 'The Development of Suburban Council Housing Estates in Liverpool between the Wars', PhD thesis (University of Liverpool, 1986), 211.
[22] Robert Ryder, 'Council House Building in County Durham, 1900–39: The Local Implementation of National Policy', in Martin J. Daunton (ed.), *Councillors and Tenants: Local Authority Housing in English Cities, 1919–1939* (Leicester: Leicester University Press, 1984), 75.
[23] E. D. Smithies, 'The Contrast between North and South in England 1918–1939: A Study of Economic, Social and Political Problems with Particular Reference to the Experience of Burnley, Halifax, Ipswich, and Luton', PhD thesis (University of Leeds, 1974), 194.
[24] Norman Williams, 'Problems of Population and Education in the New Housing Estates, with Special Reference to Norris Green', MA dissertation (Liverpool University, 1938), 36–7.
[25] Ryder, 'Council House Building in County Durham', 76.

Fig. 7.2. A Drages' hire purchase 'drawing room' furniture package
Source: Drages Ltd, 'Drages Easter Bargains in Fine Furniture', brochure (n.d., 1920s–30s), Peter Scott collection.

whom poverty made HP impractical. However, this was seen to carry the stamp of charity and was said to be unpopular with tenants.[26]

Retailers such as Drages that relied on the vigorous promotion of easy terms ensured customers that no references would be asked for and that the furniture

---

[26] Jevons and Madge, *Housing Estates*, 45; Clive Edwards, 'Buy Now—Pay Later: Credit: The Mainstay of the Retail Furniture Business?', in John Benson and Lauran Ugolini (eds), *Cultures of Selling: Perspectives on Consumption and Society since 1700* (Aldershot: Ashgate, 2006), 144.

would be delivered in plain vans, thus sparing the household the social stigma that still surrounded buying on the 'never-never'.[27] Like the house builders, HP furniture retailers learned from successful innovations in other areas of marketing to young, aspirational households. Leading HP furniture chain Smart Brothers adopted a lifestyle marketing approach—emphasizing the potential that furniture offered purchasers to achieve the sort of aspirational, domestically orientated lifestyles being promulgated in women's magazines. Large glossy brochures copied women's magazines in style and format, emphasizing the glamour, luxury, and aspirational connotations of rooms furnished with new suites.

One 80-page brochure included features such as 'Choosing Your Colour Schemes and Planning Your Room', and testimonials from movie stars. It also drew on the ideology of domesticity (a popular theme in women's magazines); for example, the section devoted to the nursery began 'Your Baby! The most valuable thing in the world—a precious symbol of mutual love and understanding.'[28] Short stories, akin to those in women's magazines, were also used to deliver the main sales message. 'Honeymoon: A complete love story by Garth Preston' drew the reader in with the tag line 'Sheila gets two surprises... they alter the whole course of her life! Thrill to this tender story of youthful love!' After a couple of paragraphs the predicament is set out:

> Gordon considered John and Arthur, now settled down with charming wives in beautiful new homes. Then he thought of his own position. Engaged to the most fascinating girl he'd ever met, and unable to marry her because he couldn't afford it. Even seeing Sheila seemed to be difficult. They couldn't be alone when he asked her to his house, because Mother and Dad were always there. It was the same at Sheila's. All they could do was go for walks or the pictures, or as they were doing to-morrow, to some dance. And these places he knew were unsatisfactory.[29]

The answer to the conundrum, provided by a similarly impecunious married friend, was, of course, Smart's furniture catalogue and four-yearly credit terms, which allowed him to 'furnish the most beautiful home in the world without waiting another day!'

There is considerable evidence of one-sided HP contracts having been exploited by unscrupulous retailers to deprive customers of their normal legal rights as purchasers, provide substandard goods at inflated prices, and, sometimes, 'snatchback' goods towards the end of the contract without any compensation, if a payment was late by even a few hours. This was perfectly legal prior to the 1938 Hire Purchase Act, as goods were technically only 'hired' until final payment had been made.[30] However, most of the life history accounts that discuss using HP

---

[27] Peter Scott collection, Drages Ltd, 'Mr & Mrs Everyman Talk Things over with Mr Drage', brochure (n.d., c.mid- to late 1920s).
[28] Geffrye Museum, Smart Brothers Ltd, 'Smarts Have Furnished a Million Homes and Won a Million Hearts', brochure (n.d., interwar).
[29] Smart Brothers, 'Smarts Have Furnished a Million Homes'.
[30] Peter Scott, 'The Twilight World of Interwar Hire Purchase', *Past and Present*, 177 (2002), 195–225.

generally describe it as a useful means of acquiring expensive items which would have otherwise been unaffordable. During a period when a substantial proportion of working- and lower-middle-class families moved from traditional inner-urban housing to new municipal or owner-occupied estates, the HP furniture multiples enabled many households to realize higher standards of material comfort and display, if at substantial financial cost—which was inevitably reflected in cutbacks to other areas of consumption.

FURNITURE ACQUISITION STRATEGIES AND COSTS

The Life Histories Database sheds some light on the furniture-purchasing strategies of families moving to the suburbs. After finding a home, acquiring the necessary furniture is shown to have typically constituted the largest single financial problem facing couples setting up new households and, for people renting accommodation, their main item of capital expenditure. A number of furniture acquisition strategies can be identified, mainly varying according to income. Some low-income families delayed purchasing much of their furniture for some time after marriage and furnished using a mix of second-hand goods, items handed down from families and friends, and home-made furniture. However, a high proportion of working-class households purchased a substantial amount of their furniture new.

New furniture was an important marker of distinction. While upper-middle-class families still often favoured antiques, these carried less social cache for lower-income groups, for whom old furniture had connotations of poverty, dirt, and vermin infestation. A few households in the database were able to save enough before marriage to purchase most or all their furniture outright. Some also had part of their furniture bought for them by their families. However, new furniture was most commonly obtained via HP and sometimes involved very large purchases at around the time of the house move. A Liverpool factory worker, earning £3 a week at the time of his marriage, recalled furnishing his house 'on overtime. A big shop, Alexander's, had everything in it, and I bought sideboard, table and chairs, everything there. They would ask my wages, then say this will take 4 years to pay for. Everybody bought things this way though, you couldn't afford any other way.'[31] Others initially purchased a limited amount of furniture, again generally on HP, which they later added to.

The small number of lower-middle-class life histories in the database suggest that a higher proportion of such families were able to fund their purchases out of savings, while—in common with some working-class households—several who could not afford to furnish their entire house concentrated on a couple of rooms (usually including the front room, which was most visible to visitors). Middle-class families also appear to have received a larger proportion of their furniture in the form of wedding presents. HP was still important for this group, though—as

---

[31] McKenna, 'Development of Suburban Council Housing Estates', appendix 13, interview 17.

far as can be discerned from this small sample—its use appears to have been significantly lower than that for working-class households.

In common with the house itself, there was significant convergence in the contents of the interwar lower-middle- and working-class suburban home, compared to their pre-1914 counterparts. The overcrowded sitting room of the typical Victorian middle-class house, packed with furniture, ornamentation, and curiosities, was much less attractive to the interwar housewife, who now generally had to do at least some of her own cleaning. Meanwhile, magazines aimed at middle-class women, and the interior designers who contributed to the women's press, typically promoted relatively simple, 'restful' room designs, using styles of furnishings that would not rapidly go out of fashion and which reflected mainstream tastes rather than individuality.[32] New furniture based on antique styles was the preferred solution—the mock Tudor house being typically furnished with Jacobean suites rather than modernist furniture.

In the Times Furnishing Co.'s mid-1930s *Good Furnishing* booklet, Christine Veasey, of the company's Advisory Bureau, suggested the following allocation of a furnishing budget (including carpets, but not soft furnishings) for a three-bedroom house: lounge 20 per cent, dining room 18 per cent, best bedroom 20 per cent, second bedroom 14 per cent, third bedroom 10 per cent, hall 8 per cent, kitchen 8 per cent, and bathroom 2 per cent.[33] The low allocation to the last two rooms reflected the trend for new houses to have built-in units.

The front reception room assumed prime importance. It inherited the status connotations of the parlour, it was still the room where visitors were customarily entertained, and its contents could be readily observed by a visitor to the front door. As such, its cleanliness and standard of furnishing was often far from representative of the rest of the house. Still generally designated the lounge or parlour, it was used for reading, children's homework, or receiving visitors. Meanwhile, the back room might be used as a dining room, for listening to the radio or gramophone, or for similar informal relaxation. A variant of this model was to use one room (typically the front room) as a dining room and the other as a general living room.[34] In either case, the front room usually represented the public face of the house and the back room its private aspect.

Suzette Worden noted a trend towards the emergence of the multipurpose living room in both middle- and working-class homes. The middle classes approached this through a reduction in the number of functional reception rooms, compared to homes designed with an assumption of live-in servants, while for the working classes it represented increased specialization from the traditional combination of the kitchen and living room that had been necessitated by the use of the range as

---

[32] Deborah Cohen, *Household Gods: The British and their Possessions* (New Haven, CT: Yale University Press, 2006), 188–9.
[33] National Library of Art, Christine Veasey (ed.), 'Good Furnishing', Times Furnishing Co., brochure (*c*.1935).
[34] Suzette A. Worden, 'Furniture for the Living Room: An Investigation of the Interaction between Society, Industry, and Design in Britain from 1919 to 1939', PhD thesis (Brighton Polytechnic, 1980), 75.

the principal means of both cooking and heating.³⁵ A combined dining/living room was a typical feature of municipal houses and as the average size of new speculative houses continued to drop over the interwar years, this combination of the family's main daytime activities in a single room proved increasingly popular.

Furniture was frequently marketed in suites: the bedroom suite, three-piece suite, and dining suite. J. B. Jefferys argues that there was a trend towards buying suites of matching furniture among higher-income sections of the working class by 1914—though the key change occurred during the interwar years.³⁶ Marketing suites was easier for chain stores, as they provided larger unit sales to cover the cost of the free carriage and other common incentives. Suites were also attractive to purchasers, as they were cheaper than buying individual items separately, provided a coordinated style, and had important status connotations.

Reception rooms were dominated by suites—the dining suite and the three-piece suite. Dining suites consisted of a table (with extending leaves, so that it could be adapted to serve between two and six people); a set of relatively simple

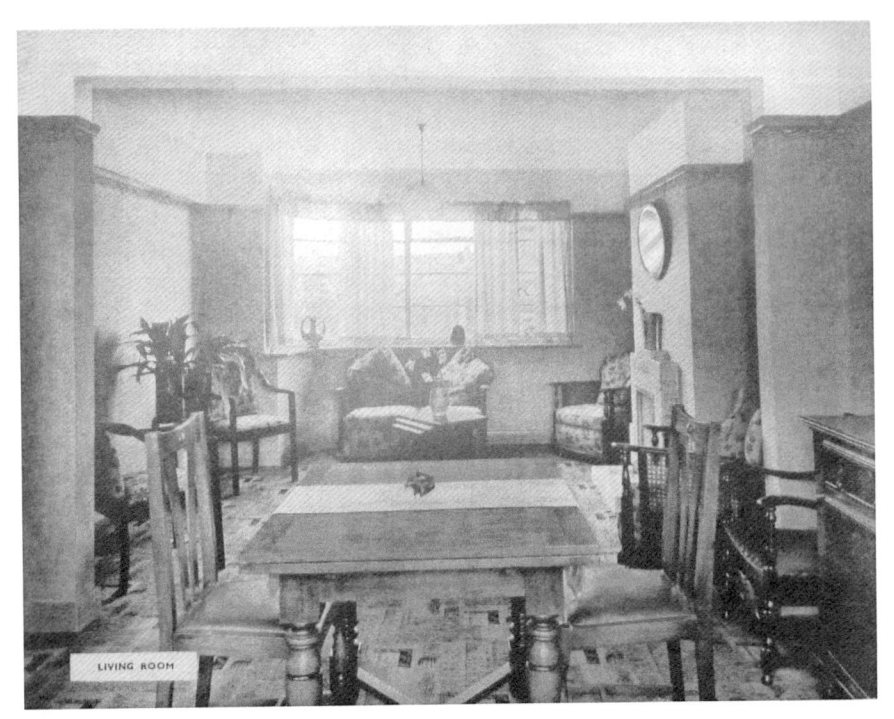

Fig. 7.3. A combined living/dining room arrangement demonstrated in a T. F. Nash show house

Source: T. F. Nash Ltd, 'Nash Houses', brochure (1938). Reproduced by kind permission of London Metropolitan Archives (LMA/4430/04/02/022).

---

[35] Worden, 'Furniture for the Living Room', 76.

[36] J. B. Jefferys, *Retail Trading in Britain: 1850–1950* (Cambridge: Cambridge University Press, 1954), 421.

dining chairs, often with upholstered seats; and the ubiquitous sideboard. It was in the sideboard that the styling of the suite found its most lavish expression, as this was generally seen as the room's principal status symbol. The sideboard was a storage unit of typically 4 ft–4 ft 6 in. in length, consisting of a varying, but usually symmetrical, combination of drawers and cupboards. It was designed to store dining crockery, cutlery, napkins, table mats, and other equipment, together with non-perishable foodstuffs such as biscuits. More expensive variants might also serve as a cocktail cabinet.

The sideboard replaced the dresser of the traditional kitchen/living room. It rapidly became an integral element of the servantless house, despite the fact that its dining-related contents might logically be better stored in the kitchen, where most would go for washing after use.[37] Indeed it was often used for more general storage purposes, especially in the combined dining/living room—where children's toys and games, household paperwork, and all manner of other small items might find their way there. Meanwhile its broad top also served as a display area for photographs, ornaments, and perhaps a clock or radio.

The three-piece suite was a particularly strong status symbol, as it indicated that the household both could afford its substantial cost and could live up to the aspirational lifestyle with which it was associated. It thus became emblematic of the transition from the traditional inner-urban terrace or rooms to the modern suburban semi. Bulky in size, luxurious in appearance, and comfortable for the user, it carried connotations of domesticity, leisure, and material affluence. Its design as a group of furniture was also very practical, as it could be arranged in a triangle around the hearth fire, providing good access for all members of the household (given the smaller size of the typical suburban family).

In council houses with only one reception room the bulky three-piece suite was often substituted by either two fireside chairs or a fireside chair and a partially upholstered settee of similar design.[38] In addition to taking up less space, such furniture was also less expensive, easier to clean, and could be added to as and when money became available. The need to economize on space in the new suburban houses (where individual room sizes were sometimes smaller than in traditional lower-middle-class housing) also led to a strong trend towards built-in furniture. Built-in units bundled up part of the cost of furnishing the house with the purchase price (thus offering repayment over 25 years, rather than the typical 4-year HP term), economized on space, and reduced housework—as they eliminated dust traps.[39]

Fitted kitchen furniture was particularly popular, pioneered by firms such as the Hygena Cabinet Co. More expensive houses sometimes provided elaborate built-in kitchens. For example, John Laing introduced a 'De Luxe' kitchen in some of their homes. This early form of fitted kitchen saved space via extensive use of 'Peerless'

---

[37] Worden, 'Furniture for the Living Room', 92.
[38] Worden, 'Furniture for the Living Room', 102.
[39] Lynne Constable, 'An Industry in Transition: The British Domestic Furniture Trade 1914–1939', PhD thesis (Brunel University, 2000), 136.

Fig. 7.4. A three-piece suite advertised by Catesbys of Tottenham Court Road for 15 guineas
Source: Catesbys, 'Easter Furnishings', brochure (n.d., 1930s), Peter Scott collection.

wall fitments, such as a drop-down or pull-out table with folding double seat at one side and a 'put-away' ironing board.[40] Another popular space-saving option was multifunctional furniture, such as the bed-settee, or chairs with built-in bookshelves or tables.

The piano remained an essential element of almost all middle-class homes until at least the late 1920s. In addition to its entertainment value, being able to play was considered an important social grace, especially for young women. In working-class households—where the piano had been a particularly expensive luxury in the

Fig. 7.5. Laing's 'De Luxe' kitchen, as illustrated in a 1935 estate brochure
Source: Northamptonshire Record Office, John Laing plc Archives, L/9/1/292, 'Laings Enfield West Estate: The Most Beautiful Estate in North London', brochure (November 1935), 6. Reproduced by kind permission of the Laing Charitable Trust.

---

[40] Northampton Record Office, John Laing plc Archives, L9/1/292, 'Laings Enfield West Estate: The Most Beautiful Estate in North London', brochure (November 1935).

Edwardian era—the picture was more mixed. Many interwar suburban families were content with a gramophone and, especially from the late 1920s, a radio. Radio sets became ubiquitous in suburban working-class houses during the 1930s, serving the piano's traditional function as the focal point of the living room.[41] In 1928 annual sales of pianos were still estimated to be as high as 100,000, yet gramophone sales were estimated at 500,000. By 1930 an estimated 600,000 radios were being purchased annually and in the following year annual sales jumped to 1.26 million.[42]

LABOUR-SAVING APPLIANCES IN LABOUR-SAVING HOMES

Interwar Britain witnessed a rapid diffusion of mains electricity, which was transformed from an expensive luxury to a 'necessity' for many families. Electricity prices fell from 6.5d per 'unit' (kilowatt-hour) in 1920 to 4d in 1923 and around 1.5d in 1938, while gas and coal prices actually rose in real terms. Meanwhile the installation costs of a modest electrical lighting system fell from £11–20 in 1919 to £7–8 by the late 1920s and £5–6 in the 1930s, while new housing estates proved significantly more economical to wire than single existing houses.[43] Prior to the 1926 Electricity Supply Act the high cost of wiring had deterred some councils from installing electricity in municipal estates; for example, a 1925 London County Council investigation found that electrical installations cost approximately £20 per house, while the gas companies charged only £1–3 for 'carcassing' homes for gas. Yet from the late 1920s most councils included both gas and electricity in new developments and some houses were retrospectively wired, while mains electricity was a standard feature of almost all new interwar owner-occupied suburban houses.[44]

Yet the rapid expansion in electricity supply was not matched by rapid diffusion of electrical appliances. Most wired working-class homes used electricity only for lighting plus, perhaps, a wireless set, clock, and domestic iron (the only widely diffused 'labour-saving' electrical appliance, having reached 77 per cent of wired homes by 1939). Less than 40 per cent of wired homes had vacuum cleaners, 27 per cent had electric fires (generally for supplementary heating), 16 per cent had kettles, 14 per cent

---

[41] Radio license statistics substantially underestimate the diffusion of radios, owing to license evasion; see Peter Scott, 'Patent Monopolies, Antitrust, and the Divergent Development Paths of the British and American Interwar Radio Equipment Industries', *Business History Review*, Table 1 (forthcoming).

[42] Sources: pianos and gramophones, see Alan A. Jackson, *The Middle Classes 1900–1950* (Nairn: David St John Thomas, 1991), 275–6; radios, Peter Scott, 'The Determinants of Competitive Success in the Interwar British Radio Industry', *Economic History Review*, 65 (2012), 1306, based on trade estimates.

[43] Leslie Hannah, *Electricity before Nationalisation: A Study of the Development of the Electricity Supply Industry in Britain to 1948* (London: Macmillan, 1979), 187; Peter Scott and James Walker, 'Power to the People: Working-Class Demand for Household Power in 1930s Britain', *Oxford Economic Papers*, 63 (2011), 600–1.

[44] Anne Glendenning, *Demons of Domesticity: Women and the English Gas Industry, 1889–1939* (Aldershot: Ashgate, 2004), 219–28.

had electric cookers (which were, in any case, widely considered inferior to their gas counterparts), and less than 5 per cent had wash boilers or electric water heaters.[45] This contrasts with the much more rapid diffusion of entertainment durables, such as the radio and gramophone. As a report on a Birmingham municipal estate noted: 'Almost every house has a wireless set which is being or has been paid for week by week. Even the poorest seem to regard a wireless set as something of a necessity.'[46]

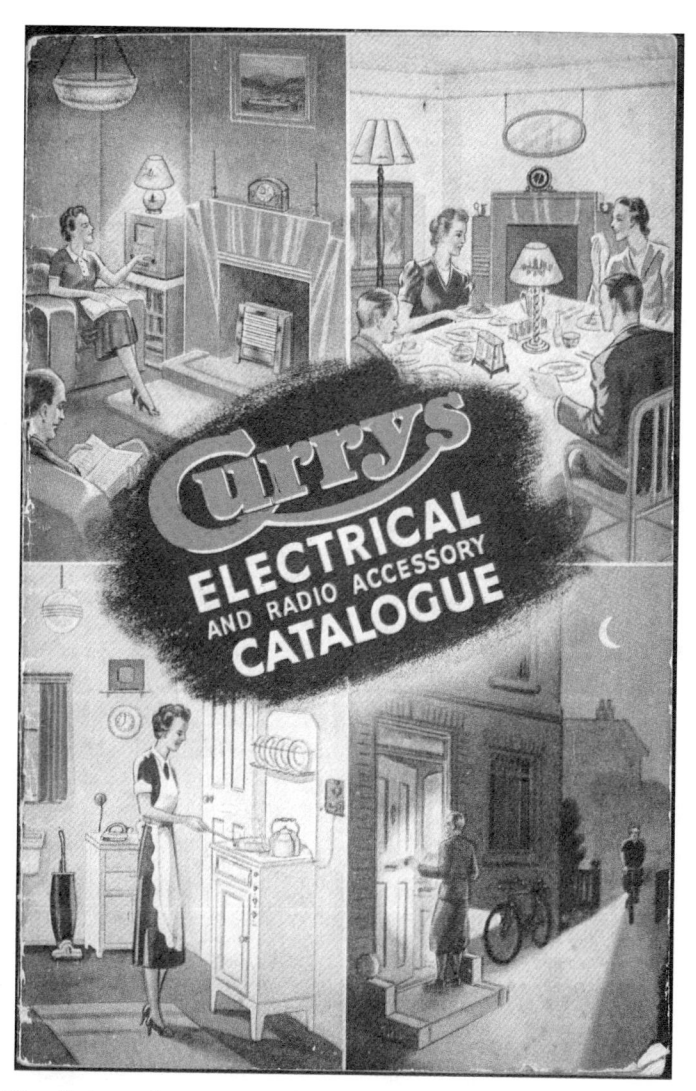

Fig. 7.6. The all-electric home, as promoted by Currys
Source: Currys Ltd, 'Currys Electrical and Radio Accessory Catalogue 1939–40' (1939), Peter Scott collection.

---

[45] Political and Economic Planning, *Report on the Supply of Electricity in Great Britain* (London: PEP, 1936), 84; Hannah, *Electricity before Nationalisation*, 208.
[46] Soutar, Wilkins, and Florence, *Nutrition and Size of Family*, 41.

Purchase costs for washing machines, fridges, or even vacuum cleaners were generally prohibitive for the working class and the lowest strata of the middle classes, given their other financial commitments, while power-hungry appliances such as electric fires had very high running costs. Many higher-income middle-class households were also reluctant to purchase the new labour-saving durables, preferring to employ someone to do the work for them. According to estimates by Elizabeth Roberts, 10.5 per cent of interwar mothers in Barrow, 18 per cent in Preston, and 18 per cent in Lancaster went out to do part-time work cleaning and/or washing.[47] The limited diffusion of electrical 'gadgets' was reflected in what appears, by modern standards, a rather parsimonious supply of power points in most 'wired' homes. While houses costing in excess of £1,000 were often generously supplied, a house bought for £500–700 in the mid-1930s, or a council house of the same period, might have power points only in the living and dining rooms, or even be limited to electric lighting.[48] Yet even houses with only electric lighting could use appliances such as electric irons and vacuum cleaners, via an adaptor fitted to the light socket.

Working-class housewives on new suburban estates were major participants in the interwar consumer durables revolution—though principally via built-in or installed, rather than plugged-in, appliances. In-built water heating, bathrooms, electric lighting, and modern cookers were typical of the facilities provided in both owner-occupied and, by the 1930s, local authority estates. These reduced the burden of housework both by cutting out much laborious work previously involved in heating water and then moving it around the house and by removing the soot created by coal fires and gas light.[49]

Built-in utilities, especially hot water systems and bathrooms, also represented a higher order of priority for most migrants in terms of their amenity value and social prestige. Bathrooms had begun to be introduced in significant numbers of new architecturally designed houses only in the 1870s. However, it was a decade or two before they constituted a typical feature of new middle-class speculative housing.[50] Yet the Edwardian era witnessed the rapid transformation of the bathroom from an innovation to a necessity in middle-class homes and the Tudor Walters council house of the early 1920s did much to popularize it among higher paid sections of the working classes. By the 1930s large numbers of working-class families had come to view the bathroom as a necessity, integral to new working-class notions of respectability that required regular bathing to ensure high standards of personal cleanliness.[51]

---

[47] Cited in Sue Bowden and Avner Offer, 'The Technological Revolution That Never Was: Gender, Class and the Diffusion of Household Appliances in Interwar England', in Victoria de Grazia and Ellen Furlough (eds), *The Sex of Things: Gender and Consumption in Historical Perspective* (Berkeley: University of California Press, 1996), 264.

[48] Gerald Carr, 'Lost Chances in New Houses', *Electrical Trading* (February 1937), 57–8.

[49] Lesley Whitworth, 'Men, Women, Shops, and "Little, Shiny Homes": The Consuming of Coventry 1930–1939', PhD thesis (University of Warwick, 1997), 227.

[50] John Burnett, *A Social History of Housing 1815–1885*, 2nd edn (London: Methuen, 1986), 214–15.

[51] Elizabeth Shove, *Comfort, Cleanliness and Convenience: The Social Organization of Normality* (Oxford: Berg, 2003), 100–6.

Manufacturers of electrical goods saw new suburban estates as particularly fertile ground and targeted much promotional effort at their occupiers and developers. In 1925 GEC opened a complete 'all-electric' show home for the public at their headquarters, Magnet House, in London's Kingsway. Later, in the 1930s, they printed a brochure, 'Electricity Sells Modern Houses', aimed at house-builders.[52] However, it was the suppliers of electrical power, and of gas, who were the chief players in the battle for the appliance budgets of new estate occupants. Each concern, whether a private company or a municipal undertaking, had a local monopoly over its own utility, but faced competition from the rival utility. Getting appliances into people's homes was seen as a key means of both increasing power sales and blocking competition. Electricity and gas undertakings thus became the most important retailers of power-hungry electrical appliances such as cookers, fires, wash-boilers, and fridges, often selling them at little or no profit in order to reap their main gain from increased power sales.

Electricity suppliers played a major role in promoting the concept of the professional housewife. Their advertising claimed that electrical appliances could take the hard work out of housework; allow women to reallocate their time towards motherhood and other 'caring' aspects of their housewife role; improve their standards of cleanliness and hygiene; and reduce their dependence on paid help.[53] For example, in the 1920s the Electrical Development Association (EDA) commissioned the propaganda film *Edward and Eda*, in which an engaged couple overcame the financial barriers to marriage by Eda volunteering to do her own housework, with the aid of electric labour-saving appliances, rather than employing a domestic servant.[54]

In reality, the economics of middle-class household management were not nearly as favourable to the new consumer durables as their marketing suggested. A 'daily', employed for three days a week or less, could be expected to take care of cleaning all rooms, washing the kitchen floor and tables, cleaning the doorsteps, polishing brass and silver, and doing the family's washing and ironing (possibly augmented by the use of a commercial laundry for items such as bed linen). This would leave the housewife with lighter tasks such as making beds, laying the fireplace, preparing (and washing up after) meals, tidying rooms, and shopping.[55]

In the mid-1930s monthly payments on a high-powered Hoover vacuum costing £20 would be around £1, while it would also incur power costs (claimed by Hoover in 1936 to be around a penny per hour).[56] A GEC electric washer and wringer cost about as much again, within minimum monthly payments of 18s 6d.

---

[52] Bodleian Library, Ms Marconi 3780, 'The "Magnet" Electric Home at Magnet House, Kingway, London', GEC brochure (1925); 'Electricity Sells Modern Houses', GEC brochure (reprinted May 1934).
[53] Bowden and Offer, 'Technological Revolution that Never Was', 266.
[54] Hannah, *Electricity before Nationalisation*, 204.   [55] Jackson, *Middle Classes*, 118.
[56] Peter Scott collection, Hoover Ltd, 'On Judging a Vacuum Cleaner', leaflet (n.d., c.1936).

A more prestigious Hotpoint electric washer/wringer cost £1 3s 10d monthly over 2 years, while a model that also included an ironer would cost £1 13s 3d per month.[57] Both were power-hungry and would thus have substantially higher electricity costs than the Hoover. Total monthly costs of substituting even the daily's core cleaning and washing/ironing tasks would therefore amount to over 45s per month (including an allowance for maintenance) for the first 2 years. After this they would fall considerably, though depreciation had to be factored in, given their short expected lifespans (6–8 years for vacuum cleaners).[58]

The same outlay could fund around 55 hours' work by a daily (paid around 10d per hour) each month, or just over 12 hours per week.[59] Meanwhile her services had a number of major advantages. She would do the tasks in their entirety, while washing, wringing, and ironing clothes remained a laborious chore for the housewife even with the aid of the available primitive electric machinery. She was also much more flexible—both in the range of tasks she could do and in the number of hours worked. When finances were tight, her services could be reduced or dispensed with, while HP payments had to be met—if the public disgrace of repossession and a county court summons was to be avoided.[60] Employing a daily also had more positive social connotations, in an era when middle-class status was still commonly associated with having servants, while the vacuum cleaner under the stairs or the electric washer/wringer in the kitchen were hardly well-located from the perspective of impressing the neighbours.

Electrical appliances thus required active marketing ('pushing') to a public characterized by strong consumer inertia and indifference. One of the most important arenas for this was the building estate show house, where suppliers used methods similar to those of the furniture retailers. Electricity suppliers were keen to foster good relations with estate builders. As a representative of London's Northmet company told his electricity industry colleagues:

> Areas with new housing developments will know the value of keeping in close contact with the builders, who usually provide a furnished show house on each estate. We can help the builder to sell the houses by floodlighting the show house and the illumination of his advertising signs and boards. In turn, we can expect co-operation on his part to take the form of a representative display of electrical appliances installed in each show house in surroundings similar to those in the house of the prospective purchaser.[61]

Gas suppliers (which were in fierce competition with electrical concerns) similarly sought to get their products into builders' show houses.[62] Like the electricity concerns,

---

[57] Peter Scott, collection, GEC, 'GEC Household Electrical Appliances', brochure (1936), 29; Hotpoint, ' "Monday I Wash": A Book of Practical Information based on Tested Methods' (1935).
[58] 'The Replacement Market', *Electrical Trading* (March 1938), 69.
[59] Elizabeth Craig, *Keeping House with Elizabeth Craig* (London: Collins, 1936), 203.
[60] See Scott, 'Twilight World of Hire Purchase.'
[61] Manchester Museum of Science and Industry, ESI 73, British Electrical Development Association, Report on Electricity Supply Sales Managers Conference London, 31 January–2 February 1938. Paper on 'Planned Selling' by G. E. Barrett (Northmet), 59–80.
[62] Glendenning, *Demons of Domesticity*, 269.

they installed appliances in show houses free of charge, often aiming to cram in 'as many…as are practicable for display purposes.'[63] Having a salesman at the show house provided an excellent opportunity to canvass not only prospective estate occupants, but visitors who were looking round with no real intention to move there. Given that on a pleasant weekend several hundred people might visit an estate, this arrangement proved particularly attractive. Gas undertakings might even provide cookery demonstrators for a week when the estate became more than half-completed, something welcomed by the builder, as it constituted an extra visitor attraction.[64]

Gas undertakings regularly advertised in the registers and guides prepared by the larger firms of estate agents, in return for which they received regular (often weekly) lists of names and addresses of customers who had been sold or let properties by the agency—which were then used for canvassing. Close cooperation with agents and builders also enabled them to lobby developers not to omit flues from living and sleeping rooms (without which some gas apparatus would have been impossible to install).[65] Stretford and District Gas Board even went so far as to make their advertising expertise available to speculative builders, assisting them with copy and design.[66]

Direct financial incentives were also offered; for example, Bournemouth Gas and Water Co. gave speculative builders a trade discount of 15 per cent on the cost of apparatus sold to house purchasers, in return for recommending them to install gas appliances.[67] Financial incentives for occupiers could also influence builders' decisions. Stretford and District Gas Board varied the service charge for supplying gas to a new estate according to the number of appliances installed—houses with extensive appliances having much lower service charges than those with only basic fittings. This encouraged builders to provide gas as the only cooking fuel and, in houses costing below £450, this policy succeeded in persuading builders not to install kitchen coal ranges as standard.[68] Both gas and electricity concerns typically offered appliances to householders on HP and/or hire terms. These were usually more generous than those of the furniture companies, since utility concerns were primarily interested in expanding power usage rather than in making direct profits from appliance sales.

Speculative developers had to balance the enticements of competing utility providers against the demands of their customers, while local authorities had to consider the political influence of each supplier (one, but very rarely both, of which might be municipally owned). An increasingly common solution was to provide both. A survey of new house-building during 1935 found that only 4.2 per cent of all houses (and less than 7 per cent of private sector houses) were all-electric,

---

[63] J. Harwood, 'Selling Gas Apparatus on New Building Estates', British Commercial Gas Association, *Gas Bulletin*, 33 (January 1934), 40.
[64] Harwood, 'Selling Gas Apparatus', 41.
[65] P. G. C. Moon, 'How We Do Our Local Publicity', British Commercial Gas Association, *Gas Bulletin*, 30 (July 1930), 124–6.
[66] Harwood, 'Selling Gas Apparatus', 41.
[67] Moon, 'How We Do Our Local Publicity', 124–6.
[68] Harwood, 'Selling Gas Apparatus', 40–1.

Fig. 7.7. 'Gas Fires on Hire' promotion by the Liverpool Gas Company
Source: Liverpool Gas Co., 'Gas Fires on Hire', brochure (n.d., c.1930s). Peter Scott collection.

though 38 per cent (or 55 per cent of private sector houses) were all-electric with the exception of cooking. Meanwhile 98.5 per cent of houses in the survey were wired for electric lighting.[69]

[69] Political and Economic Planning (PEP), *Report on the Supply of Electricity in Great Britain* (London: PEP, 1936), 78.

Yet even in the new suburbs the coal range still played a central role in the domestic routines of many households. A survey of sixty-two interwar London housing estates (both council and private) encompassing over 12,500 separate dwellings found that 84 per cent of houses were arranged for some cooking to be done in the living room, using a range or combination coal grate. Meanwhile 87 per cent of these houses had no hot water supply other than the coal range or copper.[70] Using a coal range created a good deal of additional housework, not only in attending to the fire (which could take up at least an hour a day, where ranges were used for cooking and heating), but in the extra work entailed in cooking in the living room and doing food preparation and washing up in the scullery.[71] Yet coal had clear cost advantages—Political and Economic Planning (PEP) calculated that the cost per useful therm of fuel for heating, for a family of four, was 1s 0.5d for coal (8.5d for anthracite), 1s 6d for gas, and 1s 9d for electricity.[72] Meanwhile another PEP report estimated that the all-in cost of hot water generation over 10 years (including installation, maintenance, and fuel) in 1938 would have been 3s 2.5d per week for a coal-fired back boiler, compared to minimum sums of 3s 9.5d for gas and 4s 11d for electricity.[73] Thus it is hardly surprising that a major 1942 survey found that only 2 per cent of households on annual incomes under £300 used electric water heating for baths, while only 18 per cent used gas to heat bath water.[74]

It is not clear whether the new appliances really transformed women's lives—at least from the perspective of the amount of time spent on household tasks. Judy Giles argues that, even when available, new labour-saving appliances did not reduce the aggregate time typically spent on housework, but instead shifted activity from functional to 'cosmetic' cleaning tasks. In other words activities such as washing windows, polishing furniture, cleaning floors, and scrubbing external sills and paths were done more often than was necessary for the removal of dirt. Her interviewees note the social importance attached to cleaning, which was felt to be the most rigorous criterion of a 'good housewife'. Cleaning (particularly tasks involving the exterior of the house, such as window cleaning and step whitening) were highly visible and acted as a yardstick by which the housewife's work could be assessed against accepted standards, in communities where a woman's status could be determined 'by as little as the condition of her windows'.[75]

CONCLUSION

Interwar retailers of furniture and household appliances found common cause with speculative developers in selling a new consumer universe of aspirational suburban

---

[70] PEP, *Report on the Gas Industry in Great Britain* (London: PEP, 1939), 86.
[71] PEP, *The Market for Household Appliances* (London: PEP, 1945), 37.
[72] PEP, *Report on the Gas Industry*, 80.
[73] PEP, *Market for Household Appliances*, 146. Gas and electricity costs varied substantially according to the systems used.
[74] PEP, *Market for Household Appliances*, 157.
[75] Margaret Judith Giles, 'Something That Bit Better: Working-Class Women, Domesticity, and "Respectability", 1919–1939', DPhil thesis (University of York, 1989), 233.

living to the lower middle and working classes. Each had much to learn from the marketing techniques used by the others and builders were able to develop successful cross-promotion strategies with suppliers of household durables, which were exhibited in their estate show houses and advertised in their brochures.

From the household's perspective, furniture generally assumed much greater importance than appliances. In 1938 the social research organization Mass Observation asked 200 of its volunteer observers (predominantly lower middle class, with a significant proportion of skilled working-class people) about the main drawbacks in their everyday lives.[76] Some 18 per cent of men and 31 per cent of women mentioned the lack of electrical appliances (excluding radios and gramophones, which were categorized separately). Yet in response to the question 'What would you do with an extra £100 a year?', such appliances were given top priority by only 3 per cent of both male and female respondents.[77]

With the exception of entertainment durables such as the radio and gramophone, furniture was far more visible than most appliances (which tended to be clustered around the kitchen). It also had fewer close substitutes, while electrical appliances could be substituted by older, cheaper, mechanical versions (such as the carpet sweeper for the vacuum cleaner, or the larder for the fridge). They could also be substituted by labour—the housewife's own, that of a daily, or the use of an external agency (such as a commercial laundry). In practice the housewife's own labour was most commonly used—in an era when, in most localities, women generally ceased paid employment on marriage—with perhaps a few hours' assistance from a char lady to spare the middle-class housewife from heavy work.

Like the house itself, its durables were available on 'easy' credit terms, typically spread over 4 years for furniture and around 5–7 years for some expensive installed appliances marketed by electricity supply undertakings. This provided an effective means of acquiring expensive durables, but at very high interest rates (typically in the region of 25 per cent or more for furniture).[78] As such, these extra elements of the suburban dream acted to further squeeze budgets and raise the costs of the new life—which had to be met through sacrifices in areas such as holidays, commercial entertainment, food, and numbers of children.

---

[76] Mass Observation Archive, File Report A10, 'Reactions to Advertising', December 1938.

[77] It appears that respondents wrote in their top priorities, rather than being presented with a range of options. Electrical equipment ranked 13th in order of first priorities, as categorized in the report.

[78] Scott, 'Mr Drage', 813.

8
The Suburban Garden

> The garden was not cultivated then, as this was a new estate, but what plans we made. We would have a lawn surrounded by flowers in front. At the back, another lawn with a vegetable garden beyond. We knew nothing about gardening, and neither did our neighbours... If you have never had a garden, or if you had never seen fruit and vegetables grow in a garden, then you might get some idea of the pride and joy one feels when one digs up one's first potato, beetroot or carrot.
>
> Grace Foakes, who moved from an inner-London tenement flat to the LCC's Becontree Estate in 1932.[1]

INTRODUCTION

Gardens were not common in most Victorian towns and cities. In northern Britain most small houses lacked gardens even in the suburbs, while for larger urban houses front gardens were generally more common than rear gardens. However, there were exceptions to this broad national pattern; for example, garden provision was much more common on the outskirts of East Anglian towns, even for small houses.[2] Interwar Britain witnessed the dawn of gardening as a major national passion for all classes of society. Some four million new gardens were established, most for houses occupied by working- or lower-middle-class families.[3] There were also probably at least as many new gardeners, as the small proportion of gardens left untended were counterbalanced by households where several members of the family shared in the gardening. Gardening became Britain's most popular leisure pursuit, establishing a tradition of mass amateur gardening, which still endures despite the vastly increased range of pastimes now available to the descendents of the interwar working- and lower-middle-class garden pioneers.

The introduction of 'daylight saving' in 1916, together with a national move to a 48-(or fewer) hour week in 1919 for industrial workers—reducing the average working week by around 13 per cent—acted to substantially extend the amount of

---

[1] Grace Foakes, *My Life with Reubin* (London: Shepheard-Walwyn, 1975), 38.
[2] Stefan Muthesius, *The English Terraced House* (New Haven, CT: Yale University Press, 1982), 75–6.
[3] Brad Beaven, *Leisure, Citizenship, and Working-Class Men in Britain 1850–1945* (Manchester: Manchester University Press, 2005), 137–8.

free daylight time available to the typical manual worker. White-collar workers experienced a similar reduction in working hours, typically finishing work an hour earlier each day.[4] The absence of traditional working-class community-based leisure outlets, such as pubs and working men's clubs, in the vicinity of many suburban estates also encouraged people to turn to gardening as a means of spending their free time which avoided lengthy journeys.

Jackson found that suburban London semis priced below around £900 typically had standard rectangular gardens 80–200 ft long and 20–40 ft wide.[5] Municipal estates were built at somewhat higher densities, thus compressing garden space; 54 per cent of back gardens on the LCC's Becontree, Roehampton, and Watling estates were 20–30 ft, and 44 per cent 12–20 ft, in length.[6] However, many provincial council estates had much more generous gardens, as shown in the aerial view of part of Nottingham's Aspley Estate in Figure 8.1. Back gardens were integrated into the aesthetics and functioning of the house. Most suburban houses were developed so that the back garden was easily visible from the most frequently used rooms, the living room usually being placed at the back for this reason. Owner-occupied houses often had French doors from the living room to the back garden, while the kitchen typically had a window facing the rear of the property, so that mothers could keep a watchful eye on their children.[7]

Families were often attracted to suburban estates by their semi-rural settings. Migrants were all too familiar with the health problems of urban living. The typical interwar industrial town suffered from very poor air quality and severe pollution. Solid impurities in the air above central London, for example, fell to earth at the rate of 475 tons per square mile per annum, Westminster being covered by heavy smoke for a third of the year.[8] Given the prevalence of tuberculosis and other respiratory diseases, particularly among the working classes, the health benefits of a suburban house were a high priority for large numbers of urban families. Road traffic was also a significant danger in towns, at a time when road safety was in its infancy. Deaths on Britain's roads peaked at 7,305 in 1930 (compared to only 1,850 in 2010).[9]

Yet contemporary social investigators also noted that semi-rural living was popular in its own right. As a report on Manchester's Wythenshawe estate noted, 'The rural atmosphere of the estate, the park, the grass and trees, and the general atmosphere of peace and quiet are a constant source of pleasure to numbers who are living there, and many expressions of this pleasure were made known to the

---

[4] See Peter Scott and Anna Spadavecchia, 'Did the 48-Hour Week Damage Britain's Industrial Competitiveness?', *Economic History Review*, 64 (2011).

[5] Alan A. Jackson, *Semi-Detached London: Suburban Development, Life, and Transport, 1900–39*, 2nd edn (Didcot: Wild Swan, 1991), 124.

[6] Andrzej Olechnowicz, *Working Class Housing in England between the Wars: The Becontree Estate* (Oxford: Oxford University Press, 1997), 209.

[7] Georgina E. Couch, 'The Cultural Geography of the Suburban Garden: Landscape and Life History in Nottingham, c.1920–1970', PhD thesis (University of Nottingham, 2004), 151.

[8] Paul Oliver, 'The Galleon on the Front Door', in Paul Oliver, Ian Davis, and Ian Bentley, *Dunroamin: The Suburban Semi and its Enemies* (London: Pimlico, 1981), 155.

[9] Sources: British Road Federation, *Basic Road Statistics: Great Britain* (London: British Road Federation, 1950), 9; Department for Transport, *Reported Road Casualties in Great Britain: Main Results 2010: Statistical Release* (London: National Statistics, 2011), 1.

The Suburban Garden 177

Fig. 8.1. Aerial view of the Minver Crescent section of Nottingham's Aspley municipal estate, *c.*1930

Source: Courtesy of Nottingham City Council and <http://www.picturethepast.org.uk>.

investigators.'[10] A similar preference for rural surroundings emerges strongly from life history accounts. As a London postal worker who moved to an owner-occupied estate in Sidcup recalled, their house

> was right in the country... Behind us was a big market garden which grew all kinds of vegetables and flowers. One big mass of flowers most of the spring... And all around here it was just bluebells, wood, streams, kids, frogs, and... there was always hedgehogs in the garden and we had an owl who used to sit on the lamppost, a gas lamp used to be outside here, and every night an owl used to sit on it and go woop, woop, woop... and there was pigs just round the back and often they used to get out of the pens... there was no houses, nothing, it was all open... Often you'd go out in the back garden... and you'd find a big pig wandering around.[11]

---

[10] Manchester and Salford Better Housing Council, *The Report of an Investigation on Wythenshawe* (Manchester: privately published, 1935), 14–15.

[11] Museum of London Archives, material collected for Gavin Weightman and Steve Humphries, *The Making of Modern London 1914–1939* (London: Sidgwick & Jackson, 1984), interview with G.R. Matthews.

Fig. 8.2. The rural charms of suburban living, as depicted by Charles Paine for London Underground in 1929
Source: Reproduced courtesy of London Transport Museum.

A wish to move closer to the countryside was part of a broader interwar passion for rural activities on the part of city-dwellers that encompassed pastimes such as motor and coach touring, cycling, hiking, camping, and mountaineering. For example, there were estimated to be over half a million hikers in Britain by the late 1930s, while the recently formed youth hostels movement encompassed four associations with 107,000 members.[12] Suburban gardens brought what many families saw as the 'countryside' right to their door, while also providing a sense of 'ownership' over their own little patch of British soil in which to grow produce, flowers, or lawn (or, commonly, all three).

---

[12] Harvey Taylor, *A Claim on the Countryside: A History of the British Outdoor Movement* (Edinburgh: Keele University Press, 1997), 252.

GARDENS IN MUNICIPAL SUBURBIA

Gardens had perhaps the largest social impacts on municipal tenants. Most had migrated from houses lacking gardens and had no previous experience of gardening. Meanwhile, their typically lower incomes, compared to working-class owner-occupiers, led them to highly prize access to this low-cost leisure and food resource. As an early migrant to Liverpool's Larkhill estate recalled, 'Arthur loved the garden. I hardly saw him the first year we moved in, he was out in the garden all hours. You see, our generation had never had gardens, before the First World War, everyone came from a terrace house with just a little back yard.'[13]

George Cadbury had ensured that houses on his pioneering Bourneville model workers' village came with large gardens (averaging one-eighth of an acre), as he viewed gardening as a preferable evening pastime to the public house.[14] Many councils were motivated by a similar philosophy. Some, such as Nottingham, invested considerably both in gardens and in shrubberies, greens, recreational areas, and trees, to create an attractive environment for their estates.[15] Nottingham Corporation ran annual gardening competitions for its tenants with prizes of up to £2, plus a silver cup for the first prizewinner (held for one year), together with a miniature silver replica for them to keep permanently.[16] Liverpool's Housing Committee also encouraged tenant garden competitions, in a belief that working-class moral standards would be improved if leisure time was spent in the garden rather than in the public house.[17] Similarly, Bristol Corporation viewed the provision of gardens on municipal estates as a major moral regenerator, a well-kept garden being an important marker of a good tenant.[18] In Birmingham both the council and estate community associations organized gardening competitions.[19]

The encouragement of gardening has been described as the interwar council estate's most important contribution to modifying working-class leisure.[20] Very few inner-city houses of the type municipal tenants typically moved from had gardens. Backyards, often in communal use, hosted outside toilets, coal houses, and, sometimes, washing facilities, while providing a storage area for a variety of

---

[13] Madeline McKenna, 'The Development of Suburban Council Housing Estates in Liverpool between the Wars', PhD thesis (University of Liverpool, 1986), 383.

[14] Mark Swenarton, *Homes Fit for Heroes: The Politics and Architecture of Early State Housing in Britain* (Gateshead: Heinemann, 1981), 8.

[15] Couch, 'Cultural Geography', 88.

[16] Couch, 'Cultural Geography', 126–7.

[17] Margaret Judith Giles, 'Something That Bit Better: Working-Class Women, Domesticity, and "Respectability", 1919–1939', DPhil thesis (University of York, 1989), 215; McKenna, 'Development of Suburban Council Housing Estates', 89.

[18] Madge Dresser, 'Housing Policy in Bristol, 1919–30', in Martin J. Daunton (ed.), *Councillors and Tenants: Local Authority Housing in English Cities, 1919–1939* (Leicester: Leicester University Press, 1984), 207.

[19] '"Manors from Heaven": The Municipal Housing Boom and the Challenge of Community Building on a New Estate, 1929–1939', *Suburban Birmingham* website, <http://www.suburbanbirmingham.org.uk/spaces/housing-essay.htm>.

[20] Olechnowicz, *Working Class Housing*, 208–9.

items that could not be conveniently kept within their small rooms. As the London postal worker quoted earlier recalled, as a child:

> First, we lived in the Old Kent Road in a rented house and there was seven children upstairs and seven children downstairs...Well it was purgatory actually. There was one toilet down in the yard. And eh, the old boy down below worked in the gas company down at Old Kent Road, and if he got in the toilet first with his dirty old pipe on, reading the paper...you'd have four or five kids all waiting outside all trying to go to the toilet.[21]

The carrot of competitions and other encouragement was matched by the stick of council regulations designed to protect the municipality's housing investment. All councils made looking after the garden a condition of tenancy and tenants were often banned from keeping poultry or pigeons. Yet, while some tenants may have wished to keep more livestock than was permitted, the majority were keen to cultivate their own little patch of land. The garden ranks highest on the positive features of new housing mentioned in Life History Database testimonies, for both municipal tenants and owner-occupiers (see Table 3.3). A similar appreciation of tenants' new gardens was also highlighted by contemporary investigators.

Manchester's Housing Director reported in 1933 that only 50 tenants out of 20,000 had neglected their gardens, and over 12 years only six notices to quit had been served for 'non-cultivation of garden', plus a further ten for 'arrears of rent and non-cultivation of garden'.[22] Some 90 per cent of 430 Wythenshawe householders, interviewed in 1934, stated they appreciated their gardens.[23] Similarly some 49 per cent of gardens on three large LCC out-county estates, surveyed by Mass Observation between August 1941 and April 1942, were classified as 'well-kept', while only 17 per cent were classified as 'neglected'.[24] Enthusiasm for gardens was also strong among slum clearance tenants; as a report on York's Huntington Road estate, produced for Rowntree's *Poverty and Progress* survey, noted:

> tenants...have been drawn from slum clearance areas...They are mostly in poor circumstances, a large number being either unemployed or on casual labour. Despite this, both homes and gardens are generally well kept, the latter especially. An arrangement has been made whereby, by the payment of a few pence per week, tenants can obtain garden tools from the Corporation, and the Parks Superintendent gives demonstrations and advice for free.[25]

A 1939 Birmingham municipal estate survey found that tenants were generally keener on maintaining their materially useful back gardens than their ornamental front gardens: 'while the back garden is regarded as an asset because of its [food] product and its use for sitting in, the front garden is definitely a liability which

---

[21] Museum of London Archives, material collected for Weightman and Humphries, *Making of Modern London*, interview with G. R. Matthews.
[22] Olechnowicz, *Working Class Housing*, 210.
[23] Manchester and Salford Better Housing Council, *Report of an Investigation*, 14.
[24] Mass Observation, *An Enquiry into People's Homes* (London: John Murray, 1943), 167.
[25] Borthwick Institute, York, Rowntree Archive, PP2/1. 'Report on Huntington Road No. 1 Estate, York', 24 August 1935.

must be kept up for appearances' sake'. Yet it noted that, while there were examples of gardens left untended:

> on the whole the people are interested in and proud of their gardens. Several of the newer tenants interviewed were fully conscious of the value of the garden. Having themselves been brought up in the centre of the city they laid great store by their patch of grass and felt that it was a great advantage for their children to grow up in such open and green surroundings.[26]

Marion Fitzgerald's 1939 survey of Brighton's three Moulsecoomb municipal estates produced similar findings. Back gardens were cultivated almost without exception; many tenants grew vegetables, some having erected greenhouses to produce tomatoes in the hope that sales might augment family budgets during times of slack work. Conversely, she found that front gardens were relatively neglected, a problem exacerbated by the council's unwillingness to provide fencing (despite charging particularly high rents). Tenants' attempts to provide their own fencing were often rather ramshackle, though they did at least serve to 'keep children and dogs out'.[27]

GARDENING IN OWNER-OCCUPIED SUBURBIA

Rural settings were a major attraction for house purchasers. As Mrs Morton, who moved out with her husband to the Middlesex suburb of Eastcote in 1934 (purchasing a newly built semi on the Eastcote Park Estate for £850), recalled, they were initially put off by the distance from central London and the long walk from the train station. Nevertheless, their first site of the estate won them over:

> All the trees were in leaf, the houses that they had finished on the approach to the Estate were double fronted detached ones...[By the time they reached the show house] I was getting thrilled with the idea, it could have been ten miles from the station, I wanted to come and live on Eastcote Park. It's so funny because all the time I had the garden that I was going to make in my mind...we looked over the house and I looked at the back garden first almost before I looked at the house. Because it was the garden I wanted, it was such a nice shape, no corners, rectangle and quite big enough for me.[28]

Developers sought to capitalize on the power of greenery and gardens to sell houses. A brochure for Costain's Croham Heights estate in South Croydon—offering houses priced from £800 to £950—had a front cover showing the view of open country from the estate, rather than the houses, and devoted the first two pages of

---

[26] M. S. Soutar, E. H. Wilkins, and P. Sargant Florence, *Nutrition and Size of Family: Report on a New Housing Estate—1939, Prepared for the Birmingham Social Survey Committee* (London: George Allen & Unwin, 1942), 13.

[27] Marion Fitzgerald, *Rents in Moulsecoomb: A Report on Rents and Other Costs of Living in Three Brighton Housing Estates* (Brighton: Southern Publishing, 1939), 21.

[28] Museum of London archives, material collected for Weightman and Humphries, *Making of Modern London*, interview with Mrs Morton.

text to singing the praises of its rural situation. It was even claimed that the estate had been 'especially recommended by physicians as being equally beneficial [to the seaside] by reason of the chalk subsoil and average altitude of 500 feet' and that many residents 'have testified as to their improved health, and in some cases complete recovery from serious illness since living in Croham Heights.'[29]

Costain also pointed to attractive gardens already established on their estates as examples of what might be achieved. As a circular to potential visitors to their Rylands estate in Dagenham began:

> You will find clean paved roads when you visit Rylands, and work progressing in the gardens of early occupied houses, getting ready for spring. There is still time for you to do this, and become the possessor of your own home for the small cash payment of £15. If you make your call this week-end you can be sure of one of the large gardens, and get to work in it before you move in. If you have not sufficient loose cash ready at the moment the reservation can be made for a £1, and the balance easily saved before you move in.[30]

Yet neither speculative nor municipal developers generally extended their activities to garden preparation—other than basic provision of paths, boundary fences, and walls. Moreover the topsoil was often buried under sub-soil excavated for the house's foundation, plus builder's rubble. The months and years following the move into a newly built house thus represented the greatest challenge for new gardeners, who were often faced with back-breaking work to get their gardens into shape. Potatoes were thus a popular first crop, well-known for their properties of breaking up the soil and bringing stones to the surface. Estate landscaping was also often rather basic. G. W. Mitchell acknowledged Wimpey's relative neglect of garden preparation:

> I agree [about] the importance of shrubbery and trees. On some of our latter estates we ran a front garden competition, giving a prize, so as to induce people to enter for it and get their front gardens looking well; and, at Barn Hill only I think, we paid a contractor about £3 a house to plant trees and do the front gardens before we sold them. Comben and Wakeling (who are very skilled in this) always tried to get an open green or 'feature' at the entrance to any new estate; they immediately planted this before they started to build, almost walled it in so that no one could damage it, and paid immense attention to getting it into something like shape by the time they were prepared to start selling houses.[31]

Laing's carefully planned their estates to incorporate landscaping—through preserving existing trees and taking advantage of natural features. Central gardens were also included in the layouts of some estates, such as their Golders Green development. Laing's provided privet hedges (new occupants being issued with leaflets on how to look after them) and ran gardening competitions on some

---

[29] Richard Costain & Sons Ltd, 'Croham Heights, South Croydon', undated brochure, c.1927.
[30] Richard Costain & Sons Ltd, circular letter re. Rylands Estate, Dagenham (n.d., 1930s).
[31] Circa Trust, George Wimpey archives, G. W. Mitchell, letter file. Comments by G. W. Mitchell on E. V. Collins, 'Interim Report Concerning Speculative House Construction', 1 May 1944.

Fig. 8.3. A depiction of the ideal house set in the ideal garden on the front cover of E. L. Berg's 1936 'Ideal Home' brochure
Source: Peter Scott collection.

estates.[32] Competitions were seen as a valuable means of encouraging early purchasers to maintain attractive gardens, thus increasing the appeal to potential buyers who visited at later stages of development. As the builder F. J. C. Ingram wrote to his new householders:

---

[32] Roy Coad, *Laing. A Biography of Sir John W. Laing, CBE (1879–1978)* (London: Hodder & Stoughton, 1979), 107.

Dear Sir or Madam.

From time to time as I walk along Walmington Fold I cannot help feeling how the Estate has benefited by work put in on front gardens by Purchasers. To further this and at the same time create a little interest and friendship amongst the residents on the Estate, I am offering three prizes in the Spring, and three prizes in the Summer for the best front gardens[33]

Prizes of £1, £2, and £3 were offered, based on a points system which awarded 5 potential points for the lawn and maintenance, 5 for general layout and upkeep, 5 for colour schemes, and 5 for the quality of blooms. Mindful of the strained finances of some purchasers, Ingram added that they had given only a quarter of potential points to blooms, 'so that the least expensive garden is quite likely to take a prize.'[34] Estate garden competitions appear to have been very popular, while for the keenest gardeners local horticultural shows, with prizes for flowers, fruit, vegetables, and home-made food such as preserves, provided a broader stage for their competitive instincts.

SOURCES OF INFORMATION, ADVICE, AND EQUIPMENT

A shared enthusiasm for gardening fostered one of the most successful social institutions on new estates—gardening clubs—which sometimes constituted an estate's only active social organization. On Manchester's municipal Anson estate a gardening society was formed by tenants as early as 1922. By 1932 there were just under 200 members, on an estate of over 800 houses, paying an annual subscription of 2s 6d. Another Manchester municipal estate, Ladybarn, had almost 400 members out of a residential population of around 4,750, with an annual turnover from the sale of seeds, equipment, etc., of over £100. The staff of Manchester Corporation Parks Department assisted municipal estate gardening societies with advice, lectures, and by acting as judges for estate flower shows and gardening competitions.[35]

Georgina Couch found that around one quarter of gardeners on Nottingham's Aspley municipal estate joined gardening clubs or societies, while just over a third of gardeners in two owner-occupied Nottingham suburbs were members.[36] Gardening clubs served a number of functions, including the provision of advice, sharing of equipment, and facilitating exchanges of plants and seeds. Couch found that Nottingham municipal tenants virtually all shared cuttings, produce, advice, or tools with neighbours, reflecting their strong sense of community (and, presumably,

---

[33] Barnet Local Studies and Archives Centre, circular letter to house purchasers, F. J. C. Ingram, developer of 'Woodside Park Garden Suburb', 1 December 1931.

[34] Barnet Local Studies and Archives Centre, circular letter to house purchasers, F. J. C. Ingram, developer of 'Woodside Park Garden Suburb', 1 December 1931.

[35] Frances Thompson, 'A Study of the Development of Facilities for Recreation and Leisure Occupation on New Housing Estates, with Special Reference to Manchester', Diploma in Social Studies dissertation (University of Manchester, 1937), 57–8.

[36] Couch, 'Cultural Geography', 298.

their greater financial imperative to pool resources). Meanwhile in private Nottingham estates gardeners regularly swapped materials and advice (though less commonly than their municipal counterparts) while sharing tools and produce was less usual. Some local garden associations purchased tools specifically for loaning to members, while further reducing gardeners' costs via the collective purchase of seeds and compost. Such arrangements were particularly important on council estates, where the costs of equipping the household with a range of basic garden tools might otherwise prove problematic.

Councils also provided direct advice to tenants on garden maintenance and cultivation—to encourage good standards, to show how gardens could be developed on limited budgets, and to foster some degree of conformity in design. A 1934 tenants' handbook for the LCC's Bellingham and Downham estates advised that 'a garden can be made to look attractive by the expenditure of a few shillings annually', and that, for summer competitions, gardens should be 'as full of successful blooming plants as possible... suitably arranged to cover every possible available space.' However, they were cautioned to avoid an 'artificial effect. Boarded edging and concrete paths do not give the restful effect of turf with neatly trimmed edges.'[37] Meanwhile, fencing was subject to tighter regulation—being limited to 2 ft or less in height and to light wood creosoted or painted dark brown.

Contemporary social surveys and the Life Histories Database emphasize the prevalence of both neighbourly cooperation and sharing in gardening (via both clubs and informal arrangements between neighbours), which appears at odds with the general pattern of restraint and keeping yourself to yourself emphasized in these sources for other areas of neighbourly relations. Yet, as Andrzej Olechnowicz noted, the popularity of such clubs partly reflected the fact that they facilitated, rather than replaced, privatized leisure.[38] Neighbourly cooperation also mitigated the risks of neighbours neglecting their gardens to such an extent that this lowered the tone of the street. A Mass Observation study of a Bolton municipal estate noted that differences in gardening standards could become a source of conflict—people who cared for their gardens resenting neighbours who allowed theirs

> to run to weeds. The brotherhood of gardeners regards with scowls & mutterings the expanses of chickweed, sorrel, dandelion etc. of their non-gardening neighbours. There is an intangible barrier between the non-gardener & the gardener that is ever present... Amongst the gardeners themselves, the spirit is really friendly at most times; help between each other & gifts of plants etc. being manifestations of this feeling. At competition times... this comradeship is marred by petty spite, particularly if a prize has been won by having recourse to plants bought from nurserymen.[39]

In addition to advice from fellow gardeners, a variety of printed literature informed the new suburban gardener. Seed catalogues were particularly popular among gardeners

---

[37] London Metropolitan Archives, LCC/HSG/GEN/03/012, London County Council, *Bellingham & Downham Tenants' Handbook: A Handbook of Useful Information for Tenants* (July 1934), 18–19.
[38] Olechnowicz, *Working Class Housing*, 212.
[39] Mass Observation Archive, Worktown Project, Box 44A, 'The Housing Estate', observer account (n.d., *c*.1938).

with limited means. Suppliers varied from local seed merchants and nurseries to national firms such as Carter's, Suttons, Thompson and Morgan, and Unwins. Catalogues were often lavishly illustrated and were valued by suburban gardeners as a tool for planning, a source of inspiration, and a vehicle for 'armchair gardening' during the winter months.[40] Some general household management guidebooks, typically aimed at lower-middle- or upper-working-class people setting up new households, also provided advice on gardening. *The Complete Illustrated Home Book*, published by Associated Newspapers in 1936, devoted 68 pages to various gardening topics, from sowing and planting flowers and vegetables to making a pond, rockery, garden path, or swing.[41] Similarly the Daily Express's *The Home of Today* (1934) provided 125 pages of advice, including a week-by-week guide to the annual gardening cycle.[42]

There were also a variety of more specialist gardening books, including some that explicitly targeted the new suburban gardener—such as *Planning the Suburban Garden* (1922), *Gardens for Town and Suburb* (1934), and *Suburban Gardens* (1934).[43] More affluent or enthusiastic gardeners might turn to magazines such as *Amateur Gardening* and *Popular Gardening*. Meanwhile, national and local newspapers appreciated the value of gardening columns, in both serving their readership and gaining advertising for garden-related goods and services.

The BBC pioneered garden broadcasting from 1923, though the big breakthrough had to wait until May 1931, when Cecil H. Middleton began his celebrated career as the first identifiable radio gardener with the words, 'Good afternoon. Well, it's not much of a day for gardening, is it?'[44] Middleton, who adopted a more personal and conversational style than his predecessors, pitched his talks at people lacking either much experience or deep pockets (in contrast to some of his Royal Horticultural Society broadcasting predecessors). In September 1934 he was given his own series, *In the Garden*, which proved hugely popular and established the BBC as one of the key sources of advice for the British gardener. Middleton's advice was also disseminated to his enthusiastic followers via *Mr Middleton Talks about Gardening* (1935) and several subsequent books.

The boom in suburban gardening led to a mushrooming in the number and range of stores which stocked garden produce. Woolworths, which claimed to be Britain's largest gardening products retailer, sold over £1 million of horticultural goods per year by the late 1930s.[45] This was facilitated by Woolworths' highly seasonal

---

[40] Couch, 'Cultural Geography', 60–1.
[41] Associated Newspapers Ltd, *The Complete Illustrated Home Book* (London: Associated Newspapers, 1936), 197–264.
[42] Daily Express, *The Home of Today* (London: Daily Express, 1934), 547–671.
[43] H. Humphrey, *Planning the Suburban Garden* (London: St. Clements Press, 1922); V. N. Solly, *Gardens for Town and Suburb* (London: Ernest Benn, 1926); T. G. W. Henslow, *Suburban Gardens* (London: Rich & Gowan, 1934). For a thorough guide to interwar amateur gardening literature, see Couch, 'Cultural Geography', Appendix II.
[44] Cited in Jeff Walden, 'Middleton, Cecil Henry (1886–1945)', *Oxford DNB*, <http://www.oxforddnb.com/view/article/65428>.
[45] Woolworths virtual museum, <http://www.woolworthsmuseum.co.uk>; Shop Direct plc, Woolworths company archival papers, Woolworths Buyers Committee minute book no. 1, 87–98 (1 October 1937); 99–119 (21–25 January 1938); 194–214 (19 January 1939).

The Suburban Garden 187

Fig. 8.4. The seed catalogue as advice manual—Daniel Bros' *Illustrated Guide for Amateur Gardeners*, Spring 1930
Source: Peter Scott collection.

approach to stock selection, which meant that at times of peak demand a substantial proportion of their shelving would be devoted to gardening. For example, following the end of their 'back to school' season, they would launch their 'autumn bulb' season, with about a sixth of all their September shelf-space being taken up by bulbs, shrubs, plant pots, and bulb fibre.[46] Boots, Marks & Spencer, and other

---

[46] Woolworths virtual museum, <http://www.woolworthsmuseum.co.uk/hg-bloominggood.htm>.

> **That New Garden-To-Be!**
> **—I know just how you feel**
>
> YES, I know exactly your thoughts as you survey that unlovely patch of "No man's land" you have purchased along with the house. It is usually enough to damp the ardour of the most enthusiastic. But, provided it is tackled in the right way, the mountains are soon scaled down into mole-hills. And this is where I can help you.
>
> My job is a sort of Gardeners' Good Samaritan. I simply revel in shewing people how to get the best out of their gardens. Take me into your confidence. Ask me about this and about that. Every square inch of ground is, to me, a potential patch of loveliness or utility.
>
> Why not send me a rough dimensioned sketch of the plot—I will lay out the ground for you entirely without obligation of any sort.
>
> But whatever your gardening doubt or difficulty do please "Write to Adam about it." Please enclose stamped and self-addressed envelope for reply.
>
> Always at your service
>
> *Adam*
> C/o Bees Ltd,
> Mill Street,
> LIVERPOOL.
>
> Five magnificent catalogues are published each year: (1) SEED—ready Jan.; (2) ROSES, PLANTS, SHRUBS, Etc., —ready Feb.; (3) BEDDING—ready April; (4) BULB—ready Aug.; (5) ROSES, PLANTS, SHRUBS, Etc.,—ready Sept., any or all of which will be gladly sent post free on receipt of P.C.
>
> **BEES LTD.**
> NURSERYMEN & SEEDSMEN
> 173-181 MILL ST.,
> LIVERPOOL
>
> **1937 AWARDS**
> Only a Few Results are available at the time of going to press.
> • GOLD MEDAL & CUP at the Great Chelsea Show, London.
> • FIRST PRIZE & LARGE GOLD MEDAL at the Royal Agricultural Show.
> • TWO FIRST PRIZES at the Great Yorkshire Show, York.
> • CUP, also FOUNDERS' MEDAL, at the Famous Alderley Edge Show.
> • LARGE GOLD MEDAL at the Three Counties Agricultural Show, Hereford.
> • LARGE GOLD MEDAL at the British Delphinium Society's Show.
> • TWO FIRST PRIZES at the Lincolnshire Agricultural Show.

Fig. 8.5. 'Adam', 'The Gardeners' Good Samaritan', offers his help to new suburban householders via Bees Ltd

Source: Odhams Press Ltd, *The Ideal Home Book of Garden Plans* (London: Odhams, 1937), 1.

chain stores also stocked gardening produce, as did local greengrocers and general hardware stores.[47]

More mainstream gardening shops provided both produce and advice, as did seed catalogues. Nurseries were often inaccessible to households without cars, though many nurserymen also used market stalls to sell their produce and some operated a mail order trade.[48] Meanwhile, more affluent middle-class families could access a range of garden design, construction, and garden labour services, relying on the market to provide what their less prosperous suburban counterparts had to do individually or cooperatively.

GARDEN STYLES, DESIGNS, AND FUNCTIONS

Life history accounts show that gardens served a number of distinct functions for suburban families—the mix of these being determined by the family's composition, interests, and resources. Gardens were seen as a valuable resource by

[47] Couch, 'Cultural Geography', 58. [48] Couch, 'Cultural Geography', 53–4.

most families who pioneered the movement from inner-city to suburban living. As the Wythenshawe study noted: 'To the majority of tenants the garden is unquestionably an enormous asset. It provides a place for small children to play in near the house; it is a hobby and a recreation and it is also a source of fresh vegetables. In more than one case it was mentioned what an advantage the garden had proved during periods of unemployment, both as an occupation and a source of food.'[49]

Gardens served an important function in providing spaces where children could play safely, without transgressing the social mores of the estate. As a Liverpool council tenant recalled, in contrast to their old inner-city life, on their new estate, 'if the children played out it was in their own gardens, not in the street.'[50] The back garden was generally used for this purpose, houses being designed with the kitchen at the back so that the housewife could easily monitor the children, who would also be out of sight of the neighbours. An area was often laid out as lawn for this purpose, sometimes with the addition of a swing or sandpit.

Gardens also provided venues for types of play that would not have been possible in the street, such as picnics, tea parties, putting on plays for the neighbours, and camping. Meanwhile, adults mentioned using the garden for activities such as sunbathing and entertaining guests. Back gardens also served as venues for a series of household tasks, including traditional activities such as drying clothes, repairing household furniture and equipment, and keeping pets and livestock. Lawns constituted flexible garden floorspace which was relatively cheap and simple to maintain, complemented areas for growing plants or vegetables, and, at the front of the house, constituted what rapidly came to be seen as a clear and highly visible marker of respectability.[51] Thus the housewife's traditional ritual of polishing the front doorstep of the terrace was partially replaced by the husband's weekly chore of mowing the front lawn.

The other main function of the garden was, of course, horticulture. The broad division of garden space by function tended to follow a relatively uniform pattern. A study of Manchester's giant Wythenshawe estate noted: 'a profusion of flowers in front and a considerable crop of vegetables at the back—a matter for great pride on the part of the family concerned. In summer the estate is a blaze of flowers.'[52] The life histories corroborate a clear territorial division on both owner-occupied and municipal estates between lawn and flowers in the front garden and back gardens typically containing a substantial element of fruit and vegetables. Growing produce was particularly common on municipal estates, the garden providing a valued means of supplementing tight food budgets.

Just as suburban owner-occupied housing drew strongly on the English vernacular architectural style and the image of the rural cottage, so the dominant design influence for interwar suburban gardens was the British cottage garden

---

[49] Manchester and Salford Better Housing Council, *Report of an Investigation*, 14–15.
[50] McKenna, 'Development of Suburban Council Housing Estates', 456.
[51] Couch, 'Cultural Geography', 67.
[52] Manchester and Salford Better Housing Council, *Report of an Investigation*, 14–15.

tradition.[53] Gertrude Jekyll's 'arts and crafts' gardening philosophy, involving a combination of formal layouts and informal planting arrangements within them, revived interest in this style. Such influences were reflected in the variety of features and furniture that became popular in middle-class gardens, such as containers, sundials, rose gardens, winding paths, statues, pergolas, trellis work, garden arches, and rockeries. Conversely, working-class gardens generally had fewer features of this type—on account of income constraints, smaller plots, and a more functional and produce-orientated gardening philosophy.

Gardens also rapidly accumulated a variety of more functional 'furniture', such as sheds, workshops, and garages (often added by owner-occupiers after construction, and popular even in homes without cars—for holding motorbikes and bicycles or for general storage). Garages added significantly to house prices. By the late 1920s many London suburban builders would provide brick garages as an 'extra', at a cost of £30–60, while even during the 1930s only in houses priced above £850 could a purchaser expect to find an integral garage as standard.[54] Yet many owner-occupied houses had garage spaces and prefabricated garages fell in price from around £33–110 in 1920 to as little as £10 5s in the mid-1920s.[55]

Joanna Bourke has argued that while men did not necessarily do more traditional housework—childcare, cooking, and cleaning—between the 1890s and 1950s, they did experience a considerable expansion in other forms of domestic labour—such as gardening and household maintenance and improvement.[56] These can be viewed as masculine forms of housework, while also constituting a hobby and a competitive arena for demonstrating skill and creativity to neighbours. Like some housework roles traditionally assigned to women, such as childcare, cooking, and baking, it is difficult to categorize such activity as 'leisure' or 'work'. The most meaningful distinction is from the perspective of the participant's own utility—do they gain enjoyment from the activity itself, or is it of positive value to them only in terms of what their labour produces?[57]

A significant minority of men embraced gardens as their main leisure interest. As Ruby Dunn recalled, 'Dad was proud of his work in the garden, and it became his chief hobby. I remember the fruit bushes and trees, and the harvests of black, red, and white currants, the gooseberries, blackberries, loganberries and apples. The front garden was always ablaze with colour in the summer, and one year Dad won a prize in the Annual Gardens Competition.'[58] Many more had a real, though less zealous, interest in gardening, while the Life Histories Database indicates that only a relatively small minority resented having to keep their garden

---

[53] Couch, 'Cultural Geography', 44.   [54] Jackson, *Semi-Detached London*, 125–7.

[55] David Jeremiah, *Architecture and Design for the Family in Britain, 1900–70* (Manchester: Manchester University Press, 2000), 49.

[56] Joanna Bourke, *Working Class Cultures in Britain 1890–1960: Gender, Class and Ethnicity* (London: Routledge, 1994), 84.

[57] Reuben Gronau, 'Leisure, Home Production, and Work—The Theory of the Allocation of Time Revisited', *Journal of Political Economy*, 85 (1977), 1104.

[58] Ruby Dunn, *Moulsecoomb Days: Learning and Teaching on a Brighton Council Estate 1922–1947* (Brighton: Queenspark, 1990), 5.

I'm glad we bought our house through the Halifax Building Society—they gave us splendid terms.

Large funds are available for Home-buying. Last year this famous Society advanced over £21,000,000 for Property-purchase.

ASK FOR THE LATEST BOOKLET

LOCAL AGENT
EDGAR STURMAN, 18, Long Causeway, PETERBOROUGH

Fig. 8.6. 'Conspicuous gardening'—as depicted in a 1935 Halifax mortgage advert
Source: Courtesy of Lloyds Banking Group plc Archives.

neat and tidy to meet the demands of the council inspector or the expectations of neighbours.

Yet while gardening was primarily a male activity, it was one which wives shared in to a greater extent than was typical for most traditional working-class male leisure pursuits. Women often took on the lighter gardening work and the planting of flowers, while digging, mowing, and growing vegetables was generally the preserve of the husband. As such, gardening represented a merging of what had previously been regarded as essentially separate spheres of male and female leisure for married working-class people, reflecting the broader trend towards shared and home-centred leisure in the new suburbs.

Gardening also acted as a potent and highly visible signalling device regarding the household's status, both reinforcing the signals sent by the physical character of the house and differentiating the status message from neighbouring houses of similar design. Like conspicuous consumption, or cleaning, gardening reflected fine gradations in behaviour, from the basic maintenance of a tidy, neat garden to the provision of driveways, garages, and elaborate landscaping.

Back gardens, by contrast, were regarded as private spaces, something which was often secured by the introduction of higher fences than those provided by the builder. Adding trellises, over which plants could be trained, was a customary method of raising the fence by another two or three feet without making it too obvious to the neighbours that the main intention was to screen out their gaze.[59] Yet even the back garden had some status functions, often being visible to at least immediate neighbours.

Many life histories mention keeping pets or livestock in the back garden, hens and rabbits being particularly popular. Council restrictions often limited the ambitions of municipal tenants; for example, some councils allowed tenants to keep hens, but not a cockerel. Others limited the number of hens which could be kept, with council inspectors checking periodically to see that this was not exceeded.[60] Some councils prohibited keeping poultry altogether, though this was sometimes successfully ignored.

Commentators have pointed to regulations regarding livestock, or requirements to keep gardens tidy, as evidence of an overly paternalistic and authoritarian attitude on the part of local authorities towards their tenants. However, this view ignores the fact that restrictive covenants to prevent what were viewed as undesirable practices were also commonplace on owner-occupied estates.[61] Indeed there was a long-established British tradition of including covenants and restrictive clauses in the title deeds of houses, the success of which has been taken as evidence of the strong community of interest between developer and resident in maintaining 'respectable' standards.[62]

CONCLUSION

Substantial gardens were an integral feature of the interwar suburban semi. They asserted its lineage from the country cottage and English vernacular architectural tradition, brought the countryside appeal of the suburbs right up to suburbanites' front and back doors, and offered an important arena for home-centred leisure and

---

[59] Ian Bentley, 'The Owner Makes His Mark: Choice and Adaption', in Paul Oliver, Ian Davis, and Ian Bentley, *Dunroamin: The Suburban Semi and its Enemies* (London: Pimlico, 1981), 142.
[60] Age Exchange, Reminiscence Theatre Archive, London, interview with Robert Hodgkinson conducted for 'Just Like the Country' project (c.1987).
[61] Jackson, *Semi-Detached London*, 138.   [62] Muthesius, *English Terraced House*, 32–3.

recreation in an environment where social convention, physical isolation from urban centres, and limited budgets made traditional working- and lower-middle-class leisure pursuits less accessible. The majority of this first generation to benefit from the massive extension in garden provision appear to have greatly valued this new resource, utilizing it in ways that have remained broadly characteristic of British popular gardening.

Gardening also constituted an important collective pastime, providing an arena for cooperative activities both within the family and between neighbours. These included some functions already served by the traditional backyard (hobbies, storage, housework, and children's play), together with a series of new activities that the backyard had been poorly equipped for—entertaining guests, recreation, horticulture, and asserting the family's respectability and status. As such, gardening mirrored other 'conspicuous' aspects of household behaviour in both uniting people with those they saw as being like themselves and dividing them from those they deemed to be different.

9

Visible and Invisible Walls: Social Differentiation and Conflict in Interwar Suburbia

INTRODUCTION

A series of influential studies in the 1950s and 1960s highlighted the emergence of a new 'affluent' working class in post-war Britain.[1] While acknowledging that this phenomenon was most clearly evident in new residential communities, such as new towns and suburban council estates, this literature focused on economic and social factors specific to the post-1945 era. Mass affluence, the economic security offered by full employment and the welfare state, plus the boost to household incomes from the entry of married women into the labour market, were seen as key factors behind the new patterns of consumption and related behaviour of 'affluent worker' households.

This chapter takes issue both with the timing of the initial transition from a 'traditional' to 'new' working class and with the underlying factors that initiated this process. It demonstrates that the main features identified in the affluent worker studies—aspirational, family- and home-centred lifestyles; an increased emphasis on conspicuous consumption as a means of asserting status; and a more distant approach to neighbours—were already clearly evident on new suburban estates during the 1920s and 1930s.

Drawing on the work of Pierre Bourdieu, the chapter also explores how migration to new residential communities both undermined the habitus which governed traditional working-class consumption patterns in inner-urban communities and substituted new, more materially and domestically orientated values. Meanwhile, alongside more privatized, family-centred, and materially orientated lifestyles there emerged an intolerance towards neighbours who did not share these values and were perceived to threaten their new suburban life and aspirations for their children. As discussed earlier, people moved to suburbia partly on account of preferences for more aspirational and privatized lifestyles and often had to make heavy

---

[1] See, for example, Michael Young and Peter Willmott, *Family and Kinship in East London* (Harmondsworth: Penguin, 1957); Peter Willmott and Michael Young, *Family and Class in a London Suburb* (London: Routledge & Kegan Paul, 1960); Ferdynand Zweig, *The Worker in an Affluent Society: Family Life and Industry* (London: Heinemann, 1961).

material sacrifices to sustain their new lifestyles—in terms of reducing consumption of food, fuel, and lighting, and/or engaging in family limitation. Given these sacrifices, they became particularly intolerant towards in-comers who might threaten the 'suburban dream' that was being so dearly purchased.

Such tensions led to a process of social filtering into successively fine gradations of 'rough' and 'respectable' communities, together with antipathy towards adjoining estates, or sections of a particular estate, that were perceived to have markedly different social standards. The few instances of physical barriers erected between communities, such as Oxford's infamous Cutteslowe Walls, formed merely the tip of an iceberg of anxiety regarding proximity to people perceived as 'rough'. Like the emergence of privatized lifestyles, this social filtering process has often been neglected in accounts of interwar socio-economic change. Studies have generally concentrated on tensions between middle- and working-class suburbia, or viewed friction between tenants on new council estates as essentially replicating existing rough/respectable divisions within the working class.[2]

THE AFFLUENT WORKER THESIS

Early post-war studies of migration from traditional working-class communities to new residential areas highlighted major accompanying social changes, forming part of a broader post-war revolution in working-class attitudes and behaviour. A pioneering contribution was Young and Willmott's seminal 1957 study, *Family and Kinship in East London*, which charted the social impacts of out-migration from Bethnal Green in London's East End to the new LCC housing estate of 'Greenleigh' in Essex. Moves to the estate were found to be accompanied by a transition towards more privatized, home- and family-centred relationships; domestically orientated leisure; aspirational, future-oriented values; and a much more central role for material consumption in status competition.[3]

Ferdynand Zweig's *The Worker in an Affluent Society* noted the emergence by the late 1950s of a general trend (though especially strong on new council estates and aspirational neighbourhoods) towards privatized lifestyles centred around the nuclear family, with neighbourly relations characterized as 'Friendly but not too close' or 'Keep apart from neighbours, but be friendly', and activities such as house visiting being discouraged.[4] Zweig argued that the 'fully employed welfare state' and the entry of married women into the formal labour market were transforming the British working class. Workers were adjusting to a climate of greater economic security by developing a more future orientated outlook, based around rising material expectations; more home- and family-based lifestyles; higher standards of

---

[2] See, for example, Andrzej Olechnowicz, *Working Class Housing in England between the Wars: The Becontree Estate* (Oxford: Oxford University Press, 1997), 121–5.
[3] Young and Willmott, *Family and Kinship*; Willmott and Young, *Family and Class*.
[4] Zweig, *Worker in an Affluent Society*, 116 & 194.

domestic comfort in better, well-furnished houses with modern consumer durables; and higher aspirations for the next generation.[5]

By the late 1960s the affluent worker thesis, at least in its strong form—that 'as manual workers and their families achieve relatively high incomes and living standards, they assume a way of life which is more characteristically "middle class" and become in fact progressively assimilated into middle-class society'[6]—was being challenged by a weaker-form hypothesis (which accords much more strongly with the findings of this study for the interwar period). Work by Goldthorpe and his collaborators during the 1960s produced a more qualified view of the social changes evident in 'new' working-class communities. Rather than a trend towards the assimilation of manual workers into the middle class, they identified a less dramatic process of convergence in certain aspects of working- and middle-class life (evident in values, aspirational behaviour, and a trend towards more individualistic outlooks and lifestyles). Meanwhile, important differences remained in terms of attitudes to work, and some aspects of socializing, aspirations, and social perspectives. Working-class families were thus socially transformed without becoming 'middle class' in any meaningful sense. However, full employment and post-war affluence were still viewed as the key factors behind this process.[7]

More recent studies have tended to corroborate Goldthorpe et al.'s findings that these changes fell short of 'embourgeoisement' and have also called into question the rapidity and magnitude of the decline of 'traditional' working-class communities and values. However, there is a strong consensus among both the early studies and more recent critiques that new residential communities were in the vanguard of changes in working-class social relations and that these changes were strongly linked to post-war affluence.[8] Yet oral history-based studies of working-class migration to new *interwar* residential communities have found strikingly similar socio-economic impacts on household behaviour, despite the fact that the households concerned could not be considered 'affluent' by post-war definitions.[9] This calls into question the importance of the fully employed post-war welfare state as an essential instigator of these trends.

COMMUNITIES AND SOCIAL NORMS

The interactions between local communities and social norms have been illuminated by the work of sociologist Pierre Bourdieu. Bourdieu views consumption preferences as being shaped by the pursuit of lifestyles that are subjectively

---

[5] Zweig, *Worker in an Affluent Society*, 205.
[6] J. H. Goldthorpe et al., *The Affluent Worker: Industrial Attitudes and Behaviour* (Cambridge: Cambridge University Press, 1968), 1.
[7] J. H. Goldthorpe and D. Lockwood, 'Affluence and the British Class Structure', *Sociological Review*, 11:2 (1963); Goldthorpe et al., *Affluent Worker*.
[8] There is an extensive literature in this area. For a summary of the early literature, see Goldthorpe et al., *Affluent Worker*, 12–14. A good review of more recent studies is provided in Avram Taylor, *Working Class Credit and Community since 1918* (Houndmills: Palgrave Macmillan, 2002), 13–45.
[9] Margaret Judith Giles, 'Something That Bit Better: Working-Class Women, Domesticity, and "Respectability", 1919–1939', DPhil thesis (University of York, 1989); A. Hughes and K. Hunt, 'A

acceptable given individuals' economic, social, and cultural 'capital' constraints. These pre-dispose people with similar 'capitals' to develop shared consumption orientations, a process reinforced by strategies of distinction in which individuals understand their own consumption orientations in relation to their interpretations of social groups with which they identify, or contrast themselves.

Thus, social differentiation is determined not only by individuals' 'capital' endowments but by peer group pressure.[10] This is, in turn, governed by the habitus ('taken for granted' common sense social norms and habits which mould daily behaviour and practices). As Bourdieu noted, as a product of history and perceived material realities for a person and their reference group, the habitus generates a series of positively sanctioned 'reasonable', 'common sense' behaviours, encompassing what is possible within the limits of these realities, while excluding all '"extravagances"...behaviours that would be negatively sanctioned because they are incompatible with the objective conditions'.[11]

The most powerful reference group was the local residential community. A major characteristic of traditional working-class life was close and frequent contact with neighbours. High housing densities and, often, the use of the same outdoor water taps, toilets, and courts brought neighbours into frequent and unavoidable contact. Commonalities in terms of workplaces and upbringing reinforced this familiarity, thus strengthening channels for enforcing prevailing norms. Research on traditional working-class communities has highlighted an economically conservative and culturally static value set, with respectability construed in terms of independence from state or charitable assistance via mutual aid networks, thrift, living within one's means, and, if necessary, tightening one's belt during hard times. As Szreter notes, such values made working-class communities relatively closed and each a law unto themselves, while ambitions for social status and consumer aspirations were contained within the very modest limits considered appropriate to the circumstances of the group.[12] Bourdieu highlighted this policing role of local communities as a powerful mechanism for enforcing conformism:

> The calls to order ('Who does she think she is?' 'That's not for the likes of us') which reaffirm the principle of conformity...and aim to encourage the 'reasonable' choices that are in any case imposed by the objective conditions also contain a warning against the ambition to distinguish oneself by identifying with other groups, that is, they are a reminder of the need for class solidarity...Other people's expectations are so many reinforcements of dispositions imposed by the objective conditions.[13]

Culture Transformed? Women's Lives in Wythenshawe in the 1930s', in A. Davies and S. Fielding (eds), *Worker's Worlds: Cultures and Communities in Manchester and Salford, 1880–1939* (Manchester: Manchester University Press 1992); Lesley Whitworth, 'Men, Women, Shops and "Little, Shiny Homes", the Consuming of Coventry 1930–1939', PhD thesis (University of Warwick, 1997).

[10] M. Harvey et al., 'Between Demand and Consumption: A Framework for Research', CRIC Discussion Paper 40, CRIC, University of Manchester and UMIST (2001), 43.

[11] Pierre Bourdieu, *The Logic of Practice* (Cambridge: Stanford University Press, 1990), 54–6.

[12] Simon Szreter, *Fertility, Class and Gender in Britain, 1860–1940* (Cambridge: Cambridge University Press, 1996), 528.

[13] Pierre Bourdieu, *Distinction: A Social Critique of the Judgement of Taste* (London: Harvard University Press, 1984), 380–1.

Such pressures greatly narrowed the range of consumption patterns evident in each community. Yet by the interwar period socio-economic changes were offering some working-class households both a model of an alternative lifestyle and the resources to pursue this (if at the cost of considerable sacrifices in other areas of expenditure). This period saw an expansion of working-class 'economic capital', with a substantial increase in incomes for those in work. Real wages rose by an average of 1.21 per cent per annum over 1913–38, while wage differentials between un/semi-skilled workers and their skilled counterparts narrowed.[14] There was also some limited increase in working-class 'cultural capital', via improvements in education standards and opportunities (though most people in the Life Histories Database appear to have had a typical working-class education and did not stay at school beyond the minimum leaving age).

Furthermore—contrary to some traditional depictions—the interwar years, and particularly the 1930s, witnessed a marked expansion in working-class occupational, geographical, and (within constraints imposed by their material circumstances and class position) social mobility.[15] There was less of a chasm between white-collar lifestyles and those associated with expanding sectors of manual work—such as transport and communications or engineering-related manufacturing, than was the case with declining sectors such as mining, shipbuilding, or steel. A marked convergence between the working and middle classes was also evident in their manner of dress and other aspects of observed behaviour. As the *New Survey of London Life and Labour* noted in 1930:

> the visible signs of class distinctions are disappearing... The dress of the younger generation of working men and women, so far from having any distinctive note of its own, tends merely to copy, sometimes to exaggerate, any particular fashion current in the West End. In the same way paint and powder, once regarded in this class as the marks of the prostitute, are freely used by respectable working girls... The Cockney dialect and rhyming slang are slowly disappearing while the Cockney twang is spreading to other classes. In fact the whole demeanour of the different social classes has tended towards a closer approximation in the past generation.[16]

Nevertheless, compared to the post-war era, class differentials were still marked. While both the working class and middle class might patronize 'popular' retailers such as Marks & Spencer and Woolworths, a clear working-/middle-class divide

---

[14] George R. Boyer, 'Living Standards, 1860–1939', in Roderick Floud and Paul Johnson (eds), *The Cambridge Economic History of Modern Britain*, Vol. II: *Economic Maturity, 1860–1939* (Cambridge: Cambridge University Press, 2004), 284–7.

[15] Dudley Baines and Paul Johnson, 'In Search of the "Traditional" Working Class: Social Mobility and Occupational Continuity in Interwar London', *Economic History Review*, 52 (1999); Selina Todd, *Young Women, Work, and Family in England 1918–1950* (Oxford: Oxford University Press, 2005), 113–44; Peter Scott, 'Internal Migration, the State, and the Growth of New Industrial Communities in Interwar Britain', *English Historical Review*, 115 (2000).

[16] London School of Economics, *The New Survey of London Life and Labour*, Vol. I: *Forty Years of Change* (London: P. S. King, 1930), 192.

was still evident in areas such as education, participation in many sport and social organizations, and the types of catering establishments, pubs (or areas within pubs), and, in some cases, even shops that people felt comfortable attending. For example, in 1936 electrical appliance sales managers were advised by an industry colleague that showrooms aimed at working-class customers required 'careful avoidance of anything that savours of an ornate or luxury atmosphere. In large towns this may mean that special showrooms are advisable, situated more in the working-class district and equipped in a plainer way than the central showrooms.'[17]

As noted earlier, suburban estates were characterized by 'domesticated' lifestyles, encompassing a high standard of personal and domestic hygiene, family- and home-centred lifestyles even for adult males, and an increased commitment of material and psychological resources to the welfare and material advancement of children. Individual suburban estates tended to draw their populations from many inner-urban districts, creating what were often initially communities of strangers. Lacking the long acquaintance necessary for a life-portrait assessment of status, and often already being strongly influenced by modern notions of respectability, people rapidly moved to a status system based on a mixture of material markers and 'restrained' forms of social behaviour—creating 'consumption communities', tied together not by background, workplace, or religion, but by shared material values.[18]

Aspirational behaviour and social mobility (mainly for the next, rather than the current, generation) became both legitimate and laudable goals for a 'new respectable working class' that coalesced on these estates. A substantial number of the 170 working-class life histories discuss moves to suburbia in terms of creating a better life, especially for their children, yet only one account makes any mention of a desire to rise from the working to the middle class. Families sought 'respectability' within the broad parameters of this new, suburban, aspirational working class, rather than embourgeoisement.[19]

Bourdieu's model encompasses the process by which 'needs' are modified, involving their emergence from the unconscious realm of the habitus into a conscious arena where they are open to debate, modification, and incorporation into lifestyles as 'wants' before being re-submerged into the habitus as new needs.[20] A range of influences, including the advertising and communications industries, the state, and social reform movements, drew many interwar working-class households who had hitherto excluded themselves from 'middle-class' standards of housing, hygiene, and domesticity, into this new value set.

---

[17] Manchester Museum of Science and Industry Archives, ESI 73, British Electrical Development Association, J. I. Bernard, 'Selling Electrical Service for the Small Household', paper presented at 1936 Electricity Supply Sales Managers Conference.
[18] D. J. Boorstin, *The Americans: The Democratic Experience* (New York: Vintage, 1973), 145–8.
[19] For the post-war embourgeoisement thesis, see Young and Willmott, *Family and Kinship*; Willmott and Young, *Family and Class*; Zweig, *Worker in an Affluent Society*.
[20] R. Wilk, 'Towards A Useful Multigenic Theory of Consumption', *European Council for an Energy Efficient Economy Summer Study Proceedings*, Panel 3: 7 (1999).

Recent studies have noted how changing practices regarding indoor plumbing, hot water, and bathrooms have been underpinned by the powerful symbolic linking of personal hygiene with respectability, virtue, and citizenship—promulgated by agencies ranging from social reformers and health professionals to commercial interests.[21] The 1920s council house had played a pivotal role in showing that healthy semi-rural surroundings, well-tended gardens, and clean, spacious, generously fenestrated houses, with bathrooms and other modern utilities, could be extended to the working classes. These values were reinforced by the promotion of the 'ideology of domesticity' and the 'professional housewife' in the new mass-circulation women's magazines, women's sections in national newspapers, the Ideal Home Exhibition (and various similar local and regional exhibitions), and the marketing of housing, furniture, and other consumer durables.

Propaganda in favour of new values can bring people to consciously question the values of their existing reference group. Yet Bourdieu's emphasis on the policing function of local social norms implies that non-conforming social values and preferences are suppressed by the negative reactions of neighbours. Migration constituted a means of escaping such constraints and selecting communities more in accordance with the new value set.

New working-class households were typically formed on or after marriage and housing location choices were thus taken jointly. Working-class women who were attracted to this new value cluster often looked for similar values in their future husbands. As Bourdieu noted, 'Taste is a match-maker... discouraging socially discordant relationships, encouraging well-matched relationships, without these operations ever having to be formulated other than in the socially innocent language of likes and dislikes... Love is also a way of loving one's own destiny in someone else and so of feeling loved in one's own destiny.'[22] This is strongly reflected in the Life Histories Database. Most husbands did not drink heavily and were not extensively involved in community activities, while the accounts indicate relatively little conflict between husbands and wives regarding housing preferences, consumption priorities, or leisure choices. As a housewife on Manchester Corporation's Wythenshawe estate recalled:

> I've been laughed at in the guild. Oh leave your Harold, he'll be alright. But no, I said to my husband, we agreed in the beginning that I joined the guild, I could have that night out... His was his union night and he went out that night and I took over and that was it. And I always joined on the understanding that I never left him.[23]

The constraining influence of inner-urban community norms is clearly signalled in several life history testimonies as a major factor behind house moves. Another

---

[21] Frank Trentmann and Vanessa Taylor, 'From Users to Consumers: Water Politics in Nineteenth-Century London', in Frank Trentmann (ed.), *The Making of the Consumer: Knowledge, Power and Identity in the Modern World* (Oxford: Berg, 2006); Elizabeth Shove, *Comfort, Cleanliness and Convenience: The Social Organization of Normality* (Oxford: Berg, 2003), 100–6.
[22] Bourdieu, *Distinction*, 243.
[23] Thameside Local Studies Library, interview with Mrs Grindrod, conducted by Mike Harrison, *c*.1975–6.

migrant to Wythenshawe recounted how harassment of his wife for her conspicuous consumption had prompted the move:

> We had a beautiful house in Fallowfield, but every time she bought anything for the house the neighbours criticised it—she was very unhappy. I used to be working in town and [when] I came home the wife said the neighbours had been ridiculing her again. I realised that I would have to get her away.[24]

Occasionally hostility to 'snooty' behaviour took more extreme forms. An artisan's wife, who had moved to a Coventry municipal estate developed in the 1930s from a low rental inner-urban area, recalled that 'The children were hooligans, running around with bare feet, dirty noses and hardly any clothes on. If they saw anybody well-dressed they used to spit and the grown-ups used to call after you and I used to walk a long way round to save going down that street.'[25]

Moving from traditional neighbourhoods to the suburbs itself incurred social opprobrium, as it was interpreted as a rejection of community values. For example, a man who applied for a council house, citing health reasons, fell foul of his neighbours when health inspectors visited: 'when they knew health inspectors was in the street they wanted to lynch me'.[26] Similarly, Jane Walsh, who moved from a one-up, one-down house in an Oldham slum court to a new three-bedroom suburban owner-occupied house in around 1925, found herself ostracized by her old neighbours despite attempts to maintain contacts:

> a lot of people from our old district thought Charlie and me very 'snobby' for moving away into our new house. One or two of the women I invited out were sure I was only having them there to gloat. And yet if I *hadn't* asked them out they would have been equally wrathful with me for deserting old friends.[27]

Bourdieu highlighted the powerful social significance of housing choices; as a particularly expensive durable investment, permanently exposed to the public gaze, a family's house is one of its most important social statements.[28] Moving from inner-urban rented housing to (particularly owner-occupied) suburbia constituted a key long-term project for the household, which necessarily disrupted existing habits and routines. As Elizabeth Shove has noted, new habitual social practices both compete for time with existing ones and change daily or weekly cycles of behaviour in ways that impact on other practices. These impacts would be especially strong when new practices are time-intensive (owing to their duration, repetition, or consistency), such as commuting, or the adoption of new household technologies.[29]

---

[24] Interview with Mr Pimlott, conducted in 1989 as part of the research for Audrey Kay, 'Wythenshawe *circa* 1932–1955: The Making of a Community?', PhD thesis (University of Manchester, 1993).

[25] Coventry Local Studies Library, unpublished Coventry Sociological Survey report on the Brandon Road Residential Unit, 1952.

[26] Thameside Local Studies Library, transcript of interview with Mr Pennington, conducted by Mike Harrison, *c.*1975–6.

[27] Jane Walsh, *Not Like This* (London: Lawrence & Wishart, 1953), 57. Emphasis in original.

[28] Pierre Bourdieu, *The Social Structures of the Economy* (Cambridge: Polity, 2005), 18.

[29] Elizabeth Shove, 'Habits and Their Creatures', in Alan Warde and Dale Southerton (eds), *The Habits of Consumption*, Collegium Studies Across Disciplines in the Humanities and Social Sciences, 12, available at <www.helsinki.fi/collegium/e-series/volumes/volume_12>, 100–12, esp. 106.

Migration to the suburbs could therefore be expected to have far-reaching impacts on social practices, as it physically distanced family members from inner-urban activities, implied a significant investment of time for the 'breadwinner' in daily commuting to work, and substituted the previous material realities of the inner-urban house and community with the new environment of the suburban semi.

Such disruptions, together with the removal of the constraining influence of old social norms and of a 'life portrait' yardstick for measuring status by a much narrower material yardstick, collectively served as a major system shock to the habitus. Both working- and middle-class housewives sometimes experienced strong psychological impacts following such a move; a phenomenon which, as noted in Chapter 6, entered medical terminology as 'suburban neurosis'.

This was reflected in contemporary literature. Elizabeth Bowen's short story 'Attractive Modern Homes' charts the psychological decline of middle-class housewife Mrs Watson following a move from the community in which she had grown up and where 'everyone took them for granted and thought well of them' to a 'box-like' cheap semi-detached house on an unfinished estate. Mrs Watson's transformation is shown as both a descent into depression and an awakening from the habitus into conscious analysis of her life: 'Up to now she had been happy without knowing, like a fortunate sheep or cow always in the same field. She was a woman who did not picture herself... the move had been like stepping over a cliff... She came to ask, without words, if she did exist.'[30] The loneliness of the new estate leads her to realize that her old life was not the only 'natural' way of doing things and the story ends with her meeting another housewife new to the estate whose arrival offers hope of re-establishing her social life. In response to the housewife's disorientation, she states, 'I've no doubt a place grows on one. It's really all habit, isn't it?'[31]

The heavy financial and psychological costs of, and commitment to, the new suburban house further focused families' attention on their domestic material environment. As Bourdieu noted, such housing

> tends gradually to become the exclusive focus of all investments: those involved in the—material and psychological—work required to come to terms with it in its reality, which is often so far removed from anticipations; those to which it gives rise through the sense of ownership, which determines a kind of domestication of aspirations and plans (these now end at one's own doorstep and are confined to the private sphere...); those it inspires by imposing a new system of needs... in the eyes of those who seek to live up to the (socially formed) idea they have of it.[32]

Earlier chapters have discussed how new suburban communities fostered a view of the family as a private, independent entity, with only limited and restrained contacts with neighbours, as embodied in the ubiquitous expression 'keeping ourselves

---

[30] Elizabeth Bowen, 'Attractive Modern Homes', in Elizabeth Bowen, *The Collected Short Stories of Elizabeth Bowen* (London: Anchor, 1980), 524.
[31] Bowen, 'Attractive Modern Homes', 528.
[32] Bourdieu, *Social Structures of the Economy*, 189.

to ourselves'. Zweig notes the emergence by the late 1950s of a general trend, especially strong on new council estates and aspirational neighbourhoods, towards neighbourly relations characterized as 'Friendly but not too close' or 'Keep apart from neighbours, but be friendly', with activities such as house visiting being discouraged.[33] He attributed this, in part, to post-war trends such as the entry of married women into the formal labour market and the impact of the car and television. Yet similar patterns of restrained neighbourliness were already strongly evident on interwar estates.

In new suburban communities the 'good neighbour' was defined not by active participation in mutual support networks but by activities such as keeping the garden tidy, the children neat and under control; projecting an acceptable standard of material affluence; and not bothering neighbours with unwelcome visits or borrowing. He/she might offer assistance in times of crisis, but otherwise neighbourly interaction was expected to be unintrusive and to take place outside the home.

This preference for privacy conforms to a wider trend in Western societies, of the emergence of a new 'social self' based around individuality rather than community.[34] It brought with it fear that neighbourliness might threaten privacy and lead to conflict. In traditional high-density urban neighbourhoods frequent contact with neighbours had been inevitable, but it could be avoided in the insulated suburbs. Perceived invasions of privacy included excessive and one-sided borrowing, or seeking information that would be broadcast as gossip.

Meanwhile, lacking any shared upbringing or workplace connections, people increasingly asserted status via material display, captured in another common expression in the life history accounts, 'keeping up with the Joneses'. Families often felt obliged to adopt, or at least project to the outside world, a coordinated material 'lifestyle' of new, modern goods, that encompassed all aspects of observed consumption. This foreshadowed Young and Willmott's observations of suburban migrants from London's East End in the 1950s, whose new council house proved 'only the beginning. A nice house and shabby clothes, a neat garden and an old box of a pram, do not go together... Smartness calls for smartness.'[35] Such trends tended to be markedly stronger on owner-occupied than on council estates, but are evident for both.

These priorities are indicative of a 'suburban aspiration', defined by Mark Clapson as comprising three main elements: a wish to escape from inner-city living; a desire for a suburban-style house and garden; and 'social tone'—the appeal of a high-quality residential environment, in terms of both its material qualities and type of people.[36] These aspirations were tapped into, and in the process reinforced,

---

[33] Zweig, *Worker in an Affluent Society*, 116.
[34] W. Leiss, S. Kline, and S. Jhally, *Social Communication in Advertising* (Toronto: Methuen, 1986), 52.
[35] Young and Willmott, *Family and Kinship*, 157.
[36] Mark Clapson, *Suburban Century: Social Change and Urban Growth in England and the United States* (New York: Berg, 2003), 51–2 & 69.

by building industry advertising. For example, a poster for the Planet Building Society showed a bridge spanning the chasm between a dark, dense, group of terraced streets, with small rear courts and narrow windows, and a brilliantly lit suburban neighbourhood of bungalows with large windows and generous gardens (in which a small girl rides a bicycle, out of danger of the traffic), alongside the slogan 'Bridging the gap between tenancy and ownership'.[37]

Chapters 3 and 6 revealed a willingness among suburban migrants to engage in significant short-term material and psychological hardships, including: economizing on food and heat to make up for the higher costs of suburban living; smaller families; longer commutes; and the loss of pre-existing social links in return for longer-term benefits for themselves and their children. This change in consumption time-preferences closely matches the aspirational, future-orientated mind-set described in the post-war studies.

Bourdieu found a similar pattern among French clerical workers during the early 1970s—who had both lower food expenditures than skilled manual workers and a substantially lower average number of children. He explained this in terms of different 'objective futures... The hedonism which seizes day by day the rare satisfactions ("good times") of the immediate present is the only philosophy conceivable to those who "have no future" and, in any case, little to expect from the future.'[38] Paul Johnson has developed a similar model of 'procedural rationality' governing working-class spending and saving, people conceiving their consumption behaviour in terms of either a present-orientated or future-orientated time frame—according to their economic environment.[39]

As Ross McKibbin notes, traditional differences between working- and middle-class expenditure patterns reflected not only higher middle-class incomes, but a different 'order of urgency'.[40] The emergence of working-class suburbia acted as a catalyst for a transition towards future-orientated and status-orientated consumption patterns traditionally associated with the middle class, though without (as Goldthorpe and his collaborators similarly noted for the post-war 'new working class') constituting a trend towards wholesale embourgeoisement.[41] Nevertheless, this adoption of a longer-term household planning horizon constitutes one of the strongest elements whereby interwar working-class suburban migrants broke with a 'traditional', in favour of a distinctively 'modern,' mode of living.

---

[37] J. R. Gold and M. M. Gold, '"A Place of Delightful Prospects": Promotional Imagery and the Selling of Suburbia', in L. Zonn (ed.), *Place Images in Media: Portrayal, Experience, and Meaning* (Savage, MD: Rowman & Littlefield, 1990), 169–71.

[38] Bourdieu, *Distinction*, 180–3.

[39] Paul Johnson, *Saving and Spending: The Working-Class Economy in Britain 1870–1939* (Oxford: Oxford University Press, 1985); Szreter, *Fertility, Class, and Gender*, 41.

[40] Ross McKibbin, *Classes and Cultures: England 1918–1951* (Oxford: Oxford University Press, 1998), 70.

[41] Goldthorpe and Lockwood, 'Affluence and the British Class Structure'; Goldthorpe et al., *Affluent Worker*.

SUBURBIA AS SOCIAL SEGREGATION

Two major characteristics of pre-1914 urban life were proximity both to people and to different types of people. While individual courts and streets might be dominated by certain strata of society, travel to work, shops, schools, and places of entertainment often involved use of the same thoroughfares as were taken by people from very different backgrounds. Interwar suburban estates, by contrast, were more private and segregated communities in which lower-density housing aimed at broadly similar socio-economic groups distanced people both from their neighbours and, particularly, from people of markedly different social status. People tended to value this segregation, as revealed by their reactions to new housing developments which threatened to bring different classes of people into closer proximity.

Both 'established' residents of areas undergoing suburban development and those who had moved to the area only a few years previously feared and resented new estates that might threaten the 'tone' of their area. This was evident even for middle-class in-migration. In market towns around London facing rapid suburbanization, such as Hertford, tensions arose between long-established middle-class residents and new arrivals—though these could be diffused by middle-class institutions serving both groups, such as masonic lodges, rotary clubs, and women's institutes.[42] However, such anxieties were minor compared to the threat of 'invasion' by council tenants, let alone slum clearance families.

Occupants of new municipal estates frequently encountered hostility from established local residents. This has generally been portrayed as an essentially middle-class reaction; yet, while it was most vocal among the middle classes, there was also a significant strand of hostility from 'respectable' working-class residents at the prospect of being joined by people labelled 'slum tenants' (even where this was not actually the case). A 1927 letter to the *Hendon and Finchley Times* attacking the Watling Estate—which was in fact mainly aimed at relatively prosperous manual workers—encapsulates both these elements. After first highlighting the threat to middle-class residential property values, it broadened its appeal to encompass 'respectable' middle- and working-class residents who were jointly menaced by the slum dweller:

> Thus the respectable mechanic has to live side by side with people from the slums...no one wants a house in the district now with hordes of ex-slum dwellers on the doorstep, and the threat of a greyhound track to add liveliness. Already there is a need for police protection. People in Mill Hill have found their gardens ruined by children pulling up rose standards and stripping fruit trees. The language of some of them is such that even a workman on the estate told me last week that he blushed, 'To think that such a female could use such a mouthful'.[43]

---

[42] Deborah Cohen, *Household Gods: The British and Their Possessions* (New Haven, CT: Yale University Press, 2006), 193.
[43] ADSUM (pseudonym), 'The Stranglehold on Mill Hill', *Hendon and Finchley Times* (11 November 1927), cited in A. Rubinstein (ed.), *Just Like the Country: Memories of London Families Who Settled the New Cottage Estates 1919–1939* (London: Age Exchange, c.1991), 53.

Instances of poor standards of material display, hygiene, and behaviour were quickly seized on by the local press. For example, a 1931 letter to the *Birmingham Post* produced a spate of similar complaints, one writer claiming that 'one has only to look at some of the gardens (at the back) and the windows (at the front) to imagine what the inside must be like... [why should] decent-class persons... have to live in close proximity to that class of person who can only be described as coarse and uncouth.'[44] Some council officials appear to have held similar views. Brighton's Medical Officer of Health noted in his 1928 annual report that some thirty families from the Hereford Street improvement area had been re-housed on the Council's Whitehawk estate. After criticizing this policy on the grounds that slum tenants were too poor to afford commuting into town for work, or the estate's high rents, he added: 'Still another important point is that many are dirty and unsatisfactory tenants who would quickly ruin a new house.'[45]

In many cases, local people appear to have regarded all municipal tenants as akin to slum dwellers.[46] One juvenile migrant to the LCC's Mottingham Estate recalled her surprise at this attitude, in contrast to her previous neighbourhood where her family had been accepted as respectable despite their low income:

> to be sneered at, merely because we lived in a bright new house, on a bright new estate, came as a shock to me. At the impressionable age of fifteen, I began to wonder if perhaps there was something to be ashamed of, living on a council estate. So for a time I told everyone who asked, that I lived just off Elmstead Lane, which was perfectly true but it also gave the impression that I lived in Chislehurst.[47]

Migrants reported hostility from local shopkeepers, youth organizations (which estate juveniles were often not encouraged to join), and in dealings with local services, such as education. For example, one woman who had moved to the LCC's Castelnau estate as a child recalled that children from the estate were treated as inferiors by staff at her new school. 'When it came to leaving, my mother had to go and see the Headmistress about different jobs for me. She said to my mother, "Oh, that's alright, she's only an estate girl, put her in service."'[48]

The most visible and celebrated instances of local antipathy involved the notorious walls built to segregate north Oxford's Cutteslowe Estate and the LCC's Downham Estate from their private-sector neighbours.[49] The Downham wall—a 7-ft barrier, topped with broken glass—was erected by Albert Frampton, the developer of the adjoining private Alexander Crescent estate in 1926. Frampton

---

[44] Cited in Giles, 'Something That Bit Better', 216.
[45] *Annual Report of the Medical Officer of Health for 1928* (Brighton, 1929), 73, cited in Ben Jones, 'Slum Clearance, Privatisation and Residualisation: The Practices and Politics of Council Housing in Mid-Twentieth-Century England', *Twentieth Century British History*, 21 (2010), 520.
[46] Olechnowicz, *Working Class Housing*, 7–8.
[47] Rubinstein, *Just Like the Country*, 54.
[48] Rubinstein, *Just Like the Country*, 67.
[49] Gavin Weightman and Steve Humphries, *The Making of Modern London 1914–1939* (London: Sidgwick & Jackson, 1984), 109.

was responding to complaints from his residents, who objected to 'vulgar' people using Alexander Crescent as a short cut to Bromley town centre.[50]

Oxford's Cutteslowe walls were also around 7 ft tall, but were topped with rotating iron spikes rather than glass (as shown in Fig. 9.1). Erected in 1934 by the developers of the private Urban Estate to block access to the council's Cutteslowe estate, they became an iconic symbol of middle-/working-class divisions, campaigns to demolish them featuring prominently in newspapers and newsreels. Yet evidence suggests that there was substantial overlap between the socio-economic status of many residents on the Cutteslowe Estate and the privately rented Urban Estate on the other side of the divide. A survey conducted by Peter Collison in the early 1960s indicated that skilled workers—who constituted 60 per cent of household heads at Cutteslowe—also comprised 38 per cent of Urban Estate household heads. Despite the broadness of the 'skilled' socio-economic group, the overlap appeared genuine.[51] The view that there was no substantial class difference between a significant proportion of residents on the two sides of the walls is also reflected in oral history accounts by early Cutteslowe residents.[52]

Construction of the walls had been precipitated by plans to house slum clearance tenants at Cutteslowe, allegedly in contravention of assurances the Urban Housing Co. had received when buying the land from the council. Their symbolic impact appears to have been almost as important in deterring private sector tenants as their actual numbers. When the Corporation pointed out at a public enquiry that only 28 of 298 houses on the estate were for slum clearance, the company's representative responded, 'your name "slum clearance" frightens our people'.[53] Some councils made strenuous efforts to avoid such conflicts. Leeds Council emphasized the physical distance that would be kept between its estates at Moortown and Beckett Park and new owner-occupied housing, while at Seacroft the council promised to screen its new estate via tree-planting and other landscaping devices.[54]

New suburban estates had their own complex and subtle gradations in status— each family's behavioural norms acting as the baseline for judgements of 'roughness', 'respectability', and 'snobbyness'. During the early 1920s high building costs and ambitious housing specifications produced council houses that could only be let at high rents. Meanwhile tenant selection policies filtered out families who appeared poor risks in terms of regular rental payments or conforming to council regulations. Successful applicants often had small families, were in secure jobs, and had rent books showing a good payment record. Such tenants viewed themselves

---

[50] Michael Nelson, 'Gated Communities: Class Walls', *History Today*, 61:1 (2011), available at <http://www.historytoday.com/michael-nelson/gated-communities-class-walls>.
[51] Peter Collison, *The Cutteslowe Walls: A Study in Social Class* (London: Faber & Faber, 1963), 36–9.
[52] Centre for Oxfordshire Studies, LT889, BBC radio recording, 'Voices of Oxford: Expanding Oxford', 1984, interviews with Edmund Gibbs and Jim Simmons.
[53] Collison, *Cutteslowe Walls*, 71.
[54] Robert Finnigan, 'Council Housing in Leeds, 1919–39: Social Policy and Urban Change', in Martin J. Daunton (ed.), *Councillors and Tenants: Local Authority Housing in English Cities, 1919–1939* (Leicester: Leicester University Press, 1984), 146.

Fig. 9.1. One of Oxford's two Cutteslowe walls

Source: Reproduced by kind permission of Oxfordshire County Council Photographic Archive (image D251198a).

as a select group, composed of the elite of the working class, together with a significant proportion of middle-class families.

Yet each estate had its own reputation, as did 'rough' and 'respectable' sections of the larger estates. Subsequent policy changes in favour of 'building down' to lower income groups, and moving from general housing provision to slum clearance, stoked tensions between early and more recent arrivals. As the 1939 Birmingham study noted:

> During the nine years that they have been there, the original families have put a good deal of time and money into their houses and gardens and, not unnaturally, have come to feel a sense of ownership of and right to their houses. More recently the policy of the Estates Department has changed and the estate has been used for receiving people compulsorily moved under the slum clearance and overcrowding schemes. The people now moving in have for the most part large families, and there are no requirements about their income. Families have been transferred to the estate while on public assistance.[55]

---

[55] M. S. Soutar, E. H. Wilkins, and P. Sargant Florence, *Nutrition and Size of Family: Report on a New Housing Estate—1939* (London: George Allen & Unwin, 1942), 11.

Such policies produced significant social friction. Jevons and Madge's study of Bristol municipal estates found that the imposition of slum clearance tenants 'proved disturbing to the older tenants. By the outbreak of war the prevailing tone of some estates was set, through force of numbers, by the least skilled and poorest tenants. Where this had occurred... it had become very difficult to secure co-operation between the different classes of tenants.'[56]

Private estates were generally smaller than their municipal counterparts and were developed over shorter periods. Yet many had sections of cheaper and more expensive housing, which led to similar social divisions (though these were sometimes between working- and lower-middle-class areas as well as different strata of the working class). For example, a postal worker who purchased a house for £335 on a new estate in Sidcup recalled that neighbourliness did not extend to the inhabitants of 'dearer houses, the £550 pounds/£650 pound houses, where they had to put fifty pound deposit instead of the twenty pound we had to pay, they were like clerks or the hoity toity type of people, they weren't as friendly or didn't mix with the other people in the three-hundred odd pound houses'.[57]

One common point of friction involved different social norms regarding neighbourly interaction—for example, the habit of popping in and out of other people's homes. As a Liverpool council resident recalled: 'My next door neighbour came from the rough part of town where they kept their doors open all the time. She didn't like me keeping my door closed, but you had to. You didn't want people getting to know all your business, you know, too familiar like.'[58] Even having a large family was often taken as a sign of roughness, as it contravened the suburban code of respectability based around 'spotless homes, shining ones or twos of children and a reserved bearing to neighbours'.[59]

Children could bring neighbours closer together, yet also constituted a potentially explosive point of conflict. Children from rough families were considered a greater nuisance than their parents, as—less restrained by social convention—they were more likely to reflect rough traits in anti-social behaviour. Investigations carried out by Mass Observation in 1941 revealed complaints of children 'running wild' on the Watling and Becontree estates.[60] Their nuisance value was magnified by fears that these traits might be picked up by their own children. Similarly, as noted in the previous chapter, while gardening could foster neighbourly cooperation (such as the sharing of plants and tools), it also often acted as a trigger for resentment by keen gardeners who saw their neighbour's garden running to weeds.

---

[56] Rosamond Jevons and John Madge, *Housing Estates: A Study of Bristol Corporation Policy and Practice between the Wars* (Bristol: Arrowsmith, 1946), 25.

[57] Museum of London Archive, material collected for Weightman and Humphries, *Making of Modern London,* interview with G. R. Matthews.

[58] Madeline McKenna, 'The Development of Suburban Council Housing Estates in Liverpool between the Wars', PhD thesis (University of Liverpool, 1986), Appendix 13, interview 15.

[59] Coventry Local Studies Library, unpublished Coventry Sociological Survey report on the Brandon Road Residential Unit, 1952.

[60] Mass Observation Archive, TC1/3/H, note (n.d., *c.*October 1941).

Fear of infestation by the weeds of a neighbour's garden mirrored fears of broader and less tangible infestation. The state of gardens constituted the most easily discernible marker of respectability for the houses behind them and ill-maintained gardens, like badly behaved children, reflected on both the house in question and its neighbours—implying not only rough families, but rough streets.

It has often been assumed that council tenants had little real choice of residential location—within the council housing system.[61] In fact, both the initial choice of house and, more importantly, subsequent choices to stay put or move on were strongly motivated by tenants' evaluations of how particular estates matched their own social norms. Many database accounts mention either rejecting the estate they were initially offered by the council or subsequently moving to an estate with a reputation they felt more comfortable with. Council allocation procedures did, nevertheless, play an important social filtering role, prospective tenants often being interviewed and, if considered 'rough', directed to one of the less desirable estates. Such scrutiny could influence people's perceptions of their own status; a resident of the LCC's Castleneau estate recalled that prospective tenants had to be interviewed and ' "passed" to come to this particular estate... my friend downstairs, she had to go on to the Burnt Oak estate... which wasn't very nice.'[62]

Meanwhile, many migrants who perceived that their new neighbours did not match their own standards of respectability moved on to areas dominated by people more like themselves—generating a process of successive filtering into communities of similar aspirations and behaviour. Conversely, accounts that mention having friendly neighbours stress status commonalities: 'cos... we were all of the same sort of class, you know.'[63] Positive accounts of moves to owner-occupied estates often mention both the working-class background and respectability of neighbours; the purchaser of a new £499 house in Welling, South London, described his neighbours as 'all a nice generally working class, decent working class types, and most of them worked... there were no, what we call rough types.'[64]

For families whose aspirations exceeded the social norms of municipal estates, owner occupation offered a route to a more 'select' environment. The Watling survey noted that, for many families, moving to the estate represented merely one stage of a 'pilgrimage towards suburbia', spurred on by building firms whose advertising copy stressed the advantages of home ownership and which offered 'cheap, privately built houses... which try to compensate for the inferiority of their plan, looks and solidity by the sense of superior social status which they inculcate in

---

[61] See, for example, Alison Ravetz, *Council Housing and Culture: The History of a Social Experiment* (Abingdon: Routledge, 2001), 124.

[62] Age Exchange, Reminiscence Theatre Archive, interviews conducted for 'Just Like the Country' project (*c.*1987). Interview with Mr and Mrs Wills.

[63] North Kingston Centre, Surrey, OH62, interview with Mr and Mrs Walden, conducted by Rory O'Connell and Claire Nunns (1988).

[64] Bexley Local Studies, *Bexley Between the Wars*—unpublished two-volume collection of interviews of people living in interwar Bexley (*c.*1986–7), interview with Mr and Mrs Cuthbertson.

their inhabitants'.⁶⁵ Modern estates of suburban housing rented from private landlords were also considered more exclusive than council housing.

Conversely, tenants who felt uncomfortable with the 'snobby' environments of certain municipal estates also often moved on, to estates where prevailing standards were more in keeping with their own. As a woman who had moved during childhood first to Liverpool's municipal Clubmoor Estate, then to Norris Green, recalled:

> Clubmoor was quiet, really quiet, they didn't even let the kids play out in the street, it was so posh. Our next door neighbour used to have tea on the grass, the lawn they used to call it. Some of them even had cars...and...a number used to have cleaning ladies to do for them. We never fitted in, but Norris Green, well, I loved that right off. Everybody was just ordinary working class...It was busier, noisier, lots of kids running round getting hammered by their mams; that sort of thing.⁶⁶

Conversely, the influx of such families increased pressure on more aspirational Norris Green residents to move on. As one woman who left a non-parlour Norris Green house (with a weekly rent of 9s) after 12 months for a parlour house on the council's Springwood estate (at a rent of 16s) recalled: 'Norris Green had been alright but you had got some rather low types there, barrow women in shawls, that sort of thing. It suited us...at the time, but I would not have liked to bring my daughter up amongst them. No, we felt more at home here. This estate...was very select in those days...Everybody kept their houses and gardens beautifully.'⁶⁷

One alternative to moving was adaption to the estate's prevailing norms. A 1929 survey of 100 migrants to Sheffield's Wybourn slum clearance estate, who were still on the estate after 4 years, found around two-thirds had made a good or fairly good response to the new conditions, with relatively clean and tidy homes. Meanwhile, 19 per cent were said to maintain a mediocre standard, and only 16 per cent were said to be reproducing their slum conditions. Young families were found to have generally responded best, while older people found it much harder to adapt. Low incomes and large families were also identified as factors associated with the persistence of old habits.⁶⁸

Sometimes a neighbour might take on the role of informal social worker to help new 'rough' families adjust—thus mitigating the social costs of their proximity. For example, Elizabeth Knight, a tenant on the Watling estate, recalled the arrival of poorly clothed, 'scruffy' neighbours, whom her father branded 'totters...rag and bone people'. On talking with them over the back garden fence she discerned that 'they hadn't got an idea of anything. They used to hang the washing over the line and it was as black as your hat...she would say to me, "How do you get your sheets white?" "Well I used bleach," I said, which I didn't, but after that her

---

⁶⁵ Ruth Durant, *Watling: A Survey of Social Life on a New Housing Estate* (London: King, 1939), 18.
⁶⁶ McKenna, 'Development of Suburban Council Housing Estates', Appendix 13, interview 6.
⁶⁷ McKenna, 'Development of Suburban Council Housing Estates', Appendix 13, interview 9.
⁶⁸ A. D. K. Owen, *A Report on the Housing Problem in Sheffield* (Sheffield: Sheffield Social Survey Committee, 1931), 42–3.

washing improved.'[69] She supplied her new neighbours with some curtains, as much for her sake as for theirs—'it looked better as you came through the gate.'[70] Other gifts, advice, and encouragement gradually brought them into line with the standards of the estate.

Estates of higher-value housing, only accessible to the middle classes, inevitably had a high degree of social homogeneity. At a time when access to better-paid white-collar jobs was generally limited to people from middle-class backgrounds, house prices proved a very efficient social filter. Yet even on estates of houses priced over £800, there were anxieties regarding occupants who failed to meet expected standards; as Jackson notes:

> subtle gradations of class, imperceptible to the outsider, were taken very seriously...A young widow or separated wife obliged to go out to work or take in a 'paying guest', the family who allowed their children to play in the road on Sundays (or indeed at all), the man who went to work (rather than to the station) on his bicycle...matters of this kind were a constant source of anxiety and gossip.[71]

CONCLUSION

New suburban communities offered a substantial section of the urban working class the freedom to engage in a new, materially and domestically orientated model of working-class respectability, participation in which had hitherto been suppressed by low pre-1914 working-class incomes and the policing role of traditional inner-urban social norms. Migration to the suburbs removed families from their main reference group and placed them in a new environment where traditional social values no longer held sway. On these new estates there was a rapid transition towards the new working-class social traits identified by Young, Willmott, and Zweig for the post-war period, despite the fact that the migrants could not be considered 'affluent' by any meaningful post-1950 definition.

The emergence of the 'new working class' is thus shown to be a longer-term process than accounts focusing on the second half of the twentieth century acknowledge and was not *initiated* by the marked post-1945 improvement in the levels, stability, and security of working-class incomes. These findings also highlight the key importance of new working-class suburban housing and communities in initiating the transition towards a more aspirational, domestically and future-orientated working-class value set.

---

[69] Rubinstein, *Just Like the Country*, 52. [70] Rubinstein, *Just Like the Country*, 52.
[71] Alan A. Jackson, *Semi-Detached London: Suburban Development, Life, and Transport, 1900–39*. 2nd edn (Didcot: Wild Swan, 1991), 138–9.

10

A Crisis Averted by War? Mis-selling, Consumer Protest, and the Borders Case

INTRODUCTION

Britain's speculative housing sector had long been criticized for 'jerry-building'—passing off shoddy building as good quality houses—while the growing use of non-apprenticed and unskilled labour is widely regarded as having produced a general decline in the building construction (though not design) standards of interwar homes compared to their Edwardian predecessors. The speculative housing boom of the 1930s produced widespread complaint regarding poorly built houses, which building society surveyors approved for mortgages on only the most cursory of inspections. Popular disquiet culminated in a series of 'mortgage strikes' in and around London, together with a celebrated legal case in which Elsy Borders, the wife of a London taxi driver, took on the building societies and building industry.

Mrs Borders' claim (which government counsel agreed was almost certainly right in law) was that building societies had no legal authority to accept additional collateral for mortgage loans. The case threatened to make the bulk of existing mortgages on speculative housing null and void. Meanwhile, there were growing perceptions by the late 1930s that London's speculative housing market had reached saturation and that there was a danger of a fall in property values, which a successful outcome to Mrs Borders' case might turn into a crash. Experts advised that this could threaten the financial stability of the building society movement and possibly even the clearing banks (which had made extensive loans to speculative developers).

This chapter examines the extent of jerry-building; the system of relationships between the speculative builder, building society, and purchaser which gave rise to opportunistic behaviour; the Borders case; and whether there was a real likelihood of a property crash at the end of the decade—if war had not intervened. First, however, we examine the reasons behind the building societies' close relationships with speculative builders.

BUILDING SOCIETY GROWTH AND THE MORTGAGE POOL SYSTEM

The new post-1918 British regional divide, between a prosperous South and Midlands and the depressed regions of outer Britain, upset the traditional geography of the building society movement. Prior to 1914 the movement's strongholds had been the industrial towns of northern England, with the six largest societies in 1922 all being located in the North and collectively managing 29 per cent of building society assets.[1] Even Halifax Permanent, Britain's largest building society, had substantial representation only in Yorkshire and Lancashire by 1918, with a few agencies in Durham, Lincolnshire, Nottinghamshire, and North Wales. It was not until 1924 that it opened an office in London. Yet over the decade leading to its amalgamation with Britain's second largest society, Halifax Equitable, in 1928, it established over 100 new branches and agencies.[2]

Northern societies (which had a more important function as local savings banks than their southern counterparts, partly owing to their early development of branch networks) found themselves with funds that exceeded demand for houses in the depressed regions of northern Britain. Conversely, by the end of 1922 the southern societies found that demand for mortgages was substantially outstripping available funds. Both groups thus had considerable incentives to expand into each other's territories. Southern societies had some advantage in expanding northwards, as their greater access to mortgage business enabled them to offer higher interest rates on savings than their northern rivals. Conversely, the northern societies were able to offer lower mortgage rates, on account of their stronger role as savings institutions. Nevertheless, the London societies had sufficiently higher mortgage earnings to give them a larger 'spread' between their deposit and lending rates, providing greater resources to support expansion via activities such as extensive advertising and new branch openings.[3]

The resulting competition changed the regional balance of the movement. As Table 10.1 shows, in 1922 none of the eight largest building societies were based in London; yet by 1929 there were four, with Abbey Road (which had not even featured among the top 10 in 1922) rising to second place. Meanwhile, a handful of truly national societies had emerged to dominate the sector—competing for both investment and mortgage business throughout Britain. By 1939 the twelve largest societies collectively controlled £411.3 million of the movement's total assets of £758.9 million and played a leading role in mortgage lending on speculative estates (particularly on pool schemes).[4]

Territorial expansion required national sales organizations. Martin Davis estimated that in 1938 there were only around 625 branch offices for all building societies, a figure dwarfed by the branch networks of the banks, insurance companies, and major high street retailers.[5] However, societies found other ways of

---

[1] E. J. Cleary, *The Building Society Movement* (London: Elek, 1965), 202.
[2] Oscar R. Hobson, *A Hundred Years of the Halifax* (London: Batsford, 1953), 63 and 90–101.
[3] George Speight, 'Building Society Behaviour and the Mortgage Lending Market in the Interwar Period: Risk-Taking by Mutual Institutions and the Interwar House-Building Boom', DPhil thesis (University of Oxford, 2000), 137–8.
[4] 'Building Societies since 1925', *Economist* (1 July 1939), 10–11.
[5] Martin Davis, *Every Man His Own Landlord: A History of the Coventry Building Society* (Warwick: Coventry Building Society, 1985), 64. There were a total of 12,310 UK bank branches by 1938—D. K. Sheppard, *The Growth and Role of Financial Institutions 1880–1962* (London: Methuen, 1971), 116–17.

Table 10.1. The eight largest building societies in order of asset value (£M) 1922–39

1922		1929		1939	
Society	Assets	Society	Assets	Society	Assets
Halifax Permanent[a]	13.9	Halifax	59.3	Halifax	129.1
Bradford Third	5.8	Abbey Road	19.1	Abbey Road	51.4
Halifax Equitable[a]	4.1	Leeds Permanent	12.0	Leeds Permanent	41.7
Leeds Permanent	3.7	Woolwich Equitable	11.4	Woolwich Equitable	40.1
Burnley	3.3	Bradford Third	11.3	National	35.7
Huddersfield	3.2	National	9.9	Co-op Permanent	31.2
Leicester Permanent	2.8	Huddersfield	9.8	Leicester Permanent	16.2
Bradford Second	2.2	Co-op Permanent	9.6	Bradford Third	15.5
Total	39		142.4		360.9
% of national total	36.3		45.5		46.6

Source: Herbert Ashworth, *The Building Society Story* (London: Franey, 1980), 81 and 114.

Notes: Reporting dates are to 31st December, except for Leeds Permanent and Woolwich Equitable (to 30th September); Halifax Equitable (30th June) and Halifax Permanent (31st January of the following year).

[a] The Halifax societies merged in 1928.

extending their geographical reach. Using agents was particularly popular, while some societies also employed salaried 'outside officials' to develop business in particular localities.[6] Arrangements with house-builders offered another important means of expansion, many builders effectively becoming mortgage agents for one or more building societies.

As Richard Tedlow notes, firms seeking to create mass markets require vertical systems to match marketing and distribution with production—something that can be achieved through either vertical integration or contractual relations.[7] Building societies were prevented from engaging in building work by their legal status, while many features of the house-building market involved activities, such as reducing costs via non-apprenticed piecework labour and cheaper materials, that might damage their reputation if undertaken directly. Instead, the societies developed close contractual relations with builders through the pool system. Developers effectively became retail agents for the building societies, in the same way that hire purchase traders (who also enjoyed a dubious reputation) acted as retail agents for the nationally based and much more respectable hire purchase finance houses.[8]

[6] David Paisley, 'Salesmanship and Advertising as Applicable to Building Societies', *Building Society Yearbook* (1931).

[7] R. S. Tedlow, *New and Improved: The Rise of Mass Marketing in America* (Oxford: Heinemann, 1990), 344.

[8] Peter Scott, 'The Twilight World of Interwar Hire Purchase', *Past and Present*, 177 (2002). Hire purchase contracts were often taken out with the finance house rather than the retailer, who technically acted as their agent.

A. D. McCulloch argued that building society participation in builders' pool schemes began to be important in around 1922/3.[9] Certainly by 1925 one of the most active societies, Abbey Road, had already developed a series of standard collateral offers for the builders they dealt with.[10] Yet their use appears to have intensified from the early 1930s. Collateral pool arrangements involved part of the mortgage advance being retained by the society, rather than being passed onto the builder. The sum retained was originally equal to the difference between the society's normal maximum ratio of mortgage to house price (typically 75 or 80 per cent) and the new ratio of, typically, 95 per cent. However, as competition between societies intensified, builders successfully renegotiated terms. Doing deals on a 'one in four' or 'four to one' basis (where the builder might be liable for, say, 20 per cent of the house's value but was only required to deposit a quarter of this sum with the society) soon became common.[11]

Pool deposits would nominally be repaid when the mortgage had been reduced to something between two-thirds and 70 per cent of the property's valuation. In practice builders would periodically apply to have the pool reviewed before this point and, sometimes, lump sums would be released back to the builder. Nevertheless, the pool system resulted in part of the builders' eventual profit from each estate being tied up in the building society for many years.[12] Builders were paid interest on pool deposits, usually at the current building society rate. However, George Speight argues that, given the cash-intensive nature of housing development and the prospect of receiving pool deposits back only in 10 years' time, builders had strong incentives to focus on maximizing turnover rather than on the safety of their pool funds. Builders are said to have dealt with the pool problem by increasing house prices by an amount equal to the value of their pool deposits, a practice noted even by building industry luminaries.[13] For example, in 1934 John Laing criticized the class of builder who: 'tries by reducing quality and selling at a high price to be in such a position that even if the amount of the guarantee is lost, the builder does not suffer loss.'[14]

Government sources indicate that by 1938 between 40 and 60 per cent of current building society mortgage business was being conducted via pool schemes, and a higher proportion for relatively cheap properties.[15] This is corroborated by the Life Histories Database; purchasers of new houses during the 1930s typically report

---

[9] A. D. McCulloch, 'Owner-Occupation and Class Struggle: The Mortgage Strikes of 1938–40', PhD thesis (University of Essex, 1983), 90.

[10] London Metropolitan Archives, Abbey Road Building Society papers [LMA, Abbey], 25/32, Abbey Road, Survey & Arrears committee minutes, 15 September 1925.

[11] Circa Trust, George Wimpey archives, G. W. Mitchell, letter file. 'Notes on Private Enterprise House-Building', unsigned memorandum, 5 February 1945.

[12] McCulloch, 'Owner-Occupation', 98–9; Ruth Issacharoff, 'The Building Boom of the Interwar Years: Whose Profits and Whose Cost?', in Michael Harloe (ed.), *Urban Change and Conflict* (London: CES, 1978), 308.

[13] Speight, 'Building Society Behaviour', 94–5.

[14] John Laing, 'Increased Mortgages on Builders' Guarantees', in Ernest Betham (ed.), *House Building 1934–1936* (London: Federated Employers' Press, 1934), 86–7.

[15] The National Archives [NA], CAB 27/645, Committee on Building Societies, meetings and memoranda, report of Cabinet Committee, 9 December 1938.

deposits of around 4.0–6.7 per cent of the purchase price, which were only available on pool schemes. Some building firms preferred to have several societies providing pool finance on each of their major estates. At least sixteen different societies were involved with New Ideal Homesteads' estate in Feltham, West London, and at Morrell's infamous Coney Hall estate there were nine or ten societies providing finance.[16] Some building firms, such as Wimpey, had separate pools for each estate, while others used one general pool for each building society they dealt with.

ATTEMPTS TO CONTROL COMPETITION

During the 1930s a group of major, and predominantly London-based, building societies sought to control competition in their industry via a compulsory national Building Societies Association 'Code of Ethics'.[17] This would involve agreement on standard terms for mortgage interest rates, pool arrangements, commission payments, maximum mortgage durations and loan-to-value ratios, and minimum personal stakes for mortgage borrowers.[18] The chief executives of four major London-based building societies—Abbey Road, Westbourne Park, Woolwich, and the Co-operative—initially met in May 1930. Discussions were said to have been preceded by surveys of the mortgage market in Greater London and the South of England. These revealed evidence of very low purchasers' deposits and of certain areas being 'over-built'. Moreover, 'all reports confirmed the view that the practice of selling houses on the small deposit system has had the effect of depriving purchasers of negotiating power,' a small deposit requirement making them 'practically unconcerned with the question of value'.[19]

It was recommended that collateral offers to builders on a '50/50' or 'one in three' basis should be subject to certain conditions regarding the minimum number of properties under consideration; that societies should not conduct builders' pool business on a more than 'one-in-four' basis; that mortgage contracts should be limited to 21 years; and that maximum interest rates on new deposit or guarantee accounts should be capped at 4 per cent.[20] Such measures would have drastically restricted the scope for competition between building societies. By the end of the year the National and Halifax had joined the group and it appeared increasingly likely that the large building societies would succeed in strictly regulating competition, both between themselves and from smaller societies.[21]

Cartels were common in Britain and, in the absence of any effective competition legislation, perfectly legal. Yet these large and mainly London-based societies failed in their attempts to control competition. In 1936, following 5 years of

---

[16] McCulloch, 'Owner-Occupation', 95–6. [17] Davis, *Every Man His Own Landlord*, 67.
[18] Cleary, *Building Society Movement*, 212.
[19] LMA, Abbey, 7/32, Harold Bellman, 'Proposals for Co-operation', paper to be presented to Executive Committee of National Association of Building Societies, 3 November 1931.
[20] LMA, Abbey, 7/32, Co-operation Group Committee minutes, 16 May 1930.
[21] LMS, Abbey, 7/32, Co-operation Group Committee minutes, details of agreements concluded up to 16 December 1930, tabled at meeting of 20 January 1931.

unsuccessful efforts to gain national agreement on the 'Code', a split occurred between the large London societies and a group of other societies led by the Halifax. The issue concerned a move by the large London societies to cut mortgage rates from 5 to 4.5 per cent, without first seeking agreement from the Association. This marked the culmination of a series of disputes and, in an attempt to end the impasse, the National Association of Building Societies was dissolved and reconstituted as the Building Societies Association, with the Code written into its constitution. Some fifty-five societies refused to accept the new conditions and formed the rival 'National Federation of Building Societies'.[22] When the movement later reunited in 1939, the code was formally abandoned.[23]

These attempts at cartelization had little long-term success in restraining competition between the major societies, which intensified during the 1930s. Major builders successfully played off societies against each other, as illustrated by negotiations Scotland's leading speculative house-builder, Mactaggart and Mickel, conducted separately with representatives of the Halifax, Abbey Road, National, and Leeds building societies.

Halifax had offered improved terms, but appeared unwilling to release any of the firm's existing pool deposits. They were prepared to undertake pool business on a one-in-five basis, but on the excess of 75, rather than 80, per cent of the purchase price. On a £500 house, with a £25 buyer's deposit, this would mean a pool deposit of £20 and a guarantee of £100. The £20 would be released when the loan was reduced to 70 per cent of the house value—around 10 years. For the same £500 house Abbey Road would require a pool deposit of £15 and a guarantee of £75, which would becoming releasable in about 8 years. National offered very similar terms, while stating that when they built up experience of the firm's business, they would offer better terms wherever possible. Meanwhile, the Leeds offered guarantees on a one-in-five basis, plus a repayment period of 27 years (rather than the standard 25). It was decided that 'the Halifax Building Society is hardly worthy of consideration', but that business could be done with Abbey Road and the National. Despite the Leeds' attractive proposition, the fact that it had withdrawn from the Building Societies Association made doing business problematic, as this might 'shut the door on the Abbey Road and National for any future business', or at least make it unlikely that these societies would offer similarly good terms in future.[24]

CAVEAT EMPTOR

The life histories examined for this study indicate that the great majority of interwar house-purchasers were not only happy with their new homes, but viewed their

---

[22] Glyn Davies, *Building Societies and Their Branches: A Regional Economic Survey* (London: Franey, 1981), 49–50.
[23] Davis, *Every Man His Own Landlord*, 67.
[24] Royal Commission of Ancient and Historical Monuments, Scotland, Mactaggart & Mickel papers, MS/1034/7, 'Report by Mr Grieve on Building Society terms' (referred to at Director's Meeting of 6 April 1937).

moves from cramped, unhygienic, and sometimes damp and vermin-infested housing to modern suburban accommodation as one of the most positive and important events of their lives. They also generally perceived themselves to have achieved the sort of aspirational lifestyles the developers' marketing had promised, as evidenced by many of their children having obtained jobs well beyond their own reach. For most, the 'suburban dream' offered in the estate brochures had become reality—if often at the cost of substantial daily hardships.

Yet a few accounts reported problems of the type that (together with a cavalier attitude towards the letter of the law) led the speculative house-builders and the building societies who cooperated with them into a crisis of public confidence. The builders' pool system contained a number of perverse incentives that encouraged builders to supply a low-quality product to high-risk customers at an inflated price—problems exacerbated by exaggerated, misleading, or even fraudulent statements in developers' marketing material. Public perceptions of 'jerry-built' estates were neatly summarized by the following April 1938 *Weekly Review* article describing what was said to be a typical case.

> Needing a house I study advertisements and inspect one or two estates which are being built. Knowing nothing of building, I am swayed by the convenience of the district and by the appearance and lay-out of the houses. My wife is impressed by these matters also and perhaps additionally by the chromium-plated taps and fittings. I have a consultation with the builder and his representative and am further impressed by the ease and inexpensiveness of securing ownership of one of these houses.
>
> ...The builder, or his representative, puts me in touch with a building society which will advance 90 per cent or more of the price (this is adduced as evidence of the soundness of the houses) and stresses the fact that there is no need for me to employ a surveyor as the building society will conduct a survey (at my expense) on the report of which it will advance the money—'and they don't lend money on rubbish.'
>
> ...Within a year serious defects develop and I write to the helpful builder who coldly regrets that he is no longer responsible. I then write to the building society who also regrets that it is not responsible... Perhaps I decide the defects should have been observed by the surveyor and ask the building society to let me see his report. I am here met with the refusal to divulge the nature or contents of the report even though I paid the survey fee.[25]

Building societies relied heavily on speculative builders. Pool arrangements constituted the only means through which societies could offer the 95 per cent mortgages that were key to extending the market for new houses, while the developer's retail role compensated for many building societies' limited branch networks. Developers advertised the services of those building societies offering pool mortgages on their estates, undertook face-to-face discussions with buyers, and collected their signatures to mortgage deeds. The agent relationship was formalized by commission payments (typically 1 per cent of the value of each advance)—an extension of the longer-established practice of building societies paying commission to estate agents and solicitors. Builders sometimes continued to act as the society's agent even after

---

[25] Joseph Gibbons, 'Jerry Building Societies', *Weekly Review* (21 April 1938), 109.

the mortgage was signed, collecting instalments from customers in arrears or, in some cases, from all purchasers.[26]

Yet, as in many principal–agent situations, differences in the interests of the two parties fostered opportunism. One contributory factor was the scope that 'easy terms' offered developers to inflate prices.[27] As an Inland Revenue official noted, 'The hire purchase system applied to housing has the same primary features as when applied to other commodities i.e. a nominal deposit and easy repayment terms... focusing the mind of the purchaser on his periodical rather than his capital commitments'.[28]

Malpractice was facilitated by the absence of independent expert advice. Building societies conducted their own property valuations (at the purchaser's expense), rather than employing independent, qualified, valuers—a problem identified by government as a major flaw in the system.[29] As the *Weekly Review* article noted, the purchaser was not given access to the valuation report (or even the valuation figure), despite having paid for the survey. Meanwhile, the developer's solicitor typically also acted for the purchaser and building society.[30] The survey offered no warranty and the surveyor owed no legal duty of care to the buyer (though builders sometimes encouraged buyers to believe otherwise). Building societies argued that, at the fee charged (2 or 3 guineas), no more robust survey could be provided. Indeed it was well known that surveyors typically only made a reasonably thorough inspection of the first house to be finished on a new estate, thereafter merely contenting themselves that subsequent houses were completed and decorated.[31]

The failure of collateral security, or building society surveys, to act as effective deterrents to opportunism encouraged jerry-building.[32] Developers faced few regulatory controls and their brochures sometimes included what one judge described as 'specious statements designed to leave upon the mind of the reader the impression of... high quality'.[33] Contemporary sources indicate that a significant proportion of new owner-occupied estates aimed at lower-income workers and sold on pool schemes were jerry-built and that purchasers often faced heavy unexpected repair bills.[34] This problem was tacitly acknowledged by the building society movement. As Frank Lee of the Borough Building Society noted:

---

[26] Laing, 'Increased Mortgages on Builders' Guarantees', 90.
[27] Scott, 'Twilight World', 211–12.
[28] NA, T161/945, letter by Inland Revenue official, signature illegible, to H. E. C. Gatliff, 31 March 1938.
[29] NA, HLG29/253, Note, 31 May 1938, initialled B.W.G.
[30] McCulloch, 'Owner-Occupation', 171.
[31] L. C. B. Gower, 'Building Societies and Pooling Agreements: The Borders Case and its Consequences', *Modern Law Review*, 3 (1939), 45.
[32] Frank L. Lee, 'The Changes in Building Society Practice to Meet Changed Business Conditions', *Building Societies Gazette* (October 1936), 938.
[33] NA, HLG29/23, Judgement, Third Equitable Building Society v. Borders, High Court of Justice, Chancery Division, 13 February 1939.
[34] B. S. Rowntree, *Poverty and Progress: A Second Social Survey of York* (London: Longmans, 1941), 227; 'Speculative House Building', *The Builder* (5 February 1937), 322.

The jerry builder almost invariably relies on pool terms...The excessive depreciation...is a source of considerable worry to us. It is strongly suspected that the...cash deposit towards the pool is extracted from the cost of the house and is immediately regarded in the main as being irrecoverable. Our strongest counterbalance to this probably arises through...the inherent respect with which the average British borrower treats his obligations.[35]

Perversely, builders trumpeted their pool arrangements as both proof of the value of their houses and an endorsement of their construction standards. For example, in the notorious Borders case (discussed below), the judge emphasized the misleading impact of statements such as 'a 95 per cent mortgage....proves without a shadow of doubt, the amazing value of Morrell Homes...Each house is individually inspected by the Building Society surveyor during the course of construction, and again when the last coat of paint is finished.'[36] While such problems were confined to a small proportion of houses, the publicity they attracted raised growing public concern. For example, one of Britain's leading builders, Norman Wates, stated that popular fears regarding jerry-building played a major role in tempering demand.[37]

Jerry-building could push purchasers into financial difficulties, as the move from tenancy to house purchase typically involved a substantial increase in the proportion of income devoted to accommodation, with little left over to meet unforeseen repair bills. While weekly payments were lower for a mortgaged house than an *identical* rented house, the vast majority of working-class house-buyers did not move from similar properties, but from much cheaper inner-urban accommodation. Building societies had a general 'rule of thumb' that a purchaser's housing costs, including local rates, should not exceed a quarter of net household income—a much higher figure than the typical proportion devoted to rented accommodation.[38] Prior to the introduction of rent controls, rental costs had been closer to this figure,[39] yet renting offered the flexibility to move to cheaper accommodation during times of financial hardship, while a mortgage involved both heavy sunk costs and a continuing contractual liability to meet the instalments.

---

[35] Lee, 'Changes in Building Society Practice', 938.

[36] NA, HLG29/23, Judgement, Third Equitable Building Society v. Borders, High Court of Justice, Chancery Division, 13 February 1939.

[37] NA, HLG56/157, Departmental Committee on Valuation for Rates, letter, Norman H. Walls, National Federation of Building Trades Employers, 16 February 1939.

[38] Alan A. Jackson, *Semi-Detached London: Suburban Development, Life, and Transport, 1900–39*, 2nd edn (Didcot: Wild Swan, 1991), 152–3.

[39] Rowntree (*Poverty and Progress*, 264) found that rent and rates accounted for 14.97 per cent of working-class income in York in 1900, while the national average for urban working-class families prior to 1914 has been estimated at 16 per cent (George Speight, 'Who Bought the Inter-war Semi? The Socio-economic Characteristics of New-House Buyers in the 1930s', University of Oxford, Discussion Paper in Economic and Social History 38 (December 2000), 19). However, accommodation costs were considerably higher in London and higher rents were also reported in some provincial areas—for example, rent and rates in South Tyneside in 1912 are estimated to have equalled 15–25 per cent of working-class incomes (Robert Ryder, 'Council House Building in County Durham, 1900–39: the Local Implementation of National Policy', in M. J. Daunton (ed), *Councillors and Tenants: Local Authority Housing in English Cities, 1919–1939* (Leicester: Leicester University Press, 1984), 82.

Public concern over jerry-building prompted the builders' employers association, the National Federation of Master Builders, to explore methods of ensuring minimum standards. In 1936 it established a Standards Board, chaired by Raymond Unwin, to prescribe standard specifications. A voluntary builders' registration scheme was launched in January 1937, via a National Housebuilders' Registration Council, again chaired by Unwin. The register was open to public inspection and registered firms were obliged to allow the Council's officials to inspect developments at various stages of construction and to offer a two-year warranty on completed houses. By the eve of the Second World War many of the largest developers, including Wates, New Ideal Homesteads, Laing, and Wimpey, had signed up, together with large numbers of smaller firms.[40]

ARREARS AND DEFAULTS

By raising maintenance costs, jerry-building intensified the precarious position of purchasers who had often already stretched themselves financially to meet their mortgage payments. Contemporary sources indicate that many house-buyers devoted more than a quarter of their income to accommodation.[41] Analysis of seventy-nine April 1938 household budget summaries for working-class home-buyers indicates that 17.7 per cent allocated more than 25 per cent of household expenditure to accommodation (mortgage instalments, ground rent—for leasehold premises, and rates), while 6.3 per cent allocated more than 30 per cent.[42] As the house purchases were typically made several years prior to the date of the budgets, and this had been a period of rising money wages, the proportion committing more than 25 per cent of income *at the time of purchase* is likely to have been higher.

Meanwhile, additional expenses associated with suburban living, such as higher transport costs and HP payments on furnishings, often led families into a much greater financial commitment than they had anticipated.[43] As Walter Harvey of the Burnley Building Society told his industry colleagues, 'In this pool business we are in danger of being regarded as builders' building societies rather than buyers' building societies...we are taking on in increasing numbers the type of buyer-borrower who is entering into obligations beyond his means...it is no real service to the house buyer to lend him more than he can afford to borrow.'[44] Yet competitive pressures to gain developers' business led societies into taking on many such customers.

---

[40] Jackson, *Semi-Detached London*, 128.

[41] NA, HLG56/157, Departmental Committee on Valuation for Rates, minutes of evidence of National Federation of House Builders, 16 March 1939, and National Federation of Owner-Occupiers' and Owner-Residents' Associations, 18 November 1938; Speight, 'Who Bought the Inter-war Semi?', 18–24.

[42] For a more general analysis of this data, see Table 6.4. Figures are net of any income from letting-out rooms.

[43] NA, HLG56/157. Departmental Committee on Valuation for Rates. Minutes of evidence of National Federation of House Builders, 16 March 1939.

[44] Building Societies Association, verbatim reports of National Association of Building Societies' discussions, 1934–6, reply by Walter Harvey to paper by R. Bruce Wycherley, June 1936.

Despite claims that 'you can always realize your capital on a well built house in a good district such as this,'[45] both builders and building societies were well aware that properties re-possessed during the early years of a mortgage could generally only be sold at a significant discount to their purchase price. When home-buyers came to sell, they generally faced substantial losses.[46] As 95 per cent mortgages were confined to new properties on pool schemes, home-owners trying to re-sell without the benefit of such generous terms (or the developer's extensive marketing activities) were severely disadvantaged.

The resulting increase in mortgage defaults was effectively disguised by the building societies—who pointed to official data, based on returns to the Chief Registrar of Friendly Societies, showing negligible default rates. These were limited to mortgages over a year in arrears, or properties in the possession of the society for more than a year. Societies were generally entitled to sell houses when they had accumulated only 3 months' arrears.[47] Moreover, they employed various devices to massage the default data, including using holding companies and receiverships to manage properties in possession, or using builders' pool funds to reduce arrears to below 12 months.

In 1933 the Halifax officially reported no properties in possession or mortgages in arrears of over a year, yet at the Yorkshire County Association of Building Societies' AGM it gave its ratio of mortgage defaults as 1.10 per cent.[48] Fragmentary evidence for individual societies suggests that the average annual default rate was in the region of 1–2 per cent—implying a significant likelihood of default for any particular mortgage over its typical 25-year term. Defaults were concentrated among pool-scheme clients and, therefore, among working- and lower-middle-class customers. For example, by the end of 1938 the Halifax recorded a rate of house sales following default of just under 9 per cent for mortgages introduced by its current builder-clients on pool schemes, indicating an annual default rate of about 2.5 per cent.[49]

A desire to minimize official mortgage default rates created perverse incentives for building society managers to treat borrowers abruptly when they got into difficulties, despite promises of a sympathetic attitude to customers falling on hard times.[50] A. H. Holland, Chief Master, Chancery Division, reported that court cases coming before the Division revealed a harsh attitude towards working people who had paid instalments fairly regularly for several years but got into arrears

---

[45] Brochures for the Newbold's Estate, Fallings Farm, Wolverhampton, held by Dr Duncan Nimmo (n.d., c.1934).
[46] NA, T161/945, letter by Inland Revenue official to H. E. C. Gatliff, 31 March 1938; Lee, 'Changes in Building Society Practice', 938.
[47] Speight, 'Building Society Behaviour', 93.
[48] McCulloch, 'Owner-Occupation', 157–63.
[49] Speight, 'Building Society Behaviour', 109. The default rate is calculated on the value of outstanding mortgages under pool schemes.
[50] Luke Samy, 'The Building Society Promise: The Accessibility, Risk, and Efficiency of Building Societies in England c.1880–1939', DPhil thesis (University of Oxford, 2010), 223; Colin G. Pooley and Sandra Irish, 'Access to Housing on Merseyside, 1919–39', *Transactions of the Institute of British Geographers*, new. ser., 12 (1987), 184.

of £10–£20 through illness or unemployment. Such people, Holland noted, genuinely wanted to continue payments and only asked for sufficient time. He claimed that pool agreements, by obliging the builder to buy back the property from the building society in the event of default, made societies keener to initiate repossession.[51]

Court proceedings were generally taken in the King's Bench Division of the High Court, making it difficult for people living far from London to put their case. Following appeals to the Lord Chancellor from mortgagors who had cases brought against them at very short notice, demanding repossession of their houses together with recovery of arrears of instalments and interest, jurisdiction was transferred to the Chancery Division on 12 October 1936, where it was hoped that greater consideration would be given to matters of equity. Building societies subsequently complained that procedure in the Chancery Division was less expeditious than in the Kings Bench Division where, if the defendant did not appear, judgment could be signed automatically 8 days after service of the writ.[52]

THE BORDERS CASE

The late 1930s witnessed growing public disquiet regarding the builders' pool system, culminating in the infamous Borders case and the accompanying 'mortgages strikes' on a number of estates around London which, at their height, involved about 3,000 households.[53] Elsy Borders, the wife of a London taxi driver, had purchased a house on the Coney Hall Estate, West Wickham, Kent, in 1934, under a pool arrangement between the developer, Morrells, and the Bradford Third Equitable Building Society. In common with many other houses on the estate, this soon developed serious building defects. Mrs Borders made various legal claims, but the two of greatest importance to the general relationship between building societies and speculative builders were that Bradford Third Equitable was a party to various fraudulent claims in Morrells' publicity material, and, crucially, that pool arrangements were *ultra vires*—as building societies had no legal authority to accept non-property collateral security (while Bradford Third Equitable's rules also made no provision for such collateral).[54]

Morrell's was Britain's only publicly quoted house-builder to face bankruptcy during the 1930s.[55] The firm had been founded in 1929 by three brothers who established themselves as small-scale house-builders. By 1932 Morrell's were already

---

[51] NA, CAB 27/645, memorandum by A. H. Holland, Chief Master, Chancery Division, for Cabinet Committee on Building Societies, 4 April 1938.

[52] NA, CAB 27/645, memorandum by A. H. Holland, Chief Master, Chancery Division, for Cabinet Committee on Building Societies, 4 April 1938; Cabinet Committee on Building Societies, Committee minutes, 20 June 1938.

[53] Andrew McCulloch, 'A Millstone Round Your Neck?—Building Societies in the 1930s and Mortgage Default', *Housing Studies*, 5 (1990), 49.

[54] See Gower, 'Building Societies and Pooling Agreements', 33–47.

[55] Fred Wellings, *Dictionary of British Housebuilders: A Twentieth Century History* (Trowbridge: Cromwell Press, 2006), 217.

developing major estates at Hayes, West Wickham, and Bromley Common, while they commenced development of the Petts Wood estate and the notorious Coney Hall estate in 1933. Morrell Estates was launched as a public company in 1935, with a prospectus that described it as one of Britain's largest house-builders. In fact its activities were confined to what is now the London borough of Bromley.[56] In January 1937 the firm's building subsidiary was facing voluntary liquidation and by the end of 1938 notice had also been given for the parent company to be voluntarily wound up.

An 1890 Chancery legal decision that lending more in respect of a property than would normally be lent on the security of the property itself, on account of additional collateral, was *ultra vires* was well known to the building societies, but had long been ignored.[57] While Mrs Borders' main legal argument hinged on this technicality, it was underpinned by a strong moral case, as she and her fellow occupants of the Coney Hall estate had been sold houses that were clearly not fit for purpose. As the Lord Chancellor informed the Cabinet Committee convened to deal with the crisis: 'So far as it was possible to judge, Mrs. Borders had had a most unfair deal and had been, in fact swindled by her Building Society.'[58] Official investigations found that the Borders case was only one of

> a number of scandals in the way of ramshackle properties which have been made the subject of loans well in excess of the real value of those properties. The valuation has often been utterly perfunctory. The case now in Court is of such a character...it is one where the Society in question seems to have taken special pains to put themselves in the wrong on every conceivable point...We feel that...[the building societies] must be told with authority that the Government will not introduce legislation unless there are safeguards to deal with the unsatisfactory features in the present situation.[59]

By July 1938 Mrs Borders had begun organizing a 'strike' on the estate—urging her fellow house-purchasers not to pay their instalments.[60] These tactics added a strong political dimension to her campaign, which further alarmed the government. As an official memorandum noted:

> The circumstances of the particular case add to the embarrassment of any action. As I understand, the house and estate are badly built and Mrs. Borders is a local Communist and Sir Stafford Cripps is leading for her in the action. To protect the building societies and deprive Mrs. Borders of her revenge in these circumstances would have a bad flavour.[61]

Government became so alarmed at this case and its implications for the building society movement and building industry that a special Cabinet committee was convened, chaired by the Lord Chancellor, Lord Maugham, and including Sir John

---

[56] Wellings, *Dictionary*, 217; Fred Wellings, *British Housebuilders: History and Analysis* (Oxford: Blackwell, 2006), 43.
[57] NA, HLG29/253, Note, 31 May 1938, initialled B.W.G.
[58] NA, CAB 27/645, Cabinet Committee on Building Societies, minutes, 20 June 1938.
[59] NA, HLG29/253, Note, 31 May 1938, initialled B.W.G.
[60] NA, HLG29/253, Note for Minister [of Health?], 22 July 1938.
[61] NA, HLG29/253, Note to Sir John Maude, 26 March 1938.

Simon (Chancellor of the Exchequer).[62] Government counsel advised that Mrs Borders was almost certainly right in law. Yet, as Simon informed the Cabinet, such a judgement would invalidate a large proportion of mortgages, halt new house-building, produce heated political controversy, and, possibly, start a run on building society deposits.[63]

The building society movement pressed for a bill to legalize both new and (retrospectively) existing pool advances, vigorously lobbying that a judgement declaring them *ultra vires* would affect some two million current mortgages, plus the vast majority of new advances. The majority of their new lending activities would thus be suspended, reducing the volume of house-building by at least 50 per cent. Moreover, this would 'immediately cause numerous failures in the house-building industry and widespread unemployment in that and allied trades, involving some 500,000 men. Regard should also be paid to the serious effect on the minds of investors, who exceed three million in number and whose investments, amounting to £600 millions, are withdrawable on short notice.'[64]

However, E. J. Cleary suggests that one of the building society's major fears was that builders might take advantage of pool agreements being declared ultra vires. This might enable them to withdraw their pool deposits with immediate effect and, possibly, successfully re-claim any sums previously deducted to meet short-falls between the money owed to the society on mortgages in default and that raised from selling them.[65]

When the case eventually came to trial in February 1939 it received considerable coverage in the British and even overseas press—intensifying public concern regarding jerry-building and the very limited rights of borrowers under the current mortgage system.[66] Mrs Borders (nicknamed 'Portia' by the press) argued her case in person, pitting herself against the finest brains of the Chancery Bar that building society money could buy. In a public spectacle somewhat akin to the 1997 'McLibel' trial, public sympathy swung behind this taxi driver's wife in her unequal struggle to gain redress from real and obvious hardships at the hands of the British speculative housing system.

Mrs Borders was successful in her claim that she had never executed (signed) the mortgage deed on which Bradford Third Equitable sued for possession. However, Mr Justice Bennett found that the mortgage was not beyond the statutory powers of the society, as the property constituted the primary and basic security for the mortgage. Yet he did raise the question (without expressing a view) as to whether a pooling agreement constituted a legally valid contract between the building society and builder under the 1890 legislation—concerns which were shared by the building society movement and later addressed by the 1939 Act.[67]

---

[62] NA, CAB 27/645, Cabinet Committee on Building Societies, minutes, 20 June 1938.
[63] NA, HLG29/253, memorandum to Cabinet by Chancellor of the Exchequer, 10 June 1938.
[64] NA, HLG29/253, memorandum by joint committee of the Building Societies Association, the National Federation of Building Societies and important unaffiliated societies, 12 March 1938.
[65] Cleary, *Building Society Movement*, 218–19.
[66] For an example of overseas coverage, see 'Building: Borders v. Builders', *Time Magazine* (20 March 1938), online version, <http://www.time.com/time/magazine/article/0,9171,789555,00.html>.
[67] Gower, 'Building Societies and Pooling Agreements', 33–47.

The judge also accepted that the collateral pool transaction was outside the scope of the society's rules, but held that this did not legally invalidate the transaction provided it was within the society's statutory powers. Meanwhile Justice Bennett upheld Mrs Borders' claim that Morrell's had made various misrepresentations regarding the house and the transaction, but decided that the building society could not be held responsible for this, despite their close links with Morrell's and the fact that several fraudulent claims had been made in a brochure which Bradford Third Equitable were apparently aware of. Nevertheless, he noted that:

> I confess I should have been pleased to see a Director or Manager of the Plaintiffs in the witness box, and to have a satisfactory explanation of how, if the Directors knew of the Brochure D.1. and of the statements it contained, they continued to have business associations with Morrell's.[68]

Justice Bennett thus dismissed both the action of Bradford Third Equitable and Mrs Borders' counter-action. Mrs Borders took the case to the Court of Appeal and was awarded damages against Bradford Third Equitable for knowingly allowing misrepresentations to be made about the value and quality of her house.[69] However, Bradford Third Equitable were victorious in their appeal to the House of Lords in May 1941.[70] Meanwhile, a wave of 'rent strikes' by house-purchasers who, like Mrs Borders, found themselves in possession of defective houses, had subsided following the onset of the Second World War.

Justice Bennett's original judgement had not assuaged the building societies' concerns regarding their precarious legal position. As their representative, Walter Harvey, stated in a meeting with government officials, they viewed the judgement as: ' inconclusive, it was to go to appeal and the judge's reference to the pool agreement with the builder was disturbing. Rent strikes were numerous and increasing and many societies were exceedingly restive.'[71] Similarly, Parliamentary Counsel Mr Granville Ram noted that 'Justice Bennett had used cryptic words as to the validity of the pooling agreement between the society and the builder. That issue was left in doubt.'[72]

Government thus pressed ahead with new legislation (the Building Societies Act 1939), which validated existing collateral pool arrangements. A number of safeguards for purchasers were also introduced, though some of these received at least tacit support from leading building society figures, who had long been considering the possibility of legislation to enforce compliance with their abortive 'code of ethics'.[73] The collateral builders were required to deposit under pool schemes was fixed

---

[68] NA, HLG29/23, Judgement, *Third Equitable Building Society v. Borders*, High Court of Justice, Chancery Division, 13 February 1939.
[69] Peter Craig, 'The House that Jerry Built? Building Societies, the State and the Politics of Owner-Occupation', *Housing Studies*, 1 (1986), 102.
[70] McCulloch, 'Owner-Occupation', 443.
[71] NA, HLG29/253, note of meeting of representatives of government officials, later joined by building society representatives, 14 February 1939.
[72] NA, HLG29/253, note of meeting of representatives of government officials, later joined by building society representatives, 14 February 1939.
[73] Cleary, *Building Society Movement*, 217–18.

at the full difference between the societies' normal maximum loan-to-value ratio and the pool figure (which was limited to 95 per cent of the purchase price, excluding fees) for the first five houses. Further houses could then be funded with deposits on a 'one-in-three' basis. Meanwhile, deposits would only be released when the outstanding debt fell below two-thirds of the valuation. The Act also restricted mortgage terms to 21 years (except for houses built by National House Builders Registration Council members)—partly at the behest of the Building Societies Association, which was still seeking to restrict building society competition.[74]

Various safeguards regarding survey valuations were also introduced, while commission payments to builders were prohibited. The impact of these measures was never tested, as the Second World War halted new housing development and for several decades after 1945 building societies faced tight government restrictions on new mortgage business (as an instrument of monetary policy, rather than for reasons directly connected with the housing market).

WAS THERE A LOOMING HOUSING MARKET CRISIS IN 1939?

The housing market appears to have been cooling during the late 1930s, especially in and around London. As noted in Chapter 4, several of the largest London-based speculative developers, including New Ideal Homesteads, Davis Estates, and, to a lesser extent, Wimpey and Wates, had begun to look beyond the Greater London area for some of their new developments. Several of the major house-builders also sought to diversify their target market in terms of income, 'building-down' to lower income groups than the established core market for speculative housing. While the reasons behind these diversifications are not always clear, available evidence suggests that they were often connected to perceptions that conditions in their traditional markets were becoming more difficult.[75]

Over the 6 years to March 1939 average private house completions in England and Wales were substantially in excess of both any previous year and (despite Britain's subsequent population growth) any later year. Even during the year to March 1939, despite concerns regarding a possible market downturn, some 230,600 private houses were completed in England and Wales, compared to a 1968 post-war peak, for the whole of Britain, of 222,000. A significant downturn in demand could have left large numbers of new houses unsold. Given that developers' margins (including interest costs) were in the region of only 15 per cent of the sale price, as noted in Chapter 4, the industry was ill-placed to cope with substantial price falls. Indeed, the declining profits of many leading house-builders during the latter years of the decade suggest that they were already under pressure.

By 1939 new house-building had largely redressed the balance between the stock of available housing and the number of households, at least at national level.

[74] Speight, 'Building Society Behaviour', 227–8.   [75] Wellings, *British Housebuilders*, 50–1.

At the time of the 1921 census the number of dwellings in England and Wales was equivalent to only 88 per cent of the number of private families. By the time of the next, 1931, census, it had risen to 93 per cent, though by March 1939 there were 3 per cent more houses than families.[76] The growth in household spending power was also slowing. While rearmament offset an expected recession in the late 1930s, the annual growth of real consumers' expenditure had slowed from around 2.8–2.9 per cent during the mid-1930s, to 1.7 per cent during 1937, 0.8 per cent for 1938, and only 0.5 per cent for 1939.[77] The Borders case and associated publicity regarding some of the more dubious aspects of the speculative housing market may also have had a significant impact in increasing consumer resistance to house purchase. Fears of war probably also played a role, especially in London, which was known to be vulnerable to German air attack.

Meanwhile, contractors price rings witnessed a resurgence in the mid- and late 1930s, putting upward pressure on house-building costs. The year 1935 saw the foundation of the London Builders' Conference, which sought to establish a price ring initially covering a 15-mile radius of Charing Cross (i.e., the area over which London building wages were regulated). Following some initial difficulties, agreement on new terms was reached in around July 1937, on a basis that brought most of the main players in the London market into the ring. By this time a similar body had been established for the Birmingham area and there were plans to extend the price-fixing machinery to other parts of Britain.[78]

Under the new system member firms intending to tender for competitive contracts of over £3,000 were required to inform the Conference's Chairman regarding their lowest acceptable tender price. The chairman then calculated a 'fair price'—based on the average price of the lowest two-thirds of tenders (to eliminate high tenders by firms that were not really interested in the work), plus an additional 0.1 per cent for every firm tendering. Members (together with outside firms that had been persuaded to cooperate on an ad hoc basis) would then raise their contracts by a fixed percentage, based on the amount that would bring the lowest tender up to the 'fair price'. The successful firm was then obliged to pay a percentage of the difference between their initial lowest price for the contract and the price actually obtained, which was pooled among the member firms.[79] Membership of the conference increased from 70 firms in August 1937 to almost 120 by July 1938.[80] A month later the conference was beginning to consider extending its area of operations, in the light of several important aerodrome rearmament contracts.

---

[76] Marion Bowley, *Housing and the State 1919–1944* (London: George Allen & Unwin, 1945), 269.

[77] Roger Middleton, *Towards the Managed Economy: Keynes, the Treasury, and the Fiscal Policy Debate of the 1930s* (London: Methuen, 1985), 25.

[78] Northamptonshire Record Office (NRO), John Laing plc archive (NRO, Laing), L/4/2/47, London Builders' Conference 1938–9, Sir Alfred Hurst (Chairman, London Builders' Conference), 'The London Builders' Conference: Its Origin, Objects, and Methods of Working', 16 July 1937.

[79] Hurst, 'The London Builders' Conference'; London Builders' Conference, 'Terms of Co-operation of Non-member Firms', note, March 1938.

[80] NRO, Laing, L/4/2/47, London Builders' Conference 1938–9, letter from Secretary (signature illegible), London Builders' Conference, to J. Laing & Sons Ltd, 6 July 1938.

By November it covered not only London and Middlesex, but Berkshire, Buckinghamshire, and Oxfordshire, together with part of Hampshire.[81]

George Speight argued that a severe housing market recession at the end of the 1930s would have caused significant bad debt losses for the building society movement. It was unlikely (but not impossible) that these would have directly led to the failure of any large societies. However, they might have started a run on building society deposits by savers reacting to publicity regarding rising bad debts (or to bankruptcies among the smaller, more exposed societies). These losses might in turn have compelled them to restrict mortgage lending, accentuating the housing market downturn and compounding the societies' bad debt problems. Bank of England intervention to increase liquidity for the building society movement would probably have still prevented failures among the largest societies. However, some might have been forced to cut payments to shareholders. Such a scenario would have had dire consequences for the reputation of the building society movement and their role in the housing market.[82]

Assessing the likelihood of a severe housing market crisis, had war not intervened, is inevitably a speculative exercise. However, data for the largest London-based building society, Abbey Road, provide some indication of the impact of changing market conditions to 1939. The data, in Table 10.2, show that arrears of over 13 weeks were actually lower in 1938 than in the middle of the decade and remained so in June 1939. Properties in possession and in receivership displayed a similar trend. Meanwhile, losses from sales (as a proportion of all mortgages) were lower in November 1938, the latest available figure, than the average of the available figures for 1935–7. The absolute loss per house repossessed had also fallen, from over £38 in June 1935 to less than £22 in November 1938, suggesting either that the societies were becoming more efficient at protecting themselves from losses (through, for example, builders' pool clauses which required the builder to repurchase) or that house prices remained relatively buoyant. Data for the Co-operative Permanent are also available, on an annual basis, for 1933–5. These show a loss per house similar to that for Abbey Road in June 1935, while indicating a downward trend in defaults over the early 1930s.

Moreover, there is evidence that speculative house-builders were already tempering their output to reflect the more subdued market. For example, between 1935 and 1939 Laing's speculative housing sales declined from around 1,300 houses a year on their nine estates around London, plus a further 200 on five estates in Carlisle, to around 725 houses in London and around 100 in Carlisle.[83] This cannot be explained as being due to any shortage of sites; in June 1939 seven of Laing's eight current London estates had undeveloped sites, comprising 3,964 plots, compared to 4,106 houses already sold and just 203 houses built but unsold (including

---

[81] NRO, Laing, L/4/2/47, London Builders' Conference 1938–9, letters from London Builders' Conference to John Laing & Son Ltd, 19 August, 27 October, and 7 November 1938.
[82] Speight, 'Building Society Behaviour', 247.
[83] NRO, Laing, L1/3/17, AGM review of the year 1935, 25 June 1936; L1/3/20, AGM review of the year 1938, 9 June 1939.

Table 10.2. Data on arrears, repossessions and sales (percentage of all mortgages), Abbey Road and Co-operative Permanent building societies

Date	Abbey Road Building Society					Co-operative Permanent Building Society	
	Arrears[a]	In possession	In receivership	Losses from sales	Losses per house (£)	Taken into possession[b]	Losses per house (£)
1933						3.4	33
1934						2.7	25
1935						1.6	37
June 1935	2.03	0.37	0.32	0.05	38.77		
November 1935	1.99	0.49	0.47				
February 1936	1.57	0.38	0.37	0.04	36.62		
June 1936	1.46	0.28	0.29				
September 1936	1.29	0.27	0.28	0.08	35.66		
November 1936	1.42	0.23	0.26				
February 1937	1.50	0.28	0.26	0.03	28.11		
June 1937	1.39	0.20	0.21				
September 1937	1.37	0.18	0.25	0.06	27.50		
November 1937	1.14	0.16	0.22				
March 1938	1.15	0.26	0.16				
June 1938	1.07	0.14	0.17				
September 1938	1.02	0.16	0.16	0.04	21.53		
November 1938	1.18	0.11	0.19				
February 1939	1.14	0.22	0.15				
June 1939							

Source: Abbey Road: LMA, Abbey Road papers, 30/32, Mortgage Accounts Committee minutes, agenda papers, 13 July 1937; 13 December 1938; 11 July 1939. Co-operative Permanent, Luke Samy: 'The Building Society Promise: The Accessibility, Risk, and Efficiency of Building Societies in England c.1880–1939', DPhil thesis (University of Oxford, 2010), 223.

[a] Arrears of over 13 weeks. Data for columns 2–4 are for 20th of each month; columns 5 and 6 are for 30th of each month.
[b] All repossessed properties were sold within the same year.

69 show houses).[84] It thus appears that Laing was not developing substantial numbers of units in advance of demand. Whereas earlier generations of developers might typically develop a whole terrace block, for sale once the block had been completed, interwar speculative estate development practice generally involved selling most houses 'off plan'—based on a viewing of the show house and examination of the building plot. Thus the danger of 'over-building' was substantially reduced.

It thus appears that, given the boost to economic activity in the late 1930s from rearmament, together with efforts by speculative builders to diversify into new markets (in terms of location and household income), and their practice of selling houses off-plan, there was no strong danger of a crisis in the market for new houses in the months preceding the Second World War. Instead the crisis was largely a political and PR one, based on the combination of a mis-selling scandal and a legal challenge to the financial arrangements between developers and building societies that underpinned the 95 per cent mortgage system.

CONCLUSION

The builders' pool mortgage finance system greatly facilitated access to owner occupation, but at the same time left buyers open to a variety of opportunistic practices by speculative builders. Yet it was presented to the buyer, in developers' and building societies' publicity material, as having a number of key safeguards—such as the policing of building standards by the building society and sympathetic treatment in the event of buyers encountering financial difficulties—that were actually far weaker than they appeared. Regulation was clearly needed—though, given the community of interests between the builders and the building society movement, and the absence of any strong consumer movement to counter their PR and lobbying activities, it took a national scandal and a threatened crisis to bring this about. Even then, the big building societies proved largely successful in steering the legislation so that it did not prove detrimental to their interests and mainly served to restrict mortgage competition in ways that the largest societies, with established market shares, had long been seeking.

[84] NRO, Laing, L1/3/20, note of housing estate development position as at 8 June 1939.

11
The Legacy of the Interwar Semi

THE INTERWAR HOUSING ACHIEVEMENT

Suburban estates represent the most important infrastructure legacy bequeathed to subsequent generations by the citizens of interwar Britain. While Britain failed to match the levels of investment in roads or telecommunications achieved by other leading industrial nations, it was successful in transforming both the quantity and quality of its housing stock. By 1939 around a third of all British houses had been built within the previous 20 years—mainly on suburban estates. The concept of the 'ideal home' had become closely associated with the suburban, semi-detached (and, to some extent, owner-occupied) house, while the pre-1914 terrace was generally regarded as 'obsolete' in terms of location, high plot density, limited utilities, poor fenestration, and (often) no gardens.[1]

Remarkably, the interwar semi has retained its status as the 'ideal home' for many families, almost three-quarters of a century after the last interwar houses had their foundations laid. Indeed, the 1930s house is, in a very real sense, less 'obsolete' today than the Edwardian terrace had become by the mid-1920s. The 'universal' house model discussed in Chapter 4 has proved adaptable to the major changes in family requirements since the 1930s—for example, most had designs which permitted the removal of the wall between the two reception rooms to create a larger, through living space. Public and private investment in four million such homes between the wars thus produced high long-term returns, improving the quantity and, particularly, the quality, of Britain's housing stock.

However, perhaps the most important legacy of the interwar semi is embodied in the millions of working-class children who grew up in Tudor Walters-type housing between the wars. This period is often depicted as an era of mass unemployment, chronic job insecurity, and bleak prospects for those establishing new households. For millions of families, particularly in northern Britain and Wales, this view is essentially correct. Yet for millions more this was a period of dramatic transformation in lifestyles—heralding a transition from a 'traditional' working-class mode of living based around long-established and tightly knit urban communities, making ends meet from day to day, to a recognizably 'modern' mode, centred around the nuclear family and the home, and requiring longer-term

---

[1] See, for example, Ministry of Health, *Report to the Minister of Health by the Departmental Committee on Valuation for Rates, 1939* (London: HMSO, 1944), paragraph 11; Marion Bowley, *Housing and the State 1919–1944* (London: George Allen & Unwin, 1945), 36–7.

household planning horizons. The suburban semi played a key role in this transition, as was recognized by contemporaries. For example, in 1941 George Orwell noted that:

> The modern Council house, with its bathroom and electric light, is smaller than the stockbroker's villa, but is recognizably the same kind of house, which the farm labourer's cottage is not. A person who has grown up in a Council housing estate is likely to be—indeed, visibly *is*—more middle class in outlook than a person who has grown up in a slum.[2]

Like the affluent worker studies of the 1950s and 1960s, Orwell was mistaken in conflating this with 'embourgeoisement', as it is more accurately characterized as the emergence of a new pattern of working-class family life. Yet he was correct in noting the central importance of housing in influencing wider aspects of family behaviour. As this study has shown, working-class people who made the transition from inner-urban to new suburban communities in the 1920s and 1930s perceived this to have had a marked impact on their lifestyles, encompassing how they dressed, furnished their homes, allocated their weekly finances, interacted with neighbours, socialized, and planned for their own, and their children's, future.

This transformation was most complete on the new estates of cheap owner-occupied housing, priced from around £350 to £650, which proved attractive, and accessible, to a substantial proportion of working-class married couples setting up home for the first time during the 1930s. Buying a house on mortgage entailed a substantial financial commitment, typically equivalent to around two and a half years' income, from which households could not extract themselves nearly so easily as was the case with renting. There were heavy sunk costs of the deposit and accumulated payments, plus, often, a greater psychological commitment to the new lifestyle and better prospects for their children. Thus the degree of forethought and long-term planning by such families, to develop strategies which would enable them to keep up the payments and meet the 'standards' of the estate, was markedly higher. This was reflected in, for example, a conscious effort to limit their number of children to around two—both in order to make ends meet and to give their children a better future by ensuring that the necessary resources were available.

Municipal suburban estates had broadly similar impacts on working-class migrants—though the depth of commitment to the new lifestyle was generally less strong—as it was easier to walk away from a tenancy than from a mortgage. Moreover, people typically moved to council estates at a later stage of their family lifecycle than owner-occupiers, whose purchase often represented the establishment of their new household, or a move to desired housing following a short initial period in temporary accommodation. New council tenants often already had several children—a trend accentuated by housing allocation policies which prioritized families with children and, increasingly (especially during the 1930s), those with large families. Yet the social impacts on new migrants were nevertheless profound—especially for the growing

---

[2] George Orwell, *The Lion and the Unicorn: Socialism and the English Genius* (London: Secker & Warburg, 1941), 52.

numbers of slum clearance tenants who were transferred to a very different mode of housing than they had hitherto experienced. Contrary to the myth of 'coals in the bath', contemporary and oral history evidence suggests that the majority of such families did experience a major transition in household behaviour following their moves, as they embraced the new opportunities for a more hygienic and home-centred life provided by their new bathrooms, gardens, and the other modern utilities embodied in the municipal semi.

Alison Ravetz has attacked the rise of municipal suburban housing as 'a culture transfer amounting to cultural colonisation: a vision forged by one section of society for application to another, who whom it might be more, or less, acceptable and appropriate.'[3] In fact, rather than being passive recipients of the utopian visions of the planning intelligentsia, the Tudor Walters-style suburban house, in both its council and private sector forms, encapsulated the aspirations of large numbers of working-class families, who saw it as a means of achieving a cluster of related consumption goals that collectively constituted a new form of working-class lifestyle. While some council tenants (including a large proportion of those relocated through slum clearance programmes) may have been moved to housing which did not match their existing preferences and aspirations, most interwar working-class migrants to suburbia were active participants in a project of achieving a cluster of consumption and lifestyle objectives for themselves and their children.

Perhaps the most interesting finding of this study is the degree of similarity in the behavioural changes evident in the great majority of households who moved to suburbia as a result of free choice and the significant minority who moved to council housing only because their existing 'slum' dwellings were being demolished. This suggests that while choice played a major role in the social changes outlined in this study, habitus—taken for granted social norms and practices that shape and constrain consumption choices—also played a major, and possibly dominant, role. Interwar housing that was affordable to the urban working classes was largely limited to two formats—some variant of the inner-urban terrace, or an even more narrowly defined housing type, the Tudor Walters house. This latter type almost always had the same key characteristics—suburban location, three bedrooms, front and rear gardens, modern utilities, broadly similar internal layouts, and a rectangular floorplan with longer frontage and shorter depth than the terrace. As such, households faced a choice between two distinct housing formats, rather than a spectrum of alternatives.

The particular characteristics of the interwar semi (together with the short terraces, bungalows, chalets, and maisonettes developed along Tudor Walters lines) appear to have influenced families in broadly similar ways—though this process was differentiated, to some extent, by the 'reputation' or 'tone' of the estate in question, which in turn was strongly linked to housing costs and tenure. Estates had two key common locational characteristics—they were sited some distance from where their inhabitants had previously lived and where they currently worked, and

---

[3] Alison Ravetz, *Council Housing and Culture: The History of a Social Experiment* (Abingdon: Routledge, 2001), 5.

they typically drew their populations from different inner-urban areas, rather than representing wholesale 'transplants' of communities from one location to another. These had important implications, as migration to an estate entailed a break with the social norms, values, status markers, and limits on conspicuous consumption that had governed their old communities. Disruption of the habitus interacted with the new lifestyle opportunities implicit in the physical characteristics and household budget demands of the suburban home, together with the more materialistic social norms of their new communities, to foster the cluster of values that constituted the new working-class respectability.

In practice, the influences of choice and habitus cannot be neatly unpicked. This study has shown that pre-existing preferences for some of the characteristics of suburban lifestyles were widely evident among voluntary suburban migrants, and fostered by propaganda from a range of agencies, including health professionals, print and broadcast media, and the housing and consumer durables industries. Yet the fact that such households modified their behaviour considerably following migration, often in ways they had not fully anticipated, indicates that the new conditions also played a major role in moulding habits.

Migration to suburbia constituted a major system shock to existing household routines and habits—owing to three interrelated impacts. The first involved the disruption to daily habits inherent in a transfer to a new residential environment. New commuting patterns, household power utilities, and facilities such as gardens, kitchens, and bathrooms necessarily entailed the modification of previous routines and thus often displaced existing habits by new ones. The second impact involved replacing the social norms of the old community with more privatized, domesticated, and materially orientated norms and status markers—stimulating new patterns of behaviour to meet the 'standards' of the new estate. Finally, the status of the new house as the family's key lifestyle project, requiring a major and sustained investment of monetary, time, and psychological resources, and encapsulating long-term aspirations for themselves and their children, further encouraged the rapid adoption of new habits that would boost and defend the rewards from this investment.

These lifestyle patterns are strongly similar to those identified by social studies of new residential communities in the 1950s and 1960s—suggesting that the origins of social changes commonly attributed to the post-war 'affluent' worker were already emerging among families who could not be considered affluent by any post-1945 definition. This gives further weight to two key arguments that emerge from this study—that new residential community development should be seen as a major driver of social change; and that the degree of continuity in patterns of social change during the 1930s and 1950s is markedly greater than is generally appreciated.

Yet it is important to remember that for many people setting up new households in the 1920s and 1930s there was no real opportunity to cross the bridge from inner-urban terrace to new suburban semi. The army of the unemployed, together with the large numbers of people in insecure or casual employment, lacked the means to make this move—while the consequences for such families, when compulsorily re-housed under slum clearance schemes, were sometimes negative or even tragic. Most rural workers were also locked into poor quality housing by poverty and geography. Farm workers' families suffered from very poor housing, often provided under a semi-feudal system which served both to keep them tied to the land and to minimize their employers' wage costs. The 1937/8 Ministry of Labour working-class household budgets survey found that almost 40 per cent of agricultural workers were living in accommodation provided 'rent free' (that is, regarded as part of their wages), from which they could be evicted at will. Most others rented their houses, while only 4.4 per cent owned or were buying their dwellings. Average weekly rents (or corresponding deductions from cash wages for employer-provided housing), plus rates and water charges, amounted to 4s 9d, less than half that for a typical urban working-class family.

Low rents were necessitated by low household incomes, averaging 57s 11d, compared to 86s 3d for other working-class households in employment.[4] Yet they also reflected deplorable housing conditions. Few agricultural workers' cottages had indoor plumbing, while as late as 1939 some 25 per cent of English parishes lacked any mains water supply and a higher proportion lacked mains sewerage.[5] Typically cold, damp farm cottages left families particularly vulnerable to diseases such as rheumatism, tuberculosis, and bronchitis. Meanwhile, the growing popularity of the countryside with town-dwellers reduced the stock of better-quality rural housing, often purchased by the middle classes as weekend retreats.

The other principal group of rural workers, coal miners, also continued to live under conditions viewed even by contemporaries as squalid, overcrowded, and unhealthy. In Northumberland and Durham miners lived in housing provided 'rent free' by their employers, while in other regions they typically rented their homes. South Wales had a strong tradition of owner occupation, though given the depressed state of the coal industry and the remoteness of many colliery villages, such housing did not have any great market value. The unifying characteristic of miners' housing, regardless of tenure, was its generally poor quality. Like agricultural communities, mining areas were a poor prospect for housing investment, typically characterized by isolated communities, dominated by a single industry, offering low-wage, insecure employment.[6] Even expanding coalfields, such as Kent, found it hard to attract housing development. For example, when Henry Boot's First National Housing Trust sought to build cheap rented houses in Aylesham under the Housing (Financial Provisions) Act, 1933, the building societies refused to finance the project—on the grounds that miners constituted the only local source of housing demand.[7]

---

[4] The National Archives, LAB17/7, 'Weekly Expenditure of Working-Class Households in the United Kingdom in 1937-38', Ministry of Labour and National Service, July 1949, 18–42.

[5] Peter Dewey, 'Agriculture, Agrarian Society, and the Countryside', in Chris Wrigley (ed.), *A Companion to Early Twentieth Century Britain* (Oxford: Blackwell, 2003), 281.

[6] Barry Supple, *The History of the British Coal Industry*, Vol. 4: *1913–1946: The Political Economy of Decline* (Oxford: Clarendon, 1987), 457–62.

[7] Henry Boot plc company archives, Charles Boot, 'Housing Built by Private Enterprise', memorandum for the Ministry of Health's Sub-Committee on Private Enterprise Housing, October 1943, 2.

FROM IDEAL HOME TO TOWER BLOCK

Given the outstanding success of the interwar semi, it seems counterintuitive that government largely abandoned this model of municipal housing from the 1950s. The rejection of suburban estates in favour of high-density, and often high-rise, inner-urban housing, was conceived by the planning and architectural elite even prior to the Second World War, but born and nurtured by a mixture of political expediency, false optimism, commercial lobbying, and (to an extent that will probably never be fully clear) corruption.

During the 1930s the architectural and planning elite was already becoming enamoured with high-density mass public housing projects. A growing number of its leading lights were drawn to the modern movement's idealistic view of high-rise mass housing's potential for fostering more cohesive communities, together with the visual appeal of monumental buildings that would impact on the urban skyline. A shift towards slum clearance also led some to advocate high-rise housing using industrialized building techniques on cost grounds. Yet in reality costs per home were typically more than a third higher than for suburban council houses. Indeed per square foot of floor-space, flats were found to be almost twice as expensive.[8]

Enthusiasm for mass housing was accompanied by increasing hostility towards conventional suburban estates. The semi's individuality and status connotations were seen as diametrically opposed to what many architects and planners saw as their ideal—housing which asserted community through collective expression. Indeed the very features that made speculative semis attractive to their purchasers—such as individual gardens, variegation in design, and opportunities for occupiers to further customize their external appearance—made them all the more objectionable in the architects' and planners' eyes.[9]

Delegations from various councils visited the Vienna workers' flats and similar Continental projects of the 1930s and reported back positively. It was noted that the majority of European flats examined lacked private baths or bathrooms and were smaller and less well-furnished than their British counterparts, leading to recommendations that British standards of private comfort should be combined with European levels of public amenities. The extra costs that this would impose, on what was already an expensive housing form, were largely glossed over.[10]

The estate was subsequently developed with loans from the Public Works Loan Board and from the parent company.

[8] John Burnett, *A Social History of Housing 1815–1885*, 2nd edn (London: Methuen, 1986), 247–8.

[9] For a review of this literature, see Ian Davis, 'One of the Greatest Evils... Dunroamin and the Modern Movement', in Paul Oliver, Ian Davis, and Ian Bentley, *Dunroamin: The Suburban Semi and its Enemies* (London: Pimlico, 1981).

[10] See Alison Ravetz, 'From Working-Class Tenement to Modern Flat: Local Authorities and Multi-storey Housing between the Wars', in Anthony Sutcliffe (ed.), *Multi-storey Living: The British Working Class Experience* (London: Croom Helm, 1974).

These views became more influential among policy-makers during and after the Second World War, in an environment of policy experimentation and a greatly increased reverence for the 'cult of the expert'. Yet the enthusiasm of the planning 'experts' was largely based on their own ideologies and tastes, rather than any significant body of empirical evidence. The new planning ethos had relatively little impact on the type of housing actually built during the era of the 1945–51 Labour governments (except in Greater London towards the end of this period). Severe shortages and the pressing need for new houses led central and local government to fall back on traditional solutions and over 1946–50 flats and maisonettes represented only around 10 per cent of new local authority dwellings in England and Wales, with most houses located on suburban estates and virtually no high-rise blocks being built.[11]

It was the Conservative governments of 1951–64 that launched Britain's mass housing era, the contribution of flats to new municipal homes rising to 22 per cent during 1951–5, 35 per cent over 1956–60, and 48 per cent for 1961–5.[12] Meanwhile, blocks of ten or more storeys represented 9 per cent of new public sector housing during 1953–9 and reached an all-time peak of 28 per cent during 1960–4. The reasons for the Conservatives' championing of a building form originally advocated by architects and planners influenced by socialist views of community are complex. The weight of professional opinion in the planning sector certainly played some role, as did a desire to avoid encroachment on 'good agricultural land' and an erroneous belief that industrialized building techniques would, in the long term, yield cost savings. However, the two key reasons appear to have been a switch in public housing provision from general needs to the residual functions of 'slum clearance', together with aggressive advocacy for high-density solutions by an influential group of major national contractors who received most of the tower block contracts.

In 1953 the Conservatives resumed the slum clearance programme and in 1955 it was announced that the private sector would be left to provide the bulk of new housing. Subsidies to local authorities for general needs housing were reduced and, in 1956, abolished. Henceforth councils would only receive government financial assistance for slum clearance housing, the expected character of which was signalled by a substantial reduction in housing standards. High-density, inner-urban developments constituted a politically attractive option for the Conservatives, as by concentrating slum clearance families in such areas the development of edge-of-town estates, which might raise opposition from established residents (and bring Labour voters into Conservative council wards and Parliamentary constituencies) was avoided.[13] This policy also reflected a view of slum tenants which had changed little from the negative stereotypes of the 1930s, reviewed in Chapter 9. For example, Wilfred Burns, City Planning Officer for Newcastle 1960–8 and a key figure

---

[11] A. E. Holmans, *Housing Policy in Britain* (London: Croom Helm, 1987), 114. Figures for ratios of flats to all municipal housing include new towns, but not housing associations or 'pre-fabs'.
[12] Holmans, *Housing Policy*, 114.   [13] Holmans, *Housing Policy*, 117–18.

in British post-war planning, described slum dwellers as 'almost a separate race of people... who have no initiative or civic pride. The task surely is to break up such groupings, even though the people seem to be satisfied with their miserable environment'.[14]

The big contractors launched a sustained PR and lobbying drive to persuade policy-makers that high-rise, 'system-built' blocks offered the best slum clearance solution. Most of this campaigning was aimed at politicians and officials rather than the public and a great deal involved informal contacts. As Patrick Dunleavy has noted, there were strong personal and funding links between some of the major building firms most active in public housing development and key policy-makers. Keith Joseph, heir to the Bovis fortune and their chairman 1958–9, then served as parliamentary secretary to the Minister of Housing and Local Government 1959–61. Dame Evelyn Sharp, permanent secretary at the Ministry 1955–66 and a leading champion for high-rise development, was offered a Directorship at Bovis on her retirement and was also a close friend of the contractor Neil Wates. Meanwhile, several leading contractors, such as McAlpine and Taylor Woodrow, were major long-term contributors to Conservative Party funds.[15]

Such links were also present at local authority level. Council members and officials were often invited to travel to the Continent to see new system-built housing estates—receiving hospitality from developers advocating the systems in question. Strong links between a major industry and policy-makers are not unusual, though, as the Poulson scandal was later to reveal, there were cases where local and/or and central government officials and politicians received incentives from housing contractors and their agents—including some that met the criminal definition of bribery.

Comprehensive urban development schemes, which local authorities were increasingly encouraged to employ during the late 1950s and 1960s, often involved demolishing both slums and other housing that got in their way. This eventually provoked a backlash by local residents, especially owner-occupiers of houses which they did not perceive to be slums (and, often, could not be so classified by any reasonable definition). Sometimes property was condemned merely because it was old and, in the eyes of planners, 'obsolete'. A campaign against the bulldozer gathered pace during the 1960s, as relocated families became increasingly critical both of the quality of their new accommodation and of the destruction of their old communities. There was also a growing volume of empirical evidence showing that high-rise flats were both unsuitable for families and deeply unpopular, both with

---

[14] Wilfred Burns, *New Towns for Old: The Technique of Urban Renewal* (London: Leonard Hill, 1963), 93–4.
[15] Patrick Dunleavy, *The Politics of Mass Housing in Britain, 1945–1975* (Oxford: Clarendon, 1981), 20-21; Kevin Theakston 'Sharp, Evelyn Adelaide, Baroness Sharp (1903–1985), civil servant', *Oxford DNB*, <http://www.oxforddnb.com/index/31/101031672/>; Brian Harrison, 'Joseph, Keith Sinjohn, Baron Joseph (1918–1994), politician', *Oxford DNB*, <http://www.oxforddnb.com/view/article/55063>.

prospective tenants (who generally wanted conventional houses with gardens) and with those already relocated to tower blocks.[16]

Flats continued to account for about half of all new public sector housing over the decade to 1975. Much of the balance consisted of high-density, low-rise, developments. These often took the form of terraces, but, like the tower blocks, generally employed industrialized building systems that made them attractive propositions for the big contractors. Meanwhile, their appearance became markedly more standardized than interwar council houses, partly owing to the desire of local authority planners and architects to stamp out any hint of individuality (the colours of doors and, in some cases, even curtains being specified to achieve this effect). Similarly, communal areas of greenery often replaced individual gardens. Thus, as in the tower block, there was no element of external 'defensible space' whereby owners could define their own territories.[17]

Two events eventually brought an end both to the era of high-density mass housing and to public confidence in the unholy alliance of building contractors, politicians, and housing professionals who had championed this policy. The first was the partial collapse of the twenty-two-storey Ronan Point tower block in Newham, East London, on 16 May 1968—two months after its completion by Taylor-Woodrow-Anglian—when a small gas explosion demolished a load-bearing wall. This led to the deaths of five people and, at a time of growing public concern regarding tower blocks, fatally undermined confidence in their construction standards and safety.

The second, the 'Poulson scandal', broke in 1972, when the tower block era was already coming to an end, but nevertheless had a crucial impact in making the public aware of the extensive corruption which underpinned some comprehensive redevelopment schemes. The bankruptcy of architect John Poulson, which triggered a police fraud investigation and the eventual imprisonment of both Poulson and a number of his associates, shed light on the extent to which those involved with overseeing large-scale urban development had direct (and often illegal) financial interests in pushing them through. Poulson (whose career was fictionalized in the seminal BBC series *Our Friends in the North*) had built up what was, at its peak, Britain's largest architectural practice—pioneering the integration of professional services into a single building design service firm. However, his success had been fuelled by industrial-scale bribery, encompassing all ranks of local and central government from council officials to MPs and peers. His corruption trial was the largest of the century, leading to a seven-year sentence for Poulson, the conviction of twenty others, and the resignation of Home Secretary Reginald Maudling, who had chaired two of Poulson's companies.[18]

---

[16] Dunleavy, *Politics of Mass Housing*, 94.
[17] Paul Oliver, 'Introduction', in Paul Oliver, Ian Davis, and Ian Bentley, *Dunroamin: The Suburban Semi and its Enemies* (London: Pimlico, 1981), 21–3.
[18] Owen Ludler, 'Poulson, John Garlick Llewellyn (1910–1993), architect and criminal', *Oxford DNB*, online version, <http://www.oxforddnb.com/view/article/53151>.

Neither the Ronan Point disaster or the Poulson scandal was seized upon by the opposition party of the day, as both major parties were deeply implicated in the practices that were brought to light. However, the curtain which had shielded the system from public view had been torn away, resulting in an upsurge in opposition to further comprehensive redevelopment or mass housing projects. Planners and architects might still preach the merits of inner-urban mass housing solutions and attack 'reactionaries' who preferred the old semis (or the traditional terraces that had been torn down to make way for tower blocks)—but now no one was listening.

By the mid-1970s construction of high-rise blocks of ten or more storeys had virtually ceased and the limited amount of public sector dwellings built in the second half of the decade constituted vernacular houses and low-rise flats, built using traditional materials and methods.[19] In this respect public sector housing re-converged with building for owner occupation, which had never departed from traditional building forms (with the exception of flats aimed at young adults, which grew in popularity from the 1980s). However, the 1950s and 1960s left a legacy of well over 2.5 million council flats of five storeys or more, which eroded the quality and, eventually even the quantity, of the public sector housing stock—many having to be demolished within a few decades of their construction.[20]

Meanwhile, the 1970s witnessed a revival of popular interest in, and enthusiasm for, the interwar suburbs. Long viewed by the intelligentsia as dreary, monotonous, and conservative, they became rehabilitated as an environment which, while inherently nostalgic, was nevertheless central to aspirational, upwardly mobile, modern Britain.[21] Ironically, the traditional inner-urban terrace also underwent something of a popular renaissance, as—when bathrooms and modern utilities were added—many terraced streets were shown to provide better housing than the developments councils sought to put in their place. Conversely, one major long-term casualty of the comprehensive redevelopment era was public trust in planning professionals and architects who advocated new approaches to housing provision. Even now the architectural pioneers of the interwar semi, such as Ned Lutyens and Raymond Unwin, represent the last generation of British housing architects to enjoy both professional and popular acclaim.

What of the interwar suburban council estates? These experienced divergent fortunes during the post-war decades—the more desirable being transferred piecemeal to the private sector via individual house sales to incumbent tenants, while the residual became increasingly dominated by people deemed to fall outside the conventional housing market. The switch of housing policy from general needs to slum clearance in the mid-1950s revived the social tensions between established tenants and 'rough' in-comers, discussed in Chapter 9. Meanwhile, housing policy increasingly turned away from a view of the council as a responsible landlord

---

[19] Holmans, *Housing Policy*, 114–15; Dunleavy, *Politics of Mass Housing*, 353.

[20] E. W. Cooney, 'High Flats in Local Authority Housing in England and Wales since 1945', in Anthony Sutcliffe (ed.), *Multi-storey Living: The British Working Class Experience* (London: Croom Helm, 1974), 152; Ravetz, *Council Housing*, 104.

[21] Dominic Sandbrook, *State of Emergency: The Way We Were: Britain 1970–1974* (London: Penguin, 2011), 329–40.

seeking to safeguard the welfare of its tenants, towards seeing council housing as a means of addressing (or, more accurately, containing) various social ills. 'Problem families' were often concentrated on specific estates, or areas of estates—a policy which reduced negative impacts on other communities, but did much to develop a popular perception of council estates as areas of deprivation, poverty, and crime. Often there was more than a grain of truth in such perceptions; for example, early migrants to Liverpool's interwar estates, interviewed by McKenna in the 1980s, often contrasted their happiness with life there before the Second World War with their current fears, or experience, of crime and anti-social behaviour.[22]

The 1977 Homelessness Act had a major impact in marginalizing council housing, by giving priority to unintentionally homeless families.[23] An increasing focus on housing allocation according to 'needs' and 'rights' made it impossible to filter out prospective tenants who had records of anti-social, or criminal, behaviour that might create nuisance, or worse, for their neighbours. In contrast to the framework of regulations that governed life on municipal estates during the 1920s and 1930s, councils generally appeared unable, or unwilling, to effectively police tenants' behaviour.[24] As a result, the term 'estate' was stripped of its original aspirational connotations, becoming a byword for areas blighted by social decay and crime.

Council housing sales (which greatly accelerated during the 1980s, but were a longer-term feature of some councils' housing policies) intensified the trend towards associating what was left of the municipal housing stock with problem families, by removing the more affluent tenants, who generally occupied the better housing, from the tenure. Council housing eventually ceased to be a real accommodation choice for most families, sales to tenants and demolitions of the post-war tower blocks reducing the proportion of municipal tenants from 34 per cent of British families in 1981 to 19 per cent by 1996 and, under New Labour, to only 12 per cent by 2005.[25]

THE END OF AFFORDABLE AND DESIRABLE SUBURBAN HOUSING?

One of the paradoxes of modern life is that, despite a considerable rise in real incomes over the past 60 years, most families find themselves unable to afford the types of houses their forebears doing similar occupations in the 1930s would have inhabited. This applies not only to the interwar semi, but even the Edwardian

---

[22] See Madeline McKenna, 'The Development of Suburban Council Housing Estates in Liverpool between the Wars', PhD thesis (University of Liverpool, 1986), Appendix 13.

[23] Harold Carter, 'Building the Divided City: Race, Class and Social Housing in Southwark, 1945–1995', *London Journal*, 33:2 (2008), 173.

[24] Harold Carter, 'From Slums to Slums in Three Generations: Housing Policy and the Political Economy of the Welfare State, 1945–2005', University of Oxford Discussion Paper in Economic and Social History 98 (May 2012), 18 & 38–9.

[25] Office for National Statistics (ONS), *General Household Survey: Results for 2006* (Norwich: HMSO, 2008), 294.

terrace—many young professionals now finding themselves buying (or struggling to find the deposits for) houses originally built for manual labourers. This is the product of a long-term rise in house prices that has consistently outpaced the growth in real incomes and has culminated in a serious crisis of housing affordability, outlined in Table 11.1. Real house prices doubled over 1938–70, doubled again by the late 1980s, and doubled once more by 2007. Following a temporary peak after the Second World War (reflecting bomb damage and a virtual cessation of new building), the ratio of average house prices to average earnings remained relatively stable during the 1950s and 1960s. Government deliberately restricted mortgage lending—not for reasons connected with housing policy, but as part of a series of measures designed to control consumer spending—to cope with periodic balance of payments crises and defend the value of sterling.

Nevertheless owner occupation experienced growing popularity, partly due to the increasing association of council housing with high-rise flats and slum clearance tenants. Moves towards de-regulation of the housing market from the early 1970s, enabling banks to compete for mortgage business with the building societies, fuelled a series of housing booms. The ratio of average house prices to average adult earnings rose with each successive housing cycle, peaking at 4.0 in 1973, 4.2 in 1989, and, following recovery from the property crash of the early 1990s, 4.8 times average adult incomes in 2002. Yet, in an atmosphere of vigorous competition for mortgage business by banks and other financial institutions, a debt-fuelled consumer boom saw the ratio rise to an incredible 6.2 times adult incomes in 2007. Even before the 2008 credit crunch put an end to liberal mortgage lending, owner-occupation rates had already begun to fall (particularly for young people with no existing housing equity), as growing numbers found themselves financially excluded from the market. Since then the decline in owner occupation has intensified, as a collapse in property market activity has not been reflected in a similarly severe fall in house prices, while overstretched lenders have tightened up their minimum deposit and income to loan value ratios.

In some key respects the quality of post-war speculative housing has also represented a step backwards from the interwar semi. A concern to protect agricultural land and the countryside led to the introduction of a much tighter planning framework after the Second World War. Building land costs consequently rose, leading to an increase in densities even for suburban houses, with the footprints of both houses and their gardens diminishing. Soaring land costs also contributed to rapid price rises for desirable pre-1939 suburban houses, thus concentrating their ownership among higher income groups. Cost pressures for higher densities were accentuated by both population growth and a reduction in average household size. Households declined from an average of 3.72 persons in 1931 to 2.33 in 2008, reflecting both growing numbers of elderly people living alone and a substantial increase in the number of single-person or small households for people of working age.[26] Despite low fertility rates for much of this period, population growth was

[26] Source: 1931, Alan Holmans, 'Housing', in A. H. Halsey (ed.), *Twentieth Century British Social Trends* (Basingstoke: Macmillan, 2000), 470–1; 2008, ONS, *Housing and Planning Statistics 2010*

Table 11.1. Housing affordability and owner-occupation rates since 1938

Year	Real house prices (1970 = 100)	House prices/ adult earnings	Owner-occupation rate (%)
1938	49	2.7	32
1948	99	4.3	
1951	91	3.8	31
1954	72	2.8	
1958	65	2.3	
1961			44
1964	99	2.9	
1970	100	2.6	
1971			50
1973	175	4.0	
1977	111	2.7	
1982	123	2.7	58
1993	176	3.0	66
2002	308	4.8	70
2009	352	5.0	66

Sources: House prices, 1938–97, and owner-occupation rates, 1938–61, Alan Holmans, 'Housing', in A. H. Halsey (ed.), *Twentieth Century British Social Trends* (Basingstoke, Macmillan, 2000), 487 & 497. House prices, 2002–2010, Nationwide UK house price index, <http://www.nationwide.co.uk/hpi/>, based on the fourth quarter for each year. Owner-occupation rates, 1971–2010, UK, Communities and Local Government, Housing Statistics <http://www.communities.gov.uk/housing/housingresearch/housingstatistics/>. The 2009 earnings level is based on ONS, *Statistical Bulletin: 2009 Annual Survey of Hours and Earnings* (London: HMSO, 2009), using the mean gross weekly earnings for full-time employees on adult rates, whose pay was unaffected by absence. Earnings for previous years were estimated using the index for annual earnings in Lawrence H. Officer, '"What Were the UK Earnings and Prices Then?"', MeasuringWorth, 2011. Available at: <http://www.measuringworth.com/ukearncpi/>.

Notes: Owner-occupation rates for 1938–61 are for England and Wales, while figures for subsequent years are for Great Britain; house price data are for England and Wales for 1938–61 and for the UK thereafter. House prices for 1997–2009 are based on the fourth quarter. However, when estimating house price to average income ratios, second quarter house price data were used to make them compatible with the earnings data.

also substantial, owing to considerable immigration, first from the Commonwealth and, more recently, Eastern Europe.

As Britain became a progressively more affluent and crowded nation, the value placed on the countryside and on green spaces within urban areas also increased and with it the social costs of developing such sites. At the local level development often threatened to undermine the value of existing houses—thus threatening both residents' quality of life and their accumulated financial investment in what, for most owner-occupiers, constitutes the bulk of their marketable wealth. Thus political pressure to limit the development of green field areas intensified, preventing an increase in house-building in line with demand and ensuring that all but the most expensive new homes were constructed at markedly higher densities than typical interwar private or municipal estates.

(London: Department for Communities and Local Government, 2010), 14. The 1931 figure is for England and Wales; 2008 figure is for England only.

Households appear to have become reconciled to devoting a rising proportion of their income to accommodation, in a competitive scramble to secure the most attractive housing within their reach. Interwar Britain already showed clear evidence of housing acting as a strong 'positional good' (a good which people prize because it demonstrates their social ranking) for working-class households—reflecting a much longer-established pattern of such behaviour among middle-class families. Housing has ideal 'positional' characteristics—it is particularly exposed to public view, is extremely costly, and is generally seen as being integral to other key aspects of material lifestyles.[27] Rising disposable incomes and the growing scarcity of 'attractive' homes—the characteristics of which are, for many people, closely related to those of the interwar semi—has acted to increase the positional value of such housing. Meanwhile, any financial worries about taking on massive debts to fund house purchases have (until recently) been assuaged by the belief that house price rises will always beat inflation in the long term.

Given the political obstacles to substantially increasing land availability for house-building, the consequent economic attractions of medium or high densities for all but the most expensive housing developments, and the near-certainty that the trend towards rising numbers of British households will continue, there appears to be no real possibility of a general return to the low-density, semi-rural housing developments of the interwar years. The interwar semi thus seems destined to remain part of a vanished 'golden age' of British house-building, when hundreds of thousands of such homes were produced in a typical year, with generous dimensions, (usually) reasonable quality, and modest costs, for families who saw an 'ideal home' as their passport to a better life.

---

[27] Pierre Bourdieu, *The Social Structures of the Economy* (Cambridge: Polity, 2005), 189.

APPENDIX: A NOTE ON SOURCES

This study makes extensive use of personal testimonies from people who moved from inner-urban areas to new suburban estates during the 1920s and 1930s, mainly as either young adults or children. The temptation to conduct new interviews was rejected, owing to the advanced age of most surviving interwar migrants and concerns that my research agenda might influence the responses. Instead I conducted a thorough review of existing testimonies. These included published and unpublished autobiographies, together with contemporary interview survey material. However, the most important sources involved transcripts and recordings from oral history projects, compiled at various dates, from the 1970s to the recent past. Relevant information was entered into a textual database, hereafter referred to as the Life Histories Database, a summary of which (for the 170 working-class testimonies) is available online via the Economic and Social Data Service.[1]

As Paul Thompson has noted, the history of the family is a field for which oral history can provide particularly valuable source material.[2] Yet oral history evidence has sometimes been viewed as problematic for a number of reasons, including the possibility of accounts being 'polluted' by the interviewer's agenda, the fallible nature of memory and its filtering through subsequent experiences, and the possibility that interviewees might mythologize, withhold information, or otherwise distort their accounts.[3] The vetting of accounts followed Thompson's procedure of examining each interview for internal consistency, cross-checking with other sources, and evaluating in terms of wider context.[4] Problems of interviewer bias and the impact of subsequent experience on earlier memories were minimized by the use of material collected by a large number of interviewers over a period spanning several decades, and comparison with evidence from autobiographies and a few contemporary interviews.

Life histories examined for this project often provided a good deal of quantitative information regarding such things as rents, mortgage instalments, and house purchase costs. When checked against documentary sources, these revealed a very high degree of accuracy. While recollections concerning values and attitudes were less amenable to such checking, the fact that the same views emerged from large numbers of accounts, assembled over a period spanning more than half a century by different interviewers, considerably increases the weight that can be attached to them.

The Life Histories Database summarizes 170 biographical accounts of working-class people who moved from inner-urban areas to council estates or into owner occupation,

---

[1] Economic and Social Data Service, SN5085, Peter Scott, 'Analysis of 170 Biographical Accounts of Working Class People Who Moved into Owner-occupation or Suburban Council Housing During the Inter-war Period, 1919–1939' (2005), <http://www.esds.ac.uk/findingData/snDescription.asp?sn=5085&key=owner-occupation+Scott>.

[2] Paul Thompson, *The Voice of the Past: Oral History* (Oxford: Oxford University Press, 1978), 7.

[3] Thompson, *Voice of the Past*, 91–137; John Tosh, *The Pursuit of History: Aims, Methods and New Directions in Modern History*, 2nd edn (London: Longman, 1991), 213–14; Ronald J. Grele, 'Movement without Aim: Methodological and Theoretical Problems in Oral History', in R. Perks and A. Thomson (eds), *The Oral History Reader* (London: Routledge, 1998).

[4] Thompson, *Voice of the Past*, 209–21.

covering a total of 174 relevant house moves.[5] The sample composition was largely determined by the availability of sources. For example, municipal tenants account for 116 of the 174 relevant house moves, partly due to the fact that oral history studies of new estates have generally focused on large municipal estates rather than their smaller, owner-occupied, counterparts. In terms of broad regional composition, the sample achieved significant representation of the North (covering 74 moves), Midlands (26) and South (74). Yet at the level of standard economic regions the sample is heavily dominated by the South East, North West, and West Midlands.[6] This reflects both the more limited growth of working-class suburbia in regions dominated by depressed heavy staple industries or agriculture and the uneven regional coverage of oral history archives.

Council tenants' testimonies represent a very broad range of urban working-class occupations (though workers in very-low-wage or insecure jobs are under-represented). Owner-occupiers were more concentrated among workers with relatively high earnings and/or secure jobs, the sample being heavily dominated by motor vehicle and other engineering workers, public transport and utility employees, non-engineering factory workers, and building-related trades.[7] Meanwhile, they were more dominated by certain regions than the municipal sample. The 58 accounts for owner-occupiers were highly concentrated in two regions: the South East (34) and the West Midlands (15).[8] Six accounts concerned northern England (3 each from Yorkshire & Humberside and the North West); and there were 2 from the East Midlands and 1 from East Anglia.

A similar life history approach was attempted for lower-middle-class suburban migrants. However, it proved extremely difficult to find usable testimonies. Autobiographies are less common for this group and typically focus on professional, political, or other non-domestic activities. This probably reflects both the fact that lower-middle-class families typically faced a less intense struggle to make ends meet and that their domestic lives were often regarded as unsuitable topics for autobiography. Lower-middle-class households have also been neglected in both contemporary social surveys and oral history research, again reflecting the fact that this section of society was widely regarded as having private and independent lifestyles that were not deemed suitable topics for social investigation.

After an exhaustive search, some 19 testimonies were identified for middle-class families. Like the working-class sample, these sometimes provide fascinating insights into the relationships between suburban migration and household behaviour, management, priorities, and aspirations. However, the low sample size obviously limits the extent to which general conclusions can be drawn from them. Their use is, therefore, generally limited to areas where they can be corroborated by other types of evidence.

---

[5] The number of house moves is greater than the number of life histories, due to the inclusion of one interview involving two people who moved to different houses as children; two interviews involving people who had moved to both local authority and owner-occupied housing; and one interviewee who described house moves both with her parents and following her marriage.

[6] Three regions—Scotland, Wales, and the northern region—were not represented in the working-class sample. These had relatively low levels of suburbanization.

[7] For a more detailed discussion of the occupational composition of this group see Peter Scott, 'Did Owner-Occupation Lead to Smaller Families for Interwar Working-Class Households?', *Economic History Review*, 61 (2008), Appendix.

[8] Accounts concerning the South East covered a large number of expanding London suburbs and other centres; conversely, all but one of the West Midlands accounts were taken from a single city, Coventry, due to the very limited amount of suitable material for other West Midlands centres.

A broad range of more conventional historical sources are also used in this study. Council housing was viewed as an important area for contemporary social investigation and there are a number of extremely valuable studies of life on the early municipal estates. Outstanding examples are Terence Young's survey of the LCC's Becontree estate at Dagenham and Ruth Durant's survey of another major LCC estate, Watling in Hendon.[9] There are also a number of shorter, but very informative, studies of estates developed by various provincial cities, such as Manchester, Birmingham, Bristol, and Brighton.[10] Some council estates have also been subject to detailed historical investigation, including excellent studies of Becontree and Manchester's Wythenshawe estate, while studies of interwar suburban migration from particular towns or cities have also proved extremely valuable.[11] The archives of a number of contemporary social survey organizations, particularly Mass Observation and the Nuffield College Social Reconstruction survey, also yielded much useful information.

Owner-occupied estates were rarely subject to contemporary social surveys and have been less popular topics for historical investigation. Business archives initially appeared a potentially fruitful resource. Unfortunately, there are only a very limited number of speculative house-builders with extensive and accessible business archives for this period. Scotland's largest interwar housing developer, Mactaggart & Mickel, has left an excellent collection of business records, preserved at the Royal Commission of Ancient and Historical Monuments, Scotland, which proved particularly useful for this project. John Laing plc has also preserved an extensive corporate archive, held at Northampton Record Office, which again provided a good deal of very useful material. I am also very grateful to Henry Boot plc for allowing me to examine their archival records for the interwar years. Some archival evidence was also available for Wimpey, held at the Circa trust. For most other speculative builders, surviving copies of estate brochures, other publicity materials, and correspondence with purchasers provided the main sources of primary data.

Primary sources on building societies included the archives of several leading societies, including Abbey Road (at London Metropolitan Archives), Woolwich (at the Barclays Archive), and the Halifax (at Lloyds Banking Group plc Archives). The Building Societies Association Library also holds some archival material. Meanwhile, the interactions between representatives of the building trade, building society movement, and government are well-captured in records at the National Archives (see the Bibliography for documents which are specifically referenced).

---

[9] Terence Young, *Becontree and Dagenham* (London: Becontree Social Survey Committee, 1934); Ruth Durant, *Watling: A Survey of Social Life on a New Housing Estate* (London: King, 1939).

[10] Manchester and Salford Better Housing Council, *The Report of an Investigation on Wythenshawe* (Manchester: privately published, 1935); M. S. Soutar, E. H. Wilkins, and P. Sargant Florence, *Nutrition and Size of Family: Report on a New Housing Estate—1939, Prepared for the Birmingham Social Survey Committee* (London: George Allen & Unwin, 1942); Rosamond Jevons and John Madge, *Housing Estates: A Study of Bristol Corporation Policy and Practice between the Wars* (Bristol: Arrowsmith, 1946); Marion Fitzgerald, *Rents in Moulsecoomb: A Report on Rents and Other Costs of Living in Three Brighton Housing Estates* (Brighton: Southern Publishing, 1939).

[11] Andrzej Olechnowicz, *Working Class Housing in England between the Wars: The Becontree Estate* (Oxford: Oxford University Press, 1997); Audrey Kay, 'Wythenshawe circa 1932–1955: The Making of a Community?', PhD thesis (University of Manchester, 1993); Madeline McKenna, 'The Development of Suburban Council Housing Estates in Liverpool between the Wars', PhD thesis (University of Liverpool, 1986); Margaret Judith Giles, 'Something That Bit Better: Working-Class Women, Domesticity, and "Respectability", 1919–1939', DPhil thesis (University of York, 1989); Lesley Whitworth, 'Men, Women, Shops and "Little, Shiny Homes": The Consuming of Coventry, 1930–1939', PhD thesis (University of Warwick, 1997).

Local authority archives and local history libraries proved useful sources of information regarding both municipal housing development and the activities of local speculative developers (often proving a fruitful source for brochures and other builders' ephemera). Other valuable sources of ephemera included the Bodleian Library's John Johnson Collection, Middlesex University's Museum of Domestic Design & Architecture, and the National Library of Art. I assembled a significant ephemera collection over the course of the project (mainly through eBay purchases); for convenience, these items are referred to in the text as belonging to the 'Peter Scott collection'. I am also deeply indebted to a large number of individuals who generously made their research notes, oral history transcripts, and other materials available to me, as noted in the Acknowledgements.

Bibliography

ARCHIVAL SOURCES
(TOGETHER WITH ABBREVIATIONS USED)

Age Exchange, Reminiscence Theatre Archive (now held at the University of Greenwich), biographical material for the 'Just Like the Country' oral history project, c.1987.

Barclays Bank Archive, Wythenshawe: Class 1023—material for Woolwich Building Society.

Barnet Local Studies and Archives Centre, circular letter to house purchasers, F. J. C. Ingram, developer of 'Woodside Park Garden Suburb', 1 December 1931.

Bexley Local Studies and Archive Centre, London (Bexley Local Studies), oral history transcripts and estates brochures.

Bodleian Library: John Johnson Collection, Building Estates, Box 1; Marconi Archive, Ms Marconi 3780.

Borthwick Institute, York, B. S. Rowntree Archive.

British Library of Economic and Political Science Archive, Andrews-Brunner Collection, file 352.

BT Archives: POST 33/1875.

Building Societies Association Library (BSA), records of predecessor organizations.

Centre for Oxfordshire Studies, Oxford, oral history collections.

Circa Trust, George Wimpey archives, G. W. Mitchell, letter file and memoranda.

Coventry Local Studies Library, unpublished Coventry Sociological Survey report on the Brandon Road Residential Unit, 1952.

Coventry Record Office (CRO), oral history collections.

Essex Record Office, oral history collections.

Geffrye Museum, London, furniture brochure collection.

Gunnersbury Park Museum, London, oral history collections.

Henry Boot plc company archives, Sheffield. Corporate documents and brochures.

Imperial War Museum, London, 1083/88/8/1, unpublished typescript memoirs of F. J. Stephens, 1988.

John Lewis Partnership Archives, Cookham: file 2075/6–7.

London Metropolitan Archives (LMA). Papers of the Abbey Road Building Society (these papers were not fully catalogued at the time of the research and are now classified under different references); London County Council housing policy papers (LCC/HSG/GEN).

Manchester Museum of Science and Industry, British Electrical Development Association papers.

Mass Observation Archive, University of Sussex, File Report A10; Topic Collection TC1/3; Worktown Project, Boxes 44 & 44A.

Museum of Domestic Design and Architecture, University of Middlesex, collection of estate developers' promotional literature.

Museum of London Archive, oral history and autobiographical material.

National Archives, Kew (NA): CAB 27/645; HLG29/23; HLG29/253; HLG56/157; LAB17/7; T161/945.

National Library of Art, London, trade catalogue collection.

North Kingston Centre, Kingston, Surrey, oral history collections.

Northampton Record Office (NRO), John Laing plc Archives.
Nottingham Record Office, Lifetimes Oral History Project transcripts.
Nuffield College, Oxford, Nuffield College Social Reconstruction Survey Archive (NCSRS).
Peter Scott collection (ephemera collection held privately by the author).
Royal Commission of Ancient and Historical Monuments, Scotland (RCAHMS), archives of Mactaggart & Mickel Ltd.
Ruskin College Library, Oxford, autobiography collection.
Shop Direct plc, Speke, Woolworths company archival papers, Woolworths Buyers Committee minutes, 1 October 1937–19 January 1939.
Tameside Local Studies Library, transcripts of interviews of early Wythenshawe residents, conducted by Mike Harrison, c.1975–6.
University of East Anglia Archives, Pritchard papers.

WEB-BASED/DIGITAL SOURCES

Anderson, M., Jamieson, L., Bechhofer, F., and McCrone, D., 'Planning and Family Planning: Forethought and Fertility-Related Attitudes and Behaviours', summary of paper at Annual Conference of the British Society for Population Studies, Leicester, 15 September 2004, <http://www2.lse.ac.uk/socialPolicy/BSPS/pdfs/Planning_Family_Planning_Anderson.pdf>.

'Building: Borders v. Builders', *Time Magazine* (20 March 1938), online version, <http://www.time.com/time/magazine/article/0,9171,789555,00.html>.

Economic and Social Data Service, SN5085, Peter Scott, 'Analysis of 170 Biographical Accounts of Working Class People Who Moved into Owner-occupation or Suburban Council Housing During the Inter-war Period, 1919–1939' (2005), <http://www.esds.ac.uk/findingData/snDescription.asp?sn=5085&key=owner-occupation+Scott>.

Harrison, Brian, 'Joseph, Keith Sinjohn, Baron Joseph (1918–1994), politician', *Oxford DNB*, <http://www.oxforddnb.com/view/article/55063>.

Ludler, Owen, 'Poulson, John Garlick Llewellyn (1910–1993), architect and criminal', *Oxford DNB*, <http://www.oxforddnb.com/view/article/53151>.

'"Manors From Heaven": The Municipal Housing Boom and the Challenge of Community Building on a New Estate, 1929–1939', *Suburban Birmingham*, <http://www.suburbanbirmingham.org.uk/spaces/housing-essay.htm>.

Nationwide UK house price index, <http://www.nationwide.co.uk/hpi/>.

Nelson, Michael, 'Gated Communities: Class Walls', *History Today*, 61:1 (2011), <http://www.historytoday.com/michael-nelson/gated-communities-class-walls>.

Officer, Lawrence H., 'Five Ways to Compute the Relative Value of a UK Pound Amount, 1830 to Present', MeasuringWorth (2011), <http://www.measuringworth.com/ukcompare/>.

—— '"What Were the UK Earnings and Prices Then?"', MeasuringWorth (2011), <http://www.measuringworth.com/ukearncpi/>.

Shove, Elizabeth, 'Habits and their Creatures', in Alan Warde and Dale Southerton (eds), *The Habits of Consumption*, Collegium Studies Across Disciplines in the Humanities and Social Sciences, 12 (2012), 100–12, <http://www.helsinki.fi/collegium/e-series/volumes/volume_12>.

Theakston, Kevin, 'Sharp, Evelyn Adelaide, Baroness Sharp (1903–1985), civil servant', *Oxford DNB*, <http://www.oxforddnb.com/index/31/101031672/>.

UK, Communities and Local Government, Housing Statistics, <http://www.communities.gov.uk/housing/housingresearch/housingstatistics/>.

Walden, Jeff, 'Middleton, Cecil Henry (1886–1945), horticulturist and broadcaster', *Oxford DNB*, <http://www.oxforddnb.com/view/article/65428>.
Woolworths virtual museum, <http://www.woolworthsmuseum.co.uk/>.

UNPUBLISHED THESES AND DISSERTATIONS

Bundock, J. D, 'Speculative Housebuilding and Some Aspects of the Activities of the Suburban Housebuilder within the Greater London Outer Suburban Areas 1919–1939', MPhil thesis (University of Kent, 1974).

Constable, Lynne, 'An Industry in Transition: The British Domestic Furniture Trade 1914–1939', PhD thesis (Brunel University, 2000).

Couch, Georgina E., 'The Cultural Geography of the Suburban Garden: Landscape and Life History in Nottingham, c.1920–1970', PhD thesis (University of Nottingham, 2004).

Crisp, Alan, 'The Working Class Owner-Occupied House of the 1930s', MLitt thesis (University of Oxford, 1998).

Giles, Margaret Judith, 'Something That Bit Better: Working-Class Women, Domesticity, and "Respectability", 1919–1939', DPhil thesis (University of York, 1989).

Kay, Audrey, 'Wythenshawe circa 1932–1955: The Making of a Community?', PhD thesis (University of Manchester, 1993).

McCulloch, A. D., 'Owner-Occupation and Class Struggle: The Mortgage Strikes of 1938–40', PhD thesis (University of Essex, 1983).

McKee, John, 'Glasgow Working-Class Housing between the Wars, 1919–1939', MLitt thesis (University of Strathclyde, 1977).

McKenna, Madeline, 'The Development of Suburban Council Housing Estates in Liverpool between the Wars', PhD thesis (University of Liverpool, 1986).

Ryan, Deborah, 'The Daily Mail Ideal Home Exhibition and Suburban Modernity, 1908–1951', PhD thesis (University of East London, 1995).

Samy, Luke, 'The Building Society Promise: The Accessibility, Risk, and Efficiency of Building Societies in England c.1880–1939', DPhil thesis (University of Oxford, 2010).

Smithies, E. D., 'The Contrast between North and South in England 1918–1939: A Study of Economic, Social and Political Problems with Particular Reference to the Experience of Burnley, Halifax, Ipswich, and Luton', PhD thesis (University of Leeds, 1974).

Speight, George, 'Building Society Behaviour and the Mortgage Lending Market in the Interwar Period: Risk-taking by Mutual Institutions and the Interwar House-Building Boom', DPhil thesis (University of Oxford, 2000).

Thompson, Frances, 'A Study of the Development of Facilities for Recreation and Leisure Occupation on New Housing Estates, with Special Reference to Manchester', Diploma in Social Studies dissertation (University of Manchester, 1937).

Whitworth, Lesley, 'Men, Women, Shops and "Little, Shiny Homes": The Consuming of Coventry, 1930–1939', PhD thesis (University of Warwick, 1997).

Williams, Norman, 'Problems of Population and Education in the New Housing Estates, with Special Reference to Norris Green', MA dissertation (Liverpool University, 1938).

Worden, Suzette A., 'Furniture for the Living Room: An Investigation of the Interaction between Society, Industry, and Design in Britain from 1919 to 1939', PhD thesis (Brighton Polytechnic, 1980).

OFFICIAL PUBLICATIONS
(UK, UNLESS OTHERWISE STATED)

Board of Trade, Enquiry into Working Class Rents, Housing, and Retail Prices, *Report* (London: HMSO, 1908).

Board of Trade Working Party Reports, *Furniture* (London: HMSO, 1946).

Department for Transport, *Reported Road Casualties in Great Britain: Main Results 2010. Statistical Release* (London: National Statistics, 2011).

Department of Health for Scotland, *Tenth Annual Report*, 1938 (Cmd. 5969 of 1939).

Department of the Environment, *Housing Policy: Technical Volume Part I* (London: HMSO, 1977).

Ministry of Health, *Report to the Minister of Health by the Departmental Committee on Valuation for Rates, 1939* (London: HMSO, 1944).

Office of National Statistics, *General Household Survey: Results for 2006* (Norwich: HMSO, 2008).

—— *Statistical Bulletin: 2009 Annual Survey of Hours and Earnings* (London: HMSO, 2009).

—— *Housing and Planning Statistics 2010* (London: Dept. for Communities and Local Government, 2010).

Parliament, *Report of the Committee Appointed by the Local Government Board and the Secretary of State for Scotland to Consider Questions of Building Construction in Connection with the Provision of Dwellings for the Working Classes in England and Wales, and Scotland, and Report upon Methods of Securing Economy and Despatch in the Provision of Such Dwellings* (Cd. 9191 of 1918).

—— Royal Commission on the Distribution of the Industrial Population, *Report* (Cmd 6153 of 1940).

—— Royal Commission on Population: *Report* (London: HMSO, 1949).

United States, *Sixth Annual Report of the United States Commissioner of Labor* (Washington, DC: USGPO, 1890, 1891).

—— *Seventh Annual Report of the United States Commissioner of Labor* (Washington, DC: USGPO, 1891, 1892).

OTHER PRINT REFERENCES

Aldridge, Henry R., *The National Housing Manual: A Guide to National Housing Policy and Administration* (London: National Housing and Town Planning Council, 1923).

Allen, Gordon, 'Building to Sell', in Ernest Betham (ed.), *House Building 1934–1936* (London: Federated Employers' Press, 1934), 137–53.

Ashworth, Herbert, *The Building Society Story* (London: Franey, 1980).

Associated Newspapers Ltd, *The Complete Illustrated Home Book* (London: Associated Newspapers, 1936).

Baines, Dudley, and Johnson, Paul, 'In Search of the "Traditional" Working Class: Social Mobility and Occupational Continuity in Interwar London', *Economic History Review*, 52 (1999), 692–713.

Ball, Michael, *Housing Policy and Economic Power: The Political Economy of Owner Occupation* (London: Methuen, 1983).

Barnett House, *A Survey of the Social Services in the Oxford District*: II: *Local Administration in a Changing Area* (London: Oxford University Press, 1940).

Beaven, Brad, *Leisure, Citizenship, and Working-Class Men in Britain 1850–1945* (Manchester: Manchester University Press, 2005).

Bellman, Harold, *The Thrifty Three Millions: A Study of the Building Society Movement and the Story of the Abbey Road Society* (London: Abbey Road Building Society, 1935).
Bentall, Rowan, *My Store of Memories* (London: W. H. Allen, 1974).
Bentley, Ian, 'Arcadia Becomes Dunroamin: Suburban Growth and the Roots of Opposition', in Paul Oliver, Ian Davis, and Ian Bentley, *Dunroamin: The Suburban Semi and its Enemies* (London: Pimlico, 1981), 54–76.
—— 'The Owner Makes his Mark. Choice and Adaption', in Paul Oliver, Ian Davis, and Ian Bentley, *Dunroamin: The Suburban Semi and its Enemies* (London: Pimlico, 1981), 136–154.
Bingham, Adrian, *Gender, Modernity, and the Popular Press in Interwar Britain* (Oxford: Clarendon, 2004).
Boorstin, D. J., *The Americans: The Democratic Experience* (New York: Vintage, 1973).
Bourdieu, Pierre, *Distinction: A Social Critique of the Judgement of Taste* (London: Harvard University Press, 1984).
—— *The Logic of Practice* (Cambridge: Stanford University Press, 1990).
—— *The Social Structures of the Economy* (Cambridge: Polity, 2005).
Bourke, Joanna, *Working Class Cultures in Britain 1890–1960: Gender, Class and Ethnicity* (London: Routledge, 1994).
Bowden, Sue, and Offer, Avner, 'The Technological Revolution that Never Was: Gender, Class and the Diffusion of Household Appliances in Interwar England', in Victoria de Grazia and Ellen Furlough (eds), *The Sex of Things: Gender and Consumption in Historical Perspective* (Berkeley: University of California Press, 1996), 244–74.
Bowen, Elizabeth, 'Attractive Modern Homes', in Elizabeth Bowen, *The Collected Short Stories of Elizabeth Bowen* (London: Anchor, 1980), 582–90.
Bowley, Marion, *Housing and the State 1919–1944* (London: George Allen & Unwin, 1945).
Boyer, George R., 'Living Standards 1860–1939', in Roderick Floud and Paul Johnson (eds), *The Cambridge Economic History of Modern Britain*, Vol. II: *Economic Maturity, 1860–1939* (Cambridge: Cambridge University Press, 2004), 280–313.
British Road Federation, *Basic Road Statistics: Great Britain* (London: British Road Federation, 1950).
'Building Societies since 1925', *Economist* (1 July 1939), 10–11.
Burnett, John, *A Social History of Housing 1815–1985*, 2nd edn (London: Methuen, 1986).
Burns, Wilfred, *New Towns for Old: The Technique of Urban Renewal* (London: Leonard Hill, 1963).
Carpenter, Niles, 'Attitude Patterns in the Home-Buying Family', *Social Forces*, 11 (1932), 76–81.
Carr, Gerald, 'Lost Chances in New Houses', *Electrical Trading* (February 1937), 57–8.
Carter, Harold, 'Building the Divided City: Race, Class and Social Housing in Southwark, 1945–1995', *London Journal*, 33:2 (2008), 157–87.
—— 'From Slums To Slums in Three Generations: Housing Policy and the Political Economy of the Welfare State, 1945–2005', University of Oxford Discussion Paper in Economic and Social History 98 (May 2012).
Chandler, T. H., 'How Building Societies Assist the Builders', in Ernest Betham (ed.), *House Building 1934–1936* (London: Federated Employers' Press, 1934), 81–5.
'Charing Cross Showhouse', *Cabinet Maker* (21 September 1935), 482.
Chiuri, Maria Concetta, and Jappelli, Tullio, 'Financial Market Imperfections and Home Ownership: a Comparative Study', Universita Delgi Studi Di Salerno, Centre for Studies in Economics and Finance Discussion Paper 44 (2000).
Clapson, Mark, *Suburban Century: Social Change and Urban Growth in England and the United States* (New York: Berg, 2003).

Cleary, E. J., *The Building Society Movement* (London: Elek, 1965).
Coad, Roy, *Laing: A Biography of Sir John W. Laing, CBE (1879–1978)* (London: Hodder & Stoughton, 1979).
Cohen, Deborah, *Household Gods: The British and Their Possessions* (New Haven, CT: Yale University Press, 2006).
Collison, Peter, *The Cutteslowe Walls: A Study in Social Class* (London: Faber & Faber, 1963).
Cooney, E. W., 'High Flats in Local Authority Housing in England and Wales since 1945', in Anthony Sutcliffe (ed.), *Multi-storey Living: The British Working Class Experience* (London: Croom Helm, 1974), 151–80.
Craig, Elizabeth, *Keeping House with Elizabeth Craig* (London: Collins, 1936).
Craig, Peter, 'The House that Jerry Built? Building Societies, the State and the Politics of Owner-Occupation', *Housing Studies*, 1 (1986), 87–108.
Cross, George, *Suffolk Punch: A Business Man's Autobiography* (London: Faber & Faber, 1939).
'Current Furniture Advertising', *Cabinet Maker* (23 August 1930), 326–8.
Daily Express, *The Home of Today* (London: Daily Express, 1934).
Daunton, Martin J., 'Introduction', in Martin J. Daunton (ed.), *Councillors and Tenants: Local Authority Housing in English Cities, 1919–1939* (Leicester: Leicester University Press, 1984), 1–38.
Davies, Glyn, *Building Societies and Their Branches: A Regional Economic Survey* (London: Franey, 1981).
Davis, Ian, 'One of the Greatest Evils…Dunroamin and the Modern Movement', in Paul Oliver, Ian Davis, and Ian Bentley, *Dunroamin: The Suburban Semi and its Enemies* (London: Pimlico, 1981), 27–53.
—— 'A Celebration of Ambiguity: The Synthesis of Contrasting Values', in Paul Oliver, Ian Davis, and Ian Bentley, *Dunroamin: The Suburban Semi and its Enemies* (London: Pimlico, 1981), 77–103.
Davis, Martin, *Every Man His Own Landlord: A History of the Coventry Building Society* (Warwick: Coventry Building Society, 1985).
De Vries, Jan, *The Industrious Revolution: Consumer Behaviour and the Household Economy, 1650 to the Present* (Cambridge: Cambridge University Press, 2008).
Dewey, Peter, 'Agriculture, Agrarian Society, and the Countryside', in Chris Wrigley (ed.), *A Companion to Early Twentieth Century Britain* (Oxford: Blackwell, 2003), 270–85.
Dresser, Madge, 'Housing Policy in Bristol, 1919–30', in Martin J. Daunton (ed.), *Councillors and Tenants: Local Authority Housing in English Cities, 1919–1939* (Leicester: Leicester University Press, 1984), 155–216.
Dunleavy, Patrick, *The Politics of Mass Housing in Britain, 1945–1975* (Oxford: Clarendon, 1981).
Dunn, Ruby, *Moulsecoomb Days: Learning and Teaching on a Brighton Council Estate 1922–1947* (Brighton: Queenspark, 1990).
Dupuis, Ann, and Thorns, David C., 'Home, Home Ownership and the Search for Ontological Security', *Sociological Review*, 46 (1998), 24–47.
Durant, Ruth, *Watling: A Survey of Social Life on a New Housing Estate* (London: King, 1939).
Dyhouse, Carol, 'Working-class Mothers and Infant Mortality in England, 1895–1914', *Journal of Social History*, 12 (1978), 248–67.
Edwards, Clive, *Turning Houses into Homes: A History of the Retailing and Consumption of Domestic Furnishings* (Aldershot: Ashgate, 2005).

—— 'Buy Now—Pay Later. Credit: The Mainstay of the Retail Furniture Business?', in John Benson and Lauran Ugolini (eds), *Cultures of Selling. Perspectives on Consumption and Society Since 1700* (Aldershot: Ashgate, 2006), 127–52.

Eichengreen, Barry, 'The British Economy between the Wars', in Roderick Floud and Paul Johnson (eds), *The Cambridge Economic History of Modern Britain*, Vol. II: *Economic Maturity, 1860–1939* (Cambridge: Cambridge University Press, 2004), 314–43.

Feinstein, Charles, *National Income, Expenditure, and Output in the United Kingdom, 1855–1965* (Cambridge: Cambridge University Press, 1972).

Finn, Margot C., *The Character of Credit: Personal Debt in English Culture, 1740–1914* (Cambridge: Cambridge University Press, 2003).

Finnigan, Robert, 'Council Housing in Leeds, 1919–39: Social Policy and Urban Change', in Martin J. Daunton (ed.), *Councillors and Tenants: Local Authority Housing in English Cities, 1919–1939* (Leicester: Leicester University Press, 1984), 102–53.

Fisher, Kate, '"She was Quite Satisfied with the Arrangements I Made": Gender and Birth Control in Britain 1920–1950', *Past and Present*, 169 (2000), 161–93.

—— 'Uncertain Aims and Tacit Negotiations: Birth Control Practices in Britain, 1925–50', *Population and Development Review*, 26 (2000), 295–317.

Fitzgerald, Marion, *Rents in Moulsecoomb: A Report on Rents and other Costs of Living in Three Brighton Housing Estates* (Brighton: Southern Publishing, 1939).

Foakes, Grace, *My Life with Reubin* (London: Shepheard-Walwyn, 1975).

Furnell, Michael, *The Diamond Jubilee of Ideal Homes* (privately published, 1989).

'Furnishing a Show House: Coventry Furnishers Set an Example', *Cabinet Maker* (15 September 1934), 394–5.

Garside, W. R., *British Unemployment 1919–1939: A Study in Public Policy* (Cambridge: Cambridge University Press, 1990).

Gazeley, Ian, and Newell, Andrew, 'Poverty in Edwardian Britain', *Economic History Review*, 64 (2011), 52–71.

—— Newell, Andrew, and Scott, Peter, 'Why was Urban Overcrowding Much More Severe in Scotland than in the Rest of the British Isles? Evidence from the First (1904) Official Household Expenditure Survey', *European Review of Economic History*, 15 (2011), 127–51.

Gibbons, Joseph, 'Jerry Building Societies', *Weekly Review* (21 April 1938), 109–10.

Giles, Margaret J., *The Parlour and the Suburb: Domestic Identities, Class, Femininity and Modernity* (Oxford: Berg, 2004).

Gittins, Diana, *Fair Sex: Family Size and Structure, 1900–39* (London: Hutchinson, 1982).

Glendenning, Anne, *Demons of Domesticity: Women and the English Gas Industry, 1889–1939* (Aldershot: Ashgate, 2004).

Gold, J. R. and Gold, M. M., '"A Place of Delightful Prospects": Promotional Imagery and the Selling of Suburbia', in L. Zonn (ed.), *Place Images in Media: Portrayal, Experience, and Meaning* (Savage, Maryland: Rowman & Littlefield, 1990), 159–82.

—— '"Home at Last!" Building Societies, Home Ownership and the Imagery of English Suburban Promotion in the Interwar Years', in John R. Gold and Steven V. Ward (eds), *Place Promotion: The Use of Publicity and Marketing to Sell Towns and Regions* (Chichester: Wiley, 1994), 75–92.

Goldthorpe, J. H., and Lockwood, D., 'Affluence and the British Class Structure', *Sociological Review*, 11:2 (1963), 133–63.

—— et al., *The Affluent Worker: Industrial Attitudes and Behaviour* (Cambridge: Cambridge University Press, 1968).

Goodden, Susanna, *At the Sign of the Four Poster: A History of Heals* (Aldershot: Ashgate, 1984).

Gower, L. C. B., 'Building Societies and Pooling Agreements: The Borders Case and its Consequences', *Modern Law Review*, 3 (1939), 33–47.

Grebler, Leo, Blank, David M., and Winnick, Louis, *Capital Formation in Residential Real Estate* (Princeton: Princeton University Press, 1956).

Greenfield, Jill, and Reid, Chris, 'Women's Magazines and the Commercial Orchestration of Femininity in the 1930s: Evidence from Woman's Own', *Media History*, 4 (1998), 161–74.

Grele, Ronald J. 'Movement without Aim: Methodological and Theoretical Problems in Oral History', in R. Perks and A. Thomson (eds), *The Oral History Reader* (London: Routledge, 1998), 38–52.

Gronau, Reuben, 'Leisure, Home Production, and Work—the Theory of the Allocation of Time Revisited', *Journal of Political Economy*, 85 (1977), 1099–124.

Hannah, Leslie, *Electricity before Nationalisation: A Study of the Development of the Electricity Supply Industry in Britain to 1948* (London: Macmillan, 1979).

Harris, Bernard, *The Origins of the British Welfare State: Social Welfare in England and Wales 1800–1945* (Basingstoke: Palgrave Macmillan, 2004).

Harris, Richard, and Hamnett, Chris, 'The Myth of the Promised Land: The Social Diffusion of Home Ownership in Britain and North America', *Annals of the Association of Amercian Geographers*, 77 (1987), 173–90.

Harrow Gazette and Observer (9 September 1932) 15.

Harvey, M., et al., 'Between Demand and Consumption: a Framework for Research', CRIC Discussion Paper 40, CRIC, University of Manchester and UMIST (2001).

Harwood, J., 'Selling Gas Apparatus on New Building Estates', British Commercial Gas Association, *Gas Bulletin*, 33 (January 1934), 40–1.

Hatton, T. J., Boyer, G. R., and Bailey, R. E., 'The Union Wage Effect in Late Nineteenth Century Britain', *Economica*, 61 (1994), 435–66.

Heller, Michael, 'Suburbia, Marketing, and Stakeholders: Developing Ilford, Essex 1880–1914', *Urban History* (forthcoming).

Henslow, T. G. W., *Suburban Gardens* (London: Rich & Gowan, 1934).

Hobson, Oscar R., *A Hundred Years of the Halifax* (London: Batsford, 1953).

Holmans, Alan, *Housing Policy in Britain* (London: Croom Helm, 1987).

—— 'Housing', in A. H. Halsey (ed.), *Twentieth Century British Social Trends* (Basingstoke: Macmillan, 2000), 469–510.

Horrell, Sara, and Humphries, Jane, 'The Origin and Expansion of the Male Breadwinner Family: The Case of Nineteenth Century Britain', *International Review of Social History*, 42 (1997), Supplement, 25–64.

'Housing the Unskilled Worker', *The Builder* (31 March 1939), 627.

Hughes, A., and Hunt, K., 'A Culture Transformed? Women's Lives in Wythenshawe in the 1930s', in A. Davies and S. Fielding (eds), *Worker's Worlds: Cultures and Communities in Manchester and Salford, 1880–1939* (Manchester: Manchester University Press, 1992).

Humphrey, H., *Planning the Suburban Garden* (London: St Clements Press, 1922).

Humphries, Jane, 'Inter-War House Building, Cheap Money, and Building Societies: The Housing Boom Revisited', *Business History*, 29 (1987), 325–45.

Issacharoff, Ruth, 'The Building Boom of the Interwar Years: Whose Profits and Whose Cost?', in Michael Harloe (ed.), *Urban Change and Conflict* (London: CES, 1978), 280–325.

Jackson, Alan A., *Semi-Detached London: Suburban Development, Life, and Transport, 1900–39*, 2nd edn (Didcot: Wild Swan, 1991).
—— *The Middle Classes 1900–1950* (Nairn: David St John Thomas, 1991).
Jefferys, J. B., *The Distribution of Consumer Goods: A Factual Study of Methods and Costs in the United Kingdom in 1938* (Cambridge: Cambridge University Press, 1950).
—— *Retail Trading in Britain: 1850–1950* (Cambridge: Cambridge University Press, 1954).
Jeremiah, David, *Architecture and Design for the Family in Britain, 1900–70* (Manchester: Manchester University Press, 2000).
Jevons, Rosamond, and Madge, John, *Housing Estates: A Study of Bristol Corporation Policy and Practice between the Wars* (Bristol: Arrowsmith, 1946).
Johnson, Paul, *Saving and Spending: The Working-Class Economy in Britain 1870–1939* (Oxford: Oxford University Press, 1985).
—— 'Conspicuous Consumption and Working-Class Culture in Late-Victorian and Edwardian Britain', *Transactions of the Royal Historical Society*, 38:5 (1988), 27–42.
Jones, Ben, 'Slum Clearance, Privatisation and Residualisation: The Practices and Politics of Council Housing in Mid-Twentieth-Century England', *Twentieth Century British History*, 21 (2010), 510–39.
Kaldor, Nicholas, and Silverman, Rodney, *A Statistical Analysis of Advertising Expenditure and the Revenue of the Press* (Cambridge: Cambridge University Press, 1948).
Kemeny, Jim, *The Myth of Home Ownership: Private versus Public Choices in Housing Tenure* (London: Routledge & Kegan Paul, 1981).
Kentsbeer, Violet, *My Dagenham Childhood* (Bicester: Bound Biographies, 2003).
Laing, John, 'Increased Mortgages on Builders' Guarantees', in Ernest Betham (ed.), *House Building 1934–1936* (London: Federated Employers' Press, 1934), 86–91.
Lee, Clive H., *British Regional Employment Statistics, 1841–1971* (Cambridge: Cambridge University Press, 1979).
—— 'Scotland 1850–1939: Growth and Poverty', in Roderick Floud and Paul Johnson (eds), *The Cambridge Economic History of Britain*, Vol. II: *Economic Maturity, 1860–1939* (Cambridge: Cambridge University Press, 2004), 428–55.
Lee, Frank L., 'The Changes in Building Society Practice to Meet Changed Business Conditions', *Building Societies Gazette* (October 1936), 934–40.
Leiss, William, Kline, Stephen, and Jhally, Sut, *Social Communication in Advertising* (Toronto: Methuen, 1986).
Levine, David, *Reproducing Families: The Political Economy of English Population History* (Cambridge: Cambridge University Press, 1987).
London School of Economics, *The New Survey of London Life and Labour*, Vol. I: *Forty Years of Change* (London: P. S. King, 1930).
—— *The New Survey of London Life and Labour*, Vol. VI: *Survey of Social Conditions (2) The Western Area* (London: P. S. King, 1934).
Lowerson, John, 'Battles for the Countryside', in Frank Gloversmith (ed.), *Class, Culture and Social Change: A New View of the 1930s* (Brighton: Harvester, 1980), 258–80.
McCulloch, Andrew, 'A Millstone Round Your Neck?—Building Societies in the 1930s and Mortgage Default', *Housing Studies*, 5 (1990), 43–58.
McKibbin, Ross, *Classes and Cultures: England 1918–1951* (Oxford: Oxford University Press, 1998).
McLaren, A., *A History of Contraception: From Antiquity to the Present Day* (Oxford: Blackwell, 1990).

Manchester and Salford Better Housing Council, *The Report of an Investigation on Wythenshawe* (Manchester: privately published, 1935).
Marchand, Roland, *Advertising the American Dream: Making Way for Modernity, 1920–1940* (Berkeley: University of California Press, 1985).
Marshall, Howard, *Slum* (London: Heinemann, 1933).
Marshall, J. H. 'The Pattern of Housebuilding in the Inter-war Period in England and Wales', *Scottish Journal of Political Economy*, 15 (1968), 184–203.
Marshall, T. H., et al., *The Population Problem: The Experts and the Public* (London: Allen & Unwin, 1938).
Mass Observation, *An Enquiry into People's Homes* (London: John Murray, 1943).
—— *Britain and Her Birth Rate* (London: John Murray, 1945).
Massey, Philip, 'The Expenditure of 1,360 British Middle-Class Households in 1938–39', *Journal of the Royal Statistical Society*, 105 (1942), 159–96.
Matless, David, *Landscape and Englishness* (London: Reaktion, 1998).
Melling, Joseph, 'Clydeside Rent Struggles and the Making of Labour Politics in Scotland, 1900–39', in Richard Rodger (ed.), *Scottish Housing in the Twentieth Century* (Leicester: Leicester University Press, 1989), 54–88.
Merrett, Stephen, *Owner Occupation in Britain* (London: Routledge & Kegan Paul, 1982).
M'Gonigle, G. C. M., *Poverty and Public Health* (London: Gollancz, 1936).
Middleton, Roger, *Towards the Managed Economy: Keynes, the Treasury, and the Fiscal Policy Debate of the 1930s* (London: Methuen, 1985).
Mokyr, Joel, 'Why "More Work for Mother?" Knowledge and Household Behavior, 1870–1945', *Journal of Economic History*, 60 (2000), 1–41.
Moon, P. G. C., 'How We Do Our Local Publicity', British Commercial Gas Association, *Gas Bulletin*, 30 (July 1930), 124–6.
Muthesius, Stefan, *The English Terraced House* (New Haven, CT: Yale University Press, 1982).
O'Carroll, Annette, 'Social Homes, Private Homes: The Reshaping of Scottish Housing, 1914–39', in Miles Glendinning and Diane Watters (eds), *House Builders: Mactaggart & Mickel and the Scottish Housebuilding Industry* (Edinburgh: RCAHMS, 1999), 211–23.
Odhams Press Ltd, *The Ideal Home Book of Garden Plans* (London: Odhams, 1937).
Offer, Avner, 'Ricardo's Paradox and the Movement of Rents in England, c.1870–1910', *Economic History Review*, 33 (1980), 236–52.
—— *Property and Politics 1870–1914: Landownership, Law, Ideology and Urban Development in England* (Cambridge: Cambridge University Press, 1981).
—— *The Challenge of Affluence. Self-Control and Well-Being in the United States and Britain since 1950* (Oxford: Oxford University Press, 2006).
Olechnowicz, Andrzej, *Working Class Housing in England between the Wars: The Becontree Estate* (Oxford: Oxford University Press, 1997).
Oliver, Paul, 'Introduction', in Paul Oliver, Ian Davis, and Ian Bentley, *Dunroamin: The Suburban Semi and its Enemies* (London: Pimlico, 1981), 9–26.
—— 'The Galleon on the Front Door', in Paul Oliver, Ian Davis, and Ian Bentley, *Dunroamin: The Suburban Semi and its Enemies* (London: Pimlico, 1981), 155–72.
'On Purchasing Houses', *Quarterly Journal of HM Inspectors of Taxes*, 26 (1930), 227–40.
Orbach, Laurence F., *Homes for Heroes: A Study of the Evolution of British Public Housing, 1915–1921* (London: Seeley, 1977).
Orwell, George, *The Lion and the Unicorn: Socialism and the English Genius* (London: Secker & Warburg, 1941).

Owen, A. D. K., *A Report on the Housing Problem in Sheffield* (Sheffield: Sheffield Social Survey Committee, 1931).

Paisley, David, 'Salesmanship and Advertising as Applicable to Building Societies', *Building Society Yearbook* (1931), 376–81.

Pearson, Kay, *Life in Hull from Then till Now* (Hull: Bradley, 1979).

Pepper, Simon, 'John Laing's Sunnyfield Estate, Mill Hill', in Boris Ford (ed.), *Early Twentieth Century Britain: The Cambridge Cultural History* (Cambridge: Cambridge University Press, 1992), 294–306.

Pilgrim Trust, *Men without Work* (Cambridge: Cambridge University Press, 1938).

Political and Economic Planning, *Housing England* (London: PEP, 1934).

—— *Report on the Supply of Electricity in Great Britain* (London: PEP, 1936).

—— *Report on the Gas Industry in Great Britain* (London: PEP, 1939).

—— *The Market for Household Appliances* (London: PEP, 1945).

Pooley, Colin, and Harmer, Michael, *Property Ownership in Britain c.1850–1950: The Role of the Bradford Equitable Building Society and the Bingley Building Society in the Development of Home Ownership* (Cambridge: Granta, 1999).

—— and Irish, Sandra, 'Access to Housing on Merseyside, 1919–39', *Transactions of the Institute of British Geographers*, new. ser., 12 (1987), 177–90.

Prais, S. J., and Houthakker, Hendrik, S., *The Analysis of Family Budgets* (Cambridge: Cambridge University Press, 1955).

Ravetz, Alison, 'From Working-Class Tenement to Modern Flat: Local Authorities and Multi-Storey Housing between the Wars', in Anthony Sutcliffe (ed.), *Multi-storey Living: The British Working Class Experience* (London: Croom Helm, 1974), 122–50.

—— *Council Housing and Culture: The History of a Social Experiment* (Abingdon: Routledge, 2001).

Roberts, Robert, *The Classic Slum: Salford Life in the First Quarter of the Century* (Manchester: Penguin, 1971).

Rodger, Richard, 'Employment, Wages and Poverty in the Scottish Cities 1841–1914', in G. Gordon (ed.), *Perspectives on the Scottish City* (Aberdeen: Aberdeen University Press, 1985), 25–63.

—— 'The Victorian Building Industry and the Housing of the Scottish Working Class', in Martin Doughty (ed.), *Building the Industrial City* (Leicester: Leicester University Press, 1986), 152–205.

—— 'Crisis and Confrontation in Scottish Housing 1880–1914', in Richard Rodger (ed.), *Scottish Housing in the Twentieth Century* (Leicester: Leicester University Press, 1989), 25–53.

—— 'Employment, Wages, and Poverty in the Scottish Cities 1840–1914', in R. J. Morris and Richard Rodger (eds), *The Victorian City; A Reader in British Urban History* (Harlow: Longman, 1993), 73–113.

—— 'Building Development: Urbanisation and the Housing of the Scottish People, 1800–1914', in Miles Glendinning and Diane Watters (eds), *Home Builders: Mactaggart & Mickel and the Scottish Housebuilding Industry* (Edinburgh: RCAHMS, 1999), 193–210.

Routh, Guy, *Occupation and Pay in Great Britain 1906–60* (Cambridge: Cambridge University Press, 1965).

Rowntree, B. S., *Poverty and Progress: A Second Social Survey of York* (London: Longmans, 1941).

Rubinstein, A. (ed.), *Just Like the Country: Memories of London Families Who Settled the New Cottage Estates 1919–1939* (London: Age Exchange, c.1991).

Ryder, Robert, 'Council House Building in County Durham, 1900–39: The Local Implementation of National Policy', in Martin J. Daunton (ed.), *Councillors and Tenants: Local Authority Housing in English Cities, 1919–1939* (Leicester: Leicester University Press, 1984), 39–100.
Samy, Luke, 'Extending Home Ownership before the First World War: The Case of the Co-operative Permanent Building Society, 1884–1913', *Economic History Review*, 65:1 (2012), 168–93.
Sandbrook, Dominic, *State of Emergency: The Way We Were: Britain 1970–1974* (London: Penguin, 2011).
Savage, Mike, 'Working-Class Identities in the 1960s: Revisiting the Affluent Worker Study', *Sociology*, 39 (2005), 929–46.
Scott, Peter, 'Internal Migration, the State, and the Growth of New Industrial Communities in Interwar Britain', *English Historical Review*, 115 (2000), 329–53.
—— 'The Twilight World of Interwar Hire Purchase', *Past and Present*, 177 (2002), 195–225.
—— *Triumph of the South: A Regional Economic History of Britain During the Early Twentieth Century* (Aldershot: Ashgate, 2007).
—— 'Did Owner-Occupation Lead to Smaller Families for Interwar Working-Class Households?', *Economic History Review*, 61 (2008), 99–124.
—— 'Mr Drage, Mr Everyman, and the Creation of a Mass Market for Domestic Furniture in Interwar Britain', *Economic History Review*, 62 (2009), 802–27.
—— 'The Determinants of Competitive Success in the Interwar British Radio Industry', *Economic History Review*, 65 (2012), 1303–25.
—— 'Patent Monopolies, Antitrust, and the Divergent Development Paths of the British and American Interwar Radio Equipment Industries', *Business History Review* (forthcoming).
—— and Newton, Lucy, 'Advertising, Promotion, and the Rise of a National Building Society Movement in Interwar Britain', *Business History*, 54 (2012), 399–423.
—— and Spadavecchia, Anna, 'Did the 48-Hour Week Damage Britain's Industrial Competitiveness?', *Economic History Review*, 64 (2011), 1266–88.
—— and Walker, James, 'Power to the People: Working-Class Demand For Household Power in 1930s Britain', *Oxford Economic Papers*, 63 (2011), 598–624.
Seccombe, Wally, 'Starting to Stop: Working-Class Fertility Decline in Britain', *Past and Present*, 126 (1990), 151–88.
—— *Weathering the Storm: Working-Class Families from the Industrial Revolution to the Fertility Decline* (London: Verso, 1993).
Sheail, John, *Rural Conservation in Inter-War Britain* (Oxford: Oxford University Press, 1981).
Sheppard, D. K., *The Growth and Role of Financial Institutions 1880–1962* (London: Methuen, 1971).
Shove, Elizabeth, *Comfort, Cleanliness and Convenience: The Social Organization of Normality* (Oxford: Berg, 2003).
Solly, V. N., *Gardens for Town and Suburb* (London: Ernest Benn, 1926).
Soutar, M. S., Wilkins, E. H., and Florence, P. Sargant, *Nutrition and Size of Family: Report on a New Housing Estate—1939, Prepared for the Birmingham Social Survey Committee* (London: George Allen & Unwin, 1942).
'Speculative House Building', *The Builder* (5 February 1937), 322.
Speight, George, 'Who Bought the Inter-war Semi? The Socio-economic Characteristics of New-House Buyers in the 1930s', University of Oxford, Discussion Paper in Economic and Social History 38 (December 2000).

Stolper, W. F., 'British Monetary Policy and the Housing Boom', *Quarterly Journal of Economics*, 56:1 (1941), i–iv + 1–170.
Strasser, Susan, *Satisfaction Guaranteed: The Making of the American Mass Market* (New York: Pantheon, 1989).
'Suburban Neurosis up to Date' (leading article), *The Lancet* (18 January 1958), 146–7.
Supple, Barry, *The History of the British Coal Industry*, Vol. 4: *1913–1946: The Political Economy of Decline* (Oxford: Clarendon, 1987).
Swenarton, Mark, *Homes Fit for Heroes: The Politics and Architecture of Early State Housing in Britain* (Gateshead: Heinemann, 1981).
—— and Taylor, Sandra, 'The Scale and Nature of the Growth of Owner-Occupation in Britain between the Wars', *Economic History Review*, 38 (1985), 373–92.
Szreter, Simon, *Fertility, Class and Gender in Britain, 1860–1940* (Cambridge: Cambridge University Press, 1996).
Taylor, Avram, *Working Class Credit and Community since 1918* (Houndmills: Palgrave Macmillan, 2002).
Taylor, Harvey, *A Claim on the Countryside: A History of the British Outdoor Movement* (Edinburgh: Keele University Press, 1997).
Taylor, Stephen., 'The Suburban Neurosis', *The Lancet* (26 March 1938), 759–61.
Taylor, Vanessa, and Trentmann, Frank, 'Liquid Politics: Water and the Politics of Everyday Life in the Modern City', *Past and Present*, 211 (2011), 199–241.
Tedlow, R. S., *New and Improved: The Rise of Mass Marketing in America* (Oxford: Heinemann, 1990).
'The Decoration Department: Its Importance to Furnishing Houses', *Cabinet Maker* (18 January 1919), 62.
'The North London Exhibition', *St Pancras Chronicle* (11 October 1935), 10.
'The Replacement Market', *Electrical Trading* (March 1938), 69.
Thompson, Paul, *The Voice of the Past: Oral History* (Oxford: Oxford University Press, 1978).
Todd, Selina, *Young Women, Work, and Family in England 1918–1950* (Oxford: Oxford University Press, 2005).
Tosh, John, *The Pursuit of History: Aims, Methods and New Directions in Modern History*, 2nd edn (London: Longman, 1991).
Trentmann, Frank, and Taylor, Vanessa, 'From Users to Consumers: Water Politics in Nineteenth-Century London', in Frank Trentmann (ed.), *The Making of the Consumer. Knowledge, Power and Identity in the Modern World* (Oxford: Berg, 2006).
Walsh, Jane, *Not Like This* (London: Lawrence & Wishart, 1953).
Walter, Sydney J., 'British Building Society Methods of Publicity and Advertising', *Building Societies Gazette* (September 1931), 664–9.
Watters, Diane, 'Mactaggart & Mickel: A Company History', in Miles Glendinning and Diane Watters (eds), *House Builders: Mactaggart & Mickel and the Scottish Housebuilding Industry* (Edinburgh: RCAHMS, 1999), 9–192.
Weightman, Gavin, and Humphries, Steve, *The Making of Modern London 1914–1939* (London: Sidgwick & Jackson, 1984).
Wellings, Fred, *The History of Marley* (Cambridge: Woodhead, 1994).
—— *British Housebuilders: History and Analysis* (Oxford: Blackwell, 2006).
—— *Dictionary of British Housebuilders: A Twentieth Century History* (Trowbridge: Cromwell Press, 2006).
White, Valerie, *Wimpey: The First Hundred Years* (London: Wimpey News, 1980).
Wilk, R., 'Towards a Useful Multigenic Theory of Consumption', *European Council for an Energy Efficient Economy Summer Study Proceedings*, Panel 3:7 (1999).

Willmott, Peter, and Young, Michael, *Family and Class in a London Suburb* (London: Routledge & Kegan Paul, 1960).

Winter, Ian, and Bryson, Lois, 'Economic Restructuring *and* State Intervention in Holdenist Suburbia: Understanding Urban Poverty in Australia', *International Journal of Urban and Regional Research*, 22 (1998), 60–75.

Woods, Robert, *The Demography of Victorian England and Wales* (Cambridge: Cambridge University Press, 2000).

Worsdall, Frank, *The Tenement: A Way of Life: A Social, Historical, and Architectural Study of Housing in Glasgow* (Edinburgh: Chambers, 1979).

Young, Michael, and Willmott, Peter, *Family and Kinship in East London* (Harmondsworth: Penguin, 1957).

Young, Terence, *Becontree and Dagenham* (London: Becontree Social Survey Committee, 1934).

Zweig, Ferdynand, *The Worker in an Affluent Society: Family Life and Industry* (London, Heinemann, 1961).

Index

Abbey Road Building Society 34, 88, 102, 106–107, 122, 214, 215, 216, 217, 218, 230–1
Acts of Parliament:
  Artizans and Labourers' Dwellings Act (1868) 21
  Building Societies Act (1939) 227–8
  Homelessness Act (1977) 243
  Housing Act (Chamberlain Act) (1923) 43, 102
  Housing Act (1925) 62
  Housing Act (Greenwood Act) (1930) 46, 62, 65
  Housing Act (1935) 46, 62
  Housing (Additional Powers) Act (1919) 38
  Housing and Town Planning Act (Addison Act) (1919) 37–8, 41, 62
  Housing (Financial Provisions) Act (Wheatley Act) (1924) 43, 62
  Housing (Financial Provisions) Act (1933) 46, 95–6
  Housing of the Working Classes Act (1890) 21
  Increase in Rent and Mortgage Interest (Restrictions) Act (1919) 35
  Increase in Rent and Mortgage Interest (War Restrictions) Act (1915) 35
  Rent and Mortgage Interest Restrictions Act (1923) 36, 62
  Rent Restriction Act (1933) 36
Addison, Christopher 37
advertising, *see* marketing
affluent worker thesis 194, 195–6, 199, 204, 234, 236
agricultural workers 47, 237
Allen, Gordon 71, 72
Applin, R. V. K., 121
architectural styles:
  English vernacular 5, 69, 189
  international 74
  modern 48
  neo-Georgian 5, 36, 51, 69
Arding & Hobbs Ltd 155

back yards 179–80
back-to-back housing 19, 66, 152
Baines, Dudley 120
Ball, Michael 21
bathrooms 31, 58, 59, 168–9
Becontree Estate, Dagenham, *see* London County Council municipal estates
Bennett, Justice 227
Bentalls of Kingston 155–6

Bingley Building Society 88
Birkenhead 53
Birmingham 53, 63, 65, 96, 156, 157, 167, 179, 180, 206, 208
Boot, Charles 39, 79, 83, 96
Boot, Henry 79
Bolton, municipal estates 54–5, 57, 60, 157, 185
Boorstin, D. J. 137
Borders case 221, 224–9
Borders, Elsy 213, 224–8
Borough Building Society 220–1
Bourdieu, Pierre 194, 195, 199–202, 204
Bourke, Joanna 57, 190
Bourneville 31, 179
Bovis 240
Bowen, Elizabeth 202
Bowley, Marion 38
Bradford Equitable Building Society 88
Bradford Second Equitable Building Society 215
Bradford Third Equitable Building Society 90, 102, 215, 225–8
Brighton, municipal estates 67
  Moulsecoomb estates 54, 63–4, 181
  Whitehawk estate 65, 206
Bristol 10, 49–51, 55, 62, 63, 64, 115, 153, 156, 157–158, 209
Bristol Association of Building Trades Employers 39
builders' merchants 116
builders pool system, *see* building societies
building contractors 39–41; *see also* price rings
building costs 38, 46, 92–3, 229
building labour 38, 91
building materials 38, 92, 92
building societies 32–4, 88, 95–6, 102–8, 122, 129, 204, 213–32, 237
  advertising expenditure 110
  and builders pool system 104, 214–32
    dubious legal status 215
  inflationary impact on house prices 220
  and development finance 88–90
  attempts to control competition 217–18
  favourable tax treatment 102, 103
  market concentration 102, 213–14
  sales networks 214–15
  use of builders as agents 215, 219–20
  see also individual building societies
Building Societies Association 218, 249
building standards 213
Bundock, J. D. 89, 90, 91
bungalows 72, 87

Burke, Helen 124–6
Burnett, John 92, 93, 94
Burnley Building Society 102, 215, 222
Burns, Wilfred 239–40

Cadbury, George 179
Carlisle 80, 230
Catesbys of Tottenham Court Road 164
coal miners' housing 237
Coates, Wells 74
Collison, Peter 207
chalets, *see* bungalows
Chamberlain, Neville 43
Chapman's of Newcastle 154
children:
    attitudes towards 12, 28, 120, 124, 139, 141, 147–9, 189, 199, 206, 209
    impact of suburbanisation on 56, 144–51, 199, 204, 209–12, 233–5
    over-representation on municipal estates 55, 62
Clapson, Mark 60, 203
Clearing banks 90, 213
Cleary, E. J. 226
clerical workers 27, 100
Comben & Wakeling Ltd 124, 182
comprehensive urban development 240–1
Coney Hall Estate, West Wickham, Kent 56, 124, 217, 224
consumption 128–51
    communities 137–8, 199
    complex of goals 11, 137
    conspicuous 11, 138, 142, 152, 204
Co-operative Permanent Building Society 32–4, 102, 215, 217, 230–1
cost of living:
    and family size 142, 145–51
    on municipal estates 62–7
    on owner-occupied estates 141–3
Couch, Georgina 184–5
council housing, *see* municipal housing
Coventry 139, 154, 201
Coventry Permanent Building Society 113
Cross, George 89
Currys Ltd 167

Daily Mail Ideal Home Exhibition, *see* home exhibitions
Daunton, Martin 30
Davis, Arthur Felix 79
Davis Estates Ltd 79–80, 95, 114, 116, 126–7, 154, 228
Davis, Martin 214
daylight saving 175–6
De Vries, Jan 11
department stores 153–6
detached housing 72
domestic service 2, 134, 168, 169–70
Drage's Ltd 156–7, 158–9
Dunleavy, Patrick 240

Dunn, Jimmy 79, 82
Durant, Ruth 55, 60, 63, 249

E. & L. Berg Ltd 74, 117, 122, 183
Edinburgh 88
earnings, growth of 100–1, 198
electrical appliances 166–73
    running costs 168, 169–70
Electrical Development Association 169
electricity supply:
    costs 173
    impact of 3, 58, 166–73
    undertakings 169–72
estate agents 88, 90–1, 111

family limitation 142–51
family size 61–2, 142–51
female employment 2, 12, 55; *see also* domestic service
Fisher, Kate 149–50
First National Housing Trust, *see* Henry Boot & Sons Ltd
First World War 1–2, 34–6
Fitzgerald, Marion 181
flats 48
    high-rise 238–42
    see also tenements
floorspace, per dwelling 28–9, 41–2, 44
Foakes, Grace 60–1, 118, 175
food expenditure 64, 141–3
forethought 145–6, 204
forty eight hour working week, introduction 2, 175–6
Frampton, Albert 206–7
Furlongs Ltd 154
furniture and furnishings 62–3, 152–74
    acquisition strategies and costs 160–6
    retail chains 156–60

G.T. Crouch Ltd 117
garages 190
garden cities and suburbs 4, 31–2
gardens & gardening 59, 138, 175–93
    and livestock 180, 189
    broadcasting 186
    clubs 184–5
    competitions 179, 183–4, 190
    functions 180–1, 188–93
    literature 186
    neighbourly conflict 185, 209–10
    neighbourly co-operation and competition 185, 190
    plot sizes 176
    sources of information, advice, and equipment 184–92
    styles and designs 188–93
gas:
    appliances 166–73
    costs 173
    supply industry 169, 170–3

Index

Gateshead 157
Gazeley, Ian 22, 27, 28
GEC Ltd 3, 169
George Wimpey Ltd 71, 72–4, 82–3, 92–3, 182, 217, 222, 228, 249
Giles, Judy 144, 149, 173
Glasgow 26, 79, 86–87, 157
Gleesons Homes 114–16
Gold, J. R. & M. M. 127
Goldthorpe, J. H. 196, 204
Gossip 60, 61, 66
gramophones 166, 167, 174
Greenwood, Arthur 46

habitus 11, 12, 194, 202, 235–6
   definition 197
half-houses 31; *see also* maisonettes
Halifax 157
Halifax Building Society 90, 102, 122, 191, 215, 217–18, 223, 249
Halifax Equitable Building Society 214, 215
Halifax Permanent Building Society 214, 215
Hampstead Garden Suburb 32
Harvey, Alexander 32
Harvey, Walter 222, 227
Heelas of Reading 155
Henry Boot & Sons Ltd 39, 79, 83, 96, 106, 114, 237, 249
hire purchase 13, 63, 64, 152, 156–60, 169–70, 171, 174, 215, 222
Holland, A. H. 223–4
home exhibitions 111, 116, 121, 155
   Daily Mail Ideal Home Exhibition 74, 116, 121, 122, 200
   North London Exhibition 116
house-building industry, structure 20–1
household behaviour 128–51; *see also* lifestyles
housework 3, 12, 28, 59, 121, 139, 168, 169, 173, 190
housing:
   choices, social significance 201
   densities 3, 5, 19, 21, 51, 71, 244
   shortages 11, 41, 228–9
   standards 12
Houthakker, Hendrik 142
Huddersfield Building Society 102, 215
Hughes, A. 137
Hull 64
Hunt, K. 137
hygiene 11, 12
   linked to respectability 59, 120, 168–9, 199, 200

Ingram, F. J. C. 183–4
Issacharoff, Ruth 89

Jackson, Alan A. 13, 83, 92, 93, 176, 212
James & Co. (Catford) Ltd 116
Jay's Ltd 156–7
Jefferys, J. B. 162

Jekyll, Gertrude 190
Jerry-building 213, 218–22
   and house-purchasers' financial difficulties 221–4
Jevons, Rosamond 63, 156, 209
John Anslow of Coventry 154
John Laing & Sons Ltd 39, 74, 80–2, 94, 117, 135–6, 163–5, 182–3, 222, 230–2, 249
Joseph, Keith 240
Laing, John W. 80, 216
Johnson, Paul 120, 138, 145, 204

Kay, Audrey 60
Kentsbeer, Violet 130
key money 104
'keeping ourselves to ourselves' 135–40, 202–3
'keeping up with the Jones's' 123, 135–40, 141, 152, 203
kitchens 76, 126–7, 163–4

labour-saving durables 3, 121, 124, 166–74
Laidler Robsons Ltd 153–4
land developers 89–91
Leach, William 76, 83
Lee, Frank 220–1
Leeds 48, 51, 54, 65, 157, 207
Leeds Permanent Building Society 102, 215, 218
Leeds Provincial Building Society 102, 146
Leicester 51, 53
Leicester Permanent Building Society 102, 215
leisure, home-centred 61; *see also* gardens and gardening
Lewis's of Liverpool 156
lifestyles 128–51, 203, 233–6
   domesticated 11, 120–1, 139, 199, 200
Liverpool 80, 156
   municipal housing 41, 48, 52, 53, 54, 55–6, 63, 64, 179
   Individual estates:
      Clubmoor 211
      Fazakerley 57
      Larkhill 179
      Norris Green 211
      Springwood 211
lodgers, *see* sub-letting
London 46, 48, 53, 55, 157, 173, 230
   individual boroughs and districts (*see also* individual estates)
      Barnehurst 74
      Bexleyheath 77
      Brent Water 80
      Bromley 206–7, 225
      Canons Park 82
      Catford 80
      Chessington 156
      Chingford 139
      Colindale 81, 82
      Cranford 82
      Croydon 80, 96, 181–2

London (*Cont.*)
  Dagenham 80, 182
  Dartford 77
  Eastcote 181
  Edgeware 73, 82, 125
  Elstree 79, 82
  Erith 77
  Golders Green 81, 135–6, 182–3
  Harrow 89
  Hatch End 82
  Hayes 82, 225
  Ilford 31
  Kenton 90
  Kingsbury 79
  Kingston 155
  Lewisham 80
  Mill Hill 80, 82, 90
  New Malden 80
  Northolt 90
  Oprington 77
  Purley 82
  Queensbury 82, 90
  Sidcup 77, 80, 140, 177, 209
  Shooters Hill 82
  Southgate 82
  Stanmore 82
  Streatham 80
  Stretford 171
  Sudbury 80, 81, 90
  Welling 77, 210
  Woodford 81
  Woolwich 154
London Builders' Conference 229–30
London County Council municipal housing 21, 48, 49, 51, 62, 63, 180
  individual estates:
    Becontree 38, 48, 55, 60–1, 64, 65, 130, 175, 176, 209
    Bellingham 185
    Burnt Oak 210
    Castleneau 60, 206, 210
    Downham 185, 206–7
    Mottingham 206
    Roehampton 176
    St. Helier 5
    Watling 55, 60, 176, 205, 209, 210, 211
Lutyens, Ned 69, 242

Mactaggart & Mickel Ltd 86–8, 96–7, 112, 117, 123, 124, 218, 249
Madge, John 63, 156, 209
maisonettes 31, 72; *see also* half-houses
Manchester 156
  municipal estates 53, 180, 184
    Individual estates:
      Anson 52–4, 153, 184
      Wilbraham 52–4
      Wythenshawe 38, 48, 54, 55, 57, 60, 62, 64, 176, 180, 189, 200, 201
marketing 12, 30, 98–127, 200

  cross-promotion strategies 154–6, 169–72
  emphasis on 'easy terms' 112, 114, 118–20
  knowledge spillovers 111
  leisure appeal 116–20
  lifestyle 13, 120–7, 159, 203–4, 210–11
  low-pressure approach 117–18
  promotional films 117
  roadside hoardings 112
  targeting of housewives 124
  transport concerns promoting new estates 124–5, 178
  use of customers as agents 114–16
  use of emotive appeals 112
  use of print media 112, 115, 124–5, 161
  use of rural appeal 123–4, 178
  use of savings and investment appeals 114, 123
  use of standardised techniques 69, 110–11
  via estate brochures 114
marriage:
  changing nature of 150–1
  prudential 151, 200
Marshall, J. L. 86
Massey, Philip 131
Maudling, Reginald 241
Maugham, Frederic 225
McAlpine 240
McCulloch, A. D. 216
McKenna, Madeline 52, 56, 62, 63, 243
McKibbin, Ross 204
Melling, Joseph 27
Meyer, Leo 77, 78
M'Gonigle, G. C. M. 66–7
Middleton, Cecil H. 186
Miller, James and John 88
Miller Homes Ltd 88
Mitchell, Godfrey Way 71, 74, 78, 182
model workers' villages 4, 31; *see also* under individual names
Morrell Estates Ltd 124, 217, 221, 224–5
mortgage lending 32, 98–127; *see also* building societies
  arrears and defaults, 222–4
  comparison with USA 105
  impact of cheap money 103
  liberalisation of lending terms 34, 102–8
mortgage strikes 213, 225, 227
municipal housing 5, 10, 36–68, 100, 234–6
  amenities 52–9, 166–74
  design 51; *see also* Tudor Walters standard
  differential renting schemes 65–6
  furniture and furnishing 153–4
  gardens 176–7, 179–81
    advice and help for tenants 185
    and regulations 180, 192
    popularity with tenants 180–1
    standards of maintenance by tenants 180–1
  local hostility towards 205–7
  post-1945 decline 242–3

regional distribution 83–6
rent arrears and removals 62–7; *see also* rents
size and layout 48–51
tenant location choices 210–11
tenant motivations for moves into estates 57–60
tenant out-migration to owner-occupied housing 65, 210–11
tenant selection criteria 57
use of direct labour 40–1
volume of development 7, 30, 45, 47, 83–7
Muthesius, Stefan 138

National Association of Building Societies 121, 218
National Federation of Building Societies 218
National Federation of House Builders 156
National Federation of Master Builders 222
National Freehold Land and Building Society 33–4, 102, 215, 217
National Housebuilders' Registration Council 222
neighbourliness, attitudes towards 60–1, 138–40, 203, 209
New Earswick 31, 32
New Ideal Homesteads Ltd 5, 74, 77–9, 90, 95, 97, 105, 112, 114, 117–18, 123, 124, 126, 217, 222, 228
Newburn-on Tyne 49–50
Newcastle 83, 154
Newell, Andrew 21, 27, 28
Newton, Lucy 110
Nottingham 184–5
 municipal estates 51–2, 53, 179
  Aspley estate 51, 176, 177, 184

Offer, Avner 29–30, 141
Oldham 201
Olechnowicz, Andrzej 63, 185
Orbach, Laurence 37
Orwell, George 234
overcrowding 25–6, 28–9, 46–7, 65–6; *see also* slum clearance
Owen, A. D. K 66
owner occupation 7, 9, 98–151
 cost, relative to renting 107
 first-time buyers, importance of 134
 furniture and furnishings 153–6
 ideology of 98–9
 impact on wider economy 108
 levels of 23, 98–100
  by class and income 129–134
  by occupation 129–30
  international comparisons 98
 regional patterns 24–5, 131–32
 social attitudes towards 108–10, 129, 136–7
 working-class participation 22–4, 32–4, 106–8
Oxford:
 Cutteslowe walls 195, 206–8
 Urban estate 207

P. E. Cane Ltd 153
P. H. Edwards Ltd 90
Parker, Barry 32, 69
parlours 19–20, 32, 51, 138, 161
philanthropic housing trusts 21
pianos 152, 165–166
Port Sunlight 31
Poulson, John 241
Poulson scandal 240, 241–2
Prais, S. J. 142
prefabricated building techniques 39
price rings 39–41, 229–30
privacy, greater emphasis on in suburbs 60, 61, 139
privately rented housing 7, 8, 29–30, 35–6, 43, 96–7
private-sector housing 8, 43
 costs, 1938 compared to later periods 244–6
 regional distribution 83–6
 volume of development 29–30, 45, 83–6, 228
 see also privately-rented housing; speculative housing
public houses, provision on new estates 56, 176

radios 140, 166, 167, 174
Ram, Granville 227
Ravetz, Alison 235
Reading, Berkshire 155
rent controls 35–6
rent strikes 35, 66
rental costs 22–5, 29–30, 44, 52, 62
 and death rates 66–7
 in relation to incomes 23
 regional patterns 24–5
 tax disadvantages for middle-class households, relative to mortgages 110
respectability, notions of 28, 32, 59, 120, 128, 134–9, 189, 192, 197, 199, 202, 235–6
 and family size, 144
 see also social status
Richard Costain & Sons Ltd 80, 105, 181–2
Roberts, Elizabeth 168
Roger, Richard 26
Ronan Point disaster 241–2
Rotherham 157
Rowntree, Benjamin See bohm 76, 97, 146, 180
rural environment, value attached to 59, 176

Samy, Luke 32, 34
schools, provision of 55–6
Scotland 25–9, 65, 83–8, 157
 feu duties 26, 83, 87
 health impacts of poor housing 28–9
 housing costs 26–9, 83
 land development system 26
 local rates system 27, 83
 tenancy system 26–7
 tenement housing 26–9
 volume of housing development 47, 83–7

Index

Scott, Peter 27, 28,110
Seccombe, Wally 150
servants, *see* domestic service
Sharp, Evelyn 240
Sheffield 48–9, 52, 66, 67, 96, 211
Shephard, Philip Edward 77–8
shops, provision on new estates 56–7, 93–4
Shove, Elizabeth 201
Simon, John 225–6
slum clearance 11, 46–7, 62, 65, 208–9, 235, 238–42
   tenants:
      compulsory fumigation of furniture 157
      difficulty in adapting to conditions on new estates 66–7
      hostility towards 205
      return migration 67
Smart Brothers Ltd 156–7, 159
social attitudes 28, 52, 200, 203, 209
   health professionals, influence of, 12
   media, influence of 12, 120–122
   see also respectability; social status
social conflict 56, 194–212
social differentiation 194–212
social filtering 195
social segregation 205–12
social self 203
social mobility 120, 149, 198, 199
social practices 28, 201–2; *see also* habitus
social status, determinants of 11, 32, 120, 137–8, 168, 192, 207–8; *see also* respectability
speculative developers 5, 69–127, 171
   attempts to develop lower-cost housing 94–7
   costs and margins 92–3
   family firm structure 76
   links with building societies, *see* building societies
   selling 'off plan' 232
   use of unskilled labour 91
speculative housing 69–97
   building costs 92–3
   cosmetic differentiation 72–3, 74
   distinction from council housing 69–70, 122
   estate layouts 76
   estate show houses 74, 87, 116–17, 170–1
   external characteristics 69–71, 154
   gardens 181–4
   internal layouts 71–3, 233
   utilities 166–74
Speight, George 103, 216, 230
Stockton-on-Tees 66–7
Strasser, Susan 120
sub-letting 64, 142
suburban aspiration 203–4
suburban neurosis 140, 202
Sunderland 153–4, 157
'Sunspan' house 74
'suntrap' houses 74–5
Szreter, Simon 137, 142, 197

T. F. Nash Ltd 162
Taylor, Frank 76, 82
Taylor, Stephen 140
Taylor Woodrow Ltd 82, 88, 240; *see also* Ronan Point disaster
Tedlow, Richard 215
telephone 140
tenants associations 44, 64
tenements 25–9, 87; *see also* flats
terraced housing 18–19, 32, 72, 100, 135, 138–9, 233, 242
Thompson, Paul 247
Times Furnishing Co. Ltd 161
Todd, Selina 120
town planning movement 31, 238–42
transport:
   costs 52–5, 63–4, 141
   improvements, impact of 30, 31
Tyneside flats 19
Tudor Walters:
   housing standard 3, 41–2, 69, 100, 200, 233, 235
   report 3, 37

unemployment 8, 26, 61, 64, 233, 236–7
urban living, negative features 59, 176, 201
Unwin, Raymond 21, 32, 37, 69, 222, 242

Voysey, C. F. A. 69

W. H. Wedlock Ltd 114
Walsh, Jane 112, 145, 201
Wates Ltd 80, 107, 112, 222, 228
Wates, Neil 240
Wates, Norman 80, 97, 221
Watling Estate, Hendon, *see* London County Council municipal estates
Webb, Philip 69
Wellings, Fred 76, 77
Westbourne Park Building Society 34, 102, 217
Western Heritable Investment Co., *see* Mactaggart & Mickel Ltd
Wheatley, John 43, 44
Whitworth, Lesley 128, 138
Willmott, Peter 195, 203, 212
Woolwich Equitable Building Society 102, 215, 217, 249
Woolworths 186–7
Worden, Suzette 161
Worsdall, Frank 28
Wythenshawe estate, *see* Manchester

York 76, 97, 146, 180
Young, Michael 195, 203, 212
Young, Terence 63, 249

Zweig, Ferdynand 195, 203, 212

Printed in the USA/Agawam, MA
July 25, 2019

707777.030